**UPDATED
SECOND
EDITION**

Decoding the
ETHICS
CODE

To my husband Gary, who lovingly supported my ethical quests;
my children Brian and Erica, who taught me how to combine responsibility with care;
and to the memory of my parents, Helen and Norman Burg,
who taught me by example the importance of moral values.

UPDATED SECOND EDITION

Includes the 2010 APA Amendments to the Ethics Code

Decoding the
ETHICS
CODE
A PRACTICAL GUIDE
FOR PSYCHOLOGISTS

CELIA B. FISHER

Center for Ethics Education, Fordham University

Los Angeles | London | New Delhi
Singapore | Washington DC

For information:

SAGE Publications, Inc.
2455 Teller Road
Thousand Oaks, California 91320
E-mail: order@sagepub.com

SAGE Publications India Pvt. Ltd.
B 1/I 1 Mohan Cooperative
 Industrial Area
Mathura Road, New Delhi 110 044
India

SAGE Publications Ltd.
1 Oliver's Yard
55 City Road
London EC1Y 1SP
United Kingdom

SAGE Publications Asia-Pacific
 Pte. Ltd.
33 Pekin Street #02-01
Far East Square
Singapore 048763

Printed in the United States of America

Library of Congress Cataloging-in-Publication Data

Fisher, Celia B.
Decoding the ethics code : a practical guide for psychologists/
Celia B. Fisher. — 2nd ed., updated ed.
    p. cm.
Includes bibliographical references and index.
ISBN 978-1-4129-9437-8 (pbk.)
    1. Psychologists—Professional ethics. 2. Psychology—Moral and ethical aspects.
I. Title.

BF76.4.F57 2012
174'.915—dc22   2010041898

This book is printed on acid-free paper.

11   12   13   14   15   10   9   8   7   6   5   4   3   2   1

Acquisitions Editor:	Christine Cardone
Editorial Assistant:	Sarita Sarak
Production Editor:	Astrid Virding
Copy Editor:	Gillian Dickens
Typesetter:	C&M Digitals (P) Ltd.
Proofreader:	A. J. Sobczak
Indexer:	Kathy Paparchontis
Marketing Manager:	Liz Thornton
Permissions Editor:	Karen Ehrmann

Brief Table of Contents

Detailed Table of Contents

PART I: INTRODUCTION AND BACKGROUND

PART II: ENFORCEABLE STANDARDS

Topical Table of Contents for Enforceable Standards

Selected Work Settings

Psychologists Working in and Consulting to Businesses and Other Organizations

Psychologists Working in or With Health Maintenance Organizations and Other Third-Party Payors

Standard	Page	Standard	Page	Standard	Page
1.03	54	5.01b	157	8.02b	213
2.01a	69	5.01c	159	9.01a	247
2.01c	73	6.01	169	9.01b	249
2.05	84	6.02a	175	9.01c	250
3.01	92	6.02c	177, 178	9.02a	251
3.06	113	6.03	178	9.02b	254
3.07	117	6.04a	179, 181	9.03a	257
4.01	131	6.04b	181–182	9.06	270
4.02a	136, 137–138	6.04c	182	9.08a	273
4.02b	138	6.04d	182, 183	9.08b	274
4.02c	139	6.06	186, 187	10.01a	285, 288
4.05a	142, 143	6.07	188	10.09	306
4.05b	144	8.01	205	10.10a	307
4.10	134	8.02a	206	10.10c	310

Work Conducted Over the Internet and Other Electronic Media

Standard	Page	Standard	Page	Standard	Page
1.04	58	5.01b	157, 158	8.08a	229
2.01a	69	5.02a	159–160	8.10	235
2.01b	71	5.02c	160	9.01a	247
2.01c	73, 74	5.03	161	9.02a	251, 252
2.01e	75, 76	5.04	162, 163	9.02b	254
2.03	79	5.05	164	9.03a	257, 259
3.05a	100	6.02a	175	9.09a	275
3.06	113, 114	6.02b	176	9.09b	276
3.10a	121, 122	6.02c	177	9.11	279
3.12	127	7.02	194	10.01a	285, 289
4.01	131, 132	7.03a	195	10.01b	203, 293–294
4.02c	139	8.02	210	10.05	301
4.05b	144	8.03	217	10.08a	303
5.01a	155	8.05	220, 223		

Psychologists in the Military and Public Service

Standard	Page	Standard	Page	Standard	Page
1.01	67	2.05	82	3.06	68
1.02	53, 68	2.06	87	3.10a	121
2.01e	77	3.05	103, 110–111	3.10b	124
2.01f	76	3.05c	112	3.10c	124

Psychologists Working in Schools

Ethics and Law

Forensic and Other Court-Related Activities

Health Insurance Portability and Accountability Act (HIPAA)

Ethics and Additional State and Federal Laws

Counseling and Therapy

Standard	Page	Standard	Page	Standard	Page
1.03	54	3.03	95	3.11b	126
1.04	58	3.04	95, 99	3.12	127
1.05	61	3.05a	100	4.01	131
1.08	64	3.05b	111	4.02a	136
2.01a	69	3.05c	112	4.02b	138
2.01b	71	3.06	113	4.02c	139
2.01c	73	3.07	117	4.03	140
2.01e	75	3.08	118, 119	4.05a	142
2.01f	76	3.09	120	4.06	148
2.04	80	3.10a	121	5.01b	157
2.06b	85, 86	3.10b	122	5.01c	158
3.01	91	6.04a		5.06	169
4.01	60	6.04b	181	7.04	60
5.03	161	6.04c	182	8.02b	213
5.04	162	6.05	182	8.08c	229
5.05	163	6.06	185, 186	9.01a	247
5.06	164	6.07	186, 187	9.03a	257
6.01	169	7.01	187	9.07	272
6.02c	177	7.02	193	10.01–10.10	99, 285
6.03	178	7.04	194		
6.04a-e	179	7.05b	198, 199		
3.02	93	3.10d	125		

Prescription Privileges

Standard	Page	Standard	Page
2.01a	69	3.09	120
2.01e	75	8.02	214
2.05	84	9.01a	248
3.04	98	9.02a	251
3.06	113, 114	10.01a	285
3.08	118		

Psychological Testing

Standard	Page	Standard	Page	Standard	Page
1.01	51	2.01a-f	69, 73, 74	2.05	82, 83
1.03	54	2.02	79	3.01	91
1.04	58	2.03	79	3.03	95
1.06	67	2.04	82	3.04	95, 96–97

Publication

Research

Teaching

Diverse Populations

Childhood, Adolescence, and Family
(see also Psychologists Working in Schools)

Gender and Sexual Orientation

Geriatric Populations

Individuals With Acute or Chronic Health Problems

Individuals With Disabilities

Racial, Ethnic, Cultural, and Linguistic Diversity

Frequently Cited Ethical Practices and Issues

Aspirational Principles

Avoiding Harm

Confidentiality

Informed Consent

Multiple Relationships and Conflict of Interest

Acknowledgments

In August 2002, the Council of Representatives of the American Psychological Association (APA) voted unanimously to adopt the ninth revision of the APA Ethical Principles of Psychologists and Code of Conduct (APA, 2002b). The 2002 APA Ethics Code is the product of an extraordinary 5-year revision process built on APA's over 50-year tradition of applying a group dynamics approach to create a living code of conduct with which psychologists can identify and use in their everyday professional and scientific decisions (Hobbs, 1948). I was privileged to chair the APA Ethics Code Task Force (ECTF) responsible for developing, implementing, and completing the 2002 Ethics Code revision. Our mission was to create a process and product that reflected the values of the discipline and that would assist APA members in meeting ethical challenges in the new millennium.

The ECTF was composed of remarkable individuals representing the public and the diverse constituencies within APA. Each member was committed to developing an ethics code that would reflect the ideals and merit the trust of psychologists and consumers.

Over its 5-year journey, the ECTF continuously sought member input on the revision process through critical incident surveys, calls for member comments, and open meetings encouraging lively exchange among the ECTF, APA members, and observers from APA constituencies. ECTF members brought to the revision process their professional, ethical, and scientific expertise. But perhaps more important, they demonstrated a special ability to listen to member concerns and a unique willingness to challenge their own ethical preconceptions. I greatly benefited from the wisdom and friendship of the following ECTF members: Peter Appleby, Bruce Bennett, Laura Brown, Linda F. Campbell, Nabil El-Ghoroury, Dennis J. Grill, Jessica Henderson Daniel, Samuel J. Knapp, Gerald P. Koocher, Marcia Moody, Peter E. Nathan, Thomas D. Oakland, Mary H. Quigley, Julia M. Ramos-Grenier, Abigail Sivan, Steven N. Sparta, Elizabeth Swenson, Melba J. T. Vasquez, and Brian Wilcox.

The ECTF had a dedicated and talented APA staff navigating the revision process through what often felt like a voyage through the Scylla and Charybdis of seven Ethics Code drafts. Stan Jones as Director of the Ethics Office and later ECTF consultant was a treasure trove of knowledge about the history of past APA ethics codes and ethics adjudication. In the middle of the revision process, Steve Behnke dived into the role of Director of the Ethics Office with a perfect combination of scholarly expertise, administrative acumen, and personal warmth.

Debbie Felder, Revision Coordinator, was the ECTF's gatekeeper, librarian, scribe, grammarian, minutes keeper, and schedule maker and performed many other essential roles with a competence and commitment remarkable to find in a single individual. Nathalie Gilfoyle, APA General Counsel, continuously helped clarify the legal parameters and challenges of the ECTF's work, nurturing the construction of standards sensitive to but not dictated by law. Along with Lindsay Childress Beatty, then Deputy General Counsel, Nathalie made sure that the ECTF was up-to-date on continuously evolving federal regulations.

As chair of the ECTF, I also benefited from the support and guidance of the APA Board of Directors, committee chairs, and division representatives. I am particularly grateful to Pat Bricklin, Charles Brewer, Jean Carter, Stuart Cooper, Pat DeLeon, Mike Honaker, Norine Johnson, Deirdre Knapp, Ron Levant, Katherine Nordal, Russ Newman, Ruth Paige, Stuart Pizer, Norma Simon, and Phil Zimbardo and to the more than 1,300 APA members who shared their kudos and concerns with the task force.

This second edition of *Decoding the Ethics Code: A Practical Guide for Psychologists* has also benefited from the wisdom of many. Steve Behnke, Director of the APA Ethics Office, has remained a close friend and rich resource of knowledge and advice for this second edition. I wish to thank Mark Yarhouse, Carrie Nassif, and Karen Riggs Skean for their helpful comments on early drafts of chapters for the book. It is also a pleasure to record indebtedness to Jennifer Owens and Matthew Oransky for their editorial and research assistance, as well as the many Fordham University graduate students who provided valuable feedback on the first edition and continue to teach me about new and emerging ethical arenas. I am fortunate to have had the wonderful guidance and support of my editor Chris Cardone and Editorial Assistant Sarita Sarak, and the assistance of senior production editor Astrid Virding and copy editor Gillian Dickens at Sage Publications. My husband, Gary, read each draft of the book and, as he did with the first edition, dramatically reduced the number of paragraph-length sentences in the final draft. I am also grateful to my daughter Erica for providing the title for this book and to both my children, Brian and Erica, and my son-in-law, Steven Battle, for their love and support.

Preface

Welcome to the updated Second Edition of *Decoding the Ethics Code: A Practical Guide for Psychologists*. This updated edition replaces the Second Edition of this text by providing the revised language and updated discussion of the latest amendments to the American Psychological Association's (APA) Ethical Principles of Psychologists and Code of Conduct (APA, 2010a).

Following the 2002 publication of the APA Ethics Code, public revelations of psychologists' involvement in harsh national security interrogations of "enemy combatants" detained at Guantanamo ignited a heated debate among APA members regarding the proper role of psychologists in interrogation and information-gathering processes related to national security. The Second Edition of *Decoding the Ethics Code,* published in 2009, provided the most up-to-date information on the nature of the debate, the steps APA had taken to address member concern, and the relevance of 2002 Ethics Code standards to the ethical practice of psychologists working for the military. Debate continued, however, on whether the wording of two Ethics Code standards (1.02 and 1.03) were ambiguous with respect to psychologists' ethical obligations when conflicts arise between psychology ethics and law or organizational policies. In February 2010, the APA Council of Representatives voted to amend the language of these two standards to make clear that these standards can never be interpreted as permitting actions by psychologists that violate human rights.

This updated Second Edition includes the *Ethical Principles of Psychologists and Code of Conduct With the 2010 Amendments,* effective June 1 2010 (APA, 2010a), explanation in relevant sections of the book on how the amended standards should be applied in practice, expanded discussion of the resolution of the debate in Chapter 4's special section on "Involvement of Psychologists in Interrogations Related to National Security," and the addition in Appendix B of national and international resource material on the roles and responsibilities of health professionals in military interrogations and inhumane treatment or punishment.

This updated Second Edition retains the format and critical content of the Second Edition. The interval between this and the first edition has demonstrated the durability of the 2002 American Psychological Association's (APA's) Ethical

Principles of Psychologists and Code of Conduct, witnessed new insights into how it can be applied to ethical decision making in the science and practice of psychology, and faced new challenges for its application to emerging moral debates.

One motivation for producing a second edition was to incorporate the wealth of knowledge generated by articles written on the relevance of the APA Ethics Code for research and practice since the Code's publication in 2002. The success of the first edition encouraged the decision to retain the user-friendly format of the book. For this edition, all chapters have been revised to ensure they reflect the current status of scholarly efforts in all facets of ethical decision making. The wisdom of the more recent articles and chapters, incorporated into this second edition, sheds new light on the application and continued relevance and vitality of the Ethics Code to moral discourse and practical challenges characterizing the dynamic and thriving discipline of psychology.

Another motivation for a second edition was the opportunity to expand the chapter on ethical decision making. The first edition sought to detail for readers specific similarities and differences between the 1992 and 2002 codes to help ease psychologists' transition to using the new format, aspirational principles, and revised, removed, or added standards. In the years since the publication of the first edition, the discipline has successfully made this transition, providing me the opportunity to shift the emphasis on introductory chapters of this book toward the articulation and application of an ethical decision-making model that can assist psychologists as they continue to face unique ethical challenges.

A final motivation for writing a second edition was the emergence of new topics of increasing ethical import to psychology—such as involvement of psychologists in military interrogations and the integration of religion and spirituality in therapy—that could benefit from ethical analysis within the framework of the Ethics Code's aspirational principles and standards. The new "Hot Topic" sections at the end of each chapter of this second edition provided an opportunity to do so.

The Goals of This Book

The primary purpose of this book is to provide graduate students, seasoned psychologists, consumers of psychological services, and professionals in related science and professional disciplines with a practical guide to the meaning and applicability of the 2002 APA's Ethical Principles of Psychologists and Code of Conduct. The book seeks to place into practical perspective the format, choice of wording, aspirational principles, and enforceable standards of the code. It provides in-depth discussions of the rationale behind and application of each ethical standard to the broad spectrum of scientific, teaching, and professional roles and activities of psychologists. It gives clear examples of behaviors that would be in compliance with or in violation of enforceable standards.

The second edition of *Decoding the Ethics Code: A Practical Guide for Psychologists* is also intended to assist psychologists in effectively using the Ethics Code's principles and standards to conduct their work activities in ethically responsible ways, to avoid ethical violations, and to preserve and protect the fundamental rights and welfare of those with whom they work. By incorporating the most recent scholarship on ethical issues in psychology and by addressing topical issues in the field, this second edition continues the vision of the first edition in providing psychologists with information and decision-making skills they need to apply the Ethics Code to the constantly changing scientific, professional, and legal realities of the discipline.

How to Use This Book

This book was written to provide an in-depth, yet easily accessible, guide to applying the Ethical Principles of Psychologists and Code of Conduct (APA, 2002b) to psychologists' everyday ethical decision making.

The book has several features designed for easy reference to a wide range of information and practical guidance on each component of the APA Ethics Code.

How the Book Is Organized

The APA Ethics Code consists of the Introduction and Applicability section, the Preamble, five General Principles, and 10 specific sections putting forth enforceable standards for ethical conduct. Although the chapters of this book are organized around the format of the Ethics Code, the book does not have to be read from cover to cover. Each chapter and the discussion of each standard are designed to stand on their own. Cross-references to other parts of the code are provided when they are helpful to ethical decision making. The book is organized around 13 chapters.

Chapter 1. A Code of Ethics for Psychology: How Did We Get Here? Chapter 1 presents an introduction to the history, goals, controversies, major advances, and revision strategies associated with the APA Ethics Code since its inception a half century ago. It contains specific examples of the innovations and challenges characterizing the process of creating the 2002 Ethics Code. It familiarizes readers with the value of the Ethics Code to the profession and the public. This chapter also explains the history of the Ethics Code revision process that included broad APA member involvement as a critical element in the construction of a code that reflects the values of the discipline.

Chapter 2. The Introduction and Applicability Section, Preamble, and General Principles: What Do They Mean? Chapter 2 provides a guide to the practical meaning of the Ethics Code's Introduction and Applicability section, Preamble, and General Principles. It includes discussion of to whom and what activities the Ethics Code applies; the rationale and meaning of the language used in the Ethics Code; the relationship between the Ethics Code, APA guidelines, and the rules and procedures for enforcement of the code; the relevance of the Ethics Code to sanctions applied by other professional bodies and state licensure boards as well as to litigation; and the meaning and practical significance of the General Principles.

Chapter 3. The APA Ethics Code and Ethical Decision Making. The Ethical Principles and Standards provide critical guidance for ethical decision making, but there is no set formula for solving the complexity of ethical challenges psychologists will confront over the course of their careers. Chapter 3 discusses the importance of ethical commitment, ethical awareness, and ethical decision making to good and rightly practiced professional and scientific psychology. It elucidates the role of moral character and moral frameworks in the ability to prepare for, identify, and resolve ethical challenges and illustrates a step-by-step decision-making strategy to assist psychologists in applying the Ethics Code to new and emerging areas of psychology as the discipline continues to evolve.

Chapters 4–13. Enforceable Standards. Chapters 4 to 13 provide in-depth explanations and practical examples of how to apply the 151 enforceable standards. The chapter titles correspond to the titles of the 10 sections on enforceable standards in the Ethics Code: Resolving Ethical Issues, Competence, Human Relations, Privacy and Confidentiality, Advertising and Other Public Statements, Record Keeping and Fees, Education and Training, Research and Publication, Assessment, and Therapy.

Hot Topics. Since the publication of the first edition of this book, a number of issues continue to be, or have emerged for psychologists as, topics of ethical import. Chapters 4 to 13 each conclude with an in-depth ethical analysis of current "Hot Topics" in the science and practice of psychology.

- Involvement of Psychologists in Interrogations Related to National Security: Chapter 4
- Multicultural Ethical Competence: Chapter 5
- Informed Consent Involving Adults With Impaired Decisional Capacity: Chapter 6
- Confidentiality and Involvement of Parents in Mental Health Services for Children and Adolescents: Chapter 7
- Avoiding False and Deceptive Statements in Scientific and Clinical Expert Testimony: Chapter 8
- Managing the Ethics of Managed Care: Chapter 9
- Ethical Supervision of Trainees: Chapter 10
- Submitting Successful IRB Proposals: Chapter 11
- The Use of Assessments in Expert Testimony: Implications of Case Law and the Federal Rules of Evidence: Chapter 12
- Ethical Issues for the Integration of Religion and Spirituality in Therapy: Chapter 13

Topical Table of Contents for Enforceable Standards

In addition to the traditional table of contents, a topical table of contents is provided to help readers quickly identify discussions of standards relevant to five major areas: work settings (industrial-organizational and consulting activities, health maintenance organizations, hospitals, companies, and work conducted over the Internet, in the military, and in schools), ethics and law (forensic and other court-related activities, Health Insurance Portability and Accountability Act [HIPAA] regulations, and ethics and state and federal laws), work roles (counseling and therapy, prescription privileges, psychological testing, publication, research, and teaching), populations (childhood, adolescence, and family; gender and sexual orientation; religion; geriatric populations; individuals with acute or chronic health problems; individuals with disabilities; and racially, ethnically, culturally, and linguistically diverse populations), aspirational principles and frequently cited ethical practices and issues (avoiding harm, confidentiality, informed consent, and multiple relationships).

Discussion of Ethical Standards

Most of the enforceable standards in the Ethics Code were written broadly so they would apply to psychologists in varied roles and work contexts. As much as possible, this book attempts to explain the overriding purpose of each standard, help readers understand the implications of critical terminology, provide examples of the range of psychological activities to which the standard applies, and offer suggestions for ethical "do's" and "don'ts" quickly identified by these icons. In the examples of ethical do's and don'ts in this book, the terms *client* and *patient* are used interchangeably.

Psychological Activity and Work Setting Icons

The Ethics Code is divided into six general sections representing ethical standards that apply to a broad spectrum of psychological activities and four more sections putting forth ethical rules explicitly for teaching, research, assessment, and therapy. The document itself, however, does not provide a precise way to locate standards directly relevant to other common work roles and settings. To help readers quickly navigate the Ethics Code for direct application to work roles that do not have special sections in the code, this book has icons that are strategically placed before the discussion of standards in which such activities are mentioned for the following areas of psychology:

 This icon alerts readers that the standard is particularly relevant to psychologists who apply the science and practice of psychology to enhance human well-being and performance in organizational and work settings, including consulting, personnel screening and promotion, marketing research, employee counseling, executive coaching, and research on job or organization effectiveness. Throughout the Ethics Code, the term *organizational client* refers to organizations to which the psychologist provides the services described above, whereas the term *client/patient* refers to individuals receiving therapy or other health services.

This icon indicates that the standard applies to work involving forensic, court-ordered, or other activities relevant to the legal system, including forensic examinations, expert testimony, testimony as a fact witness, research on a psycholegal issue, trial behavior consultation, or court-ordered or other forensic mental health services.

When readers see this icon, it means that the standard is related to research about the schooling process, consultative services to schools, or delivery of psychological services to children, adolescents, and families to assess, remediate, or otherwise address school performance and related psychological skills or vulnerabilities.

This icon indicates that a standard is particularly relevant to psychological practice, research, training, or policy formation in military, criminal justice, correctional facilities, police work, or other public service settings.

This icon highlights standards relevant to psychologists' involvement with organized systems of care, including health maintenance organizations (HMOs), managed care organizations (MCOs), Medicaid, or Medicare.

This icon draws readers' attention to compliance with standards that will be affected by or must take into account the federal Health Insurance Portability and Accountability Act (HIPAA) to ethical practice. (See "A Word About HIPAA," below.)

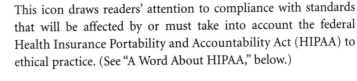

This icon alerts readers to standards that are particularly relevant to psychological services that include prescription privileges, the conduct of research on psychopharmacological medications and agents, or psychologists' involvement with psychopharmaceutical companies.

This icon draws readers' attention to standards that explicitly mention or for which examples are given for research or services using the Internet, telephone, fax machines, videoconferencing, computerized services, or other forms of electronic transmission.

This icon highlights standards that explicitly address factors associated with age, gender, gender identity, race, ethnicity, culture, national origin, religion, sexual orientation, disability, language, or socioeconomic status. It also signifies when the text offers examples for more broadly worded standards that illustrate attention to group and individual differences.

The special areas for which icons were selected are not exhaustive but represent areas outside of teaching, research, assessment, and therapy that are repeatedly referred to in the standards or in the explanations and illustrations provided in this book.

Remember, the standards within the six general sections apply to all psychological activities.

A Word About HIPAA

In 1996, Congress enacted HIPAA in response to the increasing costs associated with transmitting health records lacking standardized formatting across providers, institutions, localities, and states. Recognizing that uniform standards for creating, transmitting, and storing health care records would require additional patient protections, Congress included in HIPAA regulations standards giving patients greater access to and control of their records. The Ethics Code Task Force (ECTF) responsible for the 2002 Ethics Code revision was aware that the scope and detail of HIPAA regulations would change the nature of health care practice and research in the United States.

The ECTF sought to ensure that ethical standards would reflect sensitivity to and avoid inconsistency with the new HIPAA regulatory landscape.

Throughout this book, the relationship between HIPAA and relevant Ethics Code standards is identified and explained. A brief overview of the regulations and relevant terminology is provided below. Additional information regarding HIPAA appears throughout this book under discussion of individual standards. Readers can also obtain more detailed information about HIPAA from the U.S. Department of Health and Human Services (http://www.hhs.gov/ocr/hipaa/finalreg.html, http://aspe.hhs.gov/admnsimp/, and http://www.cms.hhs.gov/HIPAAGenInfo/), the American Psychological Association Insurance Trust (www.apait.org/hipaa), or the American Psychological Association Practice Directorate (www.apa.org/practice).

HIPAA standards. HIPAA has three components: (a) *privacy standards* for the use and disclosure of individually identifiable private health information (Privacy Rule, effective April 14, 2003), (b) *transaction standards* for the electronic exchange of health information (Transaction Rule, effective October 16, 2003), and (c) *security standards* to protect the creation and maintenance of private health information (Security Standards, effective April 21, 2003; compliance date April 21, 2005). These rules seek to protect individually identifiable health information through regulations that

- standardize the format of electronically transmitted records related to individually identifiable health information,
- secure the electronic transaction and storage of individually identifiable health information,

- limit the use and release of individually identifiable health information,
- increase patient control of use and disclosure of private health information,
- increase patients' access to their health records,
- establish legal accountability and penalties for unauthorized use and disclosure and violation of transaction and security standards,
- identify public health and welfare needs that permit use and disclosure of individually identifiable health information without patient authorization.

To what does HIPAA apply? HIPAA regulations apply to *protected health information* (PHI), defined as oral, written, typed, or electronic individually identifiable information related to (a) a person's past, present, or future physical or mental health; (b) provision of health care to the person; or (c) past, present, or future payment for health care. For health information to come under the definition of PHI, it must be created by an employer or by the following *covered entities:* a health plan, a health care clearinghouse, or a health care provider who transmits any health information in electronic form in connection with financial or administrative activities related to health care. Educational records covered by the Family Educational Rights and Privacy Act (FERPA), employment records held by a covered entity in its role as employer, and de-identified records (in which all individually identifiable information has been removed) are *not* considered PHI.

What do covered entities need to do to comply with HIPAA? Under HIPAA, covered entities must (a) provide information to patients about their privacy rights and the covered entity's privacy practices, called a *notice of privacy practices;* (b) permit patient access to records and upon patient request provide an *accounting of disclosures* of PHI made to others over the past 6 years; (c) obtain patient *authorization* for use and disclosures to others in a manner and for purposes specified in the regulations; (d) implement clear privacy procedures for electronic transmission and storage of PHI; (e) designate a *privacy officer;* (f) implement security procedures that prevent unauthorized access to health records; (g) train and ensure that employees comply with privacy, transaction, and security procedures; (h) reasonably ensure that business associates, individual contractors, consultants, collection agencies, third-party payors, and researchers with whom PHI is shared comply with privacy and transaction rules; and (i) attempt to correct violations by these other entities if they occur or cease the relationship.

Are researchers, industrial-organizational, or consulting psychologists affected by HIPAA? Most researchers or members of their team who create, use, or disclose PHI as part of a randomized clinical trial or other forms of health-relevant intervention research will be considered covered entities. Researchers who are not involved in intervention research but who plan to use in their research or consulting services PHI created by a covered entity must provide to the covered entity written assurance that they will comply with HIPAA standards.

PART I

Introduction and Background

CHAPTER 1

A Code of Ethics for Psychology

How Did We Get Here?

In a field so complex, where individual and social values are yet but ill defined, the desire to play fairly must be given direction and consistency by some rules of the game. These rules should do much more than help the unethical psychologist keep out of trouble; they should be of palpable aid to the ethical psychologist in making daily decisions.

—Hobbs (1948, p. 81)

Beginnings

The American Psychological Association (APA) has had over five decades of experience constructing and revising an ethics code that strives to reflect both the aspirations and practical aspects of ethical decisions made by members of the profession. The creation and each subsequent revision of the APA Ethics Code has been driven by the desire for standards that would encourage the highest endeavors of psychologists, ensure public welfare, promote sound relationships with allied professions, and promote the professional standing of the discipline (Hobbs, 1948).

Discussions within APA regarding the need for an ethics code in psychology arose in response to an increase in professional activity and public visibility of its members before and after World War II. During this period, the societal value of the still young discipline of psychology was evidenced as psychologists developed group tests to help the armed services quickly determine the draft eligibility of young men in wartime and provided mental health services to hospitalized soldiers when they returned home. In 1947, the first APA Committee on Ethical Standards for Psychologists was appointed. The committee, chaired by Edward Tolman, wanted to create a code of ethics for psychologists that would be more than a document with an imposing title (Hobbs, 1948). The members were committed to producing professional standards that would provide psychologists with a set of values and practical techniques for identifying and resolving moral problems.

To achieve these goals, the committee decided to draw on the knowledge of the field to create a process of developing a code that would "be effective in modifying human behavior" (Hobbs, 1948, p. 82). According to Hobbs, "This is an old and familiar task to psychologists, their very stock in trade, in fact. The only difference here is that human behavior means specifically the behavior of psychologists" (p. 82). Drawing on the knowledge of group processes during that period, the committee conceived the task of developing ethical standards as one of group dynamics (Hobbs, 1948). The process chosen was the critical incident method (Flanagan, 1954), a technique that involved asking the members of the APA to describe a situation they knew of firsthand, in which a psychologist made a decision having ethical implications, and to indicate the ethical issues involved.

A second committee, chaired by Nicholas Hobbs, reviewed more than 1,000 such incidents submitted by APA members. The committee identified major ethical themes emerging from the incidents that focused on psychologists' relationships with and responsibilities to others, including patients, students, research participants, and other professionals. Many of the incidents reflected the political climate of the postwar period, including confrontations between academic freedom and McCarthyism and dilemmas faced by psychologists working in industry asked to design tests for the purpose of maintaining racial segregation in the workforce. As different segments of the code were created, drafts were submitted to the membership for critique and revision. A final draft was adopted by APA in 1952 and published in 1953.

Revisions Preceding the 2002 Ethics Code

At the time of the adoption of the first Ethics Code, continual review and revision based on the experience and perspectives of members was seen as integral to maintaining the value of the Ethics Code for both the profession and the public (Adkins, 1952). As a result, the Ethics Code of the APA has undergone nine revisions since 1953. The 1953 version was more than 170 pages long and included case examples illustrating each ethical standard. The standards themselves were written broadly, using aspirational rather than narrow legalistic language. Subsequent revisions eliminated the cases from the text itself and moved toward more specific language.

From the beginning of its more than 50-year history, each revision of the APA's Ethical Principles of Psychologists and Code of Conduct has been guided by the following objectives (Hobbs, 1948):

- To express the best ethical practices in the field as judged by a large representative sample of members of the APA

- To reflect an explicit value system as well as clearly articulated decisional and behavioral rules
- To be applicable to the full range of activities and role relationships encountered in the work of psychologists
- To have the broadest possible participation among psychologists in its development and revisions
- To influence the ethical conduct of psychologists by meriting widespread identification and acceptance among members of the discipline

Aspirational Principles and Enforceable Standards

At its heart, an ethics code should reflect the moral principles underlying the values of the profession. For most professions, ethical behaviors are generally those that fulfill the fundamental moral obligations to do good, to do no harm, to respect others, and to treat all individuals honestly and fairly. For some, statements of general principles are sufficient to guide the ethical behavior of persons devoted to the ideals of their profession. For others, however, statements describing specific types of behaviors that meet these ideals are necessary to maximize the code's utility and to provide a means of evaluating its efficacy (Schur, 1982).

The form in which ethical guidelines are written will determine whether an ethics code is an aspirational or enforceable document. Although all codes should have a foundation in moral principles, the document can take one of three forms. An aspirational code is composed of statements of broadly worded ideals and principles that do not attempt to define with any precision right and wrong behaviors. An educational code combines ethical principles with more explicit interpretations that can help individual professionals make informed decisions in morally ambiguous contexts. An enforceable code includes a set of standards that specifically describes behaviors required and proscribed by the profession and is designed to serve as a basis for adjudicating grievances (Frankel, 1996).

Prior to the 1992 revision, the APA Ethics Code combined statements of aspirational principles with general guidelines and enforceable standards for ethical behavior (APA, 1981). By the late 1980s, the increasing legalistic reaction of consumers and psychologists involved in charges of ethical violations by psychologists raised concerns about the fairness of subjective interpretations of such broadly worded principles and standards. Moreover, a rise in the number of appeals to decisions made by the APA Ethics Committee and regulatory bodies (such as state licensing boards) that relied on the APA Ethics Code for their disciplinary procedures suggested that adjudicatory decisions based on this type of format would be increasingly difficult to enforce and thus a disservice to the APA membership (Bersoff, 1994). Accordingly, to strengthen both the enforceability and credibility of APA ethical guidelines, crafters of the 1992 APA Ethics Code separated the enforceable standards from the aspirational principles to make the standards simple, behaviorally focused, and representative of unitary concepts (Canter, Bennett, Jones, & Nagy, 1994).

During the revision process leading to the 1992 Ethics Code, some psychologists argued that adjudication based on specific ethical standards rather than general principles would diminish the moral foundation on which the APA Ethics Committee charged with adjudicating ethics complaints could base its decisions. Others supported the move toward separate enforceable standards, arguing that in practice, limiting the standards to legally and procedurally unenforceable wording would dilute the ethical goals intended by the foundational principles (Fisher & Younggren, 1997).

The 1992 Ethics Code represented a radical change from its predecessors in both structure and content. For the first time, clear distinctions were made between aspirational principles that articulated foundational values of the discipline and specific decision rules articulated in 180 distinct ethical standards that would be subject to enforcement by the APA, other organizations, and licensing boards that adopted them (Canter et al., 1994).

The Process of Developing the 2002 Ethics Code

Since its inception in 1953, each revision of the APA Ethics Code has been driven by the evolving roles and responsibilities of psychologists within a constantly changing sociocultural, economic, political, and legal landscape. Major trends influencing revisions leading to the 2002 Ethics Code included (a) the growth and influence of health maintenance organizations (HMOs) on the provision of health services, (b) the advent of Internet-mediated research and practice and the use of other electronic media, (c) greater sensitivity to the needs of culturally and language-diverse populations in research and practice, (d) increasing participation of psychologists in the legal system, and (e) the sea change from paternalistic to autonomy-based public attitudes and federal regulations affecting industries, organizations, health care, research, and educational institutions.

In 1996, the APA Ethics Committee appointed the Ethics Code Task Force (ECTF), a 14-member committee whose membership reflected the scientific, educational, professional, gender, ethnic, and geographic diversity of the discipline. Over the 5-year period, members included Celia B. Fisher (Chair), Peter Appleby, Bruce Bennett, Laura Brown, Linda F. Campbell, Nabil El-Ghoroury, Dennis J. Grill, Jessica Henderson Daniel, Samuel J. Knapp, Gerald P. Koocher, Marcia Moody, Peter E. Nathan, Thomas D. Oakland, Mary H. Quigley, Julia M. Ramos-Grenier, Abigail Sivan, Steven N. Sparta, Elizabeth Swenson, Melba J. T. Vasquez, and Brian Wilcox.

The Purpose of an Ethics Code

The mission of the task force was to develop and implement a plan for revision of the 1992 Ethics Code. In its deliberations, the ECTF considered the importance of both the purpose and process of ethics code development, recognizing that such consideration would determine the content and format of the code and ultimately whether psychologists would support it.

The many goals identified by the ECTF to guide the 2002 Ethics Code revision process included the professional, educational, public, and enforcement values of a code of ethics. These values guided decisions regarding inclusion and exclusion of ethical requirements and prohibitions and the language used to craft the General Principles and Ethical Standards.

Establishing the Integrity of a Profession. One purpose of an ethics code is to help establish and maintain the viability of a profession. An ethics code reflects a collective decision that a profession is better off when ethical standards are not based solely on individual assessments of what is or is not morally acceptable. Adoption of a set of core values that reflect consensus among members of a discipline distinguishes psychology as a "community of common purpose" and enhances public confidence in individuals who have been trained to meet the profession's ethical standards (Callahan, 1982; Frankel, 1996; Seitz & O'Neill, 1996). Acceptance of an identified set of core values by individual psychologists across the broad spectrum of psychological activities also helps to protect the integrity of the profession by focusing the attention of individual psychologists on their responsibilities and duties to others and expectations that all members of the profession have a stake in behaving by the rules.

A core value of the discipline of psychology, as articulated in the Preamble of the 2002 Ethics Code, is the welfare and protection of the individuals and groups with whom psychologists work.

Education and Professional Socialization. A second purpose of an ethics code is its professional socialization function. A document reflecting the profession's values and standards provides a guide to what psychologists should reasonably expect of themselves and one another. A code can be conceived as an enabling document that acts as a support and guide to individual psychologists in their efforts to resolve ethical dilemmas (Frankel, 1996; Sinclair, Poizner, Gilmour-Barrett, & Randall, 1987). A code of ethics also serves to deter psychologists from engaging in unethical conduct before a problem develops by specifically proscribing what the profession has identified as unethical behaviors (Fisher & Younggren, 1997). In addition, it assists faculty and supervisors in communicating the values of the profession to graduate students and to new Ph.D.s with limited professional experience.

Public Trust. A third purpose of an ethics code is to gain public trust by demonstrating that psychologists are members of a responsible and substantial profession with high standards. A code can serve a public relations value by being seen as a contract with society to act in consumers' best interest. A professional ethics code also provides standards against which the public can hold psychologists accountable. It thus offers a means by which members of the public can draw on norms prescribed by the profession itself to evaluate the conduct of scientists, educators, consultants, and practitioners with whom they interact.

Enforcement Value. A profession that demonstrates it can monitor itself is less vulnerable to external regulation. A fourth purpose of an ethics code is to provide a clear statement of the types of behaviors considered ethical violations to guide psychologists in avoiding such behaviors, assist consumers in making ethical complaints, and ensure that such complaints can be adjudicated clearly and fairly by the APA and other organizations (Fisher & Younggren, 1997). The APA Ethics Code also serves as a guide for licensing boards, courts, and other institutions for the evaluation of the responsible conduct of psychology and is thus a means of avoiding capricious standards set by nonpsychologists. The Ethics Code can also help psychologists defend their decisions to courts, institutions, or government agencies that would encourage them to go against the values of the profession.

The Revision Process

The ECTF was committed to an open and collaborative revision process that would be guided by the objectives articulated by the first ethics code committee (Hobbs, 1948).

In response to the continually evolving legal landscape of ethics adjudication and federal regulation of science and health practices, the ECTF also concluded that although law should not dictate the content of the ethics code, sensitivity to law would protect the integrity of the document as a useful tool for the everyday ethical decisions of psychologists. The 2002 Ethics Code revision process involved the following:

• Collecting from psychologists engaged in a broad spectrum of scientific and professional activities critical incidents describing ethical challenges they had encountered, actual or ideal ethical approaches to these challenges, and the extent to which the existing 1992 Ethics Code could be applied to these challenges

• Establishing an open call for and review of comments from the membership, graduate students, state psychological associations, licensing boards, and the public on the adequacy of the 1992 Ethics Code and on the content and format of each of seven drafts produced by the ECTF

• Opening ECTF meetings to observers from different APA constituencies so as to benefit from their insights and perspectives

• Ongoing legal review by APA General Counsel and outside defense, plaintiff, Federal Trade Commission, and federal regulatory attorneys

• Ongoing feedback from consumers, students, APA divisions and committees, the APA Ethics Committee, the APA Board of Directors, and the APA Council of Representatives

Following extensive discussion on the role of psychologists in military interrogations, effective June 1, 2010, Standards 1.02 and 1.03 were amended to make clear that these standards could never be used to justify or defend violating human rights (APA, 2010a; 2010b). Modifications based on these amendments appear in the relevant sections of this book.

Distinctive Features of the 2002 APA Ethics Code

Why Does the Ethics Code Separate General Principles From Enforceable Standards?

The 2002 Ethics Code retains the division of aspirational principles and enforceable standards pioneered in the 1992 version. In the development of the current code, the language of the General Principles was modified to more closely impart core moral values reflecting the highest ideals of the profession: promoting the welfare and protecting the rights of others, doing no harm, and acting faithfully and responsibly with integrity and fairness. The General Principles thus provide a conceptual framework that expresses the aspirational values of the common community of psychologists, and the behavioral rules articulated in the standards flow from these principles.

The 2002 Ethics Code reaffirmed the importance of clearly stated standards of ethical conduct that can provide APA members with sufficient due notice of the ethical behaviors required and prohibited by the APA, lend support to members' ability to defend their ethical actions, and increase the APA's success in sustaining decisions by the APA Ethics Committee in court, thus strengthening both the enforceability and credibility of APA's ethical oversight procedures. Revision of the enforceable standards of the 1992 Ethics Code included (a) minor grammatical modifications to reworking of language that helped clarify but did not otherwise alter the meaning of an existing standard, (b) new language that expanded the scope of the standard to additional roles or activities, (c) major wording changes that significantly altered the meaning of the standard, and (d) the inclusion of new rules for ethical conduct.

For interested readers, a table comparing the 1992 and 2002 Ethics Codes is available on the APA Ethics Office Web site (www.apa.org/ethics/codecompare .html).

What Is the Distinction Between the APA Ethics Code and Specific APA Guidelines?

The Introduction and Applicability section of the Ethics Code recommends that members refer to guidelines adopted or endorsed by scientific and professional psychological organizations as materials that may be useful in applying the Ethics Code to everyday activities. Unlike the 1992 Ethics Code (APA, 1992), specific APA guidelines to which psychologists may refer are not listed. The reason for this decision was twofold: (a) APA guidelines are frequently revised or become outdated, and (b) some statements in the older guidelines are inconsistent with standards in the 2002 Ethics Code and prevailing psychological science and practice. Professional and scientific guidelines are essential to ethical practice. As indicated earlier, the language of the Ethics Code is intentionally broad to be as applicable as possible to the wide range of activities that psychologists perform. Guidelines help psychologists place the standards in the context of their field of expertise. Guidelines will be cited throughout this book to illustrate best ethical practices in a given area.

Are Psychologists Obligated to Report Ethics Code Violations of Others?

Reporting Ethical Violations. When psychologists learn about a potential violation by another psychologist, they must attempt to resolve it informally by bringing it to the attention of the other psychologist if a resolution appears appropriate and the confidentiality rights of a research participant, client/patient, organizational client, or others are not violated (Standard 1.04, Informal Resolution of Ethical Violations). However, Standard 1.05, Reporting Ethical Violations, requires psychologists to formally report an ethical violation if it has or is likely to result in substantial harm, informal resolution is not appropriate, and the reporting would not violate confidentiality rights. This standard does not apply to psychologists retained to review another psychologist's ethical conduct.

Individuals Involved in Ethics Complaints. The integrity of the APA adjudication of ethics complaints is jeopardized when psychologists make "frivolous" complaints, and Standard 1.07, Improper Complaints, prohibits filing an ethics complaint with reckless disregard for or willful ignorance of facts that would disprove the allegation. The Ethics Code also prohibits psychologists from penalizing persons based solely on their having made or been the subject of an ethics complaint (Standard 1.08, Unfair Discrimination Against Complainants and Respondents). This standard is often relevant to situations that arise in whistle-blowing, discrimination, and sexual harassment cases.

Where Are Standards That Apply to Activities in Forensic Psychology?

The enforceable standards of the Ethics Code are organized into 10 sections: Resolving Ethical Issues, Competence, Human Relations, Privacy and Confidentiality, Advertising and Other Public Statements, Record Keeping and Fees, Education and Training, Research and Publication, Assessment, and Therapy. Many of the standards are worded broadly to apply to the broad range of work activities performed by psychologists. Unlike the 1992 code that preceded it, the 2002 Ethics Code does not have a separate section composed of enforceable standards uniquely related to forensic practice. Responding to an increase in ethics complaints to the APA Ethics Office, licensing board actions, and civil litigation related to forensic activities, the crafters of the 1992 Ethics Code concluded that ethical issues in forensic practice needed to be set out clearly and separately from other sections of the code and created a distinct section of standards devoted to forensic activities (APA, 1995, 1996; Canter et al., 1994). During the 10 years that followed, formal training, credentialing, and practice guidelines in forensic psychology advanced along with an increase in the number of psychologists without formal forensic training who were expanding their services to the legal arena or were called on to serve as fact witnesses in litigation (Perrin & Sales, 1994). As a result, the crafters of the 2002 Ethics Code decided to eliminate the forensic section and incorporate standards relevant to court-related activities into other sections. This change in format was selected to better serve the educational function of the document by alerting psychologists without formal training in forensic psychology to the ethical issues they must consider in advance of taking on roles involving the legal system.

Forensic or court-related work activities are explicitly mentioned in Standards 2.01f, Boundaries of Competence; 3.05c, Multiple Relationships; 3.10c, Informed Consent; 9.01a, Bases for Assessments; 9.03c, Informed Consent in Assessments; 9.04b, Release of Test Data; 9.10, Explaining Assessment Results; and 10.02b, Therapy Involving Couples or Families.

The topical table of contents and the forensic icons throughout this book will help readers quickly find discussions of these and other standards relevant to work within the legal system.

In addition, Hot Topics at the end of Chapters 8 and 12 provide in-depth analysis of the relevance of Ethics Code standards to testimony given by psychologists in legal settings.

Where Are Standards That Apply to Work With and Within Organizations?

Psychologists working in industry or consulting or delivering services to other organizations should refer to Standard 3.11, Psychological Services Delivered To or Through Organizations. This standard expands on requirements of the older code with respect to information that must be provided to organizational clients beforehand and, when appropriate, to those directly affected by the organizational services psychologists provide (i.e., employees). Other standards that explicitly refer to work for or within organizations include Standards 1.03, Conflicts Between Ethics and Organizational Demands; 3.07, Third-Party Requests for Services; 5.01, Avoidance of False or Deceptive Statements; 8.05, Dispensing With Informed Consent for Research; and 9.03, Informed Consent in Assessments. As with other areas of specialization, the broadly worded enforceable standards are relevant to and should be carefully read by consulting and by organizational and industrial psychologists. The topical table of contents and the industrial-organizational icons and case illustrations throughout this book are meant to assist in quickly identifying standards applicable to organizational settings.

Where Are Standards That Apply to Psychologists' Involvement With Health Management Organizations?

Psychologists' involvement with HMOs is addressed in standards throughout the Ethics Code. The implications of HMOs to standards on record keeping and fees are discussed in Chapter 9 of this book, followed by a Hot Topic devoted to the application of the Ethics Code to billing and contractual arrangements with HMOs. Involvement with HMOs is also relevant to standards on privacy and confidentiality (Standards 1.03, Conflicts Between Ethics and Organizational Demands; 3.07, Third-Party Requests for Services) and standards on informed consent (Standards 3.10, Informed Consent; 8.02, Informed Consent to Research; 9.03, Informed Consent in Assessments; and 10.01, Informed Consent to Therapy). The topical table of contents and the HMO icons and case illustrations throughout this book are meant to assist in quickly identifying standards applicable to work involving HMOs.

Are the Standards Relevant to Psychologists Working in the Military or Law Enforcement?

The ECTF was fortunate to receive comments and feedback on standards from Divisions 18 (Psychologists in Public Service) and 19 (Society for Military Psychology). This dialogue, for example, resulted in a modification of the title of Standard 1.02 to Conflicts Between Ethics and Law, Regulations, or Other Governing Legal Authority. As with other contexts in which psychologists work, the broadly worded enforceable standards are relevant to and should be carefully read by psychologists in the military and other areas of public service. The topical table of contents and military/law enforcement icons throughout this book are meant to assist in quickly identifying standards and case examples applicable to these contexts. In addition, Chapter 4 concludes with a Hot Topic on ethical issues relevant to involvement of psychologists in interrogations of detainees related to national security.

Is Sufficient Attention Given to Responsibilities of Administrators of Psychology Programs and Psychology Faculty?

The 2002 Ethics Code devotes a separate section for standards designed to highlight responsibilities of faculty and to strengthen protections for students. Below is a partial list of relevant standards.

Program Descriptions. Psychologists responsible for psychology programs must now include in program descriptions information regarding stipends and benefits and required course- or program-related counseling, psychotherapy, experiential groups, consulting projects, or community service (Standard 7.02, Descriptions of Education and Training Programs).

Student Disclosures and Therapy as a Program Requirement. Standard 7.04, Student Disclosure of Personal Information, prohibits teaching psychologists from requiring students or supervisees to disclose personal information regarding sexual history, history of child abuse or neglect, psychological treatment, or relationships with family or significant others unless such a requirement was clearly identified in the program description or the information is necessary to help a student or protect others from harm.

When therapy is a program or course requirement, students must be permitted to select a therapist unaffiliated with the program, and faculty who are likely to evaluate students are prohibited from providing that therapy (Standards 7.05a and b, Mandatory Individual or Group Therapy).

Sexual Relationships With Students. The 2002 Ethics Code strengthened the prohibition against sexual relationships with students and supervisees by extending it to any psychologist who has or is likely to have evaluative authority over these students (Standard 7.07, Sexual Relationships With Students and Supervisees).

Student Publication Credit. Standard 8.12c, Publication Credit, requires that except under unusual circumstances, a student is listed as principal author on any article substantially based on his or her dissertation. For other research collaborations, the standard requires that authorship credit accurately reflects the relative contributions of individuals involved, regardless of their relative status. The standard affords students additional protections by requiring that faculty advisers discuss publication credit with students as early as feasible and throughout the research and publication process as appropriate.

The Internet and Other Electronically Mediated Research and Services

The past two decades have witnessed an expansion in psychology's evolving use of the Internet and other electronic media for behavioral telehealth, psychological assessment, consulting, videoconferencing, public statements, and research. Throughout each section of the code, most of the broadly worded enforceable standards are applicable to these activities and do not require specific reference to the medium in which research or services are conducted. Use of the Internet and other electronically mediated forms relevant to research or services is explicitly mentioned in four standards: 3.10a, Informed Consent; 4.02c, Discussing the Limits of Confidentiality; 5.01a, Avoidance of False or Deceptive Statements; and 5.04, Media Presentations. To quickly locate discussions in this book on how other standards should be applied to work using electronic media, readers can refer to the topical table of contents and look for the electronic media icon in chapters on the enforceable standards.

Informed Consent for Research, Assessment, and Practice

Informed consent is seen by many as the primary means of ensuring the rights and welfare of those with whom psychologists work. Informed consent is designed to ensure that research participants, clients/patients, and organizational clients are provided with sufficient information to rationally and voluntarily decide whether they wish to participate in research or to receive psychological services. The general standard on informed consent provides direction on the nature of information that must be included and steps that must be taken to protect the rights of children and adults with cognitive impairments who are legally unable to provide consent (Standard 3.10, Informed Consent). Additional standards lay out information required for basic and intervention research; assessments relevant to mental health, forensic, and employment contexts; and individual and multiperson therapies, as well as additional consent safeguards for therapies for which generally recognized techniques and procedures have not been established (Standards 8.02, Informed Consent to Research; 8.03, Informed Consent for Recording Voices and Images in Research; 9.03, Informed Consent in Assessments; 10.01, Informed Consent to Therapy; 10.02, Therapy Involving Couples or Families; and 10.03, Group Therapy). The Hot Topic in Chapter 6 of this book examines specific applications of informed consent standards to adults with impaired decisional capacity.

Dispensing With Informed Consent. There are some instances in which informed consent is not necessary or not feasible as a means of protecting the rights and welfare of those with whom psychologists work. The Ethics Code provides specific descriptions of situations in which the requirement for informed consent may be waived and the additional steps needed to ensure individuals are treated with respect and concern for their welfare. These standards reflect enhanced sensitivity to naturalistic, neuropsychological, forensic, school, and industrial-organizational contexts in which psychologists provide services, conduct research, or administer assessments, including anonymous research surveys, assessments to determine decisional capacity, emergency treatment, and assessment or treatment mandated by law (Standards 3.10a, Informed Consent; 8.05, Dispensing With Informed Consent for Research; 9.03a, Informed Consent in Assessments; and 10.01, Informed Consent to Therapy).

New Standards for Research

Deception Research. The 2002 Ethics Code provides more specific guidance on when the use of deceptive research methods is ethically prohibited and adds a new requirement that participants in deception studies must be permitted to withdraw their data following dehoaxing (Standard 8.07, Deception in Research).

Debriefing Procedures. Researchers are now specifically required to take reasonable measures to alleviate psychological harm arising from experimental procedures when they are aware such harm has occurred (Standard 8.08c, Debriefing).

Data Sharing. Standard 8.14b, Sharing Research Data for Verification, explicitly prohibits psychologists who request data from other psychologists to verify substantive claims through reanalysis from using the data for any other purpose without prior written permission.

Standard 8.01, Institutional Approval, requires that psychologists obtain institutional review when it is required. Increased pressure on institutional review boards (IRBs) from the Department of Health and Human Services (DHHS) Office of Human Research Protections has led in recent years to more risk-averse IRB policies that have been viewed as an impediment to the conduct of social science research. The Hot Topic at the end of Chapter 8 of this book provides guidance for psychologists in submitting successful applications to IRBs.

Release of Test Data and Test Security

The standards that generated the most comment and debate among the APA membership are Standards 9.04a, Release of Test Data, and 9.11, Maintaining Test Security. As detailed in Chapter 10 of this book, one set of issues revolved around how to define *test data,* appropriate conditions for their release to clients/patients and qualified professionals, and how to respond to attorney requests, subpoenas, and court orders. A second set of issues focused on how to distinguish *test data* from *test materials* and how to balance the rights of clients/patients to their mental health records with the obligation to protect the integrity, security, and intellectual property rights of test materials and other assessment techniques. Of particular relevance to the final consensus on these standards was the federal Health Insurance Portability and Accountability Act (HIPAA) of 1996 establishing the rights of clients/patients to copies of their "designated record set" (medical or billing records maintained and used by the provider to make decisions about the patient). HIPAA raised questions about the extent to which health care providers could legally withhold health records from clients/patients. (HIPAA is discussed in greater detail throughout relevant chapters of this book and introduced in the Preface in the section "A Word About HIPAA.")

Definition of Test Data and Test Materials. Standard 9.04a defines *test data* as "raw and scaled scores, client/patient responses to test questions or stimuli, and psychologists' notes and recordings concerning client/patient statements and behavior during an examination." The definition of *test data* also includes the test materials or protocols if the psychologist wrote the client's/patient's responses, scores, or notes about behavior on the test protocol itself, and this information cannot be separated from the test materials in the client's/patient's record. Standard 9.11 defines *test materials* as "manuals, instruments, protocols, and test questions or stimuli that do not come under the definition of 'test data' as defined in Standard 9.04a."

Duty to Release and Right to Withhold Test Data. With few exceptions, Standard 9.04 requires psychologists to provide test data "to the client/patient or other persons identified in a client/patient release." The rationale for supporting release of test data was based on realities imposed by HIPAA regulations mandating release of health records to clients/patients, lack of APA member consensus on which professionals were and were not qualified to receive test data, and shifting societal emphasis on client's/patient's rights to the discovery process and judicial scrutiny of psychological tests. Standard 9.04 does not preclude psychologists from discussing with a client/patient the potential for misuse of the information by individuals unqualified to interpret it.

The standard also permits psychologists to withhold test data to protect the client/patient or another individual from substantial harm. At the same time, the standard includes the proviso that such decisions may be constrained by law. For example, under HIPAA, psychologists who are covered entities can deny client/patient access to designated record sets only if it is reasonably likely to endanger the life or physical safety of the individual or another person or cause equally substantial harm. Clients/patients also have the right to have the denial reviewed by a designated licensed health care professional. HIPAA regulations thus severely limit practicing psychologists' ability to exercise their professional judgment as to what constitutes substantial harm to clients/patients.

Standard 9.04a also permits withholding test data to protect misuse or misrepresentation of the data or the test. Before refusing to release test data under this clause, psychologists should carefully review relevant law. For example, when test data cannot be separated from test materials that are protected by copyright law, according to Richard Campanelli (Andberg, 2004), Director of the Office for Civil Rights at the U.S. DHHS, under Section 1172 (e), withholding protected health information would not be in violation of HIPPA if to do so would violate trade secret laws. There are other instances when HIPAA constraints are not at issue. HIPAA does not require release of records to clients/patients when information is compiled in reasonable anticipation of, or for use in, civil, criminal, or administrative actions or proceedings. In other instances, such as certain educational evaluations, the HIPAA Privacy Rule would not apply.

Terminating Therapy

A noteworthy aspect of the 2002 Ethics Code is the elimination of earlier codes' broadly worded prohibitions against abandoning the client/patient. This change reflects the widely accepted view that termination based on reasonable professional judgment and proper pretermination counseling is ethically appropriate. In fact, Standard 10.10 specifies situations in which psychologists are ethically required to terminate therapy when it becomes reasonably clear that the client/patient no longer needs the service, is not likely to benefit, or is being harmed by continued service. The standard also clarifies that it is permissible for psychologists to terminate therapy when they are threatened or otherwise endangered by a client/patient or another person with whom the client/patient has a relationship (Standard 10.10, Terminating Therapy).

The remainder of this book explains the meaning and applications of the 2002 Ethics Code to the rightly conducted science and practice of psychology. Chapter 2 explains the Ethics Code's Introduction and Applicability Section, Preamble, and General Principles. Chapter 3 discusses models of ethical decision making for applying the Ethics Code in everyday activities and to emerging ethical challenges as the discipline of psychology continues to evolve. Chapters 4 to 13 provide in-depth analysis and examples of each of the 151 enforceable Ethical Standards.

CHAPTER 2

The Introduction and Applicability Section, Preamble, and General Principles

What Do They Mean?

Psychologists are committed to increasing scientific and professional knowledge of behavior and people's understanding of themselves and others and to the use of such knowledge to improve the condition of individuals, organizations, and society. Psychologists respect and protect civil and human rights and the central importance of freedom of inquiry and expression in research, teaching, and publication. They strive to help the public in developing informed judgments and choices concerning human behavior.

—Ethical Principles of Psychologists and Code of
Conduct, American Psychological Association (APA, 2002b)

The 2002 Ethics Code begins with the Introduction and Applicability section, followed by the Preamble and a set of five General Principles reflecting the underlying values and ideals of the discipline.

The remainder of the code is composed of 151 enforceable standards that describe required, prohibited, and permitted behaviors. This chapter highlights the implications for ethical conduct of the Introduction and Applicability section, Preamble, and General Principles. Readers can refer to the appendix where the full text of the Ethics Code is provided.

Understanding the Introduction and Applicability Section and the Preamble

To Whom Does the Ethics Code Apply?

↗ Membership in the APA commits members and student affiliates to comply with the standards of the ethics code.

To What Does the Ethics Code Apply?

The answer to this question is all activities, all persons, all settings, and all communication contexts that are conducted, encountered, or used in one's role as a psychologist.

• *Activities* include, but are not limited to, clinical, counseling, and school practice; research; teaching and supervision; public service and policy development; program design, implementation, and evaluation; construction, administration, and interpretation of assessment instruments; organizational consulting; forensic activities; and administration.

• *Persons* include individual clients/patients, research participants, and students; children and adults of all ages; individuals with or without mental disorders; individuals with disabilities; persons from diverse cultural and language backgrounds; individuals within families, groups, and organizations; attorneys; and other professionals.

• *Settings* include military bases, schools, research laboratories, universities, private or group practice offices, business organizations, hospitals, managed care companies, the courts, private and public social services programs, government agencies, and public spaces where research or intervention is carried out.

• *Communication contexts* include research, consultation, and the delivery of services in person or through postal, telephone, fax, Internet, television and radio, and other electronic transmissions.

Psychologists should be aware that the Introduction and Applicability Section clearly states that lack of awareness or misunderstanding of any part of the Ethics Code is not itself a defense to a charge of unethical conduct.

Professional Versus Personal Activities. The Ethics Code applies only to psychologists' activities that are part of their scientific, educational, professional, or consulting roles. The code does not apply to the purely private conduct of psychologists, although the APA may take action against a member after his or her conviction of a felony, whether or not it directly resulted from activities performed in the member's role as a psychologist.

In some situations, distinctions between professional and personal activities may appear ambiguous. For example, if a psychology professor has a personal Web page that includes racist comments, are these comments relevant to his professional role if some of his students have access to this page? If a counseling psychologist criticizes the professionalism of a school psychologist during a parent meeting at her children's school, will other parents perceive her statements as at least partially professional? Pipes, Holstein, and Aguirre (2005) suggest some questions that may help psychologists determine when their personal actions are tilting toward their role as a psychologist and thus subject to the Ethics Code:

- Is the behavior linked to a role played by psychologists?
- Does the behavior, on its face, seem at least partially professional?
- Is there a high probability that those with whom the psychologist works will be affected?
- Does the action threaten the professional credibility of the psychologist or the discipline of psychology?

What Is the Relevance of Specific Language Used in the Ethics Code?

To fulfill the Ethics Code's professional, educational, public, and enforcement goals, the language of the Ethics Code needs to have the clarity necessary to provide adequate notice of behaviors that would be considered code violations, to be applicable across many multifaceted roles and responsibilities of psychologists, and to enhance and not impede good scientific and professional practice. The language of the Ethics Code must be specific enough to provide guidance and general enough to allow for critical thinking and professional judgment.

This section includes some general guidance for interpreting the language of the Ethics Code. The implications of specific terminology to specific standards are addressed in greater detail in relevant chapters.

Due Notice. Adjudicatory decisions based on an ethics code remain vulnerable to overturn on appeal if defendants can argue they had no forewarning that specific behaviors were ethical violations (Bersoff, 1994). For example, language in enforceable standards requiring psychologists to be "alert to," "guard against," or "respect" certain factors is problematic because the behaviors expected by these terms remain undefined and are thus vulnerable to subjective interpretation by psychologists, consumers, and ethics committees. Accordingly, the language of the enforceable standards in the 2002 Ethics Code was crafted to describe the behaviors that are required and those that are proscribed in a manner that would be reasonably understood by readers.

Applicability Across Diverse Roles and Contexts. Psychologists teach, conduct research, provide therapy, administer and interpret psychological tests, consult to business, provide legal testimony, evaluate school programs, serve in public service sectors and the military, and take on a multitude of different scientific and professional roles. An enforceable ethics code for psychologists must therefore be worded broadly enough to ensure that (a) standards apply across a broad range of activities in which psychologists are engaged, (b) role-specific standards are clearly presented as such, and (c) standards do not compromise scientific, practice, or consulting activities through inattention to or inconsistencies with the constantly changing realities of professional and legal responsibilities.

This requirement, viewed alongside the need for language providing due notice, means that some standards reflecting generally accepted ethical values in one work area were not included in the 2002 Ethics Code because they could not be worded in such a way as to prevent undue burden on psychologists working in another area. For example, the Ethics Code Task Force struggled with appropriate wording for a general "honesty" standard within the Human Relations section that would reflect the aspirational principle of integrity. However, such a general standard had to be abandoned because it risked prohibiting ethically acceptable practices such as paradoxical therapy and deception research. The principle of integrity is reflected in more circumscribed standards, including Standards 5.01, Avoidance of False or Deceptive Statements; 5.02, Statements by Others; 6.06, Accuracy in Reports to Payors and Funding Sources; and 8.10, Reporting Research Results. For additional discussion on this issue, readers may wish to refer to the Hot Topic in Chapter 8 on avoiding false and deceptive statements in scientific and clinical expert testimony.

The Use of Modifiers. A modifier is a word or phrase that qualifies the meaning of an ethical rule. Modifiers in the Ethics Code include terms such as *appropriate, potentially, to the extent feasible,* and *attempt to.* An explanation for the use of "modifiers" is provided in the Introduction and Applicability section. The use of modifiers is necessary for standards that are written broadly to allow for professional judgment across a wide range of psychological activities and contexts. For example, the term *feasible* in a standard permits psychologists to evaluate whether factors within the specific context in which they are working justify delaying or not implementing behaviors required by a particular standard. Modifiers are also used to eliminate injustice or inequality that would occur without the modifier. For example, a modifier such as *appropriate* signals that the behaviors required to comply with a standard can vary with the psychological characteristics of the persons involved, psychologists' roles, or specific situational demands. A modifier such as the term *relevant* is used in standards to guard against language that would create a rigid rule that would be quickly outdated. Below are three examples of the use of modifiers:

- Standard 10.01a, Informed Consent to Therapy, requires psychologists to obtain informed consent from clients/patients as early as is feasible in the therapeutic relationship. The phrase "as early as is feasible" provides decisional latitude when fully informed consent during an initial therapy session may not be possible or clinically appropriate. A client/patient may be experiencing acute distress that requires immediate psychological intervention and for which informed consent procedures may be clinically contraindicated. Psychologists may need to wait for feedback from a client's/patient's health maintenance organization (HMO) before consent discussions regarding fees can be completed.

- Standard 3.10b, Informed Consent, requires that for persons who are legally incapable of giving informed consent, psychologists "provide an appropriate explanation." The term *appropriate* indicates that the nature of the explanation will vary depending on, among other factors, the person's developmental level, cognitive capacities, mental status, and language preferences and proficiencies.

- Under Standard 2.01c, Boundaries of Competence, psychologists planning to engage in activities new to them must undertake relevant education, training, supervised experience, consultation, or study. By including the term *relevant*, this standard can continue to be applied to new roles, new techniques, and new technologies, as they emerge over time.

What Is "Reasonable"? In the Introduction and Applicability section, the term *reasonable* is defined as the "prevailing professional judgment of psychologists engaged in similar activities in similar circumstances, given the knowledge the psychologist had or should have had at the time." The use of this term serves two functions. It prohibits psychologists from exercising idiosyncratic ethical judgments inconsistent with the prevailing values and behaviors of members of the profession. In so doing, it provides other psychologists and recipients of psychological services, students, and research participants a professional standard against which to judge psychologists' ethical behaviors. At the same time, by requiring that criteria for compliance or violation of an Ethical Standard be judged against the prevailing practices of peers, the use of the term *reasonable* guards against unrealistic or unfair expectations of responsible conduct. The wording enables psychologists to launch a legitimate defense of their actions based on current best practices in the field and documentation of efforts to resolve problems in an ethical manner. The examples below illustrate these two applications of the term *reasonable:*

- Standard 4.07, Use of Confidential Information for Didactic or Other Purposes, prohibits psychologists from disclosing in public statements confidential and personally identifiable information about those with whom they work unless they have taken "reasonable steps to disguise the person or organization." The term *reasonable* recognizes that despite steps to protect confidentiality that would be considered ethically acceptable by other psychologists (i.e., the use of pseudonyms; disguising gender, ethnicity, age, setting, business products), persons to whom the statements refer may recognize (or erroneously attribute the description to) themselves or others may be privy to information not under the psychologist's control that leads to identification.

- Standard 2.05, Delegation of Work to Others, requires that psychologists who delegate work to employees, supervisees, research or teaching assistants, interpreters, or others take reasonable steps to authorize only those responsibilities that such persons can be expected to perform competently on the basis of their education, training, or experience, either independently or with the level of supervision being provided. In this case, a psychologist who asked a secretary who spoke the same language as a client/patient to serve as an interpreter during an assessment would not have taken steps considered reasonable in the prevailing view of the profession. On the other hand, a psychologist who hired an interpreter based on an impressive set of credentials in mental health evaluation would not be in violation if the interpreter had fabricated the credentials.

"Client/Patient" and "Organizational Client." Throughout the Ethics Code, the combined term *client/patient* refers to individual persons to whom a psychologist is providing treatment, intervention, or assessment services. The term *organizational clients, organizations,* or *clients* refers to organizations, representatives of organizations, or other individuals for whom the psychologist is providing consultation, organization or personnel evaluations, test development, research, forensic expertise, or other services that do not involve a treatment, intervention, or diagnostic professional relationship with the person to whom services are provided. For example, a bank hired a psychologist to provide counseling services to employees who had experienced trauma during a recent robbery. In this context, the bank was the psychologist's "client" or "organizational client," and the employees who sought the psychologist's counseling services were the clients/patients. To further illustrate this distinction, readers can compare the use of the term *client* in Standard 3.11, Psychological Services Delivered To or Through Organizations, with the use of the term *client/patient* in Standard 10.01, Informed Consent to Therapy.

How Is the Ethics Code Related to APA Ethics Enforcement?

The APA Ethics Committee investigates complaints against APA members alleging violations of the APA Ethics Code that was in effect at the time the conduct occurred. The APA Ethics Committee Rules and Procedures detail the ethics enforcement process and can be obtained online at www.apa.org/ethics/rules.html. Below is a brief summary of these rules and procedures.

Ethics Complaints. Complaints to the Ethics Committee may be brought by APA members or nonmembers or initiated by members of the Ethics Committee (*sua sponte* complaints) within specified time periods. A complaint may be dismissed prior to review by the Ethics Committee if it does not meet jurisdictional criteria or if, upon preliminary review, the Ethics Office director and the Ethics Committee chair or their designees fail to find grounds for action. If the Ethics Committee does have jurisdiction and the complaint provides grounds for action, the case is opened, violations of specific Ethical Standards are charged, and an investigation is begun. The psychologist against whom the complaint is made receives a charge letter and is given an opportunity to provide the committee with comment and materials regarding the allegations.

Failure of the respondent to cooperate with the Ethics Committee is itself an ethical violation (APA Ethics Code Standard 1.06, Cooperating With Ethics Committees; see Chapter 4). However, in response to a request by a respondent, the committee may proceed or stay the ethics process if the respondent is involved in civil or criminal litigation or disciplinary proceedings in other jurisdictions. Psychologists who do not wish to contest the allegations may submit to the APA an offer of "resignation while under investigation."

Sanctions. The Ethics Committee reviews the materials and resolves to either dismiss the case or recommend one of the following actions:

- *Reprimand.* A reprimand is given when a violation was not of a kind likely to cause harm to another person or to cause substantial harm to the profession and was not otherwise of sufficient gravity as to warrant a more severe sanction.

- *Censure.* The Ethics Committee may issue a censure if the violation was of a kind likely to cause harm to another person, but the violation was not of a kind likely to cause substantial harm to another person or to the profession and was not otherwise of sufficient gravity as to warrant a more severe sanction.

- *Expulsion.* A member can be expelled from the APA when the violation was of a kind likely to cause substantial harm to another person or the profession or was otherwise of sufficient gravity as to warrant such action.

- *Stipulated resignation.* Contingent on execution of an acceptable affidavit and approval by the Board of Directors, members may be offered a stipulated resignation following a committee finding that they committed a violation of the Ethics Code or failed to show good cause why they should not be expelled.

The Ethics Committee may also issue directives requiring the respondent to (a) cease and desist an activity, (b) obtain supervision or additional training or education, (c) be evaluated for and obtain treatment if appropriate, or (d) agree to probationary monitoring.

A psychologist who has been found in violation of the Ethics Code may respond to the recommendation by requesting an independent case review or, in the case of expulsion, an in-person proceeding before a formal hearing committee.

Notification. The director of the Ethics Office informs the respondent and the complainant of the final disposition in a matter, provides to the APA membership on an annual basis the names of individuals who have been expelled from membership and those who resigned from membership while under investigation, and informs the APA Council of Representatives in confidence who received a stipulated resignation and who resigned from membership while under investigation. The Board of Directors or the Ethics Committee may also determine that additional notification is necessary to protect the APA or the public or to maintain APA standards. The Ethics Office director may also notify state boards, affiliated state and regional associations, the American Board of Professional Psychology, the Association of State and Provincial Psychology Boards, the Council for the National Register of Health Service Providers in Psychology, and other appropriate parties. In addition, the APA may provide such information to any person who submits a request about a former member who has lost membership because of an ethical violation.

Show Cause Procedure. The Ethics Committee can also take action against a member if a criminal court, licensing board, or state psychological association has already taken adverse action against the member. The rationale for such actions can go beyond a violation of the Ethics Code and can include conviction of a felony or revocation of state licensure.

How Is the Ethics Code Related to Sanctions by Other Bodies?

The APA Ethics Code is widely used by other bodies regulating the ethical science and practice of psychology. It is intended to be applied by the APA Ethics Committee and by other bodies that choose to adopt specific standards. The Introduction and Applicability section states, "Actions that violate the standards of the Ethics Code may also lead to the imposition of sanctions on psychologists or students whether or not they are APA members by bodies other than APA, including state psychological associations, other professional groups, psychology boards, other state or federal agencies, and payors for health services." In contrast to the Ethical Standards, as stated in the General Principles section, the aspirational principles of the Ethics Code are not intended to represent specific obligations or the basis for imposing sanctions.

Across the country, the Ethics Code is adopted in its entirety or in part in statute in more than half the state boards responsible for licensing the practice of psychology. Insurance companies regularly require psychologists applying or reapplying for professional liability policies to reveal whether they have been the recipient of an ethics complaint or found in ethical violation by a professional organization, state board, or state or federal agency, and many retain the right to raise rates or cancel policies depending on the nature of the violation. In addition, the APA Ethics Committee may notify other bodies and individuals of sanctions it imposes for ethical violations. For information on the procedures for filing, investigating, and resolving ethics complaints, readers should refer to the Rules and Procedures of the APA Ethics Committee at www.apa.org/ethics/rules.html.

How Is the APA Ethics Code Related to Law?

Civil Litigation. The Introduction and Applicability section clearly states that the Ethics Code is not intended to be a basis of civil liability: "Whether a psychologist has violated the Ethics Code standards does not by itself determine whether the psychologist is legally liable in a court action, whether a contract is enforceable, or whether other legal consequences occur." However, psychologists should be aware that it seems highly unlikely that such a disclaimer would have any legally binding effect. Compliance with or violation of the Ethics Code may be admissible as evidence in some legal proceedings, depending on the circumstances. Similarly, although the Ethics Code states that using the General Principles as a representation of obligations or to apply sanctions distorts the meaning and purpose of the aspirational principles, attorneys may introduce into litigation the General Principles or Ethical Standards as evidence of the ethical values, requirements, or prohibitions of the discipline.

Compliance With Law. Law does not dictate ethics, but sensitivity to law protects the integrity of the profession. Whereas few standards require psychologists to comply with law, many standards were written to minimize the possibility that compliance with the Ethics Code would be in conflict with state laws and federal regulations. Those standards that require compliance with the law include the following:

- Work-related discrimination, Standard 3.01, Unfair Discrimination
- Obtaining consent from legally authorized persons for individuals legally incapable of giving such consent, Standard 3.10b, Informed Consent
- Legal prohibitions against disclosure of confidential information, Standards 4.05a and b, Disclosures
- Creation, storage, and disposal of records, Standard 6.01, Documentation of Professional and Scientific Work and Maintenance of Records
- Fee practices, Standard 6.04a, Fees and Financial Arrangements
- Care and use of animals in research, Standard 8.09, Humane Care and Use of Animals in Research
- Legal and contractual obligations, Standard 9.11, Maintaining Test Security

Although there are no specific Ethical Standards for which a criminal conviction is a violation, the Introduction and Applicability section and the APA Rules and Regulations clearly state that the APA may take action against a member after his or her conviction of a felony, including expulsion from the organization.

Conflicts Between Ethics and Law, Regulations, or Other Governing Legal Authority. In applying the Ethics Code to their scientific and professional work, psychologists may find relevant laws, regulations, or other governing legal authority that conflict with the Ethical Standards. As articulated in the Introduction and Applicability section, psychologists must comply with the Ethics Code if it establishes a higher standard of conduct than is required by law. When an Ethical Standard is in direct conflict with law, regulations, or other governing legal authority, psychologists must make known their commitment to the Ethics Code and take steps to resolve the conflict in a responsible manner. If the conflict is unresolvable via such means, psychologists are permitted to adhere to the legal requirements. The Introduction and Applicability section of the Ethics Code urges psychologists to resolve such conflicts in keeping with basic principles of human rights. In 2010 an amendment to the relevant enforceable standard, Standard 1.02, Conflicts Between Ethics and Law, Regulations, or Other Governing Legal Authority, clarified that the standard can never be used to justify or defend violating human rights. Application of the Ethics Code's aspirational language and enforceable standards related to conflicts between ethics and law has taken on added urgency in the national debate regarding the role of psychologists in the interrogation of prisoners at Guantanamo and other military installations. Readers may also wish to refer to the Hot Topic in Chapter 4 on the involvement of psychologists in interrogations related to national security.

General Principles

Ethics are principles of action based on a commonly accepted system of values, and agreement upon these principles and values must be reached before progress toward an acceptable code can be expected.

—Bixler and Seeman (1946, p. 486)

"A genuine and practical code of ethics . . . stems from a philosophy as well as a need" (Bixler & Seeman, 1946, p. 486). The moral values from which the APA Ethical Standards stem are articulated in five General Principles. These principles are aspirational, intended to inspire psychologists toward the highest ethical ideals of the profession. Unlike the Ethical Standards, they do not represent specific or enforceable behavioral rules of conduct. The General Principles articulate the moral vision of psychology's common community of purpose. Although psychologists must strive to act in accordance with all the principles, the moral priority of any one principle will be determined by the specific ethical problem. The principles are therefore listed in alphabetical order and are not hierarchically organized.

The General Principles help guide psychologists' decision making by providing an analytic framework from which to identify those Ethical Standards that are appropriate to the situation at hand. Each enforceable standard reflects one or more of these principles. Below, each principle is described and examples provided of standards in which the principle ideals are embedded.

Principle A: Beneficence and Nonmaleficence. Principle A reflects psychologists' dual obligation to strive to do good and avoid doing harm. As articulated in the Preamble and in Principle A, psychologists strive to do good by promoting the welfare of others, treating people and animals humanely, increasing scientific and professional knowledge of behavior and people's understanding of themselves, and improving the condition of individuals, organizations, and society. Examples of standards reflecting the principle of beneficence include Standards 2.02; Providing Services in Emergencies; 3.09, Cooperation With Other Professionals; 8.09, Humane Care and Use of Animals in Research; and 8.14, Sharing Research Data for Verification.

Throughout sections of the Ethics Code, psychologists are also expected to avoid or minimize harms when they are unavoidable by taking steps to remedy harms caused by misuse of their work, maintaining competence, guarding against behaviors that would lead to exploitation of those with whom they work, minimizing intrusions on privacy in reports or consultations with colleagues, providing opinions and reports based only on information or techniques sufficient to substantiate findings, and terminating therapy when the client/patient is likely to be harmed by continued services (Standards 1.01, Misuse of Psychologists' Work; 2.03, Maintaining Competence; 3.04, Avoiding Harm; 3.05, Multiple Relationships; 3.08, Exploitative Relationships; 9.01, Bases for Assessments; and 10.10, Terminating Therapy). Principle A represents the joint influences of beneficence and nonmaleficence in recognition that in rightly practiced psychology, individuals may be harmed without being wronged. For example, to preserve academic standards and ensure grading fairness, teaching psychologists may be obligated to give a student a poor or failing grade. Similarly, disclosing confidential information to protect a client/patient, student, or research participant from self-harm or from harming others may have moral priority over protecting that individual's privacy rights (see Standard 4.05, Disclosures). For additional information, readers may refer to the Hot Topics in Chapter 7 on disclosures and confidentiality relevant to parental involvement in mental health services for children and adolescents and in Chapter 10 on ethical supervision of trainees.

To maximize good and minimize harm, Principle A also calls for psychologists to be alert to and guard against personal problems that could lead to exploitation or harm to individuals or organizations with whom they work (see Standard 2.06, Personal Problems and Conflicts).

Principle B: Fidelity and Responsibility. Fidelity reflects faithfulness of one human being to another (Ramsey, 2002). In psychology, such faithfulness includes promise keeping, the discharge and acceptance of fiduciary responsibilities, and the appropriate maintenance of scientific, professional, and teaching relationships. Psychologists recognize their responsibility to obtain and maintain high standards of competence in their own work and to be concerned about the ethical compliance of their colleagues. The nature of the competencies and responsibilities of psychologists to individuals, organizations, and communities will be determined by the specific scientific or professional relationship. Many of the standards on competence discussed in Chapter 5 reflect the aspirations articulated in Principle B.

In fulfilling the ideals expressed in Principle B, psychologists seek to meet their responsibilities by consulting with other professionals when necessary and avoiding conflicts of interest that would jeopardize trust or lead to exploitation or harm (see, for example, Standards 3.09, Cooperation With Other Professionals, and 3.06, Conflict of Interest). The fiduciary and professional obligations to which Principle B asks psychologists to aspire are also reflected in the standards on resolving ethical issues (Chapter 4), record keeping and fees (Chapter 9), and education and training (Chapter 10). Readers may also whish to refer to the Hot Topics in Chapter 9 on managing managed care and in Chapter 11 on submitting research proposals to institutional review boards.

Principle C: Integrity. Maintaining integrity in psychological activities requires honest communication, truth telling, promise keeping, and accuracy in the science, teaching, and practice of psychology. It involves refraining from making professional commitments that cannot be met and avoiding or correcting misrepresentations of one's work. In following Principle C, psychologists do not steal, cheat, or engage in fraud or subterfuge. These ideals are evidenced in Standards 5.01, Avoidance of False or Deceptive Statements; 6.04, Fees and Financial Arrangements; and 8.10, Reporting Research Results.

In some scientific and professional relationships, deception may be justified to maximize knowledge gained or the welfare of individuals served. As articulated in Standard 8.07, Deception in Research, in each instance, psychologists have a serious obligation to evaluate whether deception is warranted, to decide whether negative consequences outweigh the benefits to individuals or society, and to correct any mistrust or harm that arises from the use of such techniques.

Principle D: Justice. Principle D calls for psychologists to strive to provide to all people fair, equitable, and appropriate access to treatment and to the benefits of scientific knowledge. Psychologists endeavor to be aware of and guard against their own biases and the prejudices of others that may condone or lead to unjust practices. These ideals are reflected in Standards 1.08, Unfair Discrimination Against Complainants and Respondents; 3.01, Unfair Discrimination; 3.02, Sexual Harassment; and 3.03, Other Harassment.

Principle D also calls for psychologists to select procedures and services that meet the needs of those with whom they work, recognizing that existing social and economic inequities may require different but comparable scientific and professional techniques. The principle of justice also requires that psychologists present their findings objectively and dispassionately. Enforceable standards reflecting the values of fairness articulated in Principle D include 7.06, Assessing Student and Supervisee Performance; 8.04, Client/Patient, Student, and Subordinate Research Participants; 9.01, Bases for Assessments; and 10.02, Therapy Involving Couples or Families.

Principle E: Respect for People's Rights and Dignity. Principle E calls for psychologists to "respect the dignity and worth of all people, and the rights of individuals to privacy, confidentiality, and self-determination." Standards requiring informed consent to research, assessment, and therapy (Standards 3.10, 8.02, 9.03, and 10.01) reflect respect for autonomous decision making articulated in Principle E. Psychologists must also be attentive to the circumstances of individuals who may have limited capacity for autonomous decision making and take the extra precautions necessary to safeguard these individuals' rights and welfare. This responsibility is specifically addressed in Standard 3.10b, Informed Consent. Readers may also wish to refer to the Hot Topic in Chapter 6 on informed consent involving adults with impaired decisional capacity.

Psychologists are aware of and respect cultural, individual, and role differences, including those based on age, gender, gender identity, race, ethnicity, culture, national origin, religion, sexual orientation, disability, language, and socioeconomic status. They ensure that they are familiar with the scientific and professional knowledge relevant to these differences and acquire the competencies necessary to perform their roles effectively. Psychologists strive to be aware of and eliminate from their work the effect of their own and others' prejudices. Exemplar standards reflecting the ideal of respect for individual differences are Standards 2.01, Boundaries of Competence, and 9.01, Bases for Assessments.

Principle E also addresses psychologists' duty to protect the rights of individuals to determine what and with whom personal information will be shared. This ideal is embedded in standards on privacy and confidentiality (Chapter 7), as well as Standards 6.02, Maintenance, Dissemination, and Disposal of Confidential Records of Professional and Scientific Work; 7.04, Student Disclosure of Personal Information; and 10.03, Group Therapy.

CHAPTER 3

The APA Ethics Code and Ethical Decision Making

T he American Psychological Association's (APA's) Ethics Code provides a set of aspirational principles and behavioral rules written broadly to apply to psychologists' varied roles and the diverse contexts in which the science and practice of psychology are conducted. The five aspirational principles described in Chapter 2 represent the core values of the discipline of psychology that guide members in recognizing in broad terms the moral rightness or wrongness of an act. As an articulation of the universal moral values intrinsic to the discipline, the aspirational principles are intended to inspire right action but do not specify what those actions might be. The ethical standards that will be discussed in later chapters of this book are concerned with specific behaviors that reflect the application of these moral principles to the work of psychologists in specific settings and with specific populations. In their everyday activities, psychologists will find many instances in which familiarity with and adherence to specific Ethical Standards provide adequate foundation for ethical actions. There will also be many instances in which (a) the means by which to comply with a standard are not readily apparent, (b) two seemingly competing standards appear equally appropriate, (c) application of a single standard or set of standards appears consistent with one aspirational principle but inconsistent with another, or (d) a judgment is required to determine if exemption criteria for a particular standard are met.

The Ethics Code is not a formula for solving these ethical challenges. The Ethics Code provides psychologists with a set of aspirations and broad general rules of conduct that must be interpreted and applied as a function of the unique scientific and professional roles and relationships in which they are embedded. Psychologists are not moral technocrats simply working their way through a maze of ethical rules. Successful application of the principles and standards of the Ethics Code involves a conception of psychologists as active moral agents committed to the good and just practice and science of psychology. Ethical decision making thus involves a commitment to applying the Ethics Code to construct rather than simply discover solutions to ethical quandaries.

This chapter discusses the ethical attitudes and decision-making strategies that can help psychologists prepare for, identify, and resolve ethical challenges as they continuously emerge and evolve in the dynamic discipline of psychology.

Ethical Commitment

> *The development of a dynamic set of ethical standards for psychologists'*
> *work-related conduct requires a personal commitment and lifelong effort to*
> *act ethically; to encourage ethical behavior by students, supervisees, employ-*
> *ees, and colleagues; and to consult with others concerning ethical problems.*
>
> —APA (2002b, Preamble)

Ethical commitment refers to a strong desire to do what is right because it is right (Josephson Institute of Ethics, 1999). In psychology, this commitment reflects a moral disposition and emotional responsiveness that move psychologists to creatively apply the APA's Ethics Code principles and standards to the unique ethical demands of the scientific or professional context.

The desire to do the right thing has often been associated with moral virtues or moral character, defined as a disposition to act and feel in accordance with moral principles, obligations, and ideals—a disposition that is neither principle bound nor situation specific (Beauchamp & Childress, 2001; MacIntyre, 1984). Virtues are dispositional habits acquired through social nurturance and professional education that provide psychologists with the motivation and skills necessary to apply the ideals and standards of the profession (see, e.g., Hauerwas, 1981; Jordan & Meara, 1990; May, 1984; National Academy of Sciences, 1995; Pellegrino, 1995).

Focal Virtues for Psychology

Many moral dispositions have been proposed for the virtuous professional (Beauchamp & Childress, 2001; Keenan, 1995; MacIntyre, 1984; May, 1984). For disciplines such as psychology, in which codes of conduct dictate the general parameters but not the context-specific nature of ethical conduct, conscientiousness, discernment, and prudence are requisite virtues.

- A *conscientious* psychologist is motivated to do what is right because it is right, diligently tries to determine what is right, and makes reasonable attempts to do the right thing.

- A *discerning* psychologist brings contextually and relationally sensitive insight, good judgment, and appropriately detached understanding to determine what is right.

- A *prudent* psychologist applies practical wisdom to ethical challenges leading to right solutions that can be realized given the nature of the problem and the individuals involved.

Some moral dispositions can be understood as derivative of their corresponding principles (Beauchamp & Childress, 2001). Drawing on the five APA General Principles, Table 3.1 lists corresponding virtues.

The virtues considered most salient by members of a profession will vary with differences in role responsibilities. Benevolence, care, and compassion are often associated with the provision of mental health services. "Openness to the other" has been identified as a core virtue for the practice of multiculturalism (Fowers & Davidov, 2006). Prudence, discretion, and trustworthiness have been considered salient in scientific decision making. Fidelity, integrity, and wisdom are moral characteristics frequently associated with teaching and consultation.

Can Virtues Be Taught?

No course could automatically close the gap between knowing what is right and doing it.

—Pellegrino (1989, p. 492)

Some have argued that psychology professors cannot change graduate students' moral character through classroom teaching, and therefore ethics education should focus on understanding the ethics code rather than instilling moral dispositions to right action. Without question, however, senior members of the discipline, through teaching and through their own examples, can enhance the ability of students and young professionals to understand the centrality of ethical commitment to ethical practice. At the same time, the development of professional moral character is not to simply know about virtue but to become good

Table 3.1   APA Ethics Code General Principles and Corresponding Virtues

APA General Principle	Corresponding Virtues
Principle A: Beneficence and Nonmaleficence	Compassionate, humane, nonmalevolent, and prudent
Principle B: Fidelity and Responsibility	Faithful, dependable, and conscientious
Principle C: Integrity	Honest, reliable, and genuine
Principle D: Justice	Judicious and fair
Principle E: Respect for People's Rights and Dignity	Respectful and considerate

(P. A. Scott, 2003). Beyond the intellectual virtues transmitted in the classroom and modeled through mentoring and supervision, excellence of character can be acquired through habitual practice (Begley, 2006). Thus, the virtuous graduate student and seasoned psychologist are committed to lifelong learning and practice in the continued development of moral excellence.

Ethical Awareness

In the process of making decisions regarding their professional behavior, psychologists must consider this Ethics Code, in addition to applicable laws and psychology board regulations.

—APA (2002b, Introduction)

Lack of awareness or misunderstanding of an ethical standard is not itself a defense to a charge of unethical conduct.

—APA (2002b, Introduction)

Ethical commitment is just the first step in effective ethical decision making. Good intentions are insufficient if psychologists fail to identify the ethical situations to which they should be applied. Psychologists found in violation of Ethical Standards or licensure regulations have too often harmed others or damaged their own careers or the careers of others because of ethical ignorance. Conscientious psychologists understand that identification of situations requiring ethical attention is dependent on familiarity and understanding of the APA Ethics Code, relevant scientific and professional guidelines, and laws and regulations applicable to their specific work-related activities.

Moral Values and Ethical Awareness

To identify a situation as warranting ethical consideration, psychologists must be aware of the moral values of the discipline. Although the Ethics Code's General Principles are not exhaustive, they do identify the major moral ideals of psychology as a field. Familiarity with the General Principles, however, is not sufficient for good ethical decision making. Psychologists need to be aware when situations call for consideration of these principles. Table 3.2 identifies types of ethical awareness corresponding to each General Principle.

Ethical Awareness and Ethical Planning

Too often, psychologists approach ethics as an afterthought to assessment or treatment plans, research designs, course preparation, or groundwork for forensic or

Table 3.2   APA Ethics Code General Principles and the Ethical Awareness Necessary to Apply the Principles

APA General Principle	Corresponding Ethical Awareness
Principle A: Beneficence and Nonmaleficence	Psychologists should be able to identify what is in the best interests of those with whom they work, when a situation threatens the welfare of individuals, and the competencies required to achieve the greatest good and avoid or minimize harm.
Principle B: Fidelity and Responsibility	Psychologists should be aware of their obligations to the individuals and communities affected by their work, including their responsibilities to the profession and obligations under the law.
Principle C: Integrity	Psychologists should know what is possible before making professional commitments and be able to identify when it is necessary to correct misconceptions or mistrust.
Principle D: Justice	Psychologists should be able to identify individual or group vulnerabilities that can lead to exploitation and recognize when a course of action would result in or has resulted in unfair or unjust practices.
Principle E: Respect for People's Rights and Dignity	Psychologists must be aware of special safeguards necessary to protect the autonomy, privacy, and dignity of members from the diverse populations with whom psychologists work.

consulting activities. Ethical planning based on familiarity with ethical standards, professional guidelines, state and federal laws, and organizational and institutional policies should be seen as integral rather than tangential to psychologists' work.

Ethical Standards. Familiarity with the rules of conduct set forth in the Ethical Standards enables psychologists to take preventive measures to avoid the harms, injustices, and violations of individual rights that often lead to ethical complaints. For example, psychologists familiar with the standards on confidentiality and disclosure discussed in Chapter 7 will take steps in advance to (a) develop appropriate procedures to protect the confidentiality of information obtained during their work-related activities; (b) appropriately inform research participants, clients/patients, organizational clients, and others in advance about the extent and limitations of confidentiality; and (c) develop specific plans and lists of appropriate professionals, agencies, and institutions to be used if disclosure of confidential information becomes necessary.

Guidelines. Good ethical planning also involves familiarity with guidelines for responsible practice and science. The APA and other professional and scientific organizations publish guidelines for responsible practice appropriate to particular psychological activities. Guidelines, unlike ethical standards, are essentially aspirational and unenforceable. As a result, compared with the enforceable Ethics Code standards, guidelines can include recommendations for and examples of responsible conduct with greater specificity to role, activity, and context. Guidelines shed light on specific steps that other psychologists in similar situations have taken to successfully resolve ethical quandaries. The crafters of guidelines developed by APA constituencies usually attempt to ensure that their recommendations are consistent with the most current APA Ethics Code—readers should be alert to instances in which the 2002 Ethics Code renders some guideline recommendations adopted prior to 2002 obsolete.

Laws, Regulations, and Policies. Another important element of information gathering is identifying and understanding applicable laws, government regulations, and institutional and organizational policies that may dictate or limit specific courses of actions necessary to resolve an ethical problem. There are state and federal laws and organizational policies governing patient privacy, mandated reporting, research with humans and animals, conduct among military enlistees and officers, employment discrimination, conflicts of interest, billing, and treatment. Psychologists involved in forensically relevant activities must also be familiar with rules of evidence governing expert testimony. Readers may also wish to refer to the Hot Topic in Chapter 12 on the implications of case and federal law on the use of assessments in expert testimony.

As discussed in Chapter 2, only a handful of Ethical Standards require psychologists to adhere to laws or institutional rules. However, choosing an ethical path that violates law, institutional rules, or company policy can have serious consequences for psychologists and others. Laws and policies should not dictate ethics, but familiarity with legal and organizational rules is essential for informed ethical decision making. When conflicts between ethics and law arise, psychologists consider the consequences of the decision for stakeholders, use practical wisdom to anticipate and take preventive actions for complications that can arise, and draw on professional virtues to help identify the moral principles most salient for meeting professional role obligations (Knapp, Gottlieb, Berman, & Handelsman, 2007).

Ethical Decision Making

Ethical commitment and well-informed ethical planning will reduce but not eliminate ethical challenges that emerge during the course of psychologists' work. Ethical problems often arise when two or more principles or standards appear to be in conflict and often arise from unforeseen reactions of those with whom a psychologist works or unexpected events. There is no ethical menu from which the right ethical actions simply can be selected. Many ethical challenges are unique in time, place, and persons involved. The very process of generating and evaluating alternative courses of action helps place in vivid relief the moral principles underlying such conflicts and stimulates creative strategies that may resolve or eliminate them.

Evaluating Alternatives and Consequences

Ethical decisions are neither singular nor static. They involve a series of steps, each of which will be determined by the consequences of previous steps. Evaluation of alternative ethical solutions should take a narrative approach that sequentially considers the potential risks and benefits of each action. Understanding of relevant laws and regulations as well as the nature of institutions, companies, or organizations in which the activities will take place is similarly essential for adequate evaluation of the reactions and restraints imposed by the specific ethical context.

Stakeholders. Ethical decision making requires sensitivity to and compassion for the views of individuals affected by actions taken. Discussions with stakeholders can clarify the multifaceted nature of an ethical problem, illuminate ethical principles that are in jeopardy of being violated or ignored, and alert psychologists to potential unintended consequences of specific action choices. By taking steps to understand the concerns, values, and perceptions of clients/patients, research participants, family members, organizational clients, students, corporate compliance or institutional review boards, and others with whom they work, psychologists can avoid ethical decisions that would be ineffective or harmful (Fisher, 1999, 2000).

Ethical Theories

In evaluating each alternative, psychologists should reflect on the rights and obligations of all involved and aspirational principles that can or cannot be achieved at each step. Ethical theories provide a moral framework to reflect upon conflicting obligations. Unfortunately, ethical theories tend to emphasize one idea as the foundation for moral decision making, and illustrative problems are often reduced to that one idea. Given the complexity of moral reality, these frameworks are probably not mutually exclusive in their claims to moral truth (Steinbock, Arras, & London, 2003). However, awareness of the moral frameworks guiding one's concerns can also help clarify the values underlying a choice of alternative strategies (Beauchamp & Childress, 2001; Fisher, 1999; Kitchener, 1984).

Deception Research: A Case Example for the Application of Different Ethical Theories

Since Stanley Milgram published his well-known obedience experiments, the use of deception has become normative practice in some fields of psychological research and a frequent source of ethical debate. Deceptive techniques in research intentionally withhold information or misinform participants about the purpose of the study, the methodology, or roles of research confederates (Sieber, 1982). The methodological rationale for the use of deception is that some psychological phenomena cannot be adequately understood if research participants are aware of the purpose of the study. For example, deception has been used to study the phenomenon of "bystander apathy effect," the tendency for people in the presence of others to observe but not help a person who is a victim of an attack, medical emergency, or other dangerous condition (Latane & Darley, 1970). In such experiments, emergency situations are staged without the knowledge of the research participants, whose reactions to the "emergency" are recorded and analyzed.

By its very nature, the use of deception in research is inconsistent with Principle C: Integrity and with enforceable standards requiring psychologists to obtain fully informed consent of research participants prior to study initiation (Fisher, 2005). At the same time, by approximating naturalistic contexts in which everyday behaviors take place, the use of deception research can reflect Principle A: Beneficence and Nonmaleficence by enhancing the ability of psychologists to generate scientifically and socially useful knowledge that might not otherwise be obtained.

Below are examples of how different ethical theories might lead to different conclusions about the moral acceptability of deception research. Readers should refer to Chapter 11 for a more in-depth discussion of Standard 8.07, Deception in Research.

Deontology. Deontological theory prioritizes absolute obligations over consequences (Kant, 1785/1959). In this moral framework, ethical decision making is the rational act of applying universal principles to all situations irrespective of specific relationships, contexts, or consequences. For Kant, respect for the worth of all persons was a categorical imperative. A course of action that results in a person being used simply as a means for others' gains would be ethically unacceptable. From a deontological perspective, deception in research would not be ethically permissible since, by intentionally disguising the nature of the study for the goals of research, it undermines the moral obligation to respect each participant's intrinsic worth by violating his or her right to make rational and autonomous decisions regarding participation (Fisher & Fyrberg, 1994).

Deontology has been described as "absolutist," "universal," and "impersonal." This reflects Kant's conviction that ethical decisions cannot vary or be influenced by special circumstances or relationships. Rather, a decision is "moral" only if a rational person believes the act resulting from the decision should be universally followed in all situations. With respect to deception in research, from a deontological perspective, since we would not believe it moral to intentionally deceive individuals in other contexts, neither potential benefits to society nor the effectiveness of participant debriefing for a particular deception study can morally justify intentionally deceiving persons about the purpose or nature of a research study.

Utilitarianism. Utilitarian theory prioritizes the consequences (or utility) of an act over the application of universal principles (Mill, 1861/1957). From this perspective, an ethical decision is situation specific and must be governed by a risk-benefit calculus that determines which act will produce the greatest possible balance of good over bad consequences. An "act utilitarian" makes an ethical decision by evaluating the consequences of an act for a given situation. A "rule utilitarian" makes an ethical decision by evaluating whether following a general rule in all similar situations would create the greater good. Like deontology, utilitarianism is impersonal. From this perspective, psychologists' obligations to those with whom they work can be superseded by an action that would produce a greater good for others.

A psychologist adhering to act utilitarianism might decide that the potential knowledge about social behavior generated by a specific deception study could produce benefits for many members of society, thereby justifying the minimal risk of harm and violation of autonomy rights for a few research participants. A rule utilitarian might decide against the use of deception in all research studies because the unknown benefits to society did not outweigh the potential harm to the discipline of psychology if society began to see it as an untrustworthy science.

Communitarianism. Communitarian theory assumes that right actions derive from community values, goals, traditions, and cooperative virtues. Accordingly, different populations with whom a psychologist works may require different conceptualizations of what is ethically appropriate (MacIntyre, 1989; Walzer, 1983). Unlike deontology, communitarianism rejects the elevation of individual over group rights. Whereas utilitarianism asks whether a policy will produce the greatest good for all individuals in society, communitarianism asks whether a policy will promote the kind of community we want to live in (Steinbock et al., 2003).

Scientists as members of a community of shared values have traditionally assumed that (a) the pursuit of knowledge is a universal good and that (b) consideration for the practical consequences of research will inhibit scientific progress (Fisher, 1999; Sarason, 1984; Scarr, 1988). From this "community of scientists" perspective, the results of deception research are intrinsically valuable, and standards or regulations prohibiting deceptive research would deprive society of this knowledge. Thus, communitarian theory may be implicitly reflected, at least in part, in the acceptance of deception research in the APA Ethics Code (Standard 8.07, Deception in Research) and in current federal regulations (Department of Health and Human Services, 2005) as representing the values of the scientific community.

Feminist Ethics. Feminist ethics, or an ethics of care, sees emotional commitment to act on behalf of persons with whom one has a significant relationship as central to ethical decision making. This moral theory rejects the primacy of universal and individual rights in favor of relationally specific obligations (Baier, 1985; Brabeck, 2000; Fisher, 2000; Gilligan, 1982). Feminist ethics also focuses our attention on power imbalances and supports efforts to promote equality of power and opportunity. In evaluating the ethics of deception research, feminist psychologists might view intentional deception as a violation of interpersonal obligations of trust by investigators to participants and as reinforcing power inequities by permitting psychologists to deprive persons of information that might affect their decision to participate.

Ethical Absolutism, Ethical Relativism, and Ethical Multiculturalism

The movement known as multiculturalism is reshaping moral dialogue in psychology through its emphasis on inclusion, social justice, and mutual respect (Flowers & Davidov, 2006).

Psychologists with high levels of ethical commitment and awareness are often stymied by moral complexities that surface when psychological activities are conducted in diverse contexts, cultures, or communities. For example, when applied to ethical decision making across different contexts, the universal perspective of the deontic position is indifferent to particular persons and situations. It therefore rejects the influence of culture on the identification and resolution of ethical problems in a manner that can lead to a one-size-fits-all form of ethical problem solving (Fisher, 1999). In sharp contrast, ethical relativism, often associated with some forms of utilitarianism and communitarianism, denies the existence of universal or common moral values characterizing the whole of human relationships, proposing instead that the identification and resolution of ethical problems are unique to each particular culture or community.

Ethical contextualism (Fisher, 1999, 2000; Macklin, 1999) blends the two approaches assuming that moral principles such as beneficence and respect for autonomy are universally valued across diverse contexts and cultures, but the expression of an ethical problem and the right actions to resolve it can be unique to the cultural context. From this perspective, universal moral principles can mediate our understanding of ethical meaning across diverse contexts without placing a priority on the principles themselves over the moral frameworks of others (Walker, 1992).

Culture and Informed Consent: A Case Example. Take the example of the ethical challenge of obtaining informed consent in countries where cultural mores require that women obtain permission from their fathers, husbands, or brothers before they can receive treatment or participate in research.

A psychologist who is an ethical absolutist might refuse to obtain permission from a male relative prior to obtaining consent from a female living in this culture on the grounds that any action that privileges the opinion of a third party in a treatment or research decision is a violation of a universal principle of respect for individual autonomy. The cultural relativist, on the other hand, might interpret the cultural mores dictating male privilege as evidence that respect for individual autonomy is not a moral value in this particular culture; consequently, any action consistent with the cultural norm (e.g., obtaining the male relative's permission) is ethical.

The ethical contextualist would see the problem as one that requires consideration of both a universal valuing of individual autonomy and its traditional expression within this particular culture. A psychologist adopting this position would seek to resolve the ethical problem in a manner consistent with both. For example, examining the cultural meaning of this tradition, a psychologist might find that women in this culture value the male gatekeeper role and see it as beneficial to themselves and/or the stability of their families and communities. In this scenario, principles of justice and respect for personhood might result in an ethical resolution in which psychologists first seek permission from a male relative before they approached a woman about treatment or research participation, making it clear to both the male and the prospective client/patient or research participant that the psychologist would respect the woman's decision about whether she wished to consent.

Alternatively, the ethical contextualist might find that women living in this particular cultural community view this tradition as repressive and fear harsh retaliation if they disagree with the decision of their husbands or other male relatives. In this scenario, drawing upon the principles of beneficence and nonmaleficence and respect for personhood, the psychologist might create a safe and confidential opportunity for women to learn about and consent or refuse the treatment or research participation on their own.

In both scenarios, psychologists recognize that respect for persons involves responding to informed consent dilemmas on the basis of participants' own self-conceptions and values (Dillon, 1992; Fisher, 2000; Fisher et al., 2008). For further discussion of these and related issues, readers are referred to the Hot Topics in Chapter 5 on multicultural ethical competence and in Chapter 13 on the integration of religion and spirituality in therapy.

Steps in Ethical Decision Making

A number of psychologists have proposed excellent ethical decision-making models to guide the responsible conduct of psychological science and practice (e.g., Canter et al., 1994; Kitchener, 1984; Koocher & Keith-Spiegel, 1998; Newman, Gray, & Fuqua, 1996; Rest, 1983; Staal & King, 2000). Drawing on these models and the importance of ethical commitment, awareness, and competence, an eight-step model is proposed:

Step 1: Develop and sustain a professional commitment to doing what is right.

Step 2: Acquire sufficient familiarity with the APA Ethics Code General Principles and Ethical Standards to be able to anticipate situations that require ethical planning and to identify unanticipated situations that require ethical decision making.

Step 3: Gather additional facts relevant to the specific ethical situation from professional guidelines, state and federal laws, and organizational policies.

Step 4: Make efforts to understand the perspective of different stakeholders who will be affected by the decision and consult with colleagues.

Step 5: Apply Steps 1 to 4 to generate ethical alternatives and evaluate each alternative in terms of moral theories, General Principles, and Ethical Standards.

Step 6: Select and implement an ethical course of action.

Step 7: Monitor and evaluate the effectiveness of the course of action.

Step 8: Modify and continue to evaluate the ethical plan if necessary.

Consider how these eight steps can be applied to the following ethical dilemma.

An Example of Ethical Decision Making

Dilemma. Dr. Ames is conducting a longitudinal ethnographic study on health-related attitudes and practices of street drug users. She has been conducting once-a-month interviews with the same participants for almost a year. Although Dr. Ames was careful not to recruit participants who were friends, partners, or relatives, she has recently learned that two research participants from this small community of drug users, 35-year-old James and 18-year-old Angela, have started to date one another. During an ethnographic interview, James, who had previously told the psychologist that he was HIV positive, casually mentions that Angela, who believes that both she and James are HIV negative, has become pregnant and that he is planning to continue to have regular unprotected sex with her. When asked, James tells Dr. Ames that he does not plan to tell Angela that he is HIV positive because she would leave him. He also angrily reminds Dr. Ames that she is "sworn to secrecy" because she promised that everything he told her, except child abuse, would be confidential (adapted from Fisher et al., in press).

Step 1. Dr. Ames is committed to doing the right thing. She thinks of herself as honest, judicious, respectful, and compassionate. She struggles with her desire to keep her promise to James to maintain his confidentiality and her concern about the welfare of Angela and her pregnancy.

Step 2. Dr. Ames reviews the Ethics Code standards. She realizes that since two of her research participants have unexpectedly entered into a romantic relationship that can potentially compromise her objectivity and effectiveness in performing her job, she is confronting an unforeseen potentially harmful multiple relationship that, according to Standard 3.05b, she must take reasonable steps to resolve the problem with due regard for the best interests of the affected persons. She also recognizes that while it is important to protect James's confidentiality (Standard 4.01, Maintaining Confidentiality), the Ethics Code permits her to disclose confidential information to protect others from harm (Standard 4.05, Disclosures). She is satisfied that her informed consent procedure was consistent with ethical standards since she did inform James of her legal obligation to report child abuse, and the possibility disclosure could occur to protect participants or others from harm. However, at the initiation of her research, there was no reason to assume that this type of situation would arise and she is unsure whether this situation meets the legal definition of child abuse or whether the consent language adequately informed participants that the risk of transmitting HIV would meet criteria for disclosure. (Standards 3.10, Informed Consent; 4.02, Discussing the Limits of Confidentiality; 8.02, Informed Consent to Research). She is also aware that if she decides to deviate from her planned ethical procedures, she must inform and obtain approval from the university ethics review board (Standard 8.01, Institutional Approval).

She also reviews the Ethics Code's aspirational principles. She recognizes that she has a fiduciary responsibility to both James and Angela that rests on establishing a relationship of trust (Principle B: Fidelity and Responsibility) and worries that the relationship with James will be jeopardized if she discloses his HIV status to Angela and that her relationship with Angela will be compromised if she is perceived to be colluding with James in a secret that could be harmful to Angela and her baby (Principle A: Beneficence and Nonmaleficence, Principle C: Integrity, and Principle E: Respect for People's Rights and Dignity).

Step 3. Dr. Ames consults with her university legal counsel and discovers that her state has no "duty to protect" law requiring researchers (or clinicians) to take steps to protect identified others from harm (see Chapter 7) and that mandatory child abuse reporting laws are not extended to pregnancies. There are also no laws requiring or preventing researchers from disclosing information on HIV obtained in a nonmedical context. Her institutional review board (IRB) similarly informs her that federal regulations do not dictate either maintaining confidentiality or disclosure under this situation. She reviews relevant publications and discovers that conditions requiring disclosure remain under debate within the discipline (Donner et al., 2008).

Step 4. She consults with medical colleagues regarding the probability that James will transmit the virus to Angela and the risks to her fetus and learns that infectivity rates are highly variable ranging from 1 per 1000 to 1 per 3 contacts (Powers, Poole, Pettifor & Cohen, 2008) and mother to child transmission is 15-30% occurring mostly in the last trimester (Orendi et al., 1999). She also speaks to the prenatal department of the community clinic that most of her participants go to and finds out that they routinely provide pregnant women with information regarding HIV risk protection. To ensure that she is sensitive to the cultural context from which James and Angela's reactions to her decision may be embedded, she consults with her community advisory board composed of former drug users and social service workers with experience serving this community. Some board members express the belief that the risk of HIV is well known in the community and that Angela is responsible for protecting herself. Others believe that James is violating community standards and that he has therefore given away his right to confidentiality (see Fisher et al., in press). Still, others point out that Dr. Ames may lose the trust of the rest of her participants if she violates James's confidentiality. Through all of these discussions, Dr. Ames is careful not to identify James and Angela (Standard 4.06, Consultations).

Step 5. Dr. Ames begins to contemplate alternative actions. From a deontic perspective, by maintaining confidentiality, she would fulfill her commitment to James on which his autonomous consent to participate was based. At the same time, Kant's idea of humanity as an end in itself might support taking steps to protect Angela and her fetus from harm. From a utilitarian perspective, the importance of protecting Angela and her fetus from a potentially life-threatening health risk must be weighed against the unknown probability of HIV infection to Angela and her fetus as well as Angela's reaction to the disclosure are unknown. Dr. Ames would also need to consider which decision would preserve the trust she has developed with all of her other participants and allow her to complete research she believes will ultimately provide important insights into the health needs of the drug-using community. The advisory board consultation suggested that there was not a broadly shared common moral perspective that would suggest a specific communitarian or multicultural approach to the problem. From a feminist ethics perspective, failing to disclose the information to Angela might perpetuate the powerlessness and victimization of women in this disenfranchised community. At the same time, disclosure might undermine Angela's autonomy if in fact she is aware of HIV risk factors in general and knows or suspects James' HIV positive status.

Step 6. On the basis of the previous steps, Dr. Ames decides that she will not at this point disclose James's HIV status to Angela. She concludes that her promise to James regarding confidentiality was explicitly related to his agreement to participate in the research, while her sense of obligation to protect Angela from James's behavior was not a requisite or an expectation of Angela's participation. The community board's comments suggest that Angela is most likely aware of the general risks of HIV transmission among drug users, as do some of Angela's comments in Dr. Ames's notes from previous interviews. In addition, Dr. Ames's visit to the clinic indicated there are available community medical services that routinely advise pregnant women about these risks. Dr. Ames decides that at her next interview with Angela, she will encourage her to visit the free prenatal clinic. She will also tell James of her decision not to disclose his HIV status to Angela, continue to encourage him to do so, and provide him with written information regarding prenatal risk and safer sexual practices. She informs her IRB of her decision. At the same time, disclosure might undermine Angela's autonomy if in fact she is aware of HIV risk factors in general and knows or suspects James' HIV positive status.

Step 7. Dr. Ames will monitor and evaluate the effectiveness of her course of action. She will keep apprised of whether Angela visits the prenatal clinic and whether James begins to act in ways that will be protective of Angela. She will also continue to evaluate whether the unexpected multiple relationship with James and Angela compromises her ability to maintain objectivity in her interviews and interpretation of data or to establish a trusting relationship with each of them as research participants.

Step 8. Whether or not monitoring leads Dr. Ames to modify her decision to maintain James's confidentiality, her evaluation of the effect of her course of action will influence her confidentiality and disclosure policies in the future. She plans to run a focus group of community drug users and consult with ethicists to develop procedures that can anticipate and best address this type of issue in the future.

Doing Good Well

Ethical decision making in psychology requires flexibility and sensitivity to the context, role responsibilities, and stakeholder expectations unique to each work endeavor. At their best, ethical choices reflect the reciprocal interplay between psychological activities and ethical standards in which each is continuously informed and transformed by the other. The specific manner in which the APA Ethics Code General Principles and Ethical Standards are applied should reflect a "goodness of fit" between ethical alternatives and the psychologist's professional role, work setting, and stakeholder needs (Fisher, 2002b, 2003b; Fisher & Goodman, in press). Envisioning the responsible conduct of psychology as a process that draws on psychologists' human responsiveness to those with whom they work and their awareness of their own boundaries, competencies, and obligations will sustain a profession that is both effective and ethical.

Ethics requires self-reflection and the courage to analyze and challenge one's values and actions. Ethical practice is ensured only to the extent that there is a personal commitment accompanied by ethical awareness and active engagement in the ongoing construction, evaluation, and modification of ethical actions. In their commitment to the ongoing identification of key ethical crossroads and the construction of contextually sensitive ethical courses of action, psychologists reflect the highest ideals of the profession and merit the trust of those with whom they work.

PART II

Enforceable Standards

CHAPTER 4

Standards for Resolving Ethical Issues

1. RESOLVING ETHICAL ISSUES

1.01 Misuse of Psychologists' Work

If psychologists learn of misuse or misrepresentation of their work, they take reasonable steps to correct or minimize the misuse or misrepresentation.

Psychologists have professional and scientific responsibilities to society and to the specific individuals, organizations, and communities with whom they work to ensure that their work products are not misused or misrepresented. Psychologists cannot reasonably be expected to anticipate all the ways in which their work can be wrongly used. Thus, Standard 1.01 of the American Psychological Association (APA) Ethics Code (APA, 2002b) focuses on corrective action that must be taken when psychologists learn that others have misused or misrepresented their work. To remedy misuse, psychologists can write letters to or speak with interested parties, request retraction of misrepresentations, or discuss with appropriate persons corrective measures to be taken.

Frequently, psychologists will not be aware that their work has been misrepresented, and inaction on their part would not be an ethical violation. However, when it is reasonable to expect that psychologists would be aware of misuse or misrepresentation of their work, a claim of ignorance would not be an acceptable defense against a charge of violation of this standard (Canter et al., 1994).

☑ A school psychologist completed a report summarizing her assessment of a child whose test results did not meet diagnostic criteria for serious emotional disturbance. Several days later, she learned that the principal of her school had forwarded to the superintendent of schools only those parts of the assessment report that supported the principal's desire to classify the student as emotionally disturbed to fill a special education quota. The psychologist asked the principal to send the entire report, explaining the ethical issues involved.

☑ A research psychologist learned that a special interest group had sent a listserv mailing for financial contributions that misquoted and misrepresented the psychologist's writings as supporting the group's cause. The psychologist contacted the group and asked it to cease sending this e-mail to other potential contributors and to e-mail a correction to the listserv recipients.

☑ A forensic psychologist learned that an attorney had submitted to the court a tampered version of the psychologist's written report. The psychologist, after consulting with an independent attorney, informed the court of the tampering.

☑ A health psychologist who had developed a commercially marketed instrument for assessing environmental and psychosocial risk for children diagnosed with asthma discovered that the company responsible for testing scoring had miskeyed some of the items. The psychologist contacted the company and requested that it (a) immediately correct the error for future use, (b) rescore tests that had been subject to the miskeying, and (c) send practitioners who had used the scoring service the rescored test results with a letter of explanation.

The phrase "reasonable steps" recognizes that despite their best efforts in some instances, psychologists may not be in a position to ensure their requests to correct misuse are followed. For example, if the research psychologist whose work had been misrepresented did not have access to the listserv, short of a civil suit, the psychologist would have few corrective options if the group refused requests for retraction. In other instances, it may not be possible or appropriate to actively seek a correction. For example, during a trial, attorneys may phrase questions that, by their nature, distort or otherwise lead to misrepresentation of a psychologist's testimony. In such instances, it is ethically appropriate for psychologists at the time of their testimony to rely on existing corrective mechanisms (i.e., asking the judge to permit the psychologist to provide clarification, responding as fully as possible to a related question during cross-examination) or refrain from corrective actions when an attempt to remedy the misrepresentation would violate the rules of the court or the legal rights of a complainant or defendant (see Standard 2.01f, Boundaries of Competence). Psychologists should always document the corrective efforts made to remedy known misuse or misrepresentations.

1.02 Conflicts Between Ethics and Law, Regulations, or Other Governing Legal Authority

If psychologists' ethical responsibilities conflict with law, regulations, or other governing legal authority, psychologists clarify the nature of the conflict, make known their commitment to the Ethics Code and take reasonable steps to resolve the conflict consistent with the General Principles and Ethical Standards of the Ethics Code. Under no circumstances may this standard be used to justify or defend violating human rights.

This standard, amended in 2010 (APA, 2010a), addresses instances in which the requirements of the Ethics Code may conflict with judicial authority, with state or federal laws, or with regulations governing the activities of psychologists working in the military, correctional facilities, or other areas of public service. Standard 1.02 requires psychologists take action when conflicts between the Ethics Code and laws, regulations, or governing legal authority arise. As highlighted in Chapter 3, psychologists must have sufficient understanding of the Ethics Code standards to identify such conflicts. Specific steps that may be taken include informing appropriate authorities of the conflict and explaining the rationale for the Ethics Code standard.

> ☑ A psychologist who had received a court order for confidential information sent a letter to the judge explaining the relevant confidentiality standards in the Ethics Code and requesting judicial review to determine whether a limited release of information would meet legal requirements.
>
> ☑ A correctional psychologist refused a request from the prison warden to draw upon his therapy sessions with a prisoner to help the warden recommend punishment for the client who had gotten into a fight with a fellow inmate. The psychologist explained to the warden that to do so could violate several ethical standards, including 1.01, Misuse of Psychologists' Work; 3.05, Multiple Relationships; and 4.01, Maintaining Confidentiality.

When a Conflict Cannot Be Resolved

Standard 1.02 also recognizes that legal and regulatory authorities may not always respond to specific steps taken by psychologists to resolve conflicts between ethics and law. When reasonable actions taken by psychologists do not resolve the conflict, they are permitted to make a conscientious decision regarding whether to adhere to the Ethics Code or the legal or regulatory authority, except under circumstances that result in a violation of human rights.

This permissive aspect of the standard recognizes that in some contexts, when legal ethics and professional ethics conflict, each may be equally defensible in terms of moral principles. For example, in some instances, a judicial review requested by a psychologist in response to a court order may determine that full release is required to protect the legal rights of a defendant or plaintiff to a fair trial. In such situations, Principle D: Justice is in conflict with Principle E: Respect for People's Rights and Dignity, and Standard 1.02

permits psychologists to draw upon ethical decision-making strategies as described in Chapter 3, to decide whether to obey or disobey the court order.

In other instances, abiding by the law helps to maintain the presence of psychologists in settings in which they can work to encourage and assist legal authorities develop alternative rules and procedures that will enable psychologists to fulfill their professional obligations as well as their obligations under the law.

For example, U.S. Department of Defense (DoD) regulations routinely require military psychologists to perform activities that place service to the military mission above the best interests of the individual client/patient, resulting in conflicts between DoD requirements and Ethical Standards involving confidentiality, maintenance of records, competence, and multiple relationships (Johnson, 1995).

Efforts by military psychologists to bridge the gap between APA Ethical Standards and DoD regulations regarding confidentiality resulted in implementation of DoD Directive 6490.1 (U.S. DoD, 1997a) and DoD Instruction 6490.4 (U.S. DoD, 1997b), which protect the rights of active-duty service members sent for commander-directed mental health evaluations (CDMHEs) to know why they were referred for evaluation and who will be conducting the evaluation, their right to obtain an evaluation summary and second opinion, and their right to speak with legal counsel, a chaplain, and a member of Congress regarding their situation (Orme & Doerman, 2001).

When Laws Are Unjust

It is important to note that Standard 1.02 does *not* require compliance with law. The intentional absence of such a requirement reflects the American Psychological Association's longtime commitment to the value of civil disobedience in response to unjust laws. Relatedly, psychologists should not assume that Standard 1.02 waives their obligation to adhere to other standards of the Ethics Code when laws are unjust. For example, the APA Council of Representatives adopted a resolution prohibiting psychologists from knowingly participating "*in any procedure in which torture or other forms of cruel, inhuman, or degrading treatment or cruel, inhuman, or degrading punishment is used or threatened*" (APA, 2006). Readers may also wish to refer to the Hot Topic at the end of this chapter on involvement of psychologists in interrogations involving national security.

1.03 Conflicts Between Ethics and Organizational Demands

If the demands of an organization with which psychologists are affiliated or for whom they are working conflict with this Ethics Code, psychologists clarify the nature of the conflict, make known their commitment to the Ethics Code, and take reasonable steps to resolve the conflict consistent with the General Principles and Ethical Standards of the Ethics Code. Under no circumstances may this standard be used to justify or defend violating human rights.

Psychologists working with organizations may encounter company policies, plans, or procedures that conflict with the Ethics Code. Standard 1.03 requires that psychologists inform the organization about the nature of the conflict and the ways in which policies or activities violate the Ethics Code, and they must take actions to resolve the conflict in a manner consistent with Ethics Code standards. The standard specifically requires psychologists to make known their commitment to the Ethics Code in communications with the organization.

☑ An industrial-organizational psychologist recently employed by an organization to handle employment testing discovered that the organization used a test for preemployment screening for which there was no applicable, documented validity evidence and that did not appear to be clearly job related (Standard 9.02b, Use of Assessments). The psychologist notified the employer of the problem and recommended that use of the test be suspended until a more suitable preemployment screening process could be identified and validated. The psychologist provided a specific, realistic plan for helping the employer move toward an ethical and legally defensible applicant screening process.

☑ A superintendent of schools wanted a counseling psychologist whose job it was to provide career and academic counseling to high school students in the school district to take on an added role as the Title IX officer designated to evaluate and enforce school rules regarding student-student and faculty-student sexual harassment. The psychologist explained that the dual assignment could compromise his ability to effectively conduct either role because it was likely that some students who came to the psychologist for counseling about sexual harassment would need to appear before the psychologist in his Title IX role to press or defend against sexual harassment charges (Standard 3.05, Multiple Relationships).

The phrase "to the extent feasible" recognizes that despite reasonable efforts by psychologists, an organization may refuse to change a policy that is inconsistent with the Ethics Code. This standard does not require psychologists to resign when their attempts at a resolution are unsuccessful as long as their work does not justify or defend violating human rights (APA, 2010a) (see Acuff et al., 1999, for excellent case examples).

☑ A psychologist was hired by a health maintenance organization (HMO) to implement preexisting company criteria for mental health services claims. During a utilization review, she noticed that company policy on the use of psychopharmacological medications in the absence of conjoint psychotherapy was counter to professional and scientific knowledge of the discipline for the particular disorder under review and believed the policy was potentially harmful to patients (Standards 2.04, Bases for Scientific and Professional Judgments and 3.04, Avoiding Harm). The psychologist drew the company's attention to the problem and the relevant APA Ethical Standards, but the HMO management refused to change the policy without a full review of alternative policies. The psychologist agreed to use the preexisting criteria while continuing her efforts to work with management on ways in which they could improve the utilization criteria.

> ☒ A psychologist working for an HMO was asked to develop evidence-based utilization standards for a specific class of mental health disorders. On the basis of current research, he recommended that individuals diagnosed to have this class of disorders receive psychopharmacological medications and conjoint psychotherapy. During a review of the first draft of the psychologist's recommendations, his employer told him that conjoint psychotherapy would significantly diminish the profitability of plans covering the disorder and asked the psychologist to remove the recommendation from the final draft of the report. The psychologist did not attempt to discuss with his employer the ethical issues associated with approving for reimbursement what was known to be inadequate treatment (Standards 2.04, Bases for Scientific and Professional Judgments, and 3.04, Avoiding Harm) and simply agreed to change his recommendation in the final report.

Psychologists should not assume that Standard 1.03 waives their obligation to adhere to other standards in this Ethics Code. For example, a psychologist who implemented a health care organization's policy to increase revenue by providing unwarranted treatment to Medicaid patients could be charged with Medicaid fraud and a violation of Standards 6.04b, Fees and Financial Arrangements, and 9.01a, Bases for Assessment, even if the psychologist brought the unethical nature of the policy to the organization's attention (see Acuff et al., 1999).

> ☒ A recently hired school psychologist discovered that the district-mandated test batteries for suspected learning disabilities were outdated, were inconsistent with current professional standards, and violated the intent of special education laws that require tests be selected in light of the unique characteristics of the individual child. She reasoned that as a new hire, it would be professionally risky to raise this issue with the district school psychology supervisor and decided to do her best for the children using the district's test battery (see Standard 9.02a, Use of Assessments, and Jacob & Hartshorne, 2007).
>
> ☑ A prescribing psychologist was employed by a nursing home to assess the psychological status and psychopharmacology needs of residents. She noticed that the excessive job demands placed on nurses' aides at the institution were resulting in limited and restrictive patient care, as well as an overuse of medications for patient sedation that in turn was contributing to a loss of patient independent functioning and deterioration of cognitive and other functional capacities. The psychologist recognized that current financial difficulties at the nursing home precluded the hiring of additional nurses' aides. When she approached the institutional director with her concerns about the overmedication, she offered to provide training sessions for the nurses' aides in behavioral techniques that would help reduce patient agitation and encourage greater patient functional independence without adding to the aides' work responsibilities.

Commercially Funded Research

Advances in training programs in neuropsychology, psychopharmacology, and pharmacotherapy have been accompanied by increased participation of psychologists in research on psychoactive and central nervous system medications, drugs, and chemicals. Growing involvement in the empirical assessment of psychotropic medications is likely to be paralleled by increased funding for research psychologists from pharmaceutical companies. Psychologists who are unfamiliar with private industry sponsorship of research may be unprepared for the ethical challenges that arise. While conflict-of-interest dilemmas have been spotlighted in the media and scholarly journals (see Standard 3.06, Conflict of Interest), university-affiliated research psychologists may find themselves in the type of conflict between ethics and organizational demands described in Standard 1.03 when the research sponsor attempts to control the dissemination of research findings.

It should not be surprising that conflicts between ethics and organizations may arise when psychologists' research results are inconsistent with the commercial interests of the company funding their study. For example, when unanticipated patient risks emerge during clinical trials, sponsors may attempt to prevent psychologists from fulfilling their obligation to inform their institutional review board (IRB) of the adverse events (Standard 8.01, Institutional Approval). When unanticipated risks to participants emerge during a clinical trial, psychologists are obligated to take appropriate steps to minimize such risks (Standard 3.04, Avoiding Harm). Such steps may involve actions the sponsor company objects to, including terminating or modifying the study or from informing participants about new concerns that may influence their willingness to continue in the research (see Standards 3.04, Avoiding Harm, and 8.02, Informed Consent to Research). Sponsors may also attempt to prevent publication of data that jeopardize the marketability of their product or exert pressure on the psychologists to falsify results (Standard 8.10, Reporting Research Results).

When faced with conflicts between ethics and organization demands, Standard 1.03 requires that psychologists explain to the sponsor their ethical obligations under the Ethics Code, including their commitment to participant protection and the responsible conduct of research. In so doing, they must develop a plan and take actions to resolve the conflict in a manner that permits adherence to the code. Psychologists and their universities should also be alert to research contracts that include nondisclosure or confidentiality agreements that create additional barriers to resolution of such conflicts.

The highly publicized dispute between university medical school researcher Nancy Olivieri and the commercial sponsor of her research illustrates the type of conflict between ethics and organizations that research psychologists may increasingly face and the ethical problems that can emerge when researchers and their universities fail to ensure that grants from private companies do not carry stipulations that could lead to Ethics Code violations.

Dr. Olivieri received a grant from a private drug manufacturer to begin short-term clinical trials of deferiprone, a drug thought to reduce iron overload in patients with thalessemia. To obtain the grant, she signed a confidentiality agreement that she would not publish the findings of the trials without prior approval of the company. Following success of the short-term trial, she received a second grant from the manufacturer for a larger scale study (for which she did not sign a confidentiality agreement). As the research progressed, the data suggested that deferiprone either failed to reduce iron levels or increased them. Against the wishes of the sponsor, she notified the University Research Ethics Board of the findings, and the patients were given revised consent forms telling them of the newly suspected risks. Within 72 hours, the sponsor terminated the trials and warned that the company would use legal remedies if Olivieri told patients, regulatory agencies, or the scientific community about her concerns. Expressing her ethical obligation to her research participants and to the medical science community, Olivieri discussed the risks with each participant and published the results. Although lauded for her actions by the science community, she spent years in litigation with the company and her university. For additional information on this case, readers should refer to Olivieri (2003) and Thompson, Baird, and Downie (2001).

1.04 Informal Resolution of Ethical Violations

When psychologists believe that there may have been an ethical violation by another psychologist, they attempt to resolve the issue by bringing it to the attention of that individual, if an informal resolution appears appropriate and the intervention does not violate any confidentiality rights that may be involved. (See also Standard 1.02, Conflicts Between Ethics and Law, Regulations, or Other Governing Legal Authority, and Standard 1.03, Conflicts Between Ethics and Organizational Demands.)

Professional and scientific misconduct by psychologists can harm coworkers, distort the public's ability to make decisions informed by knowledge generated by members of the profession, and harm the profession itself by instilling public distrust. When an ethical violation by another psychologist occurs, members of the profession are in the best position to recognize the violation and select a course of action that could ameliorate harm or prevent further violations. Standards 1.04 and 1.05 underscore the responsibility of psychologists to be concerned about and, where appropriate, address the scientific or professional misconduct of their colleagues (Principle B: Fidelity and Responsibility).

Standard 1.04 requires psychologists to attempt an informal resolution when they suspect an ethical violation has occurred that could be adequately addressed through discussion with and subsequent remedial actions by the violating psychologist. In such instances, psychologists should discuss the violation with the offending psychologist to confirm whether misconduct has actually occurred and, if appropriate, recommend corrective steps and ways to prevent future ethical violations. Examples of misconduct psychologists might encounter in which an informal resolution is appropriate include the following:

☑ A psychologist with no prior education, training, or supervised experience in neuropsychological assessment began to incorporate a number of such instruments into a battery of tests for elderly clients (Standard 2.01a, Boundaries of Competence). After a colleague brought this to her attention, an informal resolution was achieved when the psychologist agreed to obtain appropriate training in neuropsychological assessment before continuing to use such techniques.

☑ A psychologist working with a non-English-speaking psychotherapy client asked the client's son to serve as an interpreter during sessions. He agreed to use an independent translator after being approached by a colleague who explained that he was jeopardizing the value of the treatment by using an untrained interpreter and potentially jeopardizing the mother-son relationship (Standard 2.05, Delegation of Work to Others).

☑ A consulting psychologist hired to help management plan for a shift in organizational structure planned to take stock options in partial payment for the work. When a colleague pointed out how this might impair his objectivity and expose the company to harm (Standard 3.06, Conflict of Interest), the psychologist agreed to discuss alternative compensation with the organization.

☑ In a job application, a psychologist claimed as a credential for health service delivery a degree earned from an educational institution that was neither regionally accredited nor a basis for state licensure. When the unethical nature of this behavior was pointed out (Standard 5.01c, Avoidance of False or Deceptive Statements), the psychologist agreed to send a letter to the potential employer clarifying the nature of the degree.

☑ A professor of psychology had not established a timely or specific process for providing feedback to and evaluating student performance (Standard 7.06, Assessing Student and Supervisee Performance). After discussions with the departmental chair, the professor agreed to develop such a system.

☑ An assistant professor of psychology began data collection without submitting a research proposal to the university's IRB (Standard 8.01, Institutional Approval). After a senior faculty member brought this to the psychologist's attention, the researcher agreed to submit an IRB application and to cease data collection contingent on IRB approval.

☑ A psychologist working in a hospital had entered identifiable confidential information into a database available to other staff members (Standard 6.02b, Maintenance, Dissemination, and Disposal of Confidential Records of Professional and Scientific Work). When another psychologist working at the hospital pointed out the problem, the psychologist agreed to use a password and other procedures for protecting the information. In this last instance, psychologists should be aware that the Health Insurance Portability and Accountability Act (HIPAA) also requires that health care professionals take reasonable steps to mitigate any harmful effects of unlawful disclosure of protected health information (PHI) by an employee or business associate of which they are aware (readers may wish to refer to the section on HIPAA in the Preface to this book).

Standard 1.04 recognizes that in some instances, an informal resolution may not be feasible. For example, previous attempts to discuss ethical problems with the offending psychologist may have been ineffective, or the offending psychologist may have left the position in which he or she had committed the violation or is otherwise inaccessible. In addition, psychologists should not attempt an informal resolution if to do so would violate an individual's confidentiality rights.

☑ During a session at the university counseling center, a graduate student complained that her psychology professor required students to discuss their sexual history in a required experiential group (Standard 7.04, Student Disclosure of Personal Information). The student did not want anyone in the program to know she was receiving counseling. Although the counseling psychologist knew that the professor might be violating Standard 7.04, the psychologist did not attempt to resolve the issue because to do so would have placed the confidentiality of the counseling relationship at risk (Standard 4.01, Maintaining Confidentiality).

Peer Review

Journal editors or psychologists reviewing manuscripts or grant proposals may come across information in the submitted materials that suggests a potential ethical violation. For example, an initial reading of the manuscript might lead a reviewer to suspect that the data, presented as original in the manuscript, had been previously published in another journal (a violation of Standard 8.13, Duplicate Publication of Data). In such cases, the reviewer should alert the editor, who in turn can request from the author written clarification of the source and originality of the data and copies of previous publications if appropriate. Suspected plagiarism or data fabrication in a submitted manuscript or grant proposal may be similarly handled through a journal editor or grant program officer in situations in which there is sufficient uncertainty about whether a violation has occurred (Standards 8.10, Reporting Research Results, and 8.11, Plagiarism). If the violation is not resolved through or appropriate for informal resolution, a formal complaint may be made; however, psychologists need to investigate the confidentiality and proprietary rights of the submitted materials within the context of the specific review process. For example, editors of APA journals who have good cause to believe that an ethical violation has occurred are required to report the matter to the Chief Editorial Advisor and the APA Journal's Senior Director, even if the manuscript has been rejected (APA, 2006, Policy 1.05). By contrast, some publishing companies, especially those that publish journals from multiple disciplines, may not have formal policies in place for reporting suspected ethical violations for submitted manuscripts. In such cases, editors and reviewers should consult with the publisher's legal office to clarify reporting responsibilities and limitations. In most instances, whether or not confidentiality rights prohibit making a formal complaint to the APA or other ethics committees, this does not preclude an editor from rejecting such manuscripts or from reviewers documenting for a journal or grant committee the factual basis of their concerns (see also, however, Standard 1.07, Improper Complaints).

1.05 Reporting Ethical Violations

If an apparent ethical violation has substantially harmed or is likely to substantially harm a person or organization and is not appropriate for informal resolution under Standard 1.04, Informal Resolution of Ethical Violations, or is not resolved properly in that fashion, psychologists take further action appropriate to the situation. Such action might include referral to state or national committees on professional ethics, to state licensing boards, or to the appropriate institutional authorities. This standard does not apply when an intervention would violate confidentiality rights or when psychologists have been retained to review the work of another psychologist whose professional conduct is in question. (See also Standard 1.02, Conflicts Between Ethics and Law, Regulations, or Other Governing Legal Authority.)

Standard 1.05 requires psychologists to report ethical violations committed by another psychologist only if the violation has led to or has the potential to lead to substantial harm and informal resolution is unsuccessful or inappropriate. The extent to which most ethical violations have or are likely to cause substantial harm will depend on the professional or scientific context and the individuals involved. As a rule of thumb, behaviors likely to cause substantial harm are of a kind similar to sexual misconduct, insurance fraud, plagiarism, and blatant, intentional misrepresentation (APA, 2002b, Section 5.3.5.1.1).

Standard 1.05 also offers nonbinding examples of available reporting options, including filing a complaint with the APA or one of its state affiliates if the offending psychologist is a member of that organization, referring the case to a state licensing board if the ethical violation also violates state law, or filing a complaint with the appropriate committee in the institution or organization at which the offending psychologist works. As in Standard 1.04, Standard 1.05 prioritizes the protection of confidentiality over the duty to report an ethical violation.

☑ A psychology professor reviewing an assistant professor's promotion application materials discovered that the faculty member had several publications that blatantly plagiarized articles written by a senior colleague (8.11, Plagiarism). The psychologist presented the evidence to the chair of the department. The chair and the professor informed the faculty member that they had discovered the plagiarism and would be forwarding the information to the university committee on ethical conduct and, if the committee found that plagiarism had occurred, would inform the journal in which the articles were published.

☑ A client told a psychologist about the sexual misconduct of another psychologist with whom the client had previously been in psychotherapy (Standard 10.05, Sexual Intimacies With Current Therapy Clients/Patients). Judging that it was clinically appropriate, the psychologist discussed with the client the unethical nature of the previous therapist's behavior and the available reporting options. The psychologist, respecting the client's request to keep the sexual relationship confidential, did not pursue reporting the violation (Standard 4.01, Maintaining Confidentiality).

Psychologists may be retained to help an organization, the courts, or an individual evaluate whether the actions of a psychologist have violated the Ethics Code. Standard 1.05 preserves the ability of members of the discipline to provide expert opinion on the ethical conduct of their peers by exempting from the reporting requirement psychologists hired to review the ethical activities of another psychologist.

1.06 Cooperating With Ethics Committees

Psychologists cooperate in ethics investigations, proceedings, and resulting requirements of the APA or any affiliated state psychological association to which they belong. In doing so, they address any confidentiality issues. Failure to cooperate is itself an ethics violation. However, making a request for deferment of adjudication of an ethics complaint pending the outcome of litigation does not alone constitute noncooperation.

A profession that demonstrates it can monitor itself promotes public confidence in the services of its members. Thus, an ethics code must enable professional organizations to effectively adjudicate ethics complaints. Membership in the APA and its affiliated state psychological associations brings with it a commitment to adhere to the Ethical Standards of the profession. To ensure the validity and viability of APA ethics adjudication, Standard 1.06 requires that when called on to do so, psychologists cooperate with APA and state-affiliated ethics investigations, proceedings, and resulting requirements. During the comment phase of the Ethics Code revision, some members asked whether requiring cooperation with an ethics committee when a complaint has been brought against a psychologist raised Fifth Amendment issues regarding the right against self-incrimination. The answer to this question is no. Unlike state licensing boards and other government and judicial agencies, professional organizations are not bound by the Fifth Amendment.

Standard 1.06 recognizes that when a complaint is brought against a psychologist, the ability to respond in full to an ethics committee request for information may be limited by confidentiality responsibilities detailed in Section 4, Privacy and Confidentiality, of the Ethics Code.

> ☑ A patient submitted a complaint to the APA charging a psychologist with misinterpreting the results of an assessment battery, leading to inaccurate diagnosis and denial of disability (Standards 3.04, Avoiding Harm, and 9.06, Interpreting Assessment Results). To fully respond to the complaint, the psychologist needed to obtain the patient's written release so that the psychologist could submit to the ethics committee the test report and other information about the patient relevant to the complaint. Despite reasonable efforts, the patient refused to sign the release. The psychologist informed the APA Ethics Committee about the confidentiality limitations on fully responding to the committee's request.

Standard 1.06 permits psychologists to request that an APA or affiliated state psychological association ethics committee delay adjudication of a complaint pending the outcome of litigation related to the complaint. If, however, the ethics committee declines such a request, failure to cooperate will be considered a violation of Standard 1.06.

1.07 Improper Complaints

Psychologists do not file or encourage the filing of ethics complaints that are made with reckless disregard for or willful ignorance of facts that would disprove the allegation.

The filing of frivolous complaints intended solely to harm the respondent undermines the educative, adjudicative, and public protection purposes of the Ethics Code. Unfounded and revengeful complaints can taint a scientific or professional career, lead to unfair denial of professional liability insurance or hospital privileges (because some insurers ask if a complaint has been made), incur costly legal fees for a respondent, and dilute public trust in the profession. Feelings of hostility and intent to do harm may accompany a valid complaint against psychologists who have acted unethically. Accordingly, the language of this standard was crafted to focus on the complaining psychologist's disregard for available information that would disprove the allegation rather than on the personal motives underlying the complaint.

Examples of improper complaints to the APA Ethics Committee often involve academic colleagues, business rivals, or psychologists with opposing forensic roles who attempt to misuse the ethics adjudication process as a means of defeating a competitor rather than addressing wrongful behavior or who attempt to dilute a complaint against them through a countercomplaint. Standard 1.07 is violated if psychologists making a complaint had access to information refuting the accusation—whether or not they availed themselves of such information.

> ☒ Two academic psychologists, well known for conducting methodologically rigorous research on the validity of children's eyewitness testimony, were often asked to serve as forensic experts on opposing sides in criminal cases. The defense attorney who had retained one of the psychologists for a highly publicized child abuse case was concerned that a recent article published by the opposing psychologist would be potentially damaging to the defendant's case. At the attorney's urging, the psychologist submitted a complaint to the APA Ethics Committee claiming that the opposing psychologist had fabricated the data. The psychologist based her complaint only on the fact that the data seemed "too good to be true" (see also Standard 3.06, Conflict of Interest).

Member groups of psychologists involved in adversarial proceedings are increasingly recognizing the need to address this issue. For example, the American Academy of Clinical Neuropsychology (2003) has made the following recommendations for ethical and professional bodies considering ethical complaints made against neuropsychologists involved in adversarial proceedings: (a) Ethical complaints should be examined after the resolution of related adversarial proceedings, (b) investigators should consider the motivation of those making the complaints, (c) investigative board members should be from different geographical regions and have no prior relationships with those involved in the complaints and have expertise in clinical neuropsychology, and (d) multiple unfounded complaints against the same psychologists should not be used to substantiate unethical practices where none exist.

The discipline of psychology and the public benefit from psychologists monitoring the ethical activities of other psychologists, but both are damaged when the Ethics Code is misused as a weapon to harass or otherwise harm members of the profession.

1.08 Unfair Discrimination Against Complainants and Respondents

Psychologists do not deny persons employment, advancement, admissions to academic or other programs, tenure, or promotion, based solely upon their having made or their being the subject of an ethics complaint. This does not preclude taking action based upon the outcome of such proceedings or considering other appropriate information.

Situations arise in which employees, colleagues, students, or student applicants accuse others or are accused of sexual harassment or other forms of professional or scientific misconduct. Standard 1.08 protects the rights of individuals to make ethical complaints without suffering unfair punitive actions from psychologists responsible for their employ, academic admission, or training. The standard also protects the rights of those accused of unethical behaviors to pursue their career paths pending resolution of a complaint. As highly publicized cases of whistleblowing have revealed (Lang, 1993; Needleman, 1993; Sprague, 1993), premature punitive actions against those who make complaints or those who are the subjects of complaints can hamper the ability of a profession or organization to monitor itself and can violate the rights of those accused to have a fair hearing. The Ethics Code makes clear that psychologists have a responsibility to be concerned about the ethical compliance of their colleagues' scientific and professional conduct (Principle B: Fidelity and Responsibility; Standard 1.04, Informal Resolution of Ethical Violations; and Standard 1.05, Reporting Ethical Violations). Standard 1.08 supports the implementation of this obligation by prohibiting unfair discrimination against those who make ethics complaints.

> ☒ A psychology department voted to deny doctoral candidacy to a student in the department's master's program simply because she had filed a still pending sexual harassment complaint against a member of the faculty.

Standard 1.08 also recognizes that not all complaints have a basis in fact or rise to the threshold of an ethics violation. Therefore, the standard prohibits psychologists from unfair discrimination of individuals who have been accused of an ethical violation.

☒ A client accused a member of a group practice of misrepresenting the fee for psychotherapy. Fearful of additional litigation, regardless of whether the psychologist was ultimately found innocent or guilty, the other group members asked the psychologist to leave the practice.

The use of the term *solely* in the first sentence of Standard 1.08 permits complainants or complainees to be denied employment, professional or academic advancement, or program admission for reasons unrelated to the complaint or for reasons based on the outcome of the complaint.

☑ An assistant professor accused of student sexual harassment had a documented history of poor student teaching evaluations, which, independent of the sexual harassment accusation, was sufficient to support a denial of promotion to associate professor.

☑ A psychologist who accused a colleague of insurance fraud was found to have fabricated the evidence used against the colleague. The psychologist was fired from the group practice (Standard 1.07, Improper Complaints).

HOT TOPIC

Involvement of Psychologists in Interrogations Related to National Security

Psychologists respect and protect civil and human rights. . . .

—Preamble, APA Ethics Code (APA, 2002b)

BE IT RESOLVED that psychologists shall not knowingly participate in any procedure in which torture or other forms of cruel, inhuman, or degrading treatment or cruel, inhuman, or degrading punishment is used or threatened.

—APA (2006)

Since September 11, 2001, national debate on the morality of harsh interrogation techniques has become urgent. Within the discipline of psychology, the debate centered on how involved psychologists should be in interrogation and information-gathering processes related to national security. What is not in dispute is that psychologists should always treat those with whom they work, including detainees, humanely (Standard 3.04, Avoiding Harm).

The APA has taken a strong historical stance against psychologists' involvement in torture (American Psychiatric Association & APA, 1985; APA Council of Representatives, 1986; APA Presidential Task Force, 2005). In 2006, the APA Council of Representatives unequivocally prohibited participation of its members in torture and other cruel, inhuman, and degrading treatment or punishment and included a nonexhaustive list of 19 specifically barred interrogation techniques, including mock executions, water boarding, sexual humiliation, and exploitation of phobias or psychopathology (APA Council of Representatives, 2006). However, the extent to which APA policy went far enough in ensuring the ethical practice of psychologists working in the military aroused controversy among members (www.withholdapadues.com, last accessed June 28, 2008). Some members argued that the prohibition against torture is insufficient because it fails to explicitly prohibit the use of sleep deprivation and sensory deprivation in its list of cruel and inhuman techniques, tactics that may have long-lasting damaging psychological effects (Democracy Now, 2007). Others criticized the current APA policy as failing to follow the American Psychiatric Association and the American Medical Association in a complete prohibition of psychologists' involvement in detainee interrogations (Olson & Soldz, 2007).

The prohibition against torture does not diminish the APA's strong support for the critical role of psychologists in the military and recognition of their contributions to protecting innocent civilians from harm and ensuring that interrogation processes are safe, humane, and ethical. The 2006 council statement notes, "It is consistent with the APA Ethics Code for psychologists to serve in consultative roles to interrogation and information-gathering processes for national security-related purposes. . . . Acknowledging that engaging in such consultative and advisory roles entails a delicate balance of ethical considerations."

However, Olson, Soldz, and Davis (2008) challenged the use of analogy between domestic forensic psychology and psychologists' participation in the interrogation of detainees at U.S. detention centers such as Guantanamo, Abu Ghraib, or CIA black sites as support for psychologists' involvement in such interrogations. They argued that research and consulting forensic psychologists have traditionally worked in settings where prisoners are afforded basic protections, including the right to an attorney, habeas corpus, and the right against self-incrimination—protections not currently afforded to individuals detained for national security purposes. They also argue that military regulations, the chain of command, and other elements of security work raise often impenetrable barriers to the ability of psychologists to consult with or obtain support from colleagues when ethical issues associated with interrogation arise. Moreover, a recent congressional investigation into the alleged role of psychologists in developing harsh interrogation programs for the CIA (Steele & Morlin, 2007) raised serious questions as to whether a consultative role can be distinguished from involvement in torture if the tactic is used in the psychologist's presence or with the psychologist's awareness, or is based on techniques the psychologist has developed for the purpose of interrogation.

Other APA members questioned whether Standard 1.02, Conflicts Between Ethics and Law, Regulations, or Other Governing Legal Authority, permitted psychologists to participate in torture if legal counsel for the military or executive branch interprets such actions as falling within government regulations and psychologists are unsuccessful in their attempts to resolve the situation in a way that is consistent with the Ethics Code. During the five years of the Ethics Code revision process and in August 2002, when the Ethics Code was adopted unanimously by the APA Council of Representatives, neither the public nor APA members envisioned there would soon be national debate on the "legality" of torture as a means of interrogation by the U.S. military. Thus, at the time, there was no discussion on the relevance of Standard 1.02 to psychologists' involvement in inhumane interrogations.

The controversy was resolved in 2010 when the American Psychological Association amended the Ethics Code to make clear that its standards can never be interpreted to justify or defend violating human rights. The change in language to Standard 1.02, Conflicts Between Ethics and Law, Regulations, or Other Governing Legal Authority, effective June 1, 2010, explicitly prohibits psychologists from engaging in activities that might be used to justify or defend violating human rights (APA, 2010a, 2010b).

To Whom Does the Prohibition Apply?

Some have argued that when psychologists act in certain roles outside traditional health-service provider relationships—for example, as consultants to interrogations—they are not acting in a professional capacity as psychologists and therefore not bound by the APA Ethics Code.

In 2007, the APA Council of Representatives rejected this argument and, consistent with the Ethics Code, extended the association's unequivocal condemnation of torture to the activities of any psychologist (e.g., in the military, the CIA, consultants) whose work directly or indirectly involves lawful or unlawful enemy combatants (Okorodudu, Strickland, Van Hoorn, & Wiggins, 2007). The Introduction to the Ethics Code clearly indicates that while the code does not apply to the purely private conduct of psychologists outside of their professional, scientific, or educational roles, when individuals serve in a consultative or advisory position by virtue of their training, experience, and expertise as psychologists, the APA Ethics Code applies across all work contexts.

Misuse of Psychologists' Work

> BE IT RESOLVED that psychologists shall be alert to acts of torture and other cruel, inhuman, or degrading treatment or cruel, inhuman, or degrading punishment and have an ethical responsibility to report these acts to the appropriate authorities.
>
> —APA (2006)

There are many ways psychologists provide critical and ethical contributions to the nation's security and those charged with protecting it. For example, psychologists may use their training and experience to help U.S. military personnel withstand torture without divulging information. Psychologists may also provide treatment to military or nonmilitary victims of torture and other cruel, inhuman, or degrading treatment to prevent or relieve long-term, multiple psychological and physical problems. They may draw upon the psychological science base to help reduce the risk of terrorism by advising the military on how to detect falsehoods. Finally, they may help preserve the moral integrity of interrogations by instructing members of the military to elicit truthful information from detainees in humane ways or to be present during interrogations to alert personnel when techniques are psychologically cruel, inhuman, or degrading (Munsey, 2007).

There are also times when psychologists may learn that their contributions to national security and the welfare of individual victims of torture have been misused. For example, psychologists may discover that psychological techniques they developed to help U.S. military personnel withstand torture were used to break down a detainee's resistance to divulging information during inhumane and cruel interrogation practices. Or, a psychologist delivering mental health services may discover that military personnel had accessed a detainee's treatment records to identify the detainee's psychological vulnerabilities to specific degrading interrogation techniques.

In such instances, Standard 1.01, Misuse of Psychologists' Work, requires psychologists take reasonable steps to correct or minimize the misuse. Indeed, psychologists serving in the military have taken steps to intervene in abusive actions toward prisoners, putting their own careers at risk (Koocher, 2006).

The term *reasonable,* applied to the military context, recognizes that there may be legal and other limitations on psychologists' ability to take direct corrective action against the misuse. At minimum, when psychologists become aware that their work has been used in acts of torture, they should report the misuse to the appropriate military authorities. When possible, they should offer to remedy further misuse by advising interrogators on alternative, effective, and humane information-gathering strategies or take precautions to include only the minimal amount of information required in detainee treatment records.

Multiple Relationships

Psychologists who provide mental health treatment or other professional services directly to detainees should not take on any additional role that uses the information gained through the delivery of such services for increasing the detainee's susceptibility to interrogation (see Standards 3.04, Avoiding Harm; 3.05 Multiple Relationships; and 3.08, Exploitative Relationships). Treatment or assessment information applied to the military interrogation process may also increase the likelihood that questioning will create substantial psychological harm to detainees by instilling in them a profound sense of powerlessness that seriously impairs their ability to assert their interests and rights (APA Council of Representatives, 2006).

Such dual roles can compromise psychologists' objectivity by motivating them to focus on gathering information most relevant to the interrogation rather than to the mental health needs of the detainee. It can also lead to client/patient exploitation if the psychologist's military career will be advanced if he or she provides detainee personal information useful to the interrogation process (Standard 3.06, Conflict of Interest). In addition, dual roles reduce treatment effectiveness by contributing to detainee distrust of any future mental health services provided by the military.

In some military settings, the nature of the psychologist's professional identity and role functions may be ambiguous (APA Council of Representatives, 2006). It is the ethical responsibility of military psychologists to (a) be alert to potential role conflicts, (b) notify their superiors to the problems inherent in the multiple relationships that may arise, and (c) avoid multiple relationships whenever possible or, when this is not possible, take actions that can minimize potential harms.

Conflicts Between Ethics and Law, Regulations, or Other Governing Legal Authority

> *If psychologists' ethical responsibilities conflict with law, regulations, or other governing legal authority, psychologists make known their commitment to this Ethics Code and take steps to resolve the conflict in a responsible manner. If the conflict is unresolvable via such means, psychologists may adhere to the requirements of the law, regulations, or other governing authority in keeping with basic principles of human rights.*

> —Introduction and Applicability (APA, 2002b, p. 1062)

However, the crafting of language in Standard 1.02 and throughout the code suggests that this standard is not permissive when applied to psychologists' involvement in torture. First, as a reflection of APA's long-standing support of civil disobedience against unjust laws, neither Standard 1.02 nor any other standard prohibits psychologists from disobeying the law when it is in conflict with the Ethics Code. In addition, the Preamble to the Ethics Code states unequivocally that "psychologists respect and protect civil and human rights," Principle A: Beneficence and Nonmaleficence calls for psychologists to "safeguard the welfare and rights of those with whom they interact professionally," and Standard 3.04, Avoiding Harm, requires psychologists to avoid harming those with whom they work. Consequently, psychologists should not assume that Standard 1.02 waives their obligation to meet the highest moral standards of the profession.

A broader ethical question is whether psychologists' participation in interrogations not meeting the APA's definition of inhumane tactics is itself unethical in settings such as Guantanamo, where detainees are kept in indefinite confinement and deprived of the right of habeas corpus. Some have argued that any type of involvement of psychologists in such settings implicitly supports unethical and inhumane practices (Munsey, 2007; Olson et al., 2008). The language of the Introduction and Applicability section of the Ethics Code quoted above and the amended language to Standard 1.02 (APA, 2010b) clarifies that when law, regulations, or governing authority enforce systemic violations of detainees' basic human rights, psychologists have a moral responsibility to adhere to the Ethics Code's higher standards.

CHAPTER 5

Standards on Competence

2. COMPETENCE

2.01 Boundaries of Competence

(a) Psychologists provide services, teach, and conduct research with populations and in areas only within the boundaries of their competence, based on their education, training, supervised experience, consultation, study, or professional experience.

Psychologists benefit those with whom they work and avoid harm through the application of knowledge and techniques gained through education, training, supervised experience, consultation, study, or professional experience in the field (Principle A: Beneficence and Nonmaleficence). Competence is the lynchpin enabling psychologists to fulfill other ethical obligations required by the American Psychological Association (APA) Ethics Code (APA, 2002b). Under Standard 2.01a, psychologists must refrain from providing services, teaching, or conducting research in areas in which they have not had the education, training, supervised experience, consultation, study, or professional experience recognized by the discipline as necessary to conduct their work competently.

☒ Psychologists with doctoral degrees from programs solely devoted to research would be in violation of this standard if they provided therapy to individuals without obtaining additional education or training in practice fields of psychology.

☒ Graduates of counseling, clinical, or school psychology programs should not conduct neuropsychological assessments unless their programs, internships, or postdoctoral experiences provided specialized training in those techniques.

☒ Psychologists should not offer courses or professional workshops if their graduate education, training, or continued study is insufficient to provide students with fundamental knowledge and concepts of the topics or areas to be taught.

☒ Psychologists without applicable training in job-related counseling and assessment should not offer executive coaching services.

☒ Forensic psychologists should not offer opinions on children's ability to testify if they have not obtained requisite knowledge of developmental processes related to recollection of facts, susceptibility to leading questions, understanding of court procedures, and emotional and behavioral reactions to legal proceedings.

☒ Psychologists should not suggest to clients/patients that they alter their psychotropic medication regimen unless they have specialized training as a prescribing psychologist.

Determinations of whether psychologists are engaged in activities outside the boundaries of their competence will vary with current and evolving criteria in the relevant field. As noted in the Introduction and Applicability section of the Ethics Code, psychologists are encouraged to refer to materials and guidelines endorsed by scientific and professional psychological organizations to help identify competencies necessary for adherence to Standard 2.01a. For example:

☑ According to the Specialty Guidelines for Forensic Psychology (Committee on Ethical Guidelines for Forensic Psychologists, 1991), the legal information provided by forensic practitioners must be limited to their knowledge and experience in forensic practice. Forensic practitioners do not offer legal opinions, must explain to parties that legal information is not the same as legal advice, and encourage parties to consult with an attorney for guidance regarding relevant legal issues. (Readers may also wish to refer to the Committee on the Revision of the Specialty Guidelines for Forensic Psychology, 2008.)

☑ According to the Guidelines for Child Custody Evaluation in Divorce Proceedings (APA, 1994), custody evaluation requires specialized knowledge of psychological assessments for children, adults, and families; child and family development and psychopathology; the impact of divorce on children; applicable legal standards; and, in some instances, expertise on child abuse and neglect, domestic violence, or parental mental or physical illness.

☑ According to the Guidelines for the Evaluation of Dementia and Age-Related Cognitive Decline (see www.apa.org/practice/dementia.html), psychologists who provide evaluations for dementia and age-related cognitive decline must have education, training, experience, supervision in clinical interviews and neuropsychological testing, and training in the areas of gerontology, neuropsychology, rehabilitation psychology, neuropathology, psychopharmacology, and psychopathology in older adults.

☑ The Guidelines for Ethical Conduct in the Care and Use of Animals (APA Committee on Animal Research and Ethics, 1996; http://www.apa.org/science/anguide.html) state that psychologists conducting research with animals must be knowledgeable about the normal and species-specific behavior characteristics of their animal subjects and unusual behaviors that could forewarn of health problems.

☑ According to the task force titled the Ethical Practice in Organized Systems of Care, convened by the APA Committee for the Advancement of Professional Practice (CAPP), psychologists who are contracted providers for health maintenance organizations (HMOs) should only accept clients/patients whom they have the expertise to benefit (Acuff et al., 1999).

☑ The APA Guidelines for Education and Training at the Doctoral and Postdoctoral Levels in Consulting Psychology/Organizational Consulting Psychology (APA, 2007a) details three domains of competencies required for organizational consulting psychology: (a) individual (i.e., career and vocational planning, employee selection and promotion, employee job analysis, executive and employee coaching), (b) group (i.e., assessment and development of teams and functional and dysfunctional group behavior, work flow, technology and stress management), and (c) organization/systemwide/intersystem (i.e., organizational assessment and diagnosis, corporate-wide job analysis, centralizing and decentralizing decision making, strategic planning).

(b) Where scientific or professional knowledge in the discipline of psychology establishes that an understanding of factors associated with age, gender, gender identity, race, ethnicity, culture, national origin, religion, sexual orientation, disability, language, or socioeconomic status is essential for effective implementation of their services or research, psychologists have or obtain the training, experience, consultation, or supervision necessary to ensure the competence of their services, or they make appropriate referrals, except as provided in Standard 2.02, Providing Services in Emergencies.

Understanding the ways individual differences relate to psychological phenomena is essential to ensure the competent implementation of services and research. Insensitivity to factors associated with age, gender, gender identity, race, ethnicity, culture, national origin, religion, sexual orientation, disability, language, or socioeconomic status can result in underutilization of services, misdiagnosis, iatrogenic treatments, impairments in leadership effectiveness and member cohesion in group therapy, and methodologically unsound research designs (APA, 2000, 2003; Ridley et al., 2001; Trimble & Fisher, 2006).

Standard 2.01b requires that psychologists have or obtain special understanding and skills when the scientific and professional knowledge of the discipline establishes that an understanding of factors associated with these individual differences is essential to competent work. According to this standard, the competencies required to work with such populations are determined by the knowledge and skills identified by the scientific and professional knowledge base—not by personal differences or similarities between psychologists and those to whom they provide services or involve in research.

Under Standard 2.01b, psychologists have three sequentially related obligations:

Familiarity With Professional and Scientific Knowledge. For each activity in which they engage, psychologists must be sufficiently familiar with current scientific and professional knowledge to determine whether an understanding of factors associated with the individual characteristics listed above is necessary for effective implementation of their services or research. For example:

☑ Research and professional guidelines suggest that familiarity with the concept of cultural paranoia and culturally equivalent norms on certain scales of psychopathology is required for competent clinical assessment of African American clients/patients with presenting symptoms of subclinical paranoia (APA, 1993; Combs, Penn, & Fenigstein, 2002).

☑ Professional guidelines and research require knowledge of the mental health risks of social stigmatization and individual differences in the developmental trajectories of gay, lesbian, bisexual, and transgender youths when treating or studying depression involving these populations (see APA, 2000; Green & Mitchell, 2002; Savin-Williams & Diamond, 1999).

☑ Psychologists providing treatment must be alert to how religious ideals and internalized religious norms may positively or negatively influence clients'/patients' reactions to life events such as the death of a loved one or their attitudes and behaviors regarding sexual relationships, child rearing, and self-evaluation (APA, 2007d).

☑ There is growing awareness that research, assessment, and treatments involving girls and women need to be informed by biological, psychological, social, and political influences that may uniquely affect the development and well-being of this population. The APA Guidelines for Psychological Practice With Girls and Women (APA, 2007b) provides a historical overview as well as guidance for identifying and addressing areas in which a special understanding of factors associated with women's issues is required for competent provision of mental health services.

Appropriate Skills. If current knowledge in the field indicates that an understanding of one or more of the factors cited in Standard 2.01b is essential to conduct activities competently, psychologists must have or obtain the training, experience, consultation, or supervision necessary. The type of knowledge and training required depends on the extent to which the individual difference factor is central or peripheral to the service required as well as the psychologist's prior training or experience.

☑ A psychologist providing bereavement counseling to a recently widowed 70-year-old woman noticed that the client was reporting difficulties shopping for groceries and finding it frustrating to be among friends. While these difficulties might be attributed to depression following the loss of her husband, given the client's age, the psychologist also sought additional consultation with a geropsychologist on changes associated with and techniques for enhancing functional capacities related to age-related declines in vision, hearing, and activities of daily living.

☑ A rehabilitation psychologist who began to receive referrals for work with hearing-impaired clients sought training in sign language and other appropriate communication techniques.

☒ A clinical psychologist who typically provided either behavior or interpersonal psychotherapy for non-Hispanic White clients who met diagnostic criteria for anxiety disorder limited the treatment plan for African American clients to behavior therapy based on the psychologist's erroneous assumption that members of this cultural group were not comfortable with treatments that involved insight-oriented techniques.

Knowing When to Refrain and Refer. Under Standard 2.01b, psychologists who have not had or cannot obtain the knowledge or experience required must refrain from engaging in such activities and make referrals when appropriate, except when such services are needed but unavailable (Standard 2.02, Providing Services in Emergencies; see also Standard 2.01d).

☑ A psychologist trained only in adult assessment was asked to assess a child for learning difficulties. The psychologist referred the family to another psychologist with the specialized knowledge and experience necessary to conduct child assessments in general and developmental disabilities assessments in particular (Childs & Eyde, 2002).

☒ A counseling psychologist agreed to provide career services to a client with mild bilateral deafness. The psychologist had no education or training in career skills and opportunities available to people who are hearing impaired, employment-relevant disability law, hearing loss–appropriate counseling techniques, the use of American Sign Language and other modes of communication, and the appropriate use of interpreters (Leigh, Corbett, Gutman, & Morere, 1996).

(c) Psychologists planning to provide services, teach, or conduct research involving populations, areas, techniques, or technologies new to them undertake relevant education, training, supervised experience, consultation, or study.

Standard 2.01c applies when psychologists wish to expand the scope of their practice, teaching, or research to populations, areas, techniques, or technologies for which they have not obtained the necessary qualifications established by the field.

☑ Prior to offering rehabilitation services, a psychologist without previous training in this area obtained supervised experience with individuals with sensory impairments; burns; spinal cord, brain, and orthopedic injuries; catastrophic injury and illness; and chronically disabling conditions (Patterson & Hanson, 1995).

☑ A psychologist trained solely in individual psychotherapy obtained appropriate advanced education and training prior to extending his practice to group and family therapy work (Lakin, 1994).

☑ To deliver the short-term treatment required under the practice guidelines of the HMO for which she worked, a psychologist acquired additional supervised experience in the delivery of time-limited services (Haas & Cummings, 1991).

☑ A developmental psychologist who wished to test a theory of genetic and environmental influences on cognitive aging using an animal population obtained knowledge and supervised experience in animal models, animal care, and animal experimental techniques prior to conducting the research (APA Committee on Animal Research and Ethics, 1996).

☑ Prior to implementing an executive coaching program in a South Asian country, a consulting psychologist obtained knowledge about the culture's orientation toward collective versus independent goals, receptivity to authoritative versus collegial coaching approaches, and preferences for launching quickly into a task versus spending time getting to know the coach personally (Peterson, 2007).

☑ A teaching psychologist who planned to offer an interactive Internet course consulted with a specialist to ensure the information would be presented accurately (e.g., Graham, 2001; Randsdell, 2002).

(d) When psychologists are asked to provide services to individuals for whom appropriate mental health services are not available and for which psychologists have not obtained the competence necessary, psychologists with closely related prior training or experience may provide such services in order to ensure that services are not denied if they make a reasonable effort to obtain the competence required by using relevant research, training, consultation, or study.

Standard 2.01d applies to situations in which a psychologist without the appropriate training or experience is the only professional available to provide necessary mental health services. Such situations often arise in rural settings or small ethnocultural communities where a single psychologist serves a diverse-needs population. The standard reflects the balance, articulated in Principle A: Beneficence and Nonmaleficence, between the obligation to do good (to provide needed services) and the responsibility to do no harm (to avoid poor services provided by unqualified professionals). The standard also reflects the importance of providing fair access to services (Principle D: Justice).

Standard 2.01d stipulates two conditions in which psychologists may provide services for which they do not have the required education or experience: (a) Psychologists must have prior training or experience closely related to the service needed, and (b) having agreed to provide the service, psychologists must make reasonable efforts to obtain the knowledge and skills necessary to conduct their work effectively.

☑ A psychologist with expertise in culturally sensitive assessment of childhood personality and educational disorders was the only Spanish-speaking mental health professional with regularly scheduled appointments to a Mexican migrant worker community. A social worker serving the community asked the psychologist to evaluate a Spanish-speaking 80-year-old man for evidence of depression. The nearest mental health clinic was 500 miles away, and the elder was too feeble to travel. The psychologist's expertise in multicultural assessment of mental disorders in children was related though not equivalent to the knowledge and expertise necessary for a culturally sensitive geropsychological diagnosis. The psychologist agreed to conduct the evaluation. Prior to evaluating the elder, she consulted by phone with a geropsychologist in another state. She also informed the elder, the elder's family, and the social worker that because she did not have sufficient training or experience in treating depression in elderly persons, if treatment was necessary, it would have to be obtained from another provider.

(e) In those emerging areas in which generally recognized standards for preparatory training do not yet exist, psychologists nevertheless take reasonable steps to ensure the competence of their work and to protect clients/patients, students, supervisees, research participants, organizational clients, and others from harm.

Standard 2.01e applies when psychologists wish to develop or implement new practice, teaching, or research techniques for which there are no generally agreed upon scientific or professional training qualifications. The standard recognizes the value of innovative techniques as well as the added risks such innovations may place on those with whom psychologists work.

Psychologists must take reasonable steps to ensure the competence and safety of their work in new areas. In using the term *competence*, the standard assumes that all work conducted by psychologists in their role as a psychologist draws upon established scientific or professional knowledge of the discipline (see Standard 2.04, Bases for Scientific and Professional Judgments). Adherence to this standard requires that psychologists have the foundational knowledge and skills in psychology necessary to construct or implement novel approaches and to evaluate their effectiveness. For example:

> ☑ The growing literature in the field of executive coaching indicates that psychologists planning to offer new forms of these services must demonstrate a knowledge and expertise in (a) techniques for fostering and measuring change within business, government, nonprofit, or educational organizations; (b) the nature of executive responsibility and leadership; (c) targeted goal setting within organizational cultures; (d) succession planning; and (e) relevant factors associated with executive challenges such as information technology and globalization (Brotman, Liberi, & Wasylyshyn, 1998; Diedrich, 2008; Kampa-Kokesch & Anderson, 2001; Kilburg, 1996).
>
> ☑ As states begin to grant psychologists prescriptive authority, psychologists proposing to practice in this area will need the education and training outlined in the evolving practice guidelines for this field (Buelow & Chafetz, 1996; Chafetz & Buelow, 1994; Fox, Schwelitz, & Barclay, 1992). Psychologists who do not have prescription privileges but are knowledgeable about pharmacotherapy must continue to be cautious when discussing medications with clients/patients to ensure they are not working outside evolving professional and legal boundaries of competence (Bennett et al., 2006; DeLeon, Bennett, & Bricklin, 1997; Sechrest & Coan, 2002).

Standard 2.01e also requires that psychologists working in emerging areas take reasonable steps to protect those with whom they work from harm, recognizing that novel approaches may require greater vigilance in consumer or research protections.

> ☑ The application of neurocognitive enhancement techniques to healthy individuals and those displaying no signs of neurocognitive degeneration or dysfunction is an emerging field. To date, there is little research documenting positive effects of neurocognitive pharmacological treatments, cognitive exercises, neuroimaging, neurosurgery, and noninvasive cerebral manipulation such as transcranial magnetic

stimulation (Bush, 2006). Psychologists investigating these techniques and practitioners who wish to incorporate them into current modes of counseling or treatment must ensure they have the knowledge and skills to not only administer, assess, and monitor participant or patient reactions to these new methods but also remedy negative reactions if they arise (Standards 3.04, Avoiding Harm, and 8.08, Debriefing). Psychologists must also inform prospective research participants and patients of the experimental nature of the techniques (see Standards 8.02b, Informed Consent to Research, and 10.01b, Informed Consent to Therapy).

☑ Continuous advances in electronic and computer technology present new opportunities and ethical challenges for psychologists. At present, there are no generally accepted theories or comprehensive models for e-therapy, and the applicability of traditional therapies remains unknown (Heinlen, Welfel, Richmond, & O'Donnell, 2003). Traditional psychotherapy techniques based on oral and nonverbal cues may not transfer to Internet communications through written text (Nickelson, 1998). Additional harm to Internet clients/patients may be inflicted when psychologists misdiagnose a disorder, fail to identify suicidal or homicidal ideation, or inadvertently reinforce maladaptive behavior (e.g., social phobia) through the use of the Internet medium. Steps that psychologists using Internet-mediated assessment or therapeutic services might take to ensure the competence of their work and to protect clients/patients from harm include (a) staying abreast of advances in the field, (b) requiring in-person initial consultation, and (c) identifying professionals and health and social service agencies in the locality in which the client/patient lives who can be enlisted in crisis situations (Maheu, 2001).

(f) When assuming forensic roles, psychologists are or become reasonably familiar with the judicial or administrative rules governing their roles.

Psychologists assume forensic roles when they engage in activities intended to provide psychological expertise to the legal system. According to the Specialty Guidelines for Forensic Psychologists (Committee on Ethical Guidelines for Forensic Psychologists, 1991; Committee on the Revision of the Specialty Guidelines for Forensic Psychology, 2008), forensic roles include clinical forensic examiners, psychologists employed by correctional mental health systems, researchers who provide expert testimony on the relevance of psychological data to a psycholegal issue, trial behavior consultants, practitioners who are called to appear before the court as fact witnesses, forensic experts, or psychologists who otherwise consult with or testify before judicial, legislative, or administrative agencies acting in an adjudicative capacity.

Familiarity With Law, Regulations, and Governing Authority

The provision of competent forensic services requires not only education and training in a psychologist's specific area of expertise but also knowledge of the judicial or administrative rules governing various forensic roles.

☑ Scientific psychologists serving as expert witnesses should be familiar with federal rules of evidence regarding case law and expert testimony (e.g., *Daubert v. Merrell Dow Pharmaceuticals, Inc.,* 1993; *Kumho Tire Co., Ltd. v. Carmichael,* 1999; see also the Hot Topic on "The Use of Assessments in Expert Testimony: Implications of Case Law and the Federal Rules of Evidence" in Chapter 12).

☑ Psychologists offering trial consultation services to organizations may need to have an understanding of change in venue motions and sexual harassment or retaliation work policies and laws (Hellkamp & Lewis, 1995).

☑ Psychologists conducting custody evaluations should have sufficient understanding of the hearsay rule and what the term *best interests of the child* means in legal proceedings. They should also understand the distinction between criminal and civil law. The purpose of criminal law is to determine a person's guilt or innocence as it relates to violation of law and to determine appropriate sanctions if the defendant is found guilty. On the other hand, the purpose of civil law is to determine the best interests of minors or others who are under guardianship (e.g., child custody disputes, adoption, capacity determinations), assign responsibility for claims of harm (e.g., workers' compensation, personal injury litigation), and provide legal remedies (Bush, Connell, & Denney, 2006).

☑ Psychologists administering psychological services in correctional facilities should be familiar with guidelines and regulations governing the ratio of psychology staff to inmates as well as regulations governing access to confidential information by nonpsychologist correctional staff (American Association of Correctional Psychology, 2000).

Evolving Law and School Psychologists

School or educational psychologists asked to serve as expert witnesses in due process hearings for educational services need to be familiar with the legal foundations for special education law such as *Brown v. Board of Education* (1954) and federal regulations, including Section 504 of the Rehabilitation Act of 1973 (1993), Education for All Handicapped Children Act of 1975, the Americans with Disabilities Act of 1990, and the Individuals with Disabilities Education Improvement Act of 2004.

As district employees, school psychologists also have a legal duty to protect all students attending the school from reasonably foreseeable risk of harm such as student-on-student violence or harassment or student suicide (Reutter, 1994). The most common tort against school personnel is the claim of negligence in this duty. Jacob and Hartshorne (2007) identify four questions school psychologists may be called upon to address when testifying in a negligence suit: Was a wrong or damage done to the student's person, rights, reputation, or property? Did the school owe a duty in law to the student? Did the school breach that duty? Was there a proximate cause (causal) relationship between the injury and the breach of duty?

Forensic Assessments

Knowing the difference between clinical and forensic evaluations is also important. The clinician's goal is to help the client/patient adjust positively to life circumstances (Bush et al., 2006). The purpose of a forensic evaluation is to assist the "trier of facts" (a judge, juror, or administrative hearing officer) determine the legal question. While the forensic evaluator must respect the legal rights and welfare of defendants or litigants who they assess, techniques aimed at promoting the testee's mental health or therapeutic alliance, for example, are not necessary and in fact may be inappropriate (Greenberg & Shuman, 1997). In addition, legal definitions of mental disorders may differ from those ordinarily applied for diagnosis and treatment. For example, psychologists conducting competency assessments should know that the term *insanity* has different meanings in different jurisdictions (Hess, 1998).

According to the Specialty Guidelines for Forensic Psychology (Committee on Ethical Guidelines for Forensic Psychologists, 1991; Committee on the Revision of the Specialty Guidelines for Forensic Psychology, 2008), psychologists who conduct psychological evaluations of those accused of a crime must know how to acquire details about the defendant's intent, motivation, planning, thought processes, and general mental state at the time of the crime, without divulging information not previously known by the court that could aid prosecutorial investigation. Such "fruits of the statements" cannot be admitted into evidence except on an issue relevant to the defendant's mental condition already introduced by the defense into testimony.

Fact Witnesses

Sometimes psychologists who do not offer forensic services are asked to provide legal testimony as a fact witness. Fact witnesses are called on by the court to provide records or testify on knowledge they have about a patient's psychological functioning or treatment not originally obtained for legal purposes. For example, an independent practitioner seeing a client for anxiety-related disorders might be called as a fact witness in a workers' compensation case involving the client. Under Standard 2.01f, even when psychologists have no advance knowledge that their work will be used in a legal or administrative setting, when called on to provide such a service, they are nonetheless responsible for becoming reasonably familiar with the rules governing their forensic role.

> ☑ A licensed practitioner was called to testify as a fact witness regarding the diagnosis, treatment, and treatment progress of a child he was seeing in group therapy. Prior to going to court, the psychologist obtained consultation on rules governing privileged communications for children and for patients in group therapy in the state in which the psychologist practiced (Glosoff, Herlihy, Herlihy, & Spence, 1997; Knapp & VandeCreek, 1997).

2.02 Providing Services in Emergencies

In emergencies, when psychologists provide services to individuals for whom other mental health services are not available and for which psychologists have not obtained the necessary training, psychologists may provide such services in order to ensure that services are not denied. The services are discontinued as soon as the emergency has ended or appropriate services are available.

The Oklahoma City bombing, the September 11, 2001, attacks on the United States, and the aftermath of Hurricane Katrina illustrate the important public role of psychological expertise during disasters. Standard 2.02 recognizes that when adequate mental health services are not available during emergencies, psychologists without training in therapeutic services in or crisis intervention may still have knowledge and expertise that can benefit the public. The standard permits psychologists who do not have the necessary training to offer such services but requires they limit services to the immediate timeframe and to cease as soon as the emergency has passed or appropriate services become available. When a city or statewide disaster erupts unexpectedly, psychologists wishing to offer their immediate services should have some knowledge of the efficacy of different intervention techniques to ensure their services do not exacerbate psychological trauma.

In rare instances, psychologists who do not have education or training related to suicidality assessment or intervention may come in contact with an individual who appears imminently suicidal and for whom no mental health or other health services are immediately available. Under Standard 2.02, psychologists without the necessary competencies would be permitted to try to reduce the immediate risk of suicide. However, the psychologist should call for emergency services or attempt to obtain or refer the individual for appropriate services as soon as feasible. Unqualified psychologists should be wary of providing such services, recognizing the potentially harmful nature of uninformed interventions and the ethical inappropriateness of providing unqualified treatment if medical or other suicide crisis services are available (American Psychiatric Association, 2003).

☑ A second-year clinical psychology doctoral student was leaving her social services externship site when she received an emergency call from a guard who told her a member of the custodial staff was threatening to commit suicide. The student had never treated a suicidal patient but knew she was the only mental health provider still in the building. She immediately called her supervisor, who gave her instructions on how to provide limited support to the individual while the supervisor called the nearby hospital emergency services to send a treatment team to the building.

2.03 Maintaining Competence

Psychologists undertake ongoing efforts to develop and maintain their competence.

The scientific and professional knowledge base of psychology is continually evolving, spawning new research methodologies, assessment procedures, and forms of service delivery. Information and techniques constituting the core curricula of psychologists' doctoral education and training are often outdated and are replaced by new information and more effective practices as decades pass. Lifelong learning is fundamental to ensure that teaching, research, and practice provide an ongoing positive effect for those with whom psychologists work. Standard 2.03 requires that psychologists undertake ongoing efforts to ensure continued competence. The requirements of this standard can be met through independent study, continuing education courses, supervision, consultation, or formal postdoctoral study.

☑ School psychologists are faced with a continuously evolving knowledge base and laws relevant to effective teacher and school consultation. They must be aware of requirements for statewide reading and mathematics tests and state and local Board of Education criteria for attaining academic proficiency for all students, availability of public school choice, supplemental tutoring, and criteria for evaluating teacher proficiencies (Jacob & Hartshorne, 2007). They must also understand the requirements of and fiscal implications to schools of federal laws such as the No Child Left Behind Act (2001).

☑ Industrial-organizational psychologists developing personnel screening and employment practices must stay abreast of continually changing equal employment legislation (e.g., Title VII of the Civil Rights Act of 1964, the Americans with Disabilities Act of 1990, the Uniformed Services Employment and Reemployment Rights Act of 1994, and the Age Discrimination in Employment Amendments of 1996), administrative laws (e.g., Equal Employment Opportunity Act of 1972, Family and Medical Leave Act of 1993, Pregnancy Discrimination Act of 1978), executive orders (e.g., Executive Order No. 11246, 1964–1965), and court decisions (e.g., *Griggs v. Duke Power*, 1971; *Wards Cove Packing Company v. Antonio*, 1989; see also Cornell University Law School, 2007; Lowman, 2006; McAllister, 1991; Sireci & Parker, 2006).

☑ Forensic psychologists are often asked to assess the validity of an examinee's symptoms and presentation to determine if the examinee is attempting to manage impressions of his or her psychological status. Impression management is highly variable both between and within individual examinees, and as a consequence, accepted measures and techniques for assessing symptom validity are continuously evolving. Failing to detect malingering or failing to recognize symptoms as indicators of a valid mental health disorder results in harm to all stakeholders in the legal process. Forensic psychologists need to keep abreast of evolving research on the assessment of facetious disorders (Larrabee, 2007).

2.04 Bases for Scientific and Professional Judgments

Psychologists' work is based on established scientific and professional knowledge of the discipline (see also Standards 2.01e, Boundaries of Competence, and 10.01b, Informed Consent to Therapy).

Standard 2.04 requires psychologists to select methods and provide professional opinions firmly grounded in the knowledge base of scientific and professional psychology. Scientific knowledge refers to information generated according to accepted principles of research practice. Professional knowledge refers to widely accepted and reliable clinical reports, case studies, or observations.

Psychologists engaged in innovative activities who do not draw on established knowledge of the field risk failing to anticipate or detect aspects of such procedures that could lead to substantial misrepresentation or harm. The standard permits the use of novel approaches, recognizing that new theories, concepts, and techniques are critical to the continued development of the field. It does, however, prohibit psychologists from applying idiosyncratic ideas and techniques that are not grounded in either accepted principles or the field's cumulative knowledge of psychological research or practice.

☒ Several families who believed their children had been the victims of sexual abuse in the day care center they attended retained the services of a clinical psychologist to evaluate and testify in court that the children had been abused. During her years in practice, the psychologist had created for her own use a set of criteria for determining abuse based on her clinical observations and the writings of two leading practietioners who observed what they determined were universal syndromes of child sexual abuse. The psychologist's testimony played an important role in convicting the day care staff members. On appeal, however, the conviction was overturned based on the appellate court's finding that the psychologist's evaluation methods were invalid, unreliable, and not probative of sexual abuse. For additional discussion of these issues, see Fisher (1995), Fisher and Whiting (1998), and Kuehnle and Sparta (2006).

☒ On the day of and immediately following the attacks on September 11, 2001, psychologists from across the country who were not trained in trauma treatment rushed to provide services to victims, rescuers, and their families. An immediate controversy arose regarding their application of the popular but unvalidated Critical Incident Stress Debriefing (CISD) technique. The CISD encourages individuals to discuss their emotional reactions to a traumatic event immediately following exposure, with proponents claiming that it reduces immediate distress, prevents later adverse psychological reactions, and helps screen for individuals who are at risk for developing more serious disorders (Everly, Flannery, & Mitchell, 2000). Adversaries claimed the debriefing treatment had no efficacy or was potentially harmful to victims of the terrorist attacks (van Emmerick, Kamphuis, Hulsbosch, & Emmelkamp, 2002). By the second day, there was a public call to stop untrained "trauma tourists" from using the technique based on concerns they might have actually compounded the effects of trauma on those they "treated" (Bongar et al., 2002).

Psychologists trained in more traditional techniques also have a responsibility to keep up with evolving knowledge of the field to know under which conditions and for which disorders treatments do and do not work and which have iatrogenic risks (Pope & Vasquez, 2007; see also Standard 2.03, Maintaining Competence).

Evidence-Based Practice

The APA Presidential Task Force report on evidence-based practice in psychology (Levant, 2005) emphasized both the importance of scientific knowledge to treatment decisions and the importance of clinical judgment in determining the applicability of research findings to individual cases. The task force defined evidence-based practice in psychology (EBPP) as the integration of the best available research with clinical expertise in the context of client/patient characteristics, culture and preferences, and relevance to the client's/patient's treatment and assessment needs. Clinical expertise was defined as competence attained by psychologists through education, training, and experience resulting in effective practice and the ability to identify and integrate the best research evidence with clinical data (e.g., patient information obtained over the course of treatment or assessment; see also APA, 2002a).

Other professional groups have endorsed the integration of research and practice knowledge as an ethical obligation. For example:

☑ The National Association of School Psychologists' Principles for Professional Ethics (NASP, 2000) requires that "school psychologists use assessment techniques, counseling and therapy procedures, consultation techniques, and other direct and indirect service methods that the profession considers to be responsible, research-based practice" (IV.C.4, p. 28).

☑ The most current draft revision of the Specialty Guidelines for Forensic Psychology includes a provision that "forensic practitioners typically provide opinions and testimony that are (a) sufficiently based upon facts or data and on adequate scientific foundation; (b) the product of reliable principles and methods; and (c) based on principles and methods that have been applied reliably to the facts of the case" (Provision 4.05; www.ap-ls.org/links/22808sgfp.pdf).

2.05 Delegation of Work to Others

Psychologists who delegate work to employees, supervisees, research or teaching assistants, or who use the services of others, such as interpreters, must take reasonable steps to: (1) avoid delegating such work to persons who have a multiple relationship with those being served that would likely lead to exploitation or loss of objectivity; (2) authorize only those responsibilities that such persons can be expected to perform competently on the basis of their education, training, or experience, either independently or with the level of supervision being provided; and (3) see that such persons perform these services competently. (See also Standards 2.02, Providing Services in Emergencies; 3.05, Multiple Relationships; 4.01, Maintaining Confidentiality; 9.01, Bases for Assessments; 9.02, Use of Assessments; 9.03, Informed Consent in Assessments; and 9.07, Assessment by Unqualified Persons.)

In their obligation to protect the rights and welfare of those with whom they work, psychologists who delegate or use the services of others are responsible for ensuring that such work is performed competently. To be in compliance with Standard 2.05, psychologists should (a) evaluate whether employees, supervisees, assistants, or others whose services are used have the skills to implement the task independently or under appropriate supervision, (b) assign such individuals only those tasks for which they are qualified, and (c) monitor the activities to ensure competent implementation.

☑ Consulting and industrial-organizational psychologists who delegate employee assessments or organizational research responsibilities to others must ensure to the extent feasible that such individuals have adequate training in the testing or data collection skills necessary to implement the work proficiently.

☑ Psychologists in academia must take reasonable measures to ensure that research and teaching assistants have the knowledge and skills required to implement valid and ethical research procedures, teach or advise students, or grade exams.

☑ Psychologists in mental health settings who supervise psychologist and nonpsychologist staff (e.g., lay leaders for group work; see Glass, 1998) must take steps to determine that these individuals have the necessary training to perform or assist in therapeutic procedures (Stratton & Smith, 2006).

☑ School psychologists must read and approve before signing assessments administered and scored by or pupil reports prepared by graduate students, externs, or others under the psychologists' supervision.

Implications of HIPAA. Psychologists who are covered entities under the Health Insurance Portability and Accountability Act (HIPAA) should be aware that the act requires covered entities to train, document, and appropriately sanction employees regarding federal policies and procedures involving protected health information (DHHS 45 CFR 164.530[b][1]).

Use of Interpreters. Standard 2.05 specifically draws attention to the appropriate delegation of work to interpreters who assist psychologists in providing services for individuals who use American Sign Language or who do not speak the same language as the psychologist. Psychologists must ensure that interpreters have adequate translation skills and sufficient understanding of the psychological nature and ethical responsibilities of the duties to be performed. Some clients/patients who are deaf or do not speak English live, work, or socialize in close-knit communities in which those who serve as interpreters are known personally. In such settings, psychologists should avoid delegating work to such individuals when it will create a multiple relationship between the interpreter and the person receiving services or involved in research that could reasonably be expected to lead to breaches in confidentiality, exploitation, or loss of objectivity.

> ☒ At the beginning of the fall academic year, a public school experienced an influx of new pupils who had recently emigrated from Russia and who did not speak English. In the rush to ensure adequate academic placement for the students, the school psychologist asked a member of the custodial staff who was fluent in Russian and English to serve as an interpreter for administration of tests to determine if any of the pupils had learning disabilities.

> ☑ A research psychologist received institutional review board (IRB) approval to conduct a study concerning health knowledge and behaviors of illegal immigrants. All informed consent and interview scripts were translated into the participants' language. The psychologist realized that legal residents of the community trusted by prospective participants would be more effective participant recruiters than university staff. He placed an ad in the local papers and spent a week training newly hired recruiters in recruiting methods and in methods to protect prospective participants from coercion, to ensure confidentiality of information collected, and to avoid exploitative or otherwise harmful multiple relationships.

Reasonable Steps. The phrase "take reasonable steps" recognizes that despite their best efforts, persons to whom work is delegated may fail to perform their duties appropriately. The phrase also recognizes that sometimes psychologists working in organizations, in the military and other public service positions, or at the bequest of the legal system may be assigned assistants, employees, or interpreters insufficiently qualified to perform their duties. Psychologists must at minimum discuss their concerns and ethical obligations with those responsible for such assignments (see Standards 1.02, Conflicts Between Ethics and Law, Regulations, or Other Governing Legal Authority, and 1.03, Conflicts Between Ethics and Organizational Demands).

> ☑ A consulting psychologist was hired to conduct a job analysis to determine hiring needs for an organization. The company agreed to provide the psychologist with one of their administrative assistants to help schedule meetings and provide other clerical assistance. The consulting psychologist discovered the assistant was discussing with other employees her misimpression of the goals and preliminary findings of the job analysis in a manner that compromised the validity of future assessments. The psychologists immediately brought this matter to the assistant's attention and began to have biweekly monitoring meetings with the assistant to ensure her understanding of her role responsibilities.

> ☑ A prescribing psychologist worked in a hospital that employed nurse practitioners to conduct patient medical histories at intake. The psychologist noted that while the nurses' reports contained detailed information regarding physical health, the histories were incomplete in terms of information relevant to mental health. The psychologist requested and received approval from the medical director to run a brief training session on mental health intake procedures for the nurses.

2.06 Personal Problems and Conflicts

(a) Psychologists refrain from initiating an activity when they know or should know that there is a substantial likelihood that their personal problems will prevent them from performing their work-related activities in a competent manner.

There is a growing body of research indicating that emotional, social, health-related, and other personal problems can interfere with psychologists' ability to use their skills effectively. Substance abuse problems, acute depression or other mental disorders, chronic or life-threatening diseases, and other stressful life events such as divorce or the death of a loved one are situations that sometimes prevent psychologists from performing their work in a competent manner (O'Connor, 2001; Sherman & Thelen, 1998). Work-related stressors, such as social isolation in private practice, burnout, and vicarious traumatization encountered by some psychologists working with survivors of trauma, can lead to boundary violations and otherwise compromise effective job performance (Pearlman & Saakvitne, 1995; Skorupa & Agresti, 1993). Clients/patients, students, employers, and employees suffer when personal problems prevent psychologists from competently implementing their work, and the misconduct that is often a product of these circumstances harms public perceptions of psychology.

Standard 2.06a requires psychologists to refrain from beginning an activity when there is a substantial likelihood their personal problems may impair their ability to perform their work competently. The phrases "refrain from beginning" and "substantial likelihood" indicate that the intent of this standard is preemptive: It prohibits psychologists from taking on a professional or scientific role when their personal problems have the potential to impair their work. As signified by the phrase "or should know," psychologists suffering from problems that would reasonably be expected by members of the profession to cause work-related impairment will not avoid a finding of violation of this standard by claiming they did not know their problems could interfere with their work. Pope and Brown (1996) note that competence in the conduct of psychotherapy requires knowledge of self-monitoring techniques to identify one's own emotional strengths and weaknesses, needs and resources, and abilities and limits. Signs may include intense emotional reactions during therapy.

☑ A psychologist had just returned to independent practice following chemotherapy for a cancer that is now in remission. The psychologist believed that she had recovered from the fatigue and mental stress of the chemotherapy but recognized that such symptoms may persist. She set up a weekly consultation meeting with a colleague to help monitor her work until she was confident that the symptoms had fully abated.

> ☒   An industrial-organizational psychologist responsible for preemployment screening for an organization had begun to drink heavily and found that he needed to have several beers before seeing candidates in the morning and several more drinks periodically throughout the workday. In response to a complaint to the APA Ethics Committee filed by an applicant who was appalled by the psychologist's slurring of words during a screening, the psychologist claimed that his alcoholism prevented him from acknowledging he had a problem.

(b) When psychologists become aware of personal problems that may interfere with their performing work-related duties adequately, they take appropriate measures, such as obtaining professional consultation or assistance, and determine whether they should limit, suspend, or terminate their work-related duties. (See also Standard 10.10, Terminating Therapy.)

Standard 2.06b applies to situations in which psychologists who are already providing services, teaching, or conducting research become aware that their personal problems are interfering with their work. The standard calls for psychologists to take appropriate steps to remedy the problem and to determine whether such remedies are sufficient for them to continue work-related activities.

> ☑   A teaching psychologist who was undergoing outpatient treatment for a life-threatening medical disorder found it increasingly difficult to prepare lectures, grade papers, and mentor students effectively. The psychologist consulted with the chair of the department, who agreed to assign an experienced graduate teaching assistant for the lectures. The psychologist also asked a colleague to serve as a commenter on the two dissertations he was currently mentoring.

To comply with this standard, psychologists can also turn to the increasing number of state psychological association and other colleague assistance programs that help psychologists deal proactively with and remediate impairment (Barnett & Hillard, 2001). If such steps are not adequate to ensure competence, Standard 2.06b requires that psychologists appropriately limit, suspend, or terminate work-related duties.

> ☑   A counseling psychologist returned to her position at a college counseling center after sick leave for physical injuries incurred during a car accident. Within a week at the counseling center, the psychologist realized the pain medication she was frequently taking during the day was interfering with her ability to focus on clients' problems. She contacted a psychologist assistance program in her state that helped her taper off the medications, provided ongoing supervision to help her self-monitor her ability to perform her tasks, and provided support for the psychologist to approach the director of the counseling center to cut back on her hours.

☒ A psychologist working in a correctional facility was violently attacked by a new prisoner during a psychological assessment interview. The psychologist did not seek psychological counseling for his reaction to the assault. A month later, the psychologist was conducting an intake of a prisoner who reminded him of his attacker. Although the psychological assessment did not provide evidence of extreme dangerousness, the psychologist's report indicated the prisoner was highly dangerous and should be assigned to the most restrictive environment (adapted from Weinberger & Sreenivasan, 2003).

HOT TOPIC

Multicultural Ethical Competence

Ethical decision making in diverse cultural venues must be sensitive to cultural attitudes toward individual autonomy and communal responsibility, historical and contemporary discrimination within society and psychology as a discipline, sociopolitical factors influencing definitions of race and ethnicity, and variations in immigration history, acculturation, cultural/ethnic identity, language, and mixed race/ethnic heritage (Lyon & Cotler, 2007; Ponterotto, Casas, Suzuki, & Alexander, 2001; Sue & Sue, 2003; Trimble & Fisher, 2006). Multicultural responsibility requires "a fusion of personal and professional commitments to consider culture during ethical encounters" (Ridley, Liddle, Hill, & Li, 2001, p. 176). This Hot Topic section applies the ethical decision making model introduced in Chapter 3 to help psychologists identify key questions to consider as a means of acquiring the attitudes and knowledge essential to multicultural ethical competence.

Multicultural Ethical Commitment

Multicultural ethical commitment requires a strong desire to understand how culture is relevant to the identification and resolution of ethical problems. It demands a moral disposition and emotional responsiveness that moves psychologists to explore cultural differences and creatively apply the APA Ethics Code to each cultural context. Cultivation of these competencies thus includes motivation to consider the influence of culture in psychologists' work conscientiously, prudently, and with caring discernment.

The desire to ensure that cultural sensitivity is integrated into ethical decision making requires a willingness to reflect on how one's own cultural values and cultural identity influence the way ethics is conceived in one's activities as a psychologist (Arredondo, 1999; Helms, 1993). Furthermore, multicultural ethical competence entails recognition of harms that psychology can exert on culturally diverse groups by invalidating their life experiences, defining their cultural values or differences as deviant, and imposing the values of dominant culture upon them (Fisher, 1999; Fisher et al., 2002; Fowers & Davidov, 2006; Prilleltensky, 1997; Trimble & Fisher, 2006).

In psychological research and practice, multicultural ethical commitment involves motivation to

- Critically examine moral premises in the discipline that may largely reflect Eurocentric conceptions of the good
- Question "deficit" and "ethnic group comparative" approaches to understanding cultural differences

- Address the reality and impact of racial discrimination in the lives of cultural minorities
- Recognize that socially constructed racial labels can strip participants of their personal identity by responding to them only in terms of racial or ethnic categorizations
- Avoid conceptually grouping members of ethnic minority groups into categories that may not reflect how individuals see themselves
- Engage in self-examination of how institutional racism may have influenced each psychologist's own role, status, and motivation to develop professional identities free from these influences
- Develop the flexibility required to respond to rapid cultural diversification and fluid definitions of culture, ethnicity, and race

Multicultural Ethical Awareness

Multicultural ethical commitment is just the first step toward multicultural ethical competence. Good intentions are insufficient if psychologists fail to acquire relevant knowledge about cultural differences and how they may affect the expression of and solutions for ethical problems. Psychologists must be familiar with research, theory, and practice guidelines relevant to their work with diverse populations. This may include an understanding of the following:

- The history of ethical abuses of cultural minorities in the United States and how this may exacerbate disparities in mental health care, employment, criminal justice, and involvement in psychological research
- The impact on mental health of historical and contemporary discrimination in employment, education, housing, and other areas
- Cultural and contextual factors that may facilitate or interfere with psychological well-being or responsiveness to treatment
- Scientific, social, and political factors influencing the definitions of race, ethnicity, and culture and how these may serve as barriers to conducting psychological activities that protect individuals' rights and welfare
- Within-group as well as between-group differences that may be obscured by cultural stereotypes in society and within the discipline of psychology
- Knowledge and skills in constructing and implementing culturally valid and language-appropriate assessments, treatments, research procedures, teaching strategies, and consulting and organizational evaluation techniques
- Knowledge of relevant ethical standards in the APA Ethics Code and organizational guidelines relevant to multicultural ethical competence in research and practice
- Knowledge of antidiscrimination federal and state laws relevant to the contexts in which psychologists work

Goodness-of-Fit Ethics and Multicultural Ethical Decision Making

Multicultural ethical commitment and ethical awareness are essential but not sufficient to ensure ethical resolution of multicultural challenges. Given the dynamic nature of individual, institutional, and sociopolitical concepts of race, culture, and ethnicity, ethical decision making across different cultural contexts can be informed but may not be resolved by previous approaches to ethical problems. Many multicultural ethical challenges are unique to the culture, the salience of the culture for a particular individual in a particular context, other within-culture individual differences, the environment in which the psychological activity occurs, and the goals of that activity. In applying the steps for ethical decision making described in Chapter 3, multicultural ethical decision making includes (a) creating a goodness of fit between the cultural context and the psychologist's work setting and goals and (b) engaging in a process of colearning that ensures this fit (Fisher & Ragsdale, 2006).

Applying goodness-of-fit ethics to multicultural contexts requires reflection on the following questions:

- What are the cultural circumstances that might render individuals more susceptible to the benefits or risks of the intended psychological assessment, treatment, or research?
- Are cultural factors underestimated or overestimated in the assessment, treatment, organizational evaluation, or research plan?
- Do psychologists and members of cultural groups with whom they work have different conceptions of practice goals or research benefits?
- Are traditional approaches to informed consent and confidentiality protections compatible with the values of spirit, collectivity, and harmony characteristic of different ethnocultural populations?
- Are there aspects of the psychological work setting that are "misfitted" to the competencies, values, fears, and hopes of recipients of psychological services, examinees, employees, or research participants?
- How can the setting (including the aims and procedures to accomplish these aims) be modified to fit the requirements of culturally sensitive and responsibly conducted psychology?
- How can psychologists engage organizations and employees, clients/patients and practitioners, students and school personnel, research participants, and investigators in discussions that will help illuminate the cultural lens through which each views the psychologist's work?

Culture is a dynamic construct influenced by an ever-changing sociopolitical landscape. Ethical decision making that includes multicultural commitment and awareness can help psychologists correct cultural misimpressions and biases in their work. An openness to learning from and collaborating with stakeholders can help psychologists implement and monitor the cultural adequacy of ethical decisions and make appropriate adjustments when necessary. Multicultural ethical competence requires a process of lifelong learning that enables psychologists to make ethical decisions that reflect and respect the values of the discipline of psychology and the values of cultural communities.

CHAPTER 6

Standards on Human Relations

3. HUMAN RELATIONS

3.01 Unfair Discrimination

In their work-related activities, psychologists do not engage in unfair discrimination based on age, gender, gender identity, race, ethnicity, culture, national origin, religion, sexual orientation, disability, socioeconomic status, or any basis proscribed by law.

Psychologists respect the dignity and worth of all people and appropriately consider the relevance of personal characteristics based on such factors as age, gender, gender identity, race, ethnicity, culture, national origin, religion, sexual orientation, disability, or socioeconomic status (Principle E: Respect for People's Rights and Dignity). Much of the work of psychologists entails making valid discriminating judgments that best serve the people and organizations they work with and fulfilling their ethical obligations as teachers, researchers, organizational consultants, and practitioners. Standard 3.01 of the American Psychological Association (APA) Ethics Code (APA, 2002b) does not prohibit such discriminations.

☑ The graduate psychology faculty of a university used differences in standardized test scores, undergraduate grades, and professionally related experience as selection criteria for program admission.

☑ A research psychologist sampled individuals from specific age, gender, and cultural groups to test a specific hypothesis relevant to these groups.

☑ An organizational psychologist working for a software company designed assessments for employee screening and promotion to distinguish individuals with the requisite information technology skills to perform tasks essential to the positions from individuals not possessing these skills.

☑ A school psychologist considers such factors as age, language, and hearing or vision disability when making educational placement recommendations.

☑ A family bereavement counselor working in an elder care unit of a hospital regularly considered the extent to which factors associated with the families' culture or religious values were relevant to the treatment plan.

Standard 3.01 does not require psychologists offering therapeutic assistance to accept as clients/patients all individuals who request mental health services. Discerning and prudent psychologists know the limitations of their competence and accept to treat only those whom they can reasonably expect to help based on their education, training, and experience (Striefel, 2007). Psychologists may also refuse to accept clients/patients on the basis of their lack of commitment to the therapeutic process, problems they have that fall outside the therapists' area of competence, or their perceived inability or unwillingness to pay for services (Knapp & VandeCreek, 2003).

Psychologists must, however, exercise reasonable judgment and precautions to ensure their work does not reflect personal or organizational biases or prejudices that can lead to injustice (Principle D: Justice). For example, the APA's *Resolution on Religious, Religion-Based, and/or Religion-Derived Prejudice* (APA, 2007d) condemns prejudice and discrimination against individuals or groups based on their religious or spiritual beliefs, practices, adherence, or background.

Standard 3.01 prohibits psychologists from making unfair discriminations based on the factors listed in the standard.

☒ The director of a graduate program in psychology rejected a candidate for program admission because the candidate indicated he was a Muslim.

☒ A consulting psychologist agreed to a company's request to develop preemployment procedures that would screen out applicants from Spanish-speaking cultures based on the company's presumption that the majority of such candidates would be undocumented residents.

☒ A psychologist working in a Medicaid clinic decided not to include a cognitive component in a behavioral treatment based solely on the psychologist's belief that lower-income patients were incapable of responding to "talk therapies."

☒   One partner of a gay couple who recently entered couple counseling called their psychologist when he learned he tested positive for the HIV virus. Although when working with heterosexual couples, the psychologist strongly encouraged clients to inform their partners if they had a sexually transmitted disease, she did not believe such an approach was necessary in this situation based on her erroneous assumption that all gay men engaged in reckless and risky sexual behavior (see Palma & Iannelli, 2002).

Discrimination Proscribed by Law. Standard 3.01 prohibits psychologists from discriminating among individuals on any basis proscribed by law. For example, industrial-organizational psychologists need to be aware of nondiscrimination laws relevant to race, religion, and disability that apply to companies for which they work (e.g., Americans with Disabilities Act of 1990 [ADA], www.ada.gov; Title VII of the Civil Rights Act of 1964, www.eeoc .gov/policy/vii.html, www.eeoc.gov/types/religion.html; Workforce Investment Act of 1998, www.doleta.gov/usworkforce/wia/wialaw.txt). Psychologists conducting personnel performance evaluations should avoid selecting tests developed to assess psychopathology (see *Karraker v. Rent-a-Center,* 2005). In some instances, ADA laws for small businesses also apply to psychologists in private practice. Therefore, psychologists in independent practice should familiarize themselves with relevant federal and state ADA compliance regulations, such as wheelchair accessibility. In addition, the Health Insurance Portability and Accountability Act of 1996 (HIPAA) prohibits covered entities from discriminating against an individual for filing a complaint, participating in a compliance review or hearing, or opposing an act or practice that is unlawful under the regulation (45 CFR 164.530[g]).

3.02 Sexual Harassment

Psychologists do not engage in sexual harassment. Sexual harassment is sexual solicitation, physical advances, or verbal or nonverbal conduct that is sexual in nature, that occurs in connection with the psychologist's activities or roles as a psychologist, and that either (1) is unwelcome, is offensive, or creates a hostile workplace or educational environment, and the psychologist knows or is told this; or (2) is sufficiently severe or intense to be abusive to a reasonable person in the context. Sexual harassment can consist of a single intense or severe act or of multiple persistent or pervasive acts. (See also Standard 1.08, Unfair Discrimination Against Complainants and Respondents.)

It is always wise for psychologists to be familiar with and comply with applicable laws and institutional policies regarding sexual harassment. Laws on sexual harassment vary across jurisdictions, are often complex, and change over time. Standard 3.02 provides a clear definition of behaviors that are prohibited and considered sexual harassment under the Ethics Code. When this definition establishes a higher standard of conduct than required by law, psychologists must comply with Standard 3.02.

According to Standard 3.02, sexual harassment can be verbal or nonverbal solicitation, advances, or sexual conduct that occurs in connection with the psychologist's activities or role as a psychologist. The wording of the definition was carefully crafted to prohibit sexual harassment without encouraging complaints against psychologists whose poor judgments or behaviors do not rise to the level of harassment. Thus, to meet the standard's threshold for sexual harassment, behaviors have to be either so severe or intense that a reasonable person would deem them abusive in that context, or, regardless of intensity, the psychologist was aware or had been told that the behaviors are unwelcome, offensive, or creating a hostile workplace or educational environment.

For example, a senior faculty member who places an arm around a student's shoulder during a discussion or who tells an off-color sexual joke that offends a number of junior faculty may not be in violation of this standard if such behavior is uncharacteristic of the faculty member's usual conduct, if a reasonable person might interpret the behavior as inoffensive, and if there is reason to assume the psychologist neither is aware of nor has been told the behavior is offensive.

A hostile workplace or educational environment is one in which the sexual language or behaviors of the psychologist impairs the ability of those who are the target of the sexual harassment to conduct their work or participate in classroom and educational experiences. The actions of the senior faculty member described above might be considered sexual harassment if the psychologist's behaviors reflected a consistent pattern of sexual conduct during class or office hours, if such behaviors had led students to withdraw from the psychologist's class, or if students or other faculty had repeatedly told the psychologist about the discomfort produced.

According to this standard, sexual harassment can also consist of a single intense or severe act that would be considered abusive to a reasonable person.

> ☒ A senior psychologist at a test company sexually fondled a junior colleague during an office party.

A violation of this standard applies to all psychologists irrespective of the status, sex, or sexual orientation of the psychologist or individual harassed.

> ☒ During clinical supervision, a trainee had an emotional discussion with her female supervisor about how her own experiences recognizing her lesbian sexual orientation during adolescence were helping her counsel the gay and lesbian youths she was working with. At the end of the session, the supervisor kissed the trainee on the lips.

3.03 Other Harassment

Psychologists do not knowingly engage in behavior that is harassing or demeaning to persons with whom they interact in their work based on factors such as those persons' age, gender, gender identity, race, ethnicity, culture, national origin, religion, sexual orientation, disability, language, or socioeconomic status.

According to Principle E: Respect for People's Rights and Dignity, psychologists should eliminate from their work the effect of bias and prejudice based on factors such as age, gender, gender identity, race, ethnicity, national origin, religion, sexual orientation, disability, language, and socioeconomic status. Standard 3.03 prohibits behaviors that draw on these categories to harass or demean individuals with whom psychologists work, such as colleagues, students, research participants, or employees. Behaviors in violation of this standard include ethnic slurs and negative generalizations based on gender, sexual orientation, disability, or socioeconomic status whose intention or outcome is lowering status or reputation.

The term *knowingly* reflects the fact that evolving societal sensitivity to language and behaviors demeaning to different groups may result in psychologists unknowingly acting in a pejorative manner. The term *knowingly* also reflects awareness that interpretations of behaviors that are harassing or demeaning can often be subjective. Thus, a violation of this standard rests on an objective evaluation that a psychologist would have or should have been aware that his or her behavior would be perceived as harassing or demeaning.

This standard does not prohibit psychologists from critical comments about the work of students, colleagues, or others based on legitimate criteria. For example, professors can inform, and often have a duty to inform, students that their writing or clinical skills are below program standards or indicate when a student's classroom comment is incorrect or inappropriate. It is the responsibility of employers or chairs of academic departments to critically review, report on, and discuss both positive and negative evaluations of employees or faculty. Similarly, the standard does not prohibit psychologists conducting assessment or therapy from applying valid diagnostic classifications that a client/patient may find offensive.

3.04 Avoiding Harm

Psychologists take reasonable steps to avoid harming their clients/patients, students, supervisees, research participants, organizational clients, and others with whom they work, and to minimize harm where it is foreseeable and unavoidable.

As articulated in Principle A: Beneficence and Nonmaleficence, psychologists seek to safeguard the welfare of those with whom they work and avoid or minimize harm when conflicts occur among professional obligations. In the rightly practiced profession and science of psychology, harm is not always unethical or avoidable. Legitimate activities that may lead to harm include (a) giving low grades to students who perform poorly on exams; (b) providing a valid diagnosis that prevents a client/patient from receiving disability insurance; (c) conducting personnel reviews that lead to an individual's termination of employment; (d) conducting a custody evaluation in a case in which the judge determines one of the parents must relinquish custodial rights; or (e) disclosing confidential information to protect the physical welfare of a third party.

☑ Parents of a fourth-grade student wanted their child placed in a special education class. After administering a complete battery of tests, the school psychologist's report indicated that the child's responses did not meet established definitions for learning disabilities and therefore did not meet the district's criteria for such placement.

☑ A forensic psychologist was asked to evaluate the mental status of a prisoner who had been convicted of murder and would face the death penalty if found to be mentally competent. The psychologist conducted a thorough evaluation based on definitions of competency established by the profession of psychology and by law. While the psychologist's report noted the inmate had some cognitive deficiencies and emotional instability, it also noted these deficiencies did not meet the legal definition of mental illness that would bar execution.

☒ A psychologist conducted therapy over the Internet for clients/patients in a rural area 120 miles from her office. The psychologist had not developed a plan with each client/patient for handling mental health crises. During a live video Internet session, a client who had been struggling with bouts of depression showed the psychologist his gun and said he was going outside to "blow his head off." The psychologist did not have the contact information of any local hospital, relative, or friend to send prompt emergency assistance.

Avoiding Harm

Recognizing that such harms are not always avoidable or inappropriate, Standard 3.04 requires psychologists to take reasonable steps to avoid harming those with whom they interact in their professional and scientific roles and to minimize harm where it is foreseeable and unavoidable.

These steps often include complying with other standards in the Ethics Code, such as the following:

☑ Clarifying course requirements and establishing a timely and specific process for providing feedback to students (Standard 7.06, Assessing Student and Supervisee Performance)

☑ Selecting and using valid and reliable assessment techniques appropriate to the nature of the problem and characteristics of the individual assessed to avoid misdiagnosis and inappropriate services (Standards 9.01, Bases for Assessments, and 9.02, Use of Assessments)

☑ Ensuring that informed consent for assessments clearly describes the intended purpose of the assessment and the limits of confidentiality (Standard 9.03, Informed Consent in Assessments)

☑ When appropriate, providing information beforehand to employees and others who may be directly affected by a psychologist's services to an organization (Standard 3.11, Psychological Services Delivered To or Through Organizations)

☑ Acquiring adequate knowledge of relevant judicial or administrative rules prior to performing forensic roles to avoid violating the legal rights of individuals involved in litigation (Standard 2.01f, Boundaries of Competence)

☑ Taking steps to minimize harm when, during debriefing, a psychologist becomes aware of participant distress created by the research procedure (Standard 8.08c, Debriefing)

☑ Becoming familiar with local social service, medical, and legal resources for clients/patients and third parties who will be affected if a psychologist is ethically or legally compelled to report child abuse, suicide risk, elder abuse, or intent to do physical harm to another individual (Standard 4.05b, Disclosures)

Is Use of Aversion Therapies Unethical? Aversion therapy involves the repeated association of a maladaptive behavior or cognition with an aversive stimulus (e.g., electric shock, unpleasant images, nausea) to eliminate pleasant associations or introduce negative associations with the undesirable behavior. Aversion therapies have proved promising in treatments of drug cravings, alcoholism, and pica (Bordnick, Elkins, Orr, Walters, & Thyer, 2004; Ferreri, Tamm, & Wier, 2006; Thurber, 1985) and have been used with questionable effectiveness for pedophilia (Hall & Hall, 2007). It is beyond the purview of this volume to review literature evaluating the clinical efficacy of aversion therapies for different disorders. However, irrespective of evidence of clinical efficacy, aversion therapies have and will continue to require ethical deliberation because they purposely subject clients/patients to physical and emotional discomfort and distress. In so doing, they raise the fundamental moral issue of balancing doing good against doing no harm, Principle A: Beneficence and Nonmaleficence.

Psychologists should consider the following questions before engaging in aversion therapy:

- Have all empirically and clinically validated alternative therapeutic approaches been attempted?

- Is there empirical evidence that the aversive therapeutic approach has demonstrated effectiveness with individuals who are similar to the client/patient in mental health disorder, age, physical health, and other relevant factors? (Standard 2.04, Bases for Scientific and Professional Judgments)

- To what extent is the behavior endangering the life or seriously compromising the well-being of the client/patient?

- For this particular patient, will the discomfort and distress of the aversive treatment outweigh its potential positive effects?

- To what extent is the urgency defined by the needs of third parties rather than the client/patient? (Standards 3.05, Multiple Relationships; 3.07, Third-Party Requests for Services; and 3.08, Exploitative Relationships)

- Am I competent to administer the aversive treatment? (Standards 2.01a, Boundaries of Competence, and 2.05, Delegation of Work to Others)

- If aversive treatment is the only remaining option to best serve the needs of the client/patient, how can harm be minimized?

- Have I established appropriate monitoring procedures and termination criteria?

☑ Prescribing psychologists trained in addiction treatments opened a group practice to provide assessment and individual and group therapy for substance abuse and comorbid disorders. Occasionally, some clients who were long-term cocaine users could not overcome their cravings despite positive responses to therapy related to comorbid disorders and high levels of motivation to stop abusing drugs. In such cases, the team would offer the client a chemical aversion therapy with empirical evidence of treatment efficacy. A member of the team had acquired additional training in this technique.

☑ Prior to initiating the aversion therapy, clients were required to undergo a physical examination to rule out those for whom the treatment posed a potential medical risk. The treatment consisted of drinking a saltwater solution containing a chemical that would induce nausea. Saltwater was used to avoid creating a negative association with water. As soon as the client began to feel nausea, he or she was instructed to ingest a placebo form of crack cocaine using drug paraphernalia. A bucket was available for vomiting. Patients were monitored by a physician assistant and psychologist during the process and recovery for any medical or iatrogenic psychological side effects. Following the recommended minimum number of sessions, patients continued in individual psychotherapy, and positive and negative reactions to the aversion therapy continued to be monitored (see Bordnick et al., 2004).

Harm Caused by Violation of Other Standards

Clients/patients may be harmed when psychotherapy creates unanticipated iatrogenic reactions or when treatment is continued when it is reasonably clear that they are not likely to benefit from the services. Standard 10.10, Terminating Therapy, requires psychologists to terminate services under such conditions. However, recognizing that harm can also arise when services are prematurely terminated, Standard 10.10 also requires psychologists to provide appropriate pretermination counseling and referrals, unless precluded by the actions of clients/patients or third-party payors.

When managed care companies refuse psychologists' request to extend coverage for clients/patients whose reimbursement quotas have been reached, psychologists may be in violation of Standard 3.04 if they (a) did not take reasonable steps at the outset of therapy to estimate and communicate to patients and their insurance company the number of sessions anticipated, (b) did not familiarize themselves with the insurers' policy, (c), recognized a need for continuing treatment but did not communicate with insurers in an adequate or timely fashion, or (d) were unprepared to handle client/patient response to termination of services.

Often, violation of Standard 3.04 will occur in connection with the violation of other standards in this code that detail the actions required to perform psychological activities in an ethically responsible manner. For example:

> ☒ Providing testimony on the poor parenting skills of an individual whom the psychologist has never personally examined that contributed to that individual's loss of child custody (Standard 9.01b, Bases for Assessments)
>
> ☒ Engaging in a sexual relationship with a current therapy client/patient that was a factor leading to the breakup of the client's/patient's marriage (Standard 10.05, Sexual Intimacies With Current Therapy Clients/Patients)
>
> ☒ Asking students to relate their personal experience in psychotherapy to past and current theories on mental health treatment when this requirement was not stipulated in admissions or program materials, causing some students to drop out of the program (Standard 7.04, Student Disclosure of Personal Information)
>
> ☒ Deceiving a research participant about procedures the investigator expected would cause some physical pain (Standard 8.07b, Deception in Research)

Some contexts require more stringent protections against harm. For example, psychologists working within institutions that use seclusion or physical restraint techniques to treat violent episodes or other potentially injurious patient behaviors must ensure these extreme methods are employed only upon evidence of their effectiveness, when other treatment alternatives have failed, and when the use of such techniques is in the best interest of the patient and not for punishment, staff convenience or anxiety, or to reduce costs (Jerome, 1998).

> ☒ The director of psychological services for a children's state psychiatric in-patient ward approved the employment of timeout procedures to discipline patients who were disruptive during educational classes. A special room was set up for this purpose. The director did not, however, set guidelines for how the timeout procedure should be implemented. For example, he failed to set limits on the length of time a child could be kept in the room, did not require staff monitoring, did not ensure the room was protected against fire hazard, and did not develop policies that would permit patients to leave the room for appropriate reasons. The director was appalled to learn staff had not monitored a 7-year-old who was kept in the room for over an hour and was discovered crying and self-soiled (see, e.g., *Dickens v. Johnson County Board of Education*, 1987; *Goss v. Lopez*, 1975; *Hayes v. Unified School District*, 1989; Yell, 1994).

Equipoise and Randomized Clinical Trials

Important questions of treatment efficacy and effectiveness driving the conduct of randomized clinical trials for mental health treatments raise, by their very nature, the possibility that some participants will fail to respond to experimental treatment conditions or experience a decline in mental health during the trial. To comply with Standard 3.04, research psychologists should develop procedures to identify and address such possibilities. Such steps can include (a) scientifically and clinically informed inclusion and exclusion criteria for patient participation, (b) the establishment of a data safety monitoring board to evaluate unanticipated risks that may emerge during a clinical trial, and (c) prior to the initiation of the research, establishing criteria based on anticipated risks for when a trial should be stopped to protect the welfare of participants. For additional information on guidance from the Office of Human Research Protections, readers can refer to www.hhs.gov/ohrp/policy/AdvEvntGuid.htm.

Implications of HIPAA. Psychologists should be aware that HIPAA requires covered entities to take reasonable steps to mitigate any harmful effects of a violation of the Privacy Rule of which they are aware (45 CFR 164.530[f]).

3.05 Multiple Relationships

(a) A multiple relationship occurs when a psychologist is in a professional role with a person and (1) at the same time is in another role with the same person, (2) at the same time is in a relationship with a person closely associated with or related to the person with whom the psychologist has the professional relationship, or (3) promises to enter into another relationship in the future with the person or a person closely associated with or related to the person. A psychologist refrains from entering into a multiple relationship if the multiple relationship could reasonably be expected to impair the psychologist's objectivity, competence, or effectiveness in performing his or her functions as a psychologist, or otherwise risks exploitation or harm to the person with whom the professional relationship exists.

Multiple relationships that would not reasonably be expected to cause impairment or risk exploitation or harm are not unethical.

Individual psychologists may perform a variety of roles. For example, during the course of a year, a psychologist might see clients/patients in private practice, teach at a university, provide consultation services to an organization, and conduct research. In some instances, these multiple roles will involve the same person or persons who have a close relationship with one another and may be concurrent or sequential.

Not All Multiple Relationships Are Unethical

Multiple relationships that would not reasonably be expected to cause impairment or risk exploitation or harm are not unethical. For example, it is not unethical for psychologists to serve as clinical supervisors or dissertation mentors for students enrolled in one of their graduate classes because supervision, mentoring, and teaching are all educational roles.

Standard 3.05 does not prohibit attendance at a client's/patient's, student's, employee's, or employer's family funeral, wedding, or graduation; the participation of a psychologist's child in an athletic team coached by a client/patient; gift giving or receiving with those with whom one has a professional role; or entering into a social relationship with a colleague as long as these relationships would not reasonably be expected to lead to role impairment, exploitation, or harm. Incidental encounters with clients/patients at religious services, school events, restaurants, health clubs, or similar places are also not unethical as long as psychologists react to these encounters in a professional manner. Nonetheless, psychologists should always consider whether the particular nature of a professional relationship might lead to a client's/patient's misperceptions regarding an encounter. If so, it is advisable to keep a record of such encounters. For example:

> ☑ A client with a fluctuating sense of reality coupled with strong romantic transference feelings for a treating psychologist misinterpreted two incidental encounters with his psychologist as planned romantic meetings. The client subsequently raised these incidents in a sexual misconduct complaint against the psychologist. The psychologist's recorded notes, made immediately following these encounters, were effective evidence against the invalid accusations.

Posttermination Nonsexual Relationships. The standard does not have an absolute prohibition against posttermination *non*sexual relationships with persons with whom psychologists have had a previous professional relationship. However, such relationships are prohibited if the posttermination relationship was promised during the course of the original relationship or if the individual was exploited or harmed by the intent to have the posttermination relationship. Psychologists should be aware that posttermination relationships can become problematic when personal knowledge acquired during the professional relationship becomes relevant to the new relationship (see Anderson & Kitchener, 1996, for examples and discussion of nonromantic, nonsexual posttherapy relationships). *— I have distaste.*

> ☒ A psychologist in independent practice abruptly terminated therapy with a patient who was an editor at a large publishing company so that the patient could review a book manuscript the psychologist had submitted to the company.

Clients in Individual and Group Therapy. In most instances, treating clients/patients concurrently in individual and group therapy does not represent a multiple relationship because the practitioner is working in a therapeutic role in both contexts (R. E. Taylor & Gazda, 1991), and Standard 3.05 does not prohibit such practice. Psychologists providing individual and group therapy to the same clients/patients should consider instituting special protections against inadvertently revealing to a therapy group information shared by a client/patient in individual sessions. As in all types of professional practice, psychologists should avoid recommending an additional form of therapy based on the psychologist's financial interests rather than the client's/patient's mental health needs (Standard 3.06, Conflict of Interest).

Judging the Ethicality of Multiple Roles

Several authors have provided helpful decision-making models for judging whether a multiple relationship may place the psychologist in violation of Standard 3.04 (Brownlee, 1996; Gottlieb, 1993; Oberlander & Barnett, 2005; Younggren & Gottlieb, 2004). The majority look at multiple relationships in terms of a continuum of risk. From these models, the ethical appropriateness of a multiple relationship becomes increasingly questionable with

- Increased incompatibility in role functions and objectives;
- The greater power or prestige the psychologist has over the person with whom there is a multiple role;
- The greater the intimacy called for in the roles;
- The longer the role relationships are anticipated to last;
- The more vulnerable the client/patient, student, supervisee, or other subordinate is to harm; and
- The extent to which engaging in the multiple relationship meets the needs of the psychologist rather than the needs of the client/patient.

Potentially Unethical Multiple Relationships

Entering Into Another Role. Psychologists may encounter situations in which the opportunity to enter a new relationship emerges with a person with whom they already have an established professional role. The following examples illustrate multiple relationships that, with rare exception, would be prohibited by Standard 3.05a because each situation could reasonably be expected to impair psychologists' ability to competently and objectively perform their roles or lead to exploitation or harm.

> ☒   A psychologist agreed to see a student in the psychologist's introductory psychology course for brief private counseling for test anxiety. At the end of the semester, to avoid jeopardizing the student's growing academic self-confidence, the psychologist refrained from giving the student a legitimate low grade for poor class performance. The psychologist should have anticipated that the multiple relationship could impair her objectivity and effectiveness as a teacher and create an unfair grading environment for the rest of the class.

☒ A company hired a psychologist for consultation on how to prepare employees for a shift in management anticipated by the failing mental health of the chief executive officer (CEO). A few months later, the psychologist agreed to a request by the board of directors to counsel the CEO about retiring. The CEO did not want to retire and told the psychologist about the coercive tactics used by the board. The psychologist realized too late that this second role undermined both treatment and consultation effectiveness because the counseling role played by the psychologist would be viewed as either exploitative by the CEO or as disloyal by the board of directors.

☒ A school psychologist whose responsibilities in the school district included discussing with parents the results of their children's psychoeducational assessments regularly recommended to parents that they bring their children to his private practice for consultation and possible therapy.

☒ As part of their final class assignment, a psychologist required all students in her undergraduate psychology class to participate in a federally funded research study she was conducting on college student drinking behaviors.

☒ A psychologist treating an inmate for anxiety disorder in a correctional facility agreed with a request by the prison administrator to serve on a panel determining the inmate's parole eligibility (Anno, 2001).

☒ A graduate student interning at an in-patient psychiatric hospital asked her patients if they would agree to participate in her dissertation research.

Forensic Roles. Forensic psychologists may be called upon for a variety of assessment roles that differ in their goals and responsibilities from those of treating psychologists. Whereas the responsibility of the treating psychologist is to help clients/patients achieve mental health, the responsibility of forensic psychologists serving as experts for the court, the defense, or plaintiff is to provide objective information to assist the finder of facts in legal determinations. In most instances, psychologists who take on both roles concurrently or sequentially will be in violation of Standard 3.05a. For example, in the treatment context, the format, information sought, and psychologist–client/patient relationship are guided by the psychologist's professional evaluation of client/patient needs. Information obtained in a standardized or unstructured manner or in response to practitioner empathy and other elements of the therapeutic alliance is a legitimate means of meeting treatment goals.

However, when mixed with the forensic role, the subjective nature of such inquiries and the selectivity of information obtained impair the psychologist's objectivity and thus ability to fulfill forensic responsibilities. Moreover, the conflicting objectives of the treating and forensic roles will be confusing and potentially intimidating to clients/patients, thereby undermining the psychologist's effectiveness in functioning under either role.

> ☒   A forensic psychologist was hired by the court to conduct a psychological evaluation for a probation hearing of a man serving a jail sentence for spousal abuse. At the end of the evaluation, the psychologist suggested that if the inmate were released, he and his wife should consider seeing her for couple's therapy.

Bush et al. (2006) suggest that one potential exception to multiple relationships in forensic contexts may be seen in psychologists who transition from the role of forensic evaluator to trial consultant. For example, a psychologist retained by the defense attorney to provide only verbal feedback after conducting a client evaluation and who will not be asked to testify in court might perform consultative services to the attorney following the evaluation regarding the testimony of other psychologists during a trial. Psychologists should, however, approach such a multiple relationship with caution if, by ingratiating themselves with the attorney, they intentionally or unintentionally bias their evaluation or otherwise violate Standard 3.05a or 3.06, Conflict of Interest. (For additional discussion of the role of forensic experts, see the Hot Topics in Chapters 8 and 12 on psychologists providing testimony in courts.)

Personal-Professional Boundary Crossings Involving Clients/Patients, Students, Research Participants, and Subordinates

Boundaries serve to support the effectiveness of psychologists' work and create a safe place for clients/patients, students, employees, and other subordinates to benefit from the psychologists' services (Burian & Slimp, 2000; Russell & Peterson, 1998). Boundaries protect against a blurring of personal and professional domains that could jeopardize psychologists' objectivity and clients', students', and employees' confidence that psychologists will act in their best interests. Unethical multiple relationships often emerge after psychologists have engaged in a pattern that "progresses from apparently benign and perhaps well intended boundary crossings to increasingly intrusive and harmful boundary violations and multiple relationships" (Oberlander & Barnett, 2005, p. 51). Boundary crossings can thus place psychologists on a slippery slope leading to ethical misconduct (Gutheil & Gabbard, 1993; Norris, Gutheil, & Strasburger, 2003).

Clients/patients, students, research participants, and supervisees have less experience, knowledge, and power compared with the psychologist providing assessment, treatment, teaching, mentoring, or supervision. Consequently, they are unlikely to recognize inappropriate boundary crossings or to express their concerns. It is the psychologist's responsibility to monitor and ensure appropriate boundaries between professional and personal communications and relationships (Gottlieb, Robinson, & Younggren, 2007).

Sharing aspects of their personal history or current reactions to a situation with those they work with is not unethical if psychologists limit these communications to meet the therapeutic, educational, or supervisory needs of those they serve.

☑ A graduate student expressed to his dissertation mentor his feelings of inadequacy and frustration upon learning a manuscript he had submitted was rejected for publication. The mentor described how she often reacted similarly when first receiving such information but framed this disclosure within a "lesson" for the student on rising above the initial emotion to objectively reflect on the review and improve his chances of having a revised manuscript accepted.

☑ A psychologist in private practice was providing cognitive-behavioral therapy to help a client conquer feelings of inadequacy and panic attacks that were interfering with her desired career advancement. After several sessions, the psychologist realized the client's distorted belief regarding the ease with which other people and the psychologist in particular attained their career goals was interfering with the effectiveness of the treatment. The psychologist shared with the client a brief personal story regarding how he experienced and reacted to a career obstacle, limiting the disclosure to elements the client could use in framing her own career difficulties.

Boundary crossings can become boundary violations when psychologists share personal information with clients/patients, students, or employees to satisfy their own needs.

☒ A psychologist repeatedly confided to his graduate research assistant about the economic strains his marriage was placing on his personal and professional life. After several weeks, the graduate student began to pay for the psychologist's lunches when they were delivered to the office.

☒ A psychologist providing services at a college counseling center was having difficulties with her own college-aged son's drinking habits. She began to share her concerns about her son with her student clients and sometimes asked their advice.

Boundary crossings can also lead to bidirectional coercion, exploitation, or harm. For example, the intimacy between researchers and study participants inherent in ethnographic and participant observation research can create ambiguous or blurred personal/professional boundaries that can threaten the validity of data collected (Fisher, 2004). Study participants may feel bound by a personal relationship with an investigator to continue in a research project they find distressing, or investigators may feel pressured to yield to participant demands for involvement in illegal behaviors or for money or other resources above those allocated for participation in the research (Singer et al., 1999).

☒ A psychologist was conducting ethnographic research on the lives of female sex workers who were also raising young children. In an effort to establish a sense of trust with the sex workers, she spent many months in the five-block radius where they worked, sharing stories with them about her own parenting experiences. One day, when the police were conducting a drug raid in the area, a participant the psychologist had interviewed numerous times begged the psychologist to hold her marijuana before the police searched her, crying that she would lose her child if the drugs were discovered. The psychologist felt she had no choice but to agree to hide the drugs because of the personal worries about the safety of her own children that she had shared with the participant.

Nonsexual Physical Contact. Nonsexual physical contact with clients/patients, students, or others over whom the psychologist has professional authority can also lead to role misperceptions that interfere with the psychologist's professional functions. While Standard 3.05 does not prohibit psychologists from hugging, hand-holding, putting an arm around those with whom they work in response to a special event (e.g., graduation, termination of therapy, promotion), or showing empathy for emotional crises (e.g., death in the family, recounting of an intense emotional event), such actions can be the first step toward an easing of boundaries that could lead to an unethical multiple relationship.

Whenever such circumstances arise, psychologists should evaluate, before they act, the appropriateness of the physical contact by asking the following questions:

- Is the initiation of physical contact consistent with the professional goals of the relationship?
- How might the contact serve to strengthen or jeopardize the future functioning of the psychologist's role?
- How will the contact be perceived by the recipient?
- Does the act serve the immediate needs of the psychologist rather than the immediate or long-term needs of the client/patient, student, or supervisee?
- Is the physical contact a substitute for more professionally appropriate behaviors?
- Is the physical contact part of a continuing pattern of behavior that may reflect the psychologists' personal problems or conflicts?

Relationships With Others. Psychologists also encounter situations in which a person closely associated with someone with whom they have a professional role seeks to enter into a similar professional relationship. For example, the roommate of a current psychotherapy client/patient might ask the psychologist for an appointment to begin psychotherapy. A CEO of a company that hires a psychologist to conduct personnel evaluations might ask the psychologist to administer psychological tests to the CEO's child to determine whether the child has a learning disability. With few exceptions, entering into such relationships would risk a violation of Standard 3.05a because it could reasonably be expected that the psychologist's ability to make appropriate and objective judgments would be impaired, which in turn would jeopardize the effectiveness of services provided and result in harm.

Receiving referrals from current or recent clients/patients should raise ethical red flags. In many instances, accepting into treatment a friend, relative, or others referred by a current client can create a real or perceived intrusion on the psychologist-patient relationship. For example, a current client/patient may question whether the psychologist has information about him or her gained from the person he or she referred or whether the psychologist is siding with one person or the other if there is a social conflict. Psychologists must also guard against exploiting clients/patients by explicitly or implicitly encouraging referrals to expand their practice.

Some have suggested that treating psychologists should consider a referral from a current client/patient in the same way they would evaluate the therapeutic meaning of a "gift" (E. Shapiro & Ginzberg, 2003). In all circumstances, psychologists must evaluate the extent to which accepting a referral can impair their objectivity and conduct of their work or lead to exploitation or harm. One way of addressing this issue is to clearly state to current patients the psychologist's policy of not accepting patient referrals and, if a situation arises requiring an immediate need for treatment, to provide a professional referral to another psychologist.

When practicing psychologists receive referrals from former clients/patients, it is prudent to consider (a) whether the former client/patient may need the psychologist's services in the future, (b) whether information obtained about the new referral during the former client's/patient's therapy is likely to impair the psychologist's objectivity, and (c) the extent to which the new referral's beliefs about the former client's/patient's relationship with the psychologist is likely to interfere with treatment effectiveness.

Preexisting Personal Relationships. Psychologists may also encounter situations in which they are asked to take on a professional role with someone whom they have had a preexisting personal relationship. Such multiple relationships are often unethical because the preexisting relationship would reasonably be expected to impair the psychologist's objectivity and effectiveness.

> ☒ A psychologist agrees to spend a few sessions helping his nephew overcome anxiety about going to school.
>
> ☒ At a colleague's request, a psychologist agrees to administer a battery of tests to assess whether the colleague has adult attention deficit disorder.

Sexual Multiple Relationships. Sexual relationships with individuals with whom psychologists have a current professional relationship are always unethical. Because of the strong potential for harm involved in such multiple relationships, they are specifically addressed in several standards of the Ethics Code that will be covered in greater detail in Chapters 10 and 13 (Standards 7.07, Sexual Relationships With Students and Supervisees; 10.05, Sexual Intimacies With Current Therapy

Clients/Patients; 10.06, Sexual Intimacies With Relatives or Significant Others of Current Therapy Clients/Patients; 10.07, Therapy With Former Sexual Partners; and 10.08, Sexual Intimacies With Former Therapy Clients/Patients).

"Reasonably Expected." It is important to note that the phrase "could reasonably be expected" indicates that violations of Standard 3.05a may be judged not only by whether actual impairment, harm, or exploitation has occurred but also by whether most psychologists engaged in similar activities in similar circumstances would determine that entering into such a multiple relationship would be expected to lead to such harms.

> ☑ A judge asked a psychologist who had conducted a custody evaluation to provide 6-month mandated family counseling for the couple involved followed by a reevaluation for custody. The psychologist explained to the judge that providing family counseling to individuals whose parenting skills the psychologist would later have to evaluate could reasonably be expected to impair her ability to form an objective opinion independent of knowledge gained and the professional investment made in the counseling sessions. She also explained that such a multiple relationship could impair her effectiveness as a counselor if the parents refrained from honest engagement in the counseling sessions for fear that comments made would be used against them during the custody assessment. The judge agreed to assign the family to another psychologist for counseling.

Unavoidable Multiple Relationships

In some situations, it may not be possible or reasonable to avoid multiple relationships. Psychologists working in rural communities, small towns, American Indian reservations, or small insulated religious communities or who are qualified to provide services to members of unique ethnic or language groups for which alternative psychological services are not available would not be in violation of this standard if they took reasonable steps to protect their objectivity and effectiveness and the possibility of exploitation and harm.

Such steps might include seeking consultation by phone from a colleague to help ensure objectivity and taking extra precautions to protect the confidentiality of each individual with whom the psychologist works. Psychologists can also explain to individuals involved the ethical challenges of the multiple relationships, describe the steps the psychologist will take to mitigate these risks, and encourage individuals to alert the psychologist to relational situations of which the psychologist might not be aware and that might place his or her effectiveness at risk.

> ☑ A rabbi in a small orthodox Jewish community also served as the community's sole licensed clinical psychologist. The psychologist was careful to clearly articulate to his clients the separation of his role as a psychologist and his role as their rabbi. He was

also able to apply his understanding of the orthodox faith and community culture to help clients/patients with some of the unique psychological issues raised. He had been treating a young woman in the community for depression when it became clear that a primary contributor to her distress was her deep questioning of her faith. The psychologist knew from his years in the community that abandoning orthodox tenets would most likely result in the woman being ostracized by her family and community. As a rabbi, the psychologist had experience helping individuals grapple with doubts about their faith. However, despite the woman's requests, he was unwilling to engage in this rabbinical role as a part of the therapy, believing that helping the woman maintain her faith would be incompatible with his responsibility as a psychologist to help her examine the psychological facets of her conflicted feelings. The rabbi contacted the director of an orthodox rabbinical school who helped him identify an advanced student with experience in Jewish communal service who was willing to come to the community once a week to provide a Jewish studies seminar and meet individually with congregants about issues of faith. The psychologist explained the role conflict to his patient. They agreed that she would continue to see the psychologist for psychotherapy and meet with the visiting rabbinical student to discuss specific issues of faith. Readers may also wish to refer to the Hot Topic in Chapter 13 on the role of religion and spirituality in psychotherapy.

Correctional and Military Psychologists

Psychologists working in correctional settings and those enlisted in the military often face unique multiple relationships challenges. In some prisons, correctional administrators believe all employees should provide services as officers. As detailed by Weinberger and Sreenivasan (2003), psychologists in such settings may be asked to search for contraband, use a firearm, patrol to prevent escapes, coordinate inmate movement, and deal with crises unrelated to their role as a psychologist. Any one of these roles has the potential to undermine the therapeutic relationship a psychologist establishes with individual inmates by blurring the roles of care provider and security officer. Such potentially harmful multiple relationships are also inconsistent with the Standards for Psychological Services in Jails, Prisons, Correctional Facilities, and Agencies (Althouse, 2000).

As required by Standard 1.03, Conflicts Between Ethics and Organizational Demands, ideally prior to taking a position as a treating psychologist or whenever correctional psychologists are asked to engage in a role that will compromise their health provider responsibilities, they should clarify the nature of the conflict to the administrator, make known their commitment to the Ethics Code, and attempt to resolve the conflict by taking steps to ensure they do not engage in multiple roles that will interfere with the provision of psychological services.

☑ A psychologist working in a correctional facility had successfully established his primary role as that of mental health treatment provider with both prison officials and inmates. He was not required to search his patients for contraband or to perform any other security-related activities. As required of all facility staff, he received training in the use of firearms and techniques to disarm prisoners who had weapons. On one occasion, several newly admitted inmates suddenly began to attack some of the older prisoners with homemade knives. As one of the few correctional staff members present at the scene, the psychologist assisted the security staff in disarming the inmates. Although none of the attacking inmates were in treatment with him, he did discuss the incident with his current patients to address any concerns they might have about the therapeutic relationship.

Psychologists in the military face additional challenges. Johnson, Bacho, Heim, and Ralph (2006) highlight multiple role obligations that may create a conflict between responsibilities to individual military clients/patients and to the military organization: (a) As commissioned officers, psychologists' primary obligation is to the military mission; (b) embedded psychologists must promote the fighting power and combat readiness of individual military personnel and the combat unit as a whole; (c) since many military psychologists are the sole mental health provider for their unit, there is less room for choice of alternative treatment providers; (d) there is less control and choice regarding shifts between therapeutic and administrative role relationships (e.g., seeing as a patient a member about whom the psychologist previously had to render an administrative decision); and (e) like rural communities, military communities are often small, with military psychologists having social relationships with individuals who may at some point become patients.

To minimize the potential harm that could emerge from such multiple relationships, Johnson et al. (2006) suggest that military psychologists (a) strive for a neutral position in the community, avoiding high-profile social positions; (b) assume that every member of the community is a potential client/patient and attempt to establish appropriate boundaries accordingly, requiring limitations on self-disclosure that would be expected in common social circumstances; (c) provide informed consent immediately if a nontherapeutic role relationship transitions into a therapeutic one; (d) be conservative in the information one "needs to know" in the therapeutic role to avoid to the extent feasible threats to confidentiality that may emerge when an administrative role is required; (e) collaborate with clients/patients on how best to handle role transitions when possible and appropriate; and (f) carefully document multiple role conflicts, how they were handled, and the rationale for such decisions.

☑ A military psychologist provided therapy to an enlisted officer who was ordered to enter treatment for difficulties in job-related performance. During treatment, the client and psychologist were assigned to a field exercise in which the client would be under the psychologist's command. To reassign the client to a different officer for the exercise, the psychologist would need to speak with a superior who was not a mental health worker. Recognizing that the client's involvement in therapy would have to be revealed in such a discussion, the psychologist explained the situation to the enlisted member and asked permission to discuss the situation with her superiors. The client refused to give permission. The psychologist was the only mental health professional on the base, so transferring the client to another provider was not an option. The psychologist therefore developed a specific plan with the client for how they would relate to each other during the field exercise and how they would discuss in therapy issues that arose. (This case is adapted from one of four military cases provided by Staal & King, 2000.)

(b) If a psychologist finds that, due to unforeseen factors, a potentially harmful multiple relationship has arisen, the psychologist takes reasonable steps to resolve it with due regard for the best interests of the affected person and maximal compliance with the Ethics Code.

There will be instances when psychologists discover they are involved in a potentially harmful multiple relationship of which they had been unaware. Standard 3.05b requires psychologists take reasonable steps to resolve the potential harms that might arise from such relationships, recognizing that the best interests of the affected person and maximal compliance with other standards in the Ethics Code may sometimes require psychologists to remain in the multiple roles.

☑ A psychologist responsible for conducting individual assessments of candidates for an executive-level position discovered that one of the candidates was a close friend's husband. Because information about this prior relationship was neither confidential nor harmful to the candidate, the psychologist explained the situation to company executives and worked with the organization to assign that particular promotion evaluation to another qualified professional.

☑ A psychologist working at a university counseling center discovered that a counseling client had enrolled in a large undergraduate class the psychologist was going to teach. The psychologist discussed the potential conflict with the client and attempted to help him enroll in a different class. However, the client was a senior and needed the class to complete his major requirements. In addition, there were no appropriate referrals for the student at the counseling center. Without revealing the student's identity, the psychologist discussed her options with the department chair. They concluded that because the class was very large, the psychologist could take the following steps to protect her objectivity and effectiveness as both a teacher and counselor: (a) A graduate teaching assistant would be responsible for grading exams and for calculating the final course grade based on the average of scores on the exams, and (b) the psychologist would monitor the situation during counseling sessions and seek consultation if problems arose.

☑ A psychologist in independent practice became aware that his neighbor had begun dating one of the psychologist's psychotherapy patients. Although telling the patient about the social relationship could cause distress, it was likely the patient would find out about the relationship during conversations with the neighbor. The psychologist considered reducing his social exchanges with the neighbor, but this proved infeasible. After seeking consultation from a colleague, the psychologist decided that he could not ensure therapeutic objectivity or effectiveness if the situation continued. He decided to explain the situation to the patient, provide a referral, and assist the transition to a new therapist during pretermination counseling.

(c) When psychologists are required by law, institutional policy, or extraordinary circumstances to serve in more than one role in judicial or administrative proceedings, at the outset they clarify role expectations and the extent of confidentiality and thereafter as changes occur. (See also Standards 3.04, Avoiding Harm, and 3.07, Third-Party Requests for Services.)

Standard 3.05c applies to instances when psychologists are required to serve in more than one role in judicial or administrative proceedings because of institutional policy or extraordinary circumstances. This standard does *not* permit psychologists to take on these multiple roles if such a situation can be avoided. When such multiple roles cannot be avoided, Standard 3.05c requires, as soon as possible and thereafter as changes occur, that psychologists clarify to all parties involved the roles the psychologist is expected to perform and the extent and limits of confidentiality that can be anticipated by taking on these multiple roles.

In most situations, psychologists are expected to avoid multiple relationships in forensically relevant situations or to resolve such relationships when they unexpectedly occur (Standards 3.05a and b). When such circumstances arise (e.g., performing a custody evaluation and then providing court-mandated family therapy for the couple involved), the conflict may sometimes be resolved by explaining to a judge or institutional administrator the problematic nature of the multiple relationship.

☒ A forensic psychologist was appointed by the court to evaluate an elderly man for possible dementia for a case in which his adult children were petitioning the court to declare their father mentally incompetent to handle his estate. The man's daughter accompanied him to the psychologist's office for testing. At the end of the assessment, the psychologist suggested to the daughter that they consider entering into family treatment with him to resolve their conflicts.

☑ A consulting psychologist developed a company's sexual harassment policy. After the policy was approved and implemented, the psychologist took on the position of counseling employees experiencing sexual harassment. One of the psychologist's clients then filed a sexual harassment suit against the company. The psychologist was called on by the defense to testify as an expert witness for the company's sexual harassment policy and by the plaintiff as a fact witness about the stress and anxiety observed during counseling sessions. The psychologist (a) immediately disclosed to the company and the employee the nature of the multiple relationship; (b) described to both the problems that testifying might raise, including the limits of maintaining the confidentiality of information acquired from either the consulting or counseling roles; and (c) ceased providing sexual harassment counseling services for employees. Neither party agreed to withdraw its request to the judge for the psychologist's testimony. The psychologist wrote a letter to the judge explaining the conflicting roles and asked to be recused from testifying (see Hellkamp & Lewis, 1995, for further discussion of this type of dilemma).

3.06 Conflict of Interest

Psychologists refrain from taking on a professional role when personal, scientific, professional, legal, financial, or other interests or relationships could reasonably be expected to (1) impair their objectivity, competence, or effectiveness in performing their functions as psychologists or (2) expose the person or organization with whom the professional relationship exists to harm or exploitation.

Psychologists strive to benefit from and establish relationships of trust with those with whom they work through the exercise of professional and scientific judgments based on their training and experience and established knowledge of the discipline (Principle A: Beneficence and Nonmaleficence and Principle B: Fidelity and Responsibility). Standard 3.06 prohibits psychologists from taking on a professional role when competing professional, personal, financial, legal, or other interests or relationships could reasonably be expected to impair their objectivity, competence, or ability to effectively perform this role. Examples of conflicts of interest sufficient to compromise the psychologist's judgments include the following:

☒   Irrespective of patients' treatment needs, to save money, a psychologist reduced the number of sessions for certain patients after he had exceeded his yearly compensation under a capitated contract with a health maintenance organization (HMO).

☒   A member of a faculty hiring committee refused to recuse herself from voting when a friend applied for the position under the committee's consideration.

☒   A psychologist in private practice agreed to be paid $1,000 for each patient he referred for participation in a psychopharmaceutical treatment study.

☒   A research psychologist agreed to provide expert testimony on a contingent fee basis, thereby compromising her role as advocate for the scientific data.

☒   A psychologist who had just purchased biofeedback equipment for his practice began to overstate the effectiveness of biofeedback to his clients.

☒ A prescribing psychologist failed to disclose to patients her substantial financial investment in the company that manufactured the medication the psychologist frequently recommended.

☒ A psychologist used his professional Web site to recommend Internet mental health services in which he had an undisclosed financial interest.

☒ A school psychologist agreed to conduct a record review for the educational placement of the child of the president of a foundation that contributed heavily to the private school that employed the psychologist.

Conflicts of interest can extend to financial or other gains that accrue to psychologists indirectly through the effect of their decisions on the interests of their family members:

☒ An educational psychologist encouraged a school system she was consulting to purchase learning software from a company that employed her husband.

☒ An organizational psychologist was hired by a company to provide confidential support and referral services for employees with substance abuse problems. The psychologist would refer employees he counseled to a private mental health group practice in which his wife was a member.

Psychologists also have a fiduciary responsibility to avoid actions that would create public distrust in the integrity of psychological science and practice (Principle B: Fidelity and Responsibility). Accordingly, Standard 3.06 also prohibits taking on a role that would expose a person or organization with whom a psychologist already works to harm or exploitation. For example:

☒ A research psychologist on the board of a private foundation encouraged the foundation to fund a colleague's proposal from which he would be paid as a statistical consultant.

☒ A psychologist accepted a position on the board of directors from a company for which she was currently conducting an independent evaluation of employee productivity.

☒ A psychologist took on a psychotherapy client who was a financial analyst at the brokerage company the psychologist used for his personal investments.

Psychologists in administrative positions have a responsibility to resist explicit or implicit pressure to bias decisions regarding the adequacy of research participant or patient protections to meet the needs of the institution's financial interests.

☑ A psychologist serving on her university's institutional review board gave into pressure to approve a study with ethically questionable procedures because it would bring a substantial amount of funding dollars to the university.

☑ A school psychologist refused the district superintendent's request that she conduct training sessions for teachers at an overcrowded school that would result in the misapplication of behavioral principles to keep students docile and quiet.

Conflicts of Interest in Forensic Practice

Psychologists seek to promote accuracy and truthfulness in their work (Principle C: Integrity). Forensic psychologists hired to provide expert testimony based on forensic assessment or research relevant to the legal decision need to be aware of potential conflicts of interest that may impair their objectivity or lead them to distort their testimony. For example, psychologists providing expert testimony should not provide such services on the basis of contingent fees (fees adjusted to whether a case is won or lost) since this can exert pressure on psychologists to intentionally or unintentionally modify their reports or testimony in favor of the retaining party. However, if a psychologist is serving as a consultant to a legal team and will not be testifying in court, a contingency fee may not be unethical as long as it does not lead psychologists to distort facts in giving their advice (Heilbrun, 2001). Psychologists should also avoid charging higher fees for testimony since this may motivate writing a report that is more likely to lead to a request to testify (Heilbrun, 2001). Bush et al. (2006) suggest psychologists set fixed rates (which may be required in some states) and bill an hourly rate consistent for all activities.

Forensic psychologists hired by the defense team must also avoid explicit or subtle pressure to use more or less sensitive symptom validation measures to assess the mental status of the defendant. Psychologists should not submit to pressure by a legal team to modify a submitted report. Amendments to the original report may be added to correct factual errors, and if a report is rewritten, the rationale for the changes should be given within the report (Bush et al., 2006; Martelli, Bush, & Sasler, 2003). Interested readers may also refer to the Chapter 8 Hot Topic on "Avoiding False and Deceptive Statements in Scientific and Clinical Expert Testimony."

Corporate Funding and Conflicts of Interest. The APA Task Force on External Funding (www.apa.org/about/taskforce.html) provides a detailed history of conflicts of interest in related fields and provides specific recommendations for psychology (see also Pachter, Fox, Zimbardo, & Antonuccio, 2007). Recommendations include the following:

• When research is industry sponsored, psychologists should ensure they have input into study design, independent access to raw data, and a role in manuscript submission.

- Full public disclosure regarding financial conflicts of interest should be included in all public statements.

- Psychologists should be aware and guard against potential biases inherent in accepting sponsor-provided inducements that might affect their selection of textbooks or assessment instruments.

- Practitioners should be alert to the influence on clients/patients of sponsor-provided materials (e.g., mugs, pens, notepads) that might suggest endorsement of the sponsor's products.

The National Institutes of Health Office of Extramural Research requires every institution receiving research Public Health Service (PHS) grants to have written guidelines for the avoidance and institutional review of conflict of interest. These guidelines must reflect state and local laws and cover financial interests, gifts, gratuities and favors, nepotism, political participation, and bribery. In addition, employees accepting grants or contracts are expected to be knowledgeable of the granting and contracting organization's conflict of interest policy and to abide by it (http://grants.nih.gov/grants/policy/coi/). In addition, the PHS Regulations 42 CFR Part 50 (Subpart F) and 45 CFR Part 94 provide conflict of interest guidelines for individual investigators (http://grants/guide/notice-files/not95–179.html).

Many organizations, institutions, and federal agencies have conflict of interest policies.

- The APA *Editor's Handbook: Operating Procedures and Policies for APA Publications* (APA, 2006, Policy 1.03) requires that journal reviewers and editors avoid either real or apparent conflict of interest by declining to review submitted manuscripts from recent collaborators or students, members of their institutions, or work from which they might obtain financial gain. When such potential conflicts of interest arise or when editors or associate editors submit their own work to the journal they edit, the *Handbook* recommends that the editor (a) request a well-qualified individual to serve as ad hoc Action Editor, (b) set up a process that ensures the Action Editor's independence, and (c) identify the Action Editor in the publication of the article. APA also requires all authors to submit a Full Disclosure of Interests Form that certifies whether the psychologist or his or her immediate family members have significant financial or product interests related to information provided in the manuscript or other sources of negative or positive bias (www.apa.org/journals/authors/disclosure_of_interests.pdf).

- The APA Committee on Accreditation's Conflict of Interest Policy for Site Visitors includes prohibitions against even the appearance of a conflict of interest for committee members and faculty in the program being visited. Possible conflicts include former employment or enrollment in the program or a family connection or close friend or professional colleague in the program (www.apa.org/ed/accreditation/sitevstrconflict.html).

- The National Association of School Psychologists' (NASP's) *Professional Conduct Manual* requires psychologists to avoid conflicts of interest by recognizing the importance of ethical standards and the separation of roles and by taking full responsibility for protecting and informing the consumer of all potential concerns (NASP, 2000, V.A.1).

- According to the *Specialty Guidelines for Forensic Psychology* (see Committee on the Revision of the Specialty Guidelines for Forensic Psychology, 2008), psychologists should not provide services to parties to a legal proceeding on the basis of a contingent fee (SGFP, IV.B).

3.07 Third-Party Requests for Services

When psychologists agree to provide services to a person or entity at the request of a third party, psychologists attempt to clarify at the outset of the service the nature of the relationship with all individuals or organizations involved. This clarification includes the role of the psychologist (e.g., therapist, consultant, diagnostician, or expert witness), an identification of who is the client, the probable uses of the services provided or the information obtained, and the fact that there may be limits to confidentiality. (See also Standards 3.05, Multiple Relationships, and 4.02, Discussing the Limits of Confidentiality.)

Psychologists are often asked to conduct an assessment, provide psychotherapy, or testify in court by third parties who themselves will not be directly involved in the evaluation, treatment, or testimony.

In all these cases, Standard 3.07 requires psychologists at the outset of services to explain to both the third party and those individuals who will receive psychological services the nature of the psychologist's relationship with all individuals or organizations involved. This includes providing information about the role of the psychologist (i.e., therapist, consultant, diagnostician, expert witness), identifying whether the third party or the individual receiving the services is the client, who will receive information about the services, and probable uses of information gained or services provided.

☑ A company asked a psychologist to conduct preemployment evaluations of potential employees. The psychologist informed each applicant evaluated that she was working for the company, that the company would receive the test results, and that the information would be used in hiring decisions.

☑ A school district hired a psychologist to evaluate students for educational placement. The psychologist first clarified state and federal laws on parental rights regarding educational assessments, communicated this information to the school superintendent and the child's guardian(s), and explained the nature and use of the assessments and the confidentiality and reporting procedures the psychologist would use.

☑ A legal guardian requested behavioral treatment for her 30-year-old developmentally disabled adult child because of difficulties he was experiencing at the sheltered workshop where he worked. At the outset of services, using language compatible with the patient's intellectual level, the psychologist informed the patient that the guardian had requested the treatment, explained the purpose of the treatment, and indicated the extent to which the guardian would have access to confidential information and how such information might be used.

☑ A defense attorney hired a psychologist to conduct an independent evaluation of a plaintiff who claimed the attorney's client had caused her emotional harm. The plaintiff agreed to be evaluated. The psychologist first explained to the plaintiff that the defense attorney was the client and that all information would be shared with the attorney and possibly used by the attorney to refute the plaintiff's allegations in court. Once the evaluation commenced, the psychologist avoided using techniques that would encourage the plaintiff to respond to the psychologist as a psychotherapist (Hess, 1998).

☑ A judge ordered a convicted sex offender to receive therapy as a condition of parole. The psychologist assigned to provide the therapy explained to the parolee that all information revealed during therapy would be provided to the court and might be used to rescind parole.

Legal Representatives Seeking to Retain a Forensic Psychologist. In many instances, forensic psychologists will be retained by the attorney representing the legal party's interests. In such instances, the attorney is the psychologist's client. During the initial consultation with a legal representative seeking the psychologist's forensic services, psychologists should consider providing the following information: (a) the fee structure for anticipated services; (b) previous or current obligations, activities, or relationships that might be perceived as conflicts of interest; (c) level and limitations of competence to provide forensic services requested; and (d) any other information that might reasonably be expected to influence the decision to contract with the psychologist (see Committee on the Revision of the Specialty Guidelines for Forensic Psychology, 2008).

Implications of HIPAA. Psychologists planning to share information with third parties should also carefully consider whether such information is included under the HIPAA definition of protected health information (PHI), whether HIPAA regulations require prior patient authorization for such release, or whether the authorization requirement can be waived by the legal prerogatives of the third party (45 CFR 164.508 and 164.512). Psychologists should then clarify beforehand to both the third party and recipient of services the HIPAA requirements for the release of PHI.

3.08 Exploitative Relationships

Psychologists do not exploit persons over whom they have supervisory, evaluative, or other authority such as clients/patients, students, supervisees, research participants, and employees.

(See also Standards 3.05, Multiple Relationships; 6.04, Fees and Financial Arrangements; 6.05, Barter With Clients/Patients; 7.07, Sexual Relationships With Students and Supervisees; 10.05, Sexual Intimacies With Current Therapy Clients/Patients; 10.06, Sexual Intimacies With Relatives or Significant Others of Current Therapy Clients/Patients; 10.07, Therapy With Former Sexual Partners; and 10.08, Sexual Intimacies With Former Therapy Clients/Patients.)

Standard 3.08 prohibits psychologists from taking unfair advantage of or manipulating for their own personal use or satisfaction students, supervisees, clients/patients, research participants, employees, or others over whom they have authority. The following are examples of actions that would violate this standard:

☒ Repeatedly requiring graduate assistants to work overtime without additional compensation

☒ Requiring employees to run a psychologist's personal errands

☒ Taking advantage of company billing loopholes to inflate rates for consulting services

☒ Encouraging expensive gifts from psychotherapy clients/patients

☒ Using "bait-and-switch" tactics to lure clients/patients into therapy with initial low rates that are hiked after a few sessions

Violations of Standard 3.08 often occur in connection with other violations of the Ethics Code. For example:

☒ Psychologists exploit the trust and vulnerability of individuals with whom they work when they have sexual relationships with current clients/patients or students (Standards 10.05, Sexual Intimacies With Current Therapy Clients/Patients, and 7.07, Sexual Relationships With Students and Supervisees).

☒ Exploitation occurs when a psychologist accepts nonmonetary remuneration from clients/patients, the value of which is substantially higher than the psychological services rendered (Standard 6.05, Barter With Clients/Patients).

☒ Psychologists exploit patients with limited resources who they know will require long-term treatment plans when they provide services until the patients' money or insurance runs out and then refer them to low-cost or free alternative treatments.

☒ It is exploitative to charge clients/patients for psychological assessments for which the client/patient had not initially agreed to and that are unnecessary for the agreed on goals of the psychological evaluation (Standard 6.04a, Fees and Financial Arrangements).

☒ School psychologists exploit their students when, in their private practice, they provide fee-for-service psychological testing to students who could receive these services free of charge from the psychologist in the school district in which they work (Standard 3.05a, Multiple Relationships; see also the *Professional Conduct Manual for School Psychology,* National Association for School Psychologists, 2000, www.naspweb.org).

Standard 3.08 does not prohibit psychologists from having a sliding-fee scale or different payment plans for different types or amount of services, as long as the fee practices are fairly and consistently applied.

Recruitment for Research Participation. Institutional populations are particularly susceptible to research exploitation. Prisoners and youth held for brief periods in detention centers, for example, are highly vulnerable because of their restricted autonomy and liberty, often compounded by their low socioeconomic status, poor education, and poor health (Gostin, 2007). Incarcerated persons have few expectations regarding privacy protections and may view research participation as a means of seeking favor with or avoiding punishment from prison guards or detention officials. In-patients in psychiatric centers or nursing homes are also vulnerable to exploitive recruitment practices that touch upon their fears that a participation refusal will result in denial of other needed services. Investigators should ensure through adequate informed consent procedures and discussion with institutional staff to ensure research participation is not coerced (Fisher et al., 2002; see also Standard 8.02, Informed Consent to Research).

3.09 Cooperation With Other Professionals

When indicated and professionally appropriate, psychologists cooperate with other professionals in order to serve their clients/patients effectively and appropriately. (See also Standard 4.05, Disclosures.)

Individuals who come to psychologists for assessment, counseling, or therapy are often either receiving or in need of collateral medical, legal, educational, or social services. Collaboration and consultation with, and referral to, other professionals are thus often necessary to serve the best interests of clients/patients. Standard 3.09 requires psychologists to cooperate with other professionals when it is appropriate and will help serve the client/patient most effectively. For example, having obtained appropriate consent:

> ☑ With permission and written authorization of the parent, a clinical child psychologist spoke with a child's teacher to help determine if behaviors suggestive of attention deficit disorder exhibited at home and in the psychologist's office were consistent with the child's classroom behavior.
>
> ☑ With consent from the parent, a school psychologist contacted a social worker who was helping a student's family apply for public assistance to help determine the availability of collateral services (e.g., substance abuse counseling).
>
> ☑ A psychologist with prescribing privileges referred a patient to a physician for diagnosis of physical symptoms thought by the patient to be the result of a psychological disorder that was more suggestive of a medical condition.

In schools, hospitals, social service agencies, and other multidisciplinary settings, a psychologist may have joint responsibilities with other professionals for the assessment or treatment of those with whom they work. In such settings, psychologists should develop a clear agreement with the other professionals regarding overlapping and distinct role responsibilities and how confidential information should be handled in the best interests of the students or client/patients. The nature of these collaborative arrangements should be shared with the recipients of the services or their legal guardians.

Implications of HIPAA. Psychologists who are covered entities under HIPAA should be familiar with situations in which regulations requiring patients' written authorization for release of PHI apply to communications with other professionals (45 CFR 164.510, 164.512). They should also be aware of rules governing patients' rights to know when such disclosures have been made (45 CFR 164.520, Notice of Privacy Practices, and 45 CFR 164.528, Accounting of Disclosures of Protected Health Information).

3.10 Informed Consent

(a) When psychologists conduct research or provide assessment, therapy, counseling, or consulting services in person or via electronic transmission or other forms of communication, they obtain the informed consent of the individual or individuals using language that is reasonably understandable to that person or persons except when conducting such activities without consent is mandated by law or governmental regulation or as otherwise provided in this Ethics Code. (See also Standards 8.02, Informed Consent to Research; 9.03, Informed Consent in Assessments; and 10.01, Informed Consent to Therapy.)

Informed consent is seen by many as the primary means of protecting the self-governing and privacy rights of those with whom psychologists work. Required elements of informed consent for specific areas of psychology are detailed in Standards 8.02, Informed Consent to Research; 9.03, Informed Consent in Assessments; and 10.01, Informed Consent to Therapy. The obligations described in Standard 3.10 apply to these other consent standards. The salience of informed consent requirements for most psychological activities reflects the continuing societal sea change from a paternalistic to an autonomy-based view of professional and scientific ethics.

Language. In research, assessment, and therapy, psychologists must obtain informed consent using language reasonably understandable by the person asked to consent. For example, psychologists must use appropriate translations of consent information for individuals for whom English is not a preferred language or who use sign language. Psychologists should also adjust reading and language comprehension levels of consent procedures to an individual's developmental or educational level or reading or learning disability.

Culture. Individuals from recently immigrated or disadvantaged cultural communities may lack familiarity with assessment, treatment or research procedures, and terminology typically used in informed consent documents. These individuals may also be unfamiliar with or distrust statements associated with voluntary choice and other client/patient or research participant rights described during informed consent. Standard 3.10 requires sensitivity to the cultural dimensions of individuals' understanding of and anticipated responses to consent information and tailor informed consent language to such dimensions. This may also require psychologists to include educational components regarding the nature of and individual rights in agreeing to psychological services or research participation. For individuals not proficient in English, written informed consent information must be translated in a manner that considers cultural differences in health care or scientific concepts that present challenges in a word-for-word translation. When using interpreters to conduct informed consent procedures, psychologists must follow the requirements of Standard 2.05, Delegation of Work to Others, in ensuring their competence, training, and supervision.

Consent Via Electronic Transmission. Standard 3.10a requires informed consent be obtained when research, assessment, or therapy is conducted via electronic transmission such as the telephone or the Internet. Psychologists need to take special steps to identify the language and reading level of those from whom they obtain consent via electronic media. In addition, psychologists conducting work via e-mail or other electronic communications should take precautions to ensure that the individual who gave consent is in fact the individual participating in the research or receiving the psychologist's services (i.e., use of a participant/client/patient password).

Exemptions. Some activities are exempt from the requirements of Standard 3.10. For example, psychologists conducting court-ordered assessments or evaluating military personnel may be prevented from obtaining consent by law or governmental regulation. In addition, several standards in the Ethics Code detail conditions under which informed consent may be waived (Standards 8.03, Informed Consent for Recording Voices and Images in Research; 8.05, Dispensing With Informed Consent for Research; and 8.07, Deception in Research). HIPAA also permits certain exemptions from patient authorization requirements relevant to research and practice, which are discussed in later chapters on standards for research, assessment, and therapy.

(b) For persons who are legally incapable of giving informed consent, psychologists nevertheless (1) provide an appropriate explanation, (2) seek the individual's assent, (3) consider such persons' preferences and best interests, and (4) obtain appropriate permission from a legally authorized person, if such substitute consent is permitted or required by law. When consent by a legally authorized person is not permitted or required by law, psychologists take reasonable steps to protect the individual's rights and welfare.

Adults who have been declared legally incompetent and most children younger than age 18 do not have the legal right to provide independent consent to receive psychological services or participate in psychological research. In recognition of these individuals' rights as persons, Standard 3.10b requires that psychologists obtain their affirmative agreement to participate in psychological activities after providing them with an explanation of the nature and purpose of the activities and their right to decline or withdraw from participation. The phrase "consider such persons' preferences and best interests" indicates that although in most instances, psychologists respect a person's right to dissent from participation in psychological activities, this right can be superseded if failure to participate would deprive persons of psychological services necessary to protect or promote their welfare.

For individuals who are legally incapable of giving informed consent, psychologists must also obtain permission from a legally authorized person, if such substitute consent is permitted or required by law. Psychologists working with children in the foster care system and in juvenile detention centers and those working with institutionalized adults with identified cognitive or mental disorders leading to decisional impairment must carefully determine who has legal responsibility for substitute decision making. Psychologists should be aware that in some instances, especially for children in foster care, legal guardianship may change over time.

Emancipated and Mature Minors. There are instances when guardian permission for treatment or research is not required or possible for children younger than age 18. For example, *emancipated minor* is a legal status conferred on persons who have not yet attained the age of legal competency as defined by state law but are entitled to treatment as if they have such status by virtue of assuming adult responsibilities, such as self-support, marriage, or procreation. *Mature minor* is someone who has not reached adulthood (as defined by state law) but who, according to state law, may be treated as an adult for certain purposes (e.g., consenting to treatment for venereal disease, drug abuse, or emotional disorders). When a child is an emancipated or mature minor, informed consent procedures should follow Standard 3.10a.

Best Interests of the Child. The requirement for guardian permission may be inappropriate if there is serious doubt whether the guardian's interests adequately reflect the child's interests (e.g., cases of child abuse or neglect, genetic testing of a healthy child to assist in understanding the disorder of a sibling) or cannot reasonably be obtained (e.g., treatment or research involving runaways). In such cases, the appointment of a consent advocate can protect the child's rights and welfare by verifying the minor's understanding of assent procedures, supporting the child's preferences, ensuring participation is voluntary, and monitoring reactions to psychological procedures. Psychologists conducting research need to be familiar with federal regulations regarding waiver of parental permission (45 CFR 46.408c) and have such waivers approved by an institutional review board (Standard 8.01, Institutional Approval; Fisher, Hoagwood, & Jensen, 1996). Psychologists conducting therapy need to be familiar with their state laws regarding provision of therapy to children and adolescents without parental consent (Fisher, Hatashita-Wong, & Isman, 1999).

Adults With Cognitive Impairments Who Do Not Have Legal Guardians. There may be adults, such as those with Alzheimer's disease or developmental disabilities, who do not have a legal guardian but whose ability to fully understand consent-relevant information is impaired. For example, clinical geropsychologists frequently work with older persons with progressive dementia living in nursing homes and assisted-living and residential care facilities where substitute decision making is typically handled informally by family members or others. In addition to obtaining consent from the individual, psychologists can seek additional protections for the individual by encouraging a shared decision-making process with or seeking additional permission from these informal caretakers (Fisher, 1999, 2002b, 2003b; Fisher, Cea, Davidson, & Fried, 2006; see also the Hot Topic, "Goodness-of-Fit Ethics for Informed Consent Involving Adults With Impaired Decisional Capacity," at the end of this chapter).

HIPAA Notice of Privacy Practices. Prior to beginning treatment or treatment-relevant assessments or randomized clinical trials in which health care is provided, HIPAA-covered entities must provide patients with a Notice of Privacy Practices that describes the psychologist's policies for use and disclosure of PHI, the clients'/patients' rights regarding their PHI under HIPAA, and the provider's obligations under the Privacy Rule (45 CFR 164.520). In most instances, the notice will be given to prospective clients/patients at the same time as informed consent is obtained since the notice provides information relevant to the scope and limits of confidentiality. HIPAA requires that if, under applicable law, a person has authority to act on behalf of an individual who is an adult, an emancipated minor, or an unemancipated minor in making decisions related to health care, a covered entity must treat such a person (called a personal representative) as the individual. Exceptions are permitted if there is reason to believe the patient has been abused or is endangered by the personal representative or that treating the individual as a personal representative would not be in the best interests of the client/patient (45 CFR 164.502g). This requirement refers to court-appointed guardians or holders of relevant power of attorney of adults with impaired capacities, parents who are generally recognized as personal representatives of their minor children, and individuals designated as a representative by the patient. To comply with both Standard 3.10b and the HIPAA Notice of Privacy Practices, psychologists, when working with persons legally incapable of giving consent, should provide the Notice of Privacy Practices to both the individual's legal guardian or personal representative and the client/patient.

(c) When psychological services are court ordered or otherwise mandated, psychologists inform the individual of the nature of the anticipated services, including whether the services are court ordered or mandated and any limits of confidentiality, before proceeding.

When informed consent is prohibited by law or other governing authority, psychologists must nonetheless respect an individual's right to know the nature of anticipated services, whether the services were court ordered or mandated by another governing authority, and the limits of confidentiality before proceeding.

Military Psychologists. When regulations permit, military psychologists should inform active-duty personnel of the psychologist's duty to report to appropriate military agencies violations of the Uniform Code of Military Justice revealed during assessment or therapy.

Court-Ordered Assessments. Psychologists conducting a court-ordered forensic assessment must inform the individual tested (a) why the assessment is being conducted, (b) that the findings may be entered into evidence in court, and (c) if known to the psychologist, the extent to which the individual and his or her attorney will have access to the information. The psychologist should not assume the role of legal adviser but can advise the individual to speak with his or her attorney when asked about potential legal consequences of noncooperation.

(d) Psychologists appropriately document written or oral consent, permission, and assent. (See also Standards 8.02, Informed Consent to Research; 9.03, Informed Consent in Assessments; and 10.01, Informed Consent to Therapy.)

Standard 3.10d requires psychologists conducting research or providing health or forensic services to document they have obtained consent or assent from an individual and permission by a legal guardian or substitute decision maker. In most instances, individuals will sign a consent, assent, or permission form. Sometimes oral consent is appropriate, such as when obtaining a young child's assent, when working with illiterate populations, or when there is concern that confidentially may be at risk (i.e., in war-torn countries where consent documents may be confiscated by local authorities). In these situations, documentation can be a note in the psychologist's records.

Implications of HIPAA. Appropriate documentation can also be related to legal requirements. For example, HIPAA requires that all valid client/patient authorizations for the use and disclosure of PHI be signed and dated by the individual or the individual's personal representative (45 CFR 164.508[c][1][vi]).

3.11 Psychological Services Delivered To or Through Organizations

(a) Psychologists delivering services to or through organizations provide information beforehand to clients and when appropriate those directly affected by the services about (1) the nature and objectives of the services, (2) the intended recipients, (3) which of the individuals are clients, (4) the relationship the psychologist will have with each person and the organization, (5) the probable uses of services provided and information obtained, (6) who will have access to the information, and (7) limits of confidentiality. As soon as feasible, they provide information about the results and conclusions of such services to appropriate persons.

The informed consent procedures described in Standard 3.10, Informed Consent, are often not appropriate or sufficient for consulting, program evaluation, job effectiveness, or other psychological services delivered to or through organizations. In such contexts, Standard 3.11 requires that organizational clients, employees, staff, or others who may be involved in the psychologists' activities be provided information about the nature, objectives, and intended recipients of the services; which individuals are clients and the relationship the psychologist will have with those involved; the probable uses of and who will have access to information gained; and the limits of confidentiality. Psychologists must provide results and conclusions of the services to appropriate persons as early as is feasible.

☑ An industrial-organizational psychologist was hired to evaluate whether a company's flexible-shift policy had lowered employee absentee rates. In addition to a review of employee records, the evaluation would include interviews with supervisors and employees on the value and limits of the policy. The psychologist prepared a document for all supervisors and employees explaining (a) the purpose of the evaluation, (b) the nature of and reason for employee record review and the interviews, (c) that the evaluation would be used to help the company decide if it should maintain or modify its current flexible-shift policy, (d) that no one in the company would have access to the identities of the individuals interviewed, and (e) that the results and conclusions would be presented to the company's board of directors in a manner that protected confidentiality.

☑ A psychologist was hired by a school district to observe teacher management of student behavior during lunch and recess to help the district determine how many teachers were required for such activities and whether additional staff training was needed for these responsibilities. The psychologist held a meeting for all teaching staff who would be involved in the observations. At the meeting, the psychologist explained why the school district was conducting the research, how long it would last, the ways in which notes and summaries of observations would be written to protect the identities of individual teachers, that a detailed summary of findings would be presented to the school superintendent, and that, with the district's permission, teachers would receive a summary report.

(b) If psychologists will be precluded by law or by organizational roles from providing such information to particular individuals or groups, they so inform those individuals or groups at the outset of the service.

Standard 3.11b pertains to situations in which psychological services not requiring informed consent are mandated by law or governmental regulations, and the law or regulations restrict those affected by the services from receiving any aspect of the information listed in Standard 3.11a.

☑ A psychologist providing court-ordered therapy to a convicted pedophile submitted a report to the court regarding the therapy client's attendance and responsiveness to treatment. The therapist was prohibited from releasing the report to the client. At the beginning of therapy, the psychologist informed the client that such a report would be written and the client would not have access to the report through the psychologist.

☑ A company stipulated that the results of a personality inventory conducted as part of an employee application and screening process would not be available to applicants. Psychologists informed applicants about these restrictions prior to administering the tests.

☑ An inmate of a correctional institution was required to see the staff psychologist after repeatedly engaging in disruptive and violent behaviors that were jeopardizing the safety of the staff and other prisoners. The psychologist explained to the inmate that in this situation, she was acting on the request of prison officials to help the inmate control his behaviors. She also informed the inmate that she would be submitting formal reports on the sessions that might be used by prison officials to determine if the inmate would be assigned to a more restrictive facility.

Implications of HIPAA. Standard 3.11b may also apply to health care settings in which institutional policy dictates that testing results are sent to another professional responsible for interpreting and communicating the results to the client/patient. However, the nature of such institutional policies may be changing in light of HIPAA regulations providing greater client/patient access to PHI and control of disclosures of PHI.

3.12 Interruption of Psychological Services

Unless otherwise covered by contract, psychologists make reasonable efforts to plan for facilitating services in the event that psychological services are interrupted by factors such as the psychologist's illness, death, unavailability, relocation, or retirement or by the client's/patient's relocation or financial limitations. (See also Standard 6.02c, Maintenance, Dissemination, and Disposal of Confidential Records of Professional and Scientific Work.)

Planned and unplanned interruptions of psychological services often occur. For example, a psychologist can leave a job at a mental health care facility for a new position, take parental or family leave, interrupt services for a planned medical procedure, or retire from private practice. Clients/patients may move out of state or have a limited number of sessions covered by insurance.

When interruption of services can be anticipated, Standard 3.12 requires psychologists to make reasonable efforts to ensure needed service is continued. Such efforts can include discussing the interruption of services with the clients/patients and responding to their concerns, conducting pretermination counseling, referring the client/patient to another mental health practitioner, and, if feasible and clinically appropriate, working with the professional who will be responsible for the client's/patient's case (see also Standard 10.10, Terminating Therapy).

☑ A psychologist providing Internet-mediated psychological services to clients in a distant rural community included in her informed consent information the address of a Web site she created providing continuously updated information on the names, credentials, and contact information of local and electronically accessible backup professionals available to assist clients if the psychologist was not immediately available during an emergency.

Standard 3.12 also requires psychologists to prepare for unplanned interruptions such as sudden illness or death. In most cases, it would suffice to have a trusted professional colleague prepared to contact clients/patients if such a situation arises. Pope and Vasquez (2007) recommend that psychologists create a professional will, including directives on the person designated to assume primary responsibility, backup personnel, coordinated planning, office security and access, easy to locate schedule, avenues of communication, client records and contact information, client notification, colleague notification, professional liability coverage, attorney for professional issues, and billing records and procedures.

The phrase "reasonable efforts" reflects awareness that some events are unpredictable and even the best-laid plans may not be adequate when services are interrupted. The phrase "unless otherwise covered by contract" recognizes there may be some instances when psychologists are prohibited by contract with a commercial or health care organization from following through on plans to facilitate services.

HOT TOPIC

Goodness-of-Fit Ethics for Informed Consent Involving Adults With Impaired Decisional Capacity

The process of obtaining informed consent presents unique ethical challenges for mental health treatment and research involving adults with schizophrenia, developmental disabilities, Alzheimer's disease, and other disorders characterized by fluctuating, declining, or long-term impairments in decisional capacity. Obtaining informed consent from these populations raises a fundamental ethical question: *How can psychologists balance their ethical obligation to respect the dignity and autonomy of persons with mental disorders to make their own decisions with the obligation to ensure that ill-informed or incompetent choices do not jeopardize their welfare or leave them open to exploitation* (Cea & Fisher, 2003; Fisher, 1999; Fisher et al., 2006)?

Legal Status, Diagnostic Labels, and Consent Capacity. Some adults with serious mental disorders have been declared legally incompetent to consent. Removal of a person's legal status as a consenting adult does not, however, deprive him or her of the moral right to be involved in treatment or research participation decisions. For these adults, APA Ethics Code Standard 3.10(b) requires that psychologists obtain the appropriate permission from a legally authorized person *and* provide an appropriate explanation to the prospective client/patient or research participant, consider such person's preferences and best interests, and seek the individual's assent.

The implementation of ethically appropriate consent procedures is more complex for the many situations in which individuals diagnosed with neurological or other mental health disorders retain the legal status of a consenting adult, though their capacity for making informed, rational, and voluntary decisions may be compromised. Each person with a serious mental disorder is unique. Sole reliance on a diagnostic label to determine a client's/patient's capacity to make treatment or research participation decisions risks depriving persons with mental disorders of equal opportunities for autonomous choice.

Fitting Consent Procedures to Enhance Decisional Capacities and Protections

Thomas Grisso and Paul Appelbaum (Appelbaum & Grisso, 2001; Grisso & Appelbaum, 1998) have developed the most well-known model of consent capacity. It consists of four increasingly complex consent components: choice, understanding, appreciation, and reasoning. This model has given rise to several empirically validated instruments (Dunn, Nowrangi, Palmer, Jeste, & Saks, 2007). Assessing capacity is a necessary but insufficient basis for determining consent procedures for individuals with mental disorders. Goodness-of-fit ethics defines just and caring consent processes as those that (a) identify the consent strengths and vulnerabilities of the specific individuals or groups with whom psychologists work and (b) create consent procedures that can minimize vulnerabilities, enhance consent strengths, and provide consent supports when appropriate (Fisher, 2002a, 2002b, 2004). This section describes how psychologists can maximize person and consent context fit.

Choice

Evidencing a choice reflects the ability to actively indicate consent or dissent. For example, some adults suffering from catatonia or Parkinson's dementia may be unable to communicate a choice verbally or nonverbally. While these individuals may understand some of the consent information presented and may have a participation preference, their inability to communicate agreement or dissent will require stringent safeguards against harmful or exploitative consent procedures.

Proxy Consent. In such settings, creating a goodness of fit between person and consent context often requires respectful inclusion of a consent surrogate who has familiarity with the patient's preference history. The proxy can help ensure that the consent decision reflects, to the extent feasible, the patient's attitudes, hopes, and concerns. Once proxy consent has been obtained, respect for personhood and protection of individual welfare requires psychologists to be alert to patient-appropriate expressions of anxiety, fatigue, or distress that indicate an individual's dissent or desire to withdraw from participation.

Understanding

Understanding reflects comprehension of factual information about the nature, risks, and benefits of treatment or research. When understanding is hampered by problems of attention or retention, psychologists can incorporate consent enhancement techniques into their procedures such as incorporating pictorial representations of treatment or research procedures, presenting information in brief segments, or using repetition. Person-consent context fit also requires identifying which information is and is not critical to helping an individual make an informed choice. For example, when seeking consent for a behavioral intervention for aggressive disorders in a residence for adults with developmental disabilities, it may be important for clients to understand the specific types of behaviors targeted (e.g., hitting other residents), the reward system that will be used (e.g., points toward going to movies or other special activities), and who will be responsible for monitoring the behavior (e.g., residential staff). It may be less important for them to understand details of residential policies regarding the protection of residents' health records, especially if the confidentiality protections do not differ from those that are a natural and ongoing part of the residential experience.

Appreciation

Appreciation refers to the capacity to comprehend the personal consequences of consenting or dissenting to treatment or research. For example, an adult with a dual diagnosis may understand that treatment will require limiting aggressive behavior but not appreciate the difficulties he may have in adhering to the behavioral rules. An individual suffering from schizophrenia may understand that clinical research is testing treatment effectiveness but may not appreciate she has a disorder that requires treatment.

Sliding Scale. A sliding-scale approach based on the seriousness of personal consequences of the consent decision can be helpful in evaluating the ethical weight that should be given to the client's/patient's capacity for appreciation. For example, understanding may be sufficient for consent decisions to standard or experimental interventions that present minimal risk and are supplemental to current treatment programs. On the other hand, appreciation may be essential when the treatment or experimental intervention may expose the individual to the risk of serious side effects or offer an opportunity to receive needed services not otherwise available.

Reasoning

Reasoning reflects the ability to weigh the risks and benefits of consent or dissent. For example, an adult with schizophrenia with paranoid features may understand the nature of a treatment and appreciate its potential for reducing his anxiety but may reason that the risks outweigh the potential benefits because the psychologist offering the treatment is part of a government conspiracy to undermine his freedom.

Supported Decision Making and Enhancement. Asking individuals with questionable reasoning capacity to select a family member, friend, or other trusted person to be present during an informed consent discussion can be empowering and avoid the risk of triggering a legal competency review solely for the purposes of a single mental health treatment or research participation decision (Fisher, 2002a; Fisher et al., 2006; Roeher Institute, 1996).

Consent and Empowerment

People with longstanding, declining, or transient disorders related to decisional capacities may be accustomed to other people making decisions for them and may not understand or have experience applying the concept of autonomy. In institutional contexts, individuals with mental disorders may fear disapproval from doctors or residence supervisors or feel they must be compliant in deference to the authority of the requesting psychologist. Some may have little experience in exercising their rights or, if they are living in a community residence, may be fearful of discontinuation of other services. Psychologists can also look toward recent research demonstrating the effectiveness of brief interventions to enhance consent capacity in adult patients (Mittal et al., 2007). Modifying the consent setting to reduce the perception of power inequities, providing opportunities to practice decision making, demonstrating that other services will not be compromised, and drawing on the support of trusted family and peers can strengthen the goodness of fit between person and consent setting and ensure that informed consent is obtained within a context of justice and care.

CHAPTER 7

Standards on Privacy and Confidentiality

4. PRIVACY AND CONFIDENTIALITY

4.01 Maintaining Confidentiality

Psychologists have a primary obligation and take reasonable precautions to protect confidential information obtained through or stored in any medium, recognizing that the extent and limits of confidentiality may be regulated by law or established by institutional rules or professional or scientific relationship. (See also Standard 2.05, Delegation of Work to Others.)

Psychologists respect the privacy and dignity of persons by protecting confidential information obtained from those with whom they work (Principle E: Respect for People's Rights and Dignity). Standard 4.01 of the American Psychological Association (APA) Ethics Code (APA, 2002b) is broadly written and requires all psychologists to take reasonable precautions to maintain confidentiality. The nature of precautions required will differ according to the psychologist's role, the purpose of the psychological activity, the legal status of the person with whom the psychologist is working, federal regulations, state and local laws, and institutional and organizational policies. The term *reasonable precautions* recognizes both the responsibility to be familiar with appropriate methods of protecting confidentiality and the possibility that confidentiality may be broken despite a psychologist's best efforts. The following are general recommendations for maintaining confidentiality across a variety of psychological activities.

Use of the Internet and Other Electronic Media

When providing services, conducting distance learning, or collecting research data over the Internet, psychologists must become knowledgeable about or obtain technical assistance in employing appropriate methods for protecting confidential records concerning clients/patients, organizations, research participants, or students.

☑ When files are stored via a common server or backed up on a university system or hub server, discuss and develop security measures with appropriate personnel.

☑ Use encrypted data transmission, password-protected data storage, and firewall techniques.

☑ When confidential information is e-mailed, faxed, or otherwise electronically transmitted to scientists, professionals, or organizations, take reasonable steps to ensure that recipients of the information have an adequate confidentiality policy (see also discussion of the Health Insurance Portability and Accountability Act [HIPAA] below).

☑ Psychologists using the Internet for clinical supervision should instruct trainees on appropriate procedures to protect client/patient confidentiality.

☑ Avoid leaving telephone messages for clients/patients on answering machines. When such a message is unavoidable, take precautions to ensure the message does not reveal to others that the client/patient is in treatment or any other confidential information.

Audio, Video, or Digital Recordings of Voices or Images

Protecting confidentiality when recording voice or images of clients/patients, research participants, employees, or others may require technical advice or assistance.

☑ Store recordings in safe locations or use passwords to protect computer access.

☑ Distort voice recordings or mask faces in visual images to protect confidentiality.

☑ Destroy recordings when they are no longer needed as long as their destruction does not conflict with other ethical obligations to maintain scientific or professional records.

☑ An educational psychologist sought consent and parental permission to use teacher and student images in a Web-based instructional video for science education. To address parental concerns that students might be identified by Internet predators, she used "masking" effects on video shots of students' faces and sound editing to remove any reference to names. When there were too many faces to conceal through masking, she extracted a digital photograph from a scene in which only activities and not identities were visible and then used editing software to extract appropriate audio recordings to supplement the photographs (see Schuck & Kearney, 2006).

Research

☑ Use participant codes on all data collection materials and data entered for analysis.

☑ Maintain records linking participant codes to personal identifiers in a secure file and destroy such records once they are no longer needed.

☑ Limit access to personally identifiable information and supervise research personnel in routine confidentiality precautions.

☑ Separate consent forms from coded materials to avoid participant identification.

☑ Apply for a Certificate of Confidentiality under 301d of the Public Health Service Act of 1946 to obtain immunity from a subpoena requiring disclosure of identifying information when there is a possibility that data collected are of a sensitive nature that, if released, could result in stigmatization, discrimination, or legal action that could jeopardize an individual's financial standing, employment, or reputation (see http://www.hhs.gov/ohrp/humansubjects/guidance/certconf.htm).

☑ When publishing or otherwise disseminating research findings, consider special confidentiality protections when unnamed but small, unique samples can be identified through descriptions of demographic variables (e.g., persons with rare diseases from distinct communities).

☑ Ensure that recruitment and research procedures do not inadvertently reveal confidential information. For example, when studying addictions, mental disorders, sexually transmitted diseases, or other potentially stigmatizing conditions, approaching target populations for recruitment may result in public identification of the condition.

☑ Become familiar with and ensure HIPAA compliance when research involves the use of protected health information (PHI) obtained directly by the investigator or through a covered entity (see section on HIPAA below).

☑ Become familiar with cultural and contextual factors that may influence participant confidentiality preferences and concerns.

☑ A psychologist conducting cross-cultural research in the Amazon arranged to have individual interviews conducted in a private area of the village to protect participant confidentiality. To the psychologist's surprise, the villagers objected to these arrangements as strange and uncomfortable because they did not ordinarily conduct social or business interactions in private settings. In addition, those who did express interest in participation brought their family members to the interview. With permission from his institutional review board, he modified the procedures so that interviews were conducted in a corner of a public space within the village, and family members were permitted to be present at the invitation of the participants. Informed consent clarified to villagers the type of information to be discussed, how the discussion with each individual would be kept confidential from all who were not present during the interview, and steps the psychologist would take to ensure individual participants could not be identified by others when the study results were disseminated (adapted from Monshi & Zieglmayer, 2004).

Assessment and Psychotherapy Records

☑ Store therapy notes or client/patient records in locked file cabinets or in password-protected computer files.

☑ When working with a health maintenance organization (HMO) or within an institution, personally confirm that client/patient permission for sharing confidential information has been obtained appropriately through third-party contractual or institutional release forms.

☑ Protect the identity of clients/patients or other persons not covered by an HMO when the HMO conducts a utilization review that includes inspection of noncovered clients'/patients' records.

☑ Obtain appropriate written permission and/or signed HIPAA-compliant authorization (where appropriate) before releasing confidential information to third parties (see below).

Implications of HIPAA for Practice and Research

Practitioners and scientists whose work includes creating, using, disclosing, collecting, storing, or analyzing PHI should become familiar with requirements of the HIPAA Privacy Rule (45 CFR Parts 160–164; see also "A Word About HIPAA" in the Preface of this book). Under HIPAA, PHI is defined as information electronically transmitted or maintained in any form or medium relating to the past, present, or future physical or mental health condition, provision of care, or payment for provision of care for an individual that either identifies or can be used to identify the individual (see 45 CFR 160.103 and 164.501). The regulation applies to "covered entities" defined as a health plan, a health care clearinghouse, or a health care provider who transmits any health information in electronic form in connection with a transaction covered by the regulations (e.g., a transaction between two parties to carry out financial or administrative activities related to health care) (45 CFR 160.102[a] and 160.103).

Practice. Under HIPAA, "covered entities" must designate a "privacy officer" to oversee and ensure that HIPAA-compliant privacy procedures are developed and implemented. This requirement is "scalable," in that meeting the requirement will differ depending on whether a psychologist is in solo practice, directing a group practice, or administrating a large institutional program. Covered entities must implement security procedures that prevent unauthorized access to health records. They must also take steps to ensure that employees, business associates, individual contractors, consultants, collection agencies, third-party payors, and researchers with whom PHI is shared comply with HIPAA regulations. Psychologists transferring PHI files to or from HMOs or other companies are required to take steps to ensure that confidential records are transmitted in secure ways, for example, by means of a secured fax machine. Requirements for HIPAA compliance also vary with each state's privacy laws. The APA Insurance Trust and the APA Practice

Directorate have excellent materials to guide practitioners in HIPAA compliance (see www.apait.org/resources/hipaa).

Small Group Practices. HIPAA distinguishes between large and small health care practices, recognizing that for the latter, it is impractical to expect employees will not handle PHI. The following is a partial list of requirements when staff members have access to such records (see Rada, 2003):

• All staff must be formally trained in HIPAA regulations, including state laws relevant to faxing information that includes PHI and the group's sanction policy for violators.

• Staff must sign an employee confidentiality form, placed in their personnel record along with a record of their training.

• E-mails and fax coversheets used to communicate PHI must indicate the information is confidential.

• The fax policy must be posted beside the fax machine.

• All vendors used by the practice for accounting, legal, actuarial, billing, or other services must sign a business associate contract with the practice.

• Each group practice must have a privacy officer responsible for the development and implementation of the policies and procedures and an office manager who (a) oversees HIPAA authorizations, completion and maintenance of required records, and new staff training; (b) receives privacy complaints and mitigates harmful effects of privacy disclosures; and (c) applies sanctions when appropriate. In small clinics or practices, one person may perform both these roles.

Research Creating, Using, or Disclosing PHI. HIPAA defines research as "a systematic investigation, including research development, testing, and evaluation, designed to develop or contribute to generalizable knowledge" (45 CFR 164.501). Treatment is defined as "the provision, coordination, or management of health care and related services by one or more health care providers, including the coordination or management of health care by a health care provider with a third party; consultation between health care providers relating to a patient; or the referral of a patient for health care from one health care provider to another" (45 CFR 164.501). Psychologists who are health care providers or who employ health care providers to conduct research involving assessments or diagnoses that will be used for treatment decisions involving research participants should consider themselves or their research team covered entities under HIPAA. Investigators who are not themselves health care providers but conduct treatment research or quality improvement research for a health care facility or any other organization that is a covered entity must also ensure that their procedures are HIPAA compliant.

HIPAA permits covered entities to transmit PHI to researchers who are conducting nontherapeutic research if (a) a patient signs an authorization to release information that is project specific (*not* a general authorization for use of PHI for future unspecified research); (b) an institutional review board (IRB) or privacy board approves in writing a waiver of the requirement for such authorization, and the investigator provides the covered entity with written assurances that HIPAA-compliant procedures are in place to protect confidentiality; or (c) the records are de-identified, as specifically defined by HIPAA regulations.

HIPAA also permits covered entities to allow researchers to use PHI without patient authorization (a) for deceased patients; (b) for public health research; (c) when PHI will not leave the covered entity, will be used solely for reviews or protocol development, and the researcher conveys to the covered entity that such access is essential and that the PHI will not be removed from the premises; or (d) when research involves the use of a "limited data set" (a partially de-identified data set specifically defined by HIPAA) and the investigator has signed a "data use agreement" ensuring the covered entity that PHI will be safeguarded and used or disclosed only for limited purposes (see 45 CFR 164.512[i]).

Implications of FERPA for Psychologists Working in Schools

The Family Educational Rights and Privacy Act (FERPA) of 1974 (www.ed.gov/offices/OM/fpco/ferpa/index.html) is a federal law that protects the privacy of student education records in all schools that receive funds under an applicable program of the U.S. Department of Education. FERPA gives certain rights to parents that transfer to the student at age 18 or after leaving high school. A student's educational record may not be released without written permission from the parent or eligible student.

FERPA does allow disclosure of records without consent (a) in cases of health and safety emergencies; (b) to comply with a judicial order or with state or local authorities within the juvenile justice system; (c) to school officials with legitimate educational interest; (d) to accrediting agencies, specified officials, or organizations in connection with auditing or certain studies on behalf of the school; (e) to schools to which the student is transferring; or (f) to parties in connection with student financial aid. HIPAA regulations do not apply to records that fall under FERPA regulations. FERPA, unlike HIPAA, does not make distinctions between student health and academic records. School psychologists need to be familiar with state and district policies that may be more protective of student health privacy (e.g., HIV/AIDS).

4.02 Discussing the Limits of Confidentiality

(a) Psychologists discuss with persons (including, to the extent feasible, persons who are legally incapable of giving informed consent and their legal representatives) and organizations with whom they establish a scientific or professional relationship (1) the relevant limits of confidentiality and (2) the foreseeable uses of the information generated through their psychological activities. (See also Standard 3.10, Informed Consent.)

Legal, institutional, or professional obligations frequently place limits on the extent to which private information acquired during psychological activities can be kept confidential. Psychologists are often legally required to (a) report suspected child abuse or neglect to child protection agencies; (b) contact family members or other professionals to protect an individual from imminent self-harm; (c) warn a potential victim of a client's/patient's intent to harm him or her; (d) contact a law enforcement agency when they have foreknowledge of certain crimes; (e) assist in lawful military investigations; (f) provide companies, police departments, or military agencies psychological information to determine suitability for employment, promotion, or assignments; (g) provide treatment or assessment information in criminal or civil cases; or (h) provide information to third-party payors when mental health treatment is covered by a health plan.

Disclosure of such information can have serious material consequences for clients/patients, research participants, organizational clients, and others with whom psychologists work. Promising confidentiality without revealing its known limitations is a misrepresentation of fact that may violate a person's privacy and liberty (Bersoff, 1976). Release of confidential information poses risks to individuals and their families when disclosures lead to investigation by child protective services, arrest, conviction, institutionalization, loss of health or disability insurance, loss of child custody, or social stigmatization. Disclosures of confidential information can also lead to financial or legal risk for organizations.

Under Standard 4.02a, psychologists must discuss with persons and organizations with whom they work reporting obligations and other limits to the confidentiality of information that can be reasonably anticipated.

Persons Legally Incapable of Consent. This requirement extends to persons who are legally incapable of giving informed consent and their legal representatives. For example, psychologists conducting research with children or adults with impaired cognitive capacity must inform legal guardians and, to the extent possible, the prospective participants themselves about any limitations in confidentiality. Such limitations might include reporting requirements if investigators are state-mandated child abuse or elder abuse reporters or protective policies if the investigators have elected to disclose to guardians or professionals information about participants with serious suicidal ideation (Fisher, 2002a, 2002b, 2003a, 2003b; Fisher, Higgins-D'Alessandro, Rau, Kuther, & Belanger, 1996; O'Sullivan & Fisher, 1997). Practitioner psychologists should inform clients/patients and their legal guardians about the nature of information that will be shared with guardians and with others based on law, institutional or organizational regulations, or the psychologist's policies regarding disclosure of child or adolescent health-compromising behaviors (Fisher et al., 1999; see also the Hot Topic, "Confidentiality and Involvement of Parents in Mental Health Services for Children and Adolescents," at the end of this chapter). School psychologists may need to inform students, guardians, and school personnel about laws governing the release of school records—for example, FERPA, which establishes the right of parents to obtain copies of their children's school records (20 U.S.C. § 1232G[a][1][A]; 34 CFR § 99.11b).

Third-Party Payors. When services will be covered by third-party payors, psychologists need to inform clients/patients about information that will be shared with the third party, including treatment plans, session notes, and diagnoses. Some contractual agreements with managed care companies (HMOs) permit utilization reviews that provide HMO access to information about clients/patients not covered under the policy. Clients/patients must be informed of such limits on confidentiality if records cannot be adequately de-identified. Psychologists receiving payment through credit cards should inform persons about the possible use of this information by credit card companies that may sell their client lists to organizations specializing in self-help or other related products.

Military. In the military, there is no psychologist-client confidentiality in the traditional sense. Military psychologists are required to release information on command to assist in the lawful conduct of investigations or to determine suitability of persons for service or assignments. One of the most noteworthy gains in confidentiality and respect for the rights of the individual was the implementation of U.S. Department of Defense (DoD) Directive 6490.1 (U.S. DoD, 1997a) and DoD Instruction 6490.4 (U.S. DoD, 1997b). Thanks to the efforts of military psychologists, active-duty service members sent for commander-directed mental health evaluations now have the right to know why they were referred for the evaluation and who will be conducting that evaluation, an opportunity for a second opinion following receipt of a summary of the findings, and a right to speak with legal counsel, a chaplain, and a member of Congress regarding their situation (see Orme & Doerman, 2001).

Implications of HIPAA. Psychologists creating, transferring, analyzing, or storing PHI via electronic transmission or working with a managed care company, bill collection agency, or other organization that does so are required to provide individuals with a Notice of Privacy Practices that details the uses and disclosures of PHI and the individuals' privacy rights under relevant federal or state law (45 CFR 164.520). Notice of Privacy Practices and informed consent forms used by psychologists working in small group practices need to clarify the extent to which confidential information will be shared with other practicing professionals in the group on a regular basis and how confidentiality protections will be protected. The APA Insurance Trust and the APA Practice Directorate have available for purchase sample Notice of Privacy Practices compatible with laws governing practice in each state (see http://apait.org/hipaa, http://apa.org/practice).

(b) Unless it is not feasible or is contraindicated, the discussion of confidentiality occurs at the outset of the relationship and thereafter as new circumstances may warrant.

Clients/patients, research participants, organizations, and others are entitled to know the limits of confidentiality and its potential consequences before deciding whether or how to engage in a scientific or professional relationship with a psychologist. Standard 4.02b requires that psychologists discuss the known extent and limits of confidentiality at the outset of the relationship. The phrase "unless it is not feasible or is contraindicated" permits psychologists to delay discussion of confidentiality in cases in which the treatment needs of a new client/patient, such as acute trauma, must take priority. It also permits delays when the limits of confidentiality need to be further explored. For example, a therapist may need to call a client's/patient's health plan to determine its utilization review policies. In such situations, confidentiality is discussed as soon as the crisis has subsided or all information has been obtained.

In some instances, the scientific or professional relationship may change over time, requiring renewed discussion of confidentiality. For example, in longitudinal studies involving children extending over several years, both participants and their guardians may need to be reminded of confidentiality policies, especially if a change in such policies is warranted as the child matures into adolescence.

Psychologists whose clients/patients ask them to testify as a fact witness on their behalf should carefully explain to the clients/patients how this changes the nature of confidentiality and the implications of waiving client-therapist privilege.

(c) Psychologists who offer services, products, or information via electronic transmission inform clients/patients of the risks to privacy and limits of confidentiality.

Psychological services or transmission of records conducted over the Internet and other electronic media are vulnerable to breaches in confidentiality that may be beyond the psychologist's individual control. Under Standard 4.02c, clients/patients must be made aware of the risks to privacy and limitations of protections the psychologist can institute to guard against violations of consumer confidentiality when information is transmitted electronically (see Standard 4.01, Maintaining Confidentiality).

☑ Psychologists conducting therapy or assessments via e-mail or through secure chat rooms should inform clients/patients about the possibility of strangers hacking into secure sites or, when applicable, the extent to which institutional staff have access to secure sites on a hub server.

☑ Sometimes clients/patients may send unsolicited sensitive communications to a therapist's personal e-mail account. Once psychologists become aware such an e-mail has been sent, they should inform such clients about the risks of others reading these e-mails and discourage clients/patients from future e-mail communications if appropriate.

☑ Clients/patients who discuss sensitive information with psychologists over a cell phone should be warned about the limits of confidentiality when this medium is used.

☑ Psychologists transmitting health records to managed care companies or other health providers need to alert clients/patients to potential breaches that may occur when health information is passed through multiple systems, including utilization reviewers, case managers, bookkeepers, and accountants.

☑ Psychologists providing services on a Web site should include a visible and easy to understand privacy statement whenever a consumer's personal information is requested. The privacy statement should advise consumers of how personal information will be used (e.g., sold to other sites, used to contact the consumer at a later date) and whether they can opt out of these uses. Psychologists can download a sample privacy policy statement from the APA's Web site at http://apahelpcenter.org/about/privacy.php.

4.03 Recording

Before recording the voices or images of individuals to whom they provide services, psychologists obtain permission from all such persons or their legal representatives. (See also Standards 8.03, Informed Consent for Recording Voices and Images in Research; 8.05, Dispensing With Informed Consent for Research; and 8.07, Deception in Research.)

Psychologists who use audio, visual, or digital recordings of voices or images to provide services to individuals must obtain permission from all such persons or their legal representatives before recording begins. Although exceptions exist for informed consent to recording voices and images in research (see Standards 8.03, 8.05, and 8.07), under Standard 4.03, no such exceptions are permissible for service providers. The following are examples of violations of this standard:

> ☒ A court-appointed forensic psychologist conducting a competency evaluation of a prisoner audiotaped the assessment without informing the prisoner or the prisoner's attorney.
>
> ☒ A clinical psychologist conducting behavior therapy with a 6-year-old diagnosed with attention deficit disorder decided to videotape the therapy sessions to better analyze the child's behavioral responses to different situations. The psychologist did not obtain permission from the child's parents to videotape the session.

4.04 Minimizing Intrusions on Privacy

(a) Psychologists include in written and oral reports and consultations, only information germane to the purpose for which the communication is made.

Clients/patients, research participants, and organizational clients often share or unintentionally reveal private information to psychologists that may not be germane to the purpose of the psychological activities. Under Standard 4.04, psychologists are prohibited from including such information in their reports or consultations. Examples of potential violations of this standard include the following:

> ☒ A woman referred for a neuropsychological evaluation to assess the cause of a speech disorder immediately following a head injury was accompanied to the psychologist's office by an individual she identified as her longtime female domestic partner. The psychologist's report referred to the client as a lesbian, even though sexual orientation was not a relevant factor in the diagnosis.
>
> ☒ During a break in an assessment battery for a competency determination of an incarcerated young man, the forensic psychologist heard the man brag about the

crime to another inmate. During the competency hearing, the psychologist's expert testimony included mention of the casual admission to the crime (for further information, see Committee on Ethical Guidelines for Forensic Psychologists, 1991).

☒ A school psychologist who evaluated children with learning disabilities for academic placement typically met with parents to obtain a developmental history and information about the child's study habits at home. During one of these discussions, a parent mentioned that her husband had lost his job a few months ago. The psychologist's report included mention of the father's unemployment, although it was not a factor in the report's conclusions regarding the child's learning status and schooling needs.

Implications of HIPAA. Standard 4.04a is consistent with HIPAA regulations regarding the "minimum necessary." When disclosing or requesting PHI, a covered entity must make reasonable efforts to limit the information to the *minimum necessary* to accomplish the intended purpose of the use, disclosure, or request. This requirement does not apply to disclosures to another health care provider for treatment, disclosures to the individual client/patient, disclosures required by law, or for other purposes under the HIPAA regulation (45 CFR 164.502[b]).

(b) Psychologists discuss confidential information obtained in their work only for appropriate scientific or professional purposes and only with persons clearly concerned with such matters.

With rare exception (see Standards 4.05, Disclosures, and 4.07, Use of Confidential Information for Didactic or Other Purposes), psychologists should never discuss confidential information obtained in their work without the permission of research participants, clients/patients, organizational clients, or others who have been promised confidentiality. In some instances, consent is implicit or refers to a category of individuals, such as when research participants and patients/clients consent to have confidential information shared with members of a research team or treatment staff.

In other instances, clients/patients with psychological impairments may not have a legally appointed guardian but do have a family caregiver actively involved in their treatment with whom confidential information can be shared. Standard 4.04b requires in such situations that psychologists discuss confidential information only with persons who are clearly concerned with the matter and limit disclosures only to information that is pertinent to the scientific or professional issue at hand. The intent of the standard is to permit discussions with others necessary to competently conduct psychological activities, to prohibit unnecessary discussion of confidential information, and to avoid the use of such information as gossip among professionals.

☑ A school psychologist evaluated a fourth-grade student for placement in a special education class. With permission and a signed authorization from the child's parents, the psychologist discussed the need for such a placement with the school principal. However, the psychologist refused to discuss the child's diagnosis when questioned by several concerned teachers in the faculty dining room.

> ☑ A clinical gerontologist developed behavioral treatment plans for Alzheimer's patients at a long-term care facility. Although staff psychologists implemented the behavioral plans, it was often necessary to coordinate the patients' psychological services with staff and family members. The psychologist provided nursing staff and family members only with information they needed to ensure the consistency of the plan and carefully refrained from sharing with anyone who was not the patient's legal representative information about the patient's diagnosis or other personal information.

Implications of HIPAA. Under the HIPAA Privacy Rule, psychologists working in independent practice, group practices, or systems of health care are permitted to share PHI internally (45 CFR 164.502 and 165.506). The nature of information shared is not restricted when disclosure is with other health professionals for the purposes of providing treatment. However, psychologists must disclose only the minimum amount of information necessary to nontreatment personnel, such as staff responsible for scheduling appointments or billing, to enable them to perform their duties.

4.05 Disclosures

(a) Psychologists may disclose confidential information with the appropriate consent of the organizational client, the individual client/patient, or another legally authorized person on behalf of the client/patient unless prohibited by law.

Standard 4.05a permits but does not require psychologists to disclose confidential information if appropriate consent has been obtained from the organizational client, the individual client/patient, or another legally authorized person. Psychologists should have persons or organizations provide a signed release, provide a signed authorization if HIPAA is applicable, or otherwise document the permission or request to have confidential information disclosed. Documentation should specifically identify the persons or organizations to whom confidential information may be released, be time limited, and, where applicable, be HIPAA compliant. Psychologists should not ask individual or organizational clients to sign blanket releases for the disclosure of confidential information over an indeterminate period of time. Before releasing confidential information at the request of a hospital, organization, agency, or HMO, psychologists should confirm that the institution or organization obtained appropriate consent or authorization for the disclosure (see also the Hot Topic, "Managing the Ethics of Managed Care," in Chapter 9).

Implications of HIPAA. Standard 4.05a requires psychologists to be mindful of laws that prohibit disclosure. HIPAA requires that covered entities obtain written valid authorization from the individual or his or her personal representative prior to releasing PHI (45 CFR 164.508). The authorization must include a specific description of information to be disclosed, specific identification of the person or class of persons who can make the authorization and to whom information may be disclosed, a description of the purpose and use of the disclosure, an expiration date, and a signature (45 CFR 164.508[c]). In addition, when appropriate release and authorizations are obtained, the HIPAA Privacy Rule requires that psychologists share only the minimum amount of information necessary for billing agencies and non–health provider internal staff to perform their roles (45 CFR 164.502[b]). The APA Insurance Trust and the APA Practice Directorate have available for purchase sample HIPAA-compliant authorization forms compatible with laws governing practice in each state (see http://apait.org/hipaa, http://apa.org/practice).

Declining Requests. Under Standard 4.05a, psychologists may decline an appropriately obtained request to release confidential information if the psychologist believes disclosure will cause harm. However, psychologists should be aware that certain federal and statutory laws limit providers' rights to withhold such information. Under the HIPAA Privacy Rule, covered entities have an obligation to agree to a patient's reasonable requests for release of PHI and can deny a request only if it is reasonably likely to endanger the life or physical safety of the individual or another person or is likely to cause equally substantial harm. In addition, psychologists must allow clients/patients the right to have the denial reviewed by a designated licensed health care professional. Readers should refer to Chapter 12 for how decisions regarding disclosure of information relate to Standards 9.04, Release of Test Data, and 9.11, Maintaining Test Security.

Research. An individual's access to PHI created or obtained in the course of treatment research may be suspended temporarily for as long as the research is in progress, provided the individual has agreed to the denial of access when consenting to the research and has been promised right of access upon completion of the research (45 CFR 164.524[a][2][iii]).

Psychotherapy Notes and PHI Compiled for Legal or Administrative Action. HIPAA is highly protective of psychotherapy notes, defined as notes recorded by a health care provider who is a mental health professional documenting or analyzing the contents of a conversation during a private counseling session or a group, joint, or family counseling session and that are separated from the rest of the individual's medical record (45 CFR 164.501). Some authors (e.g., see Zuckerman, 2005) have distinguished between "progress notes" (descriptions of treatment procedures and the therapist's observations) and "process notes" (notations regarding the therapist's personal opinions or emotional reactions to patient care). The language of HIPAA does not make this distinction. Patients do *not* have the right to access psychotherapy notes, and a client/patient must provide a separate signed authorization specific to the release of psychotherapy notes when a covered entity agrees to their release. Psychologists who are or work for covered entities should also be aware that HMOs are prohibited from requiring patient authorization to disclose psychotherapy notes as a condition for evaluating eligibility.

Certain forensic records are also protected under HIPAA. Patients do not have the right of access to information compiled in reasonable anticipation of, or for use in, a civil, criminal, or administrative action or procedure (45 CFR 164.508 and 164.524[a][1]).

For information on other exceptions, see discussions of Standards 6.03, Withholding Records for Nonpayment, and 9.04, Release of Test Data.

(b) Psychologists disclose confidential information without the consent of the individual only as mandated by law, or where permitted by law for a valid purpose such as to (1) provide needed professional services; (2) obtain appropriate professional consultations; (3) protect the client/patient, psychologist, or others from harm; or (4) obtain payment for services from a client/patient, in which instance disclosure is limited to the minimum that is necessary to achieve the purpose. (See also Standard 6.04e, Fees and Financial Arrangements.)

Standard 4.05b describes those situations in which it is ethically permissible to disclose identifiable confidential information without the consent of an individual or organization. The standard is permissive rather than mandatory, leaving the decision to disclose confidential information without consent under the above listed categories to the psychologist's discretion. At the same time, the standard prohibits disclosure of confidential information without consent for any purpose other than those listed.

Clients/patients, research participants, organizational clients, and others with whom a psychologist works must be informed as early as feasible in the professional or scientific relationship about the potential for such disclosures when it is reasonable for the psychologist to anticipate disclosures may be necessary (see Standard 4.02, Discussing the Limits of Confidentiality).

Disclosures Mandated by Law

The standard permits psychologists to disclose confidential information without consent when the disclosure is mandated by law.

> ☑ Psychologists should be aware of the specific mandated child abuse reporting laws of their state. Following the Child Abuse Prevention and Treatment Act of 1976, all 50 states enacted statutes mandating mental health professionals and, in at least 13 states, researchers to report suspected child abuse or neglect, as members of the general citizenry (Liss, 1994). In addition, some states specifically require mandated reporters to alert child protection agencies when they learn about child abuse from a client/patient who is no longer a minor if other children are or may be at risk of being abused by the perpetrator of the abuse. Most statutes protect mandatory reporters from liability claims, including those for breach of confidentiality (http://childwelfare.gov/systemwide/laws_policies/state/). Some states have mandatory reporting laws for elder abuse and neglect and for knowledge of the intent to commit a criminal act.

"Duty-to-Protect" Laws. A number of states have adopted "duty-to-protect" laws following the landmark court case *Tarasoff v. Regents of the University of California* (1976). In this case, a psychologist at a university health center recognized that Prosenjhit Poddar, a client with a pathological attachment to his ex-girlfriend, Tatiana Tarasoff, was a danger to her after he made some threats. The psychologist and his supervisor notified campus police that the client was dangerous and should be committed, but after interviewing him, the police released him. Poddar did not return for therapy and murdered Tatiana 2 months later. Her parents brought a successful suit against the university, arguing that the therapist had a duty to warn Tarasoff.

Duty-to-protect laws typically require certain classes of health care providers to inform a third party of the prospect of being harmed by a client/patient if the provider has (a) a "special relationship" with the prospective assailant (i.e., a client-therapist relationship), (b) the ability to predict that violence will occur (e.g., the client/patient has made a credible threat against a third party), and (c) the ability to identify the potential victim (i.e., the client/patient has named the potential victim). Some court decisions have broadened the third requirement to a more generalized duty to protect third parties from foreseeable harm in the absence of an identifiable victim. These cases typically involve the release from hospitalization or the failure to commit for psychiatric treatment clients/patients whose dangerousness to nonidentified others is foreseeable. For an excellent overview and recommendations, see Quattrocchi and Schopp (2005).

Psychologists should remain up-to-date on controversies as to whether duty-to-protect laws apply to research or to situations involving a professional's knowledge of intentional or reckless transmission of HIV or other sexually transmitted diseases to partners or other identified victims (Appelbaum & Rosenbaum, 1989; Chenneville, 2000; Fisher et al., in press; VandeCreek & Knapp, 1993; Webber, 1999).

Psychologists providing services or conducting research over the Internet need to be familiar with state laws governing mandatory reporting in jurisdictions where recipients of Internet services or Internet-administered research instruments reside.

School Violence. In response to the rise in public awareness of school violence, statutory and case laws are increasingly recognizing the need to balance the interest of the state (school) in fulfilling its duty to protect the rights of individual children and to maintain order and ensure pupil safety. In many states, school personnel are required or permitted to detain and question students suspected of planning acts of violence. If a student poses a threat to a minor child, school psychologists may notify the threatened student's parents, supervise the potentially violent child in the school setting, take reasonable steps to encourage out-of-school supervision, and ensure the student does not have access to weapons.

Systematic assessments of foreseeable school violence may include (a) a student's past violent, menacing, or stalking acts and the precipitants to those acts; (b) recent events that might instigate violent behavior; (c) cognitive and physical capability of following through on violent intentions (e.g., availability of weapons);

and (d) protective factors in place within and outside the school to prevent the violence (Jacob & Hartshorne, 2007; Reddy et al., 2001).

Privileged Communications, Subpoenas, and Court Orders. In treatment and assessment contexts, the ethical responsibility to maintain or disclose confidential information belongs to the psychologist, but in legal settings, this information is classified as "privileged communications," and the decision to maintain or disclose such information rests with the client/patient or his or her legal guardian. There are exceptions. Therapeutic communications are often not privileged when clients/patients decide to make their mental health part of litigation or when the court has ordered psychological examinations, civil commitment hearings, or custody cases.

Practicing psychologists need to be knowledgeable about how to ethically and legally respond to subpoenas or compelled testimony for client records or test data (APA Committee on Legal Issues, 2006). A subpoena is issued by an attorney instructing the psychologist to provide documents or appear for oral testimony. Psychologists are required to respond to a subpoena, but when the subpoena asks for "privileged communications," psychologists cannot release confidential information without a signed client/patient release or authorization. If no release is forthcoming, psychologists should advise the requesting party that they are waiting for further instruction from the presiding judge (Bennett et al., 2006). A court order to provide documents or oral testimony is issued by a presiding judge, who has the power to waive client/patient privilege and legally require that mental health records be released. A court order does not preclude psychologists from communicating to the judge their confidentiality obligations and requesting limitations on the information released (see Standard 1.02, Conflicts Between Ethics and Law, Regulations, or Other Governing Legal Authority). If such requests are denied, Standard 4.05b permits psychologists to disclose records requested.

Disclosures Permitted by Law

Standard 4.05b also permits psychologists to disclose confidential information without consent if such disclosures are permitted by law *and* the disclosure is for a valid purpose. Valid purposes include those initiated to provide needed professional services; obtain appropriate professional consultation; protect the client/patient, psychologist, or others from harm; or obtain payment for services.

> ☑ It is ethically appropriate to disclose personally identifiable confidential information to another professional or family member if such notification is required to hospitalize or otherwise protect clients/patients, research participants, students, or others who have indicated credible suicidal intent or who psychologists believe to be engaged in activities that are likely to result in imminent and substantial harm.
>
> ☑ Irrespective of whether the jurisdiction in which a psychologist works has a duty-to-protect law, Standard 4.05b permits psychologists to disclose confidential information obtained by clients/patients or research participants to protect others from harm.

☑ Psychologists are permitted to report to appropriate law enforcement agencies credible threats to their welfare or to the welfare of their family or colleagues made by clients/patients, students, research participants, or others with whom they work.

☑ When a client/patient or organizational client fails to pay for a psychologist's services, the psychologist may disclose information to a bill collection agency to obtain payment. The information must be limited to the individual's or organization's name, contact information, amount of payments still outstanding, number of sessions or billable hours for which payment is due, and other factual information necessary to collect outstanding funds. Psychologists should not disclose to bill collection agencies a client's/patient's diagnosis, the nature of treatment, or other personal information. Nor should they disclose the purpose or nature of their work for a company or organization (see also Standard 6.04e, Fees and Financial Arrangements).

☑ In most states, school psychologists do not have a legal obligation to report student substance abuse or criminal acts committed by students or their parents that do not involve child abuse. However, disclosure of such information to parents or others in authority is permissible under Standard 4.05b and, in most cases, legally permissible (Jacob & Hartshorne, 2007).

☑ Military psychologists may disclose sensitive patient health information of military personnel without a client's/patient's signature for release to officers and employees in the DoD when the record is needed in the performance of their duties, such as referring military personnel for evaluation (see Jeffrey, Rankin, & Jeffrey, 1992).

Suicidal Intent. Under Standard 4.05b, psychologists are permitted to disclose confidential information to protect clients/patients from self-harm. Client/patient suicidality is a stressful experience for practitioners and a frequent cause of malpractice suits (Bennett et al., 2006). Good ethical practice in response to indications of suicidal intent requires (a) competence to recognize, manage, and treat suicidality (Standard 2.01, Boundaries of Competence); (b) identification of community resources for client/patient emergencies outside the treatment setting; (c) development of consultative relationships with other professionals (e.g., prescribing psychologists or psychiatrists) to assist in case management (Standard 3.09, Cooperation With Other Professionals); and (d) understanding of legal principles and institutional policies regarding voluntary or involuntary commitment.

Implications of HIPAA. Standard 4.05b is consistent with the HIPAA regulations under 45 CFR 164.512. The Privacy Rule permits disclosure of PHI without authorization (a) when required by law; (b) for public health activities such as for preventing or controlling disease, injury, or disability; (c) for individuals the covered entity reasonably believes to be a victim of abuse, neglect, or domestic violence; (d) for health oversight activities such as audits, criminal investigations, or licensure or disciplinary actions; (e) for judicial or administrative hearings; and (f) for activities deemed necessary by appropriate military command to ensure the proper execution of the military mission.

In some instances, HIPAA regulations may be more permissive of disclosure without client/patient consent than either state law or the Ethics Code. For example, HIPAA permits disclosure of information without consent for law enforcement purposes such as reporting wounds or other physical injuries, when issued a court-ordered subpoena, or when the information sought is relevant and material to a legitimate law enforcement inquiry. In such instances, psychologists should follow the Ethics Code as the more stringent standard.

4.06 Consultations

When consulting with colleagues, (1) psychologists do not disclose confidential information that reasonably could lead to the identification of a client/patient, research participant, or other person or organization with whom they have a confidential relationship unless they have obtained the prior consent of the person or organization or the disclosure cannot be avoided, and (2) they disclose information only to the extent necessary to achieve the purposes of the consultation. (See also Standard 4.01, Maintaining Confidentiality.)

Consultation with colleagues is an important means of ensuring and maintaining the competence of one's work and the ethical conduct of psychology. Standard 4.06 permits discussion of confidential information with colleagues without prior consent as long as the identity of the client/patient, research participant, organizational client, or other person with whom they have a confidential relationship can be adequately protected. In some instances, the obligation to provide the highest quality service or to address an ethical problem may require consultation that reveals a person's or organization's identity without prior consent. Standard 4.06 permits such actions only if the disclosure cannot be avoided and the psychologist only discloses information that is necessary to achieve the purposes of the consultation. The following is an example of how a psychologist might comply with this standard:

☑   A psychologist was hired by a bank to conduct crisis counseling for employees who had witnessed a recent armed robbery. During the course of counseling, the psychologist came across information suggesting that one of the employees helped plan the robbery. The psychologist consulted with a colleague and an attorney to help determine whether the psychologist was ethically or legally required to report this information to the company or law enforcement. Because the bank robbery had been highly publicized, the psychologist was unable to disguise the bank's identity. However, during each consultation, the psychologist took specific steps to avoid mentioning the gender, job title, or any other details about the employee in question that could lead to personal identification.

4.07 Use of Confidential Information for Didactic or Other Purposes

Psychologists do not disclose in their writings, lectures, or other public media, confidential, personally identifiable information concerning their clients/patients, students, research participants, organizational clients, or other recipients of their services that they obtained during the course of their work, unless (1) they take reasonable steps to disguise the person or organization, (2) the person or organization has consented in writing, or (3) there is legal authorization for doing so.

Professionals, students, and the public benefit when psychologists use case material and other examples from their scientific or professional work to illustrate knowledge, concepts, challenges, and techniques in psychology. Psychologists must guard against harms that can occur when such materials contain confidential, personally identifiable information disseminated without the permission of the client/patient, student, research participant, organizational client, or other service recipients. Material relevant to this standard must be both confidential (the information was shared with the psychologist under expectations that it would not be released to others) and personally identifiable (the identity of the specific person or organization described could be recognized by others).

Disguising Information. Psychologists are permitted to reveal confidential information if the person or organization has consented in writing or there is legal authorization for doing so, such as the material being authorized for release at a public hearing. When neither of these conditions is met, psychologists must take reasonable steps to adequately disguise the identity of the person or organization. When disguising information, simply using a pseudonym is often insufficient when other aspects of the case described contain details that make the individual or organization easily identifiable. Alterations in names and place should be distinct from the real names (e.g., do not use initials in creating a pseudonym). Psychologists should also consider changing the season or year of an event or modifying details of family composition and other social networks that are not essential to the didactic goal. Disguising information should not change characteristics critical to the phenomena being portrayed (VandenBos, 2001). For example, gender or ethnicity should not be changed if they play an important role in the services or research analyses described.

The term *reasonable steps* recognizes that sometimes, despite acceptable efforts to disguise information, an individual or organization might be recognized by others.

> ☑ A psychologist gave a public lecture on dream analysis that included a case example in which the occupation, family constellation, city of residence, and other patient characteristics were disguised. However, a friend of the patient in the audience was able to identify the patient because the patient had told the dream to her friend.

Privacy can also be violated when psychologists describe individuals living in small or distinct populations who can be readily identified by others in the community in which they live.

> ☒ A psychologist published ethnographic data on spiritual concerns, job stressors, and psychological distress facing gay and lesbian teachers working in religious schools. In the published report, the psychologist described the school where data were collected as a prestigious Catholic school affiliated with his university. The school was readily recognized by individuals who lived in the community, and many were able to correctly identify respondents from the specific narratives described in the report.

HOT TOPIC

Confidentiality and Involvement of Parents in Mental Health Services for Children and Adolescents

Involvement of parents is often a key factor in engaging children and adolescents in psychotherapy (Oetzel & Scherer, 2003; Weisz & Hawley, 2002). At the same time, establishing the boundaries of client/patient confidentiality is critical to establishing a trusting relationship among psychologist, child client/patient, and parents (Standard 4.01, Maintaining Confidentiality). While federal and state laws grant minors limited access to mental health services without guardian consent, they often permit (and sometimes require) parents to be involved in their child's treatment plan, provide parental access to treatment records, and permit disclosure of information to protect the child or others from harm (English & Kenney, 2003; Weithorn, 2006).

In making confidentiality and disclosure decisions, psychologists must consider practical issues such as the parent withdrawing the child from therapy for lack of access to information or children's misuse of confidentiality as a weapon in their conflict with parents. Psychologists working with children and adolescents thus need to anticipate and consistently reevaluate how they will balance confidentiality considerations with parental involvement in the child's best interests.

Establishing Confidentiality Limits at the Outset of Therapy

The nature of information that will be shared with parents should begin with a consideration of the child's cognitive and emotional maturity, presenting problem, treatment goals, and age-appropriate expectations regarding the role parents can play in facilitating treatment (D. J. Cohen & Cicchetti, 2006; Morris & Mather, 2007). For example, younger children's cognitive limitations and dependence on significant adults suggest that maintenance of strict confidentiality procedures may hinder treatment by failing to reflect the actual contexts in which children grow and develop. By contrast, increasing protection of private thoughts and feelings may facilitate treatment by demonstrating respect for older children's developing autonomy, comprehension of the nature and purpose of therapy, and ability to take a self-reflective perspective on their own thoughts and feelings (Hennan, Dornbusch, Herron, & Herting, 1997).

The Consent Conference

Engaging parents and children in discussion about the nature and rationale for confidentiality and disclosure policies is the first step to creating a trusting relationship. This can be accomplished during the consent conference when psychologists:

- explain their ethical and legal responsibilities, describe the benefits of confidentiality or information sharing relevant to the child's developmental status and treatment plan, and provide age-appropriate examples of the type of information that will and will not be confidential;
- obtain feedback from and address client's/patient's and parent's concerns; and
- tailor a confidentiality policy to the cultural and familial context in which information sharing is viewed by parent and child.

Parental Requests for Information

There will be times when parents request information the psychologist had not previously considered appropriate for disclosure. The first response should be to determine whether the parents' request relates to an issue that does not require confidentiality consideration. While parental demands should never supersede ethical, legal, and professional responsibilities to protect client/patient confidentiality, they should always be given the following respectful considerations (Fisher et al., 1999; Mitchell, Disque, & Robertson, 2002; L. Taylor & Adelman, 1989):

- Employ empathic listening skills and convey respect for parental concerns.
- Assume, unless there is information to the contrary, that parents' queries reflect a genuine concern about their child's welfare.
- Avoid turning parental requests for information into a power struggle among psychologist, parent, and client/patient.
- Guard against taking on the role of therapist or counselor to the parent (Standard 3.05, Multiple Relationships).
- Help the parent reframe confidentiality in terms of (a) the child's developing autonomy, (b) encouraging the child to share information with parents by choice rather than requirement, and (c) maintaining therapeutic trust.
- If appropriate, suggest the parent ask the child about the desired information or, with the parent's knowledge, explore with the child clinically indicated ways in which information might be shared.

Disclosing Confidential Information in Response to Client/Patient Risk Behavior

Psychologists working with children and adolescents often become aware of behaviors hidden from parents that place the child at some physical, psychological, or legal risk. Sexual activity, alcohol and drug use, gang involvement, truancy, and vandalism or theft are some of the "secret" activities that require consideration for the protection of others or whether confidentiality or disclosure is in the best therapeutic interests of the child (Standard 4.05, Disclosures).

For example, disclosures can lead to physical protections for a child who is beginning to show signs of an eating disorder or involvement in gang behavior through increased parental monitoring of behaviors in and outside the home. Alternatively, sharing such information with parents may damage the therapeutic alliance or place the child at greater risk if parental reactions can be predicted to be physically violent or emotionally abusive. For example, the consequences of disclosing to parents high-risk sexual activity of lesbian, gay, bisexual, transgendered, and questioning youth (LGBTQ) who have not discussed their sexual orientation with their parents are more complex and potentially more hazardous than would occur when disclosing information regarding a minor's heterosexual activities (Ginsberg et al., 2002; Lemoire & Chen, 2005).

Psychologists must also consider how entering into a secrecy pact with a minor client can adversely affect the therapeutic alliance and be wary when assuming that minor clients expect and desire confidentiality when they reveal during therapy that they are engaging in high-risk behaviors.

Steps to consider in deciding whether and how to disclose confidential information when clients/patients are engaging in high-risk behaviors include the following.

Step 1: Assess and Clinically Address Risk Behaviors

- Confirm that the child is actually engaging in the risk behavior and whether it is an isolated incident or a continuing pattern.
- Evaluate the danger of the behavior to the client/patient or others.
- Assess developmental, psychological, and situational factors that might impair the child's ability to terminate or reduce behaviors.
- Conduct intervention strategies to help the client/patient terminate or reduce risk levels of behavior.
- Monitor whether the client/patient has terminated or limited the behavior.

Step 2: Consider Options if Client/Patient Is Unable or Unwilling to Terminate or Reduce Behaviors

- Know federal and state laws on reporting requirements regarding prior or planned self-harming, illegal, or violent client/patient behavior.
- Weigh legal, therapeutic, social, and health consequences of confidentiality and disclosure for the client/patient.
- Anticipate, to the extent possible, parents' ability to appropriatly respond to disclosure.
- Consult with other professionals regarding alternatives to disclosure (Standard 3.09, Cooperation With Other Professionals).

Step 3: Prepare Client/Patient for Disclosure

- Frame the current need to disclose information in terms of the limits of confidentiality discussed during informed consent and the psychologist's responsibility to protect the welfare of the client/patient and others.
- Respond to the child's feelings and concerns while focusing discussion on the process of disclosure and not on ways to avoid it.
- Evaluate the client's/patient's willingness and ability to disclose information to parents.
- When appropriate, go over the steps that will be taken to share the information with parents and involve the client/patient as much as possible.

Step 4: Disclosing Information to Parents

- Involve the client/patient as much as clinically appropriate in the disclosure discussion.
- Focus on the positive actions parents can take to help their child and, whenever feasible, to place the child's actions within the context of continued treatment progress.
- Discuss additional treatment options such as joint parent-child or more frequent goal-setting sessions.

- Identify appropriate referral sources for parents to help them address their child's behaviors following disclosure.
- Empathize with and respond to the parent's feelings and concerns, and refer the parent to individual counseling if it appears necessary.
- Schedule one or more follow-up meetings with parents and clients/patients to monitor their reactions to the disclosure and the steps taken to reduce the risk behaviors and provide additional recommendations if necessary.
- If the risk increases or remains at dangerous levels, consider other therapeutic, community, and legal options.

CHAPTER 8

Standards on Advertising and Other Public Statements

5. ADVERTISING AND OTHER PUBLIC STATEMENTS

5.01 Avoidance of False or Deceptive Statements

(a) Public statements include but are not limited to paid or unpaid advertising, product endorsements, grant applications, licensing applications, other credentialing applications, brochures, printed matter, directory listings, personal resumes or curricula vitae, or comments for use in media such as print or electronic transmission, statements in legal proceedings, lectures and public oral presentations, and published materials. Psychologists do not knowingly make public statements that are false, deceptive, or fraudulent concerning their research, practice, or other work activities or those of persons or organizations with which they are affiliated.

Psychologists aspire to promote accuracy, honesty, and truthfulness in the science, teaching, and practice of psychology and do not engage in subterfuge or intentional misrepresentation of fact (Principle C: Integrity). Standard 5.01a of the American Psychological Association (APA) Ethics Code (APA, 2002b) prohibits false, deceptive, or fraudulent public statements regarding work activities or the activities of persons or organizations with which psychologists are affiliated.

The terms *avoidance* and *knowingly* exclude as violations statements that psychologists would reasonably be expected to believe are true but that they may later learn are false.

> ☑ A psychologist in a group practice distributed brochures with a listing of the group members' credentials, only to discover that one member had submitted false credentials. She ceased distribution and ordered a corrected brochure.
>
> ☑ A research psychologist gave a public lecture, a series of media interviews, and congressional testimony during which he publicly concluded that empirical evidence supported a particular policy initiative. Six months later, the release of results from a large federally funded study challenged those conclusions.

Definition of Public Statements. This standard begins with a definition of public statements. This definition applies to the use of the term *public statement* or *statement* in all standards under Section 5, Advertising and Other Public Statements. The definition refers only to statements made in the public domain. It does not apply to statements made during private professional or personal conversations with clients/patients, organizational clients, attorneys, students, colleagues, or others with whom psychologists have a professional or personal relationship.

The following are the types of statements included in this definition along with examples of false or deceptive statements that would be in violation of this standard:

> ☒ *Paid or unpaid advertising or product endorsements.* A toy company paid a school psychologist for her endorsement stating the proven effectiveness of a tape-recorded language lesson for infants that would improve reading comprehension in elementary school. There was no empirical evidence supporting this claim.
>
> ☒ *Licensing, grant applications, and other credentialing applications.* In the Preliminary Studies section of a federal grant application, an experimental psychologist listed as completed a pilot study that was still in the data collection phase.
>
> ☒ *Directory listings, personal resumes, or curricula vitae.* A psychologist with a Ph.D. in social psychology and no specialized clinical or other practice-oriented postdoctoral training listed herself in the city directory under health care providers.
>
> ☒ *Comments for use in print, electronic, or other media.* In a television interview, a psychology professor who had an academic freedom suit against his university claimed that the university refused to allow any faculty to teach courses that include discussion of human sexuality when in fact the university catalogue listed several such courses.
>
> ☒ *Statements in legal proceedings, lectures, public oral presentations, and published materials.* An industrial-organizational psychologist was hired as an expert witness by an attorney for a large retailing firm accused of discriminatory hiring practices. She testified that data on the firm's hiring of women and ethnic minority applicants were not significantly different from national data on employment practices in similar companies, despite the fact that she had not examined any of the firm's actual employment data. See the Hot Topic at the end of this chapter on "Avoiding False and Deceptive Statements in Scientific and Clinical Expert Testimony."

(b) Psychologists do not make false, deceptive, or fraudulent statements concerning (1) their train-ing, experience, or competence; (2) their academic degrees; (3) their credentials; (4) their institu-tional or association affiliations; (5) their services; (6) the scientific or clinical basis for, or results or degree of success of, their services; (7) their fees; or (8) their publications or research findings.

In contrast to Standard 5.01a, 5.01b does not include the term *knowingly* because it is assumed that psychologists would have sufficient information about the facts listed to avoid false, deceptive, or fraudulent statements.

The following are examples of violations of the eight types of statements listed under Standard 5.01b.

☒ *Training, experience, or competence.* A clinical psychologist applying to the American Board of Professional Psychology (ABPP) for diplomate status in clinical neuropsychology falsely claimed he had received specialized training in neuropsy-chology during his postdoctoral internship.

☒ *Credentials.* On a professional liability insurance application, a psychologist stated that she had obtained substance abuse certification from the APA College of Professional Psychology when in fact she only attended a workshop on substance abuse treatment at an APA meeting.

☒ *Institutional or association affiliations.* A psychologist in independent practice who rented office space from a university created a letterhead on his stationery that sug-gested he was affiliated with the institution.

☒ *Services.* A psychology group practice Web site listed family therapy as one of the services offered, even though the only psychologist offering this service had left the group more than a year ago.

☒ *Scientific or clinical basis for, or results or degree of success of, their services.* A behavioral psychologist running a weight loss program for obese adolescents stated in the program brochure that "99% of clients maintain their weight loss after they leave the program." The statement did not include the fact that for most of these clients, the maintenance of weight loss lasted for less than 3 weeks.

☒ *Brochures and printed matter.* A consulting psychologist distributed brochures to personnel departments of banks in major cities stating that he had developed a fool-proof psychological technique for preemployment integrity screening to weed out applicants who were prone to dishonesty. The claim was based on undocumented consultations conducted by the psychologist over several years.

☒ *Fees.* A child clinical psychologist presented a talk on childhood disorders at a parents' association meeting. After the talk, she handed out printed information about her practice that stated that she offered all clients a sliding scale of fees beginning at $40 a session. The handout did not mention that the $40 rate was only for clients specifically referred by the health maintenance organization with which the psychologist had a contract.

> ☒   *Publications or research findings.* A school psychologist on the faculty of a large university received a grant from an educational services company. The purpose of the funded project was to compare student academic achievement in city-administered public schools with those run by the educational services company. Data from schools in the eight cities studied indicated significant differences in favor of the city-run schools in two cities, in favor of the company-run schools in two cities, and no significant differences in the other four school districts. The psychologist published only data from the two cities in which a positive effect of company-contracted schools was found and suggested in the conclusion of the article that these results could be generalized to other cities (see also Standard 3.06, Conflict of Interest).

Comparative statements regarding the desirability of one type of service over another are not prohibited *if* there is substantial evidence to support the claim (Shead & Dobson, 2004; Standard 2.04, Bases for Scientific and Professional Judgments).

Web-Based Services. Potentially deceptive Web-based advertisements and claims regarding Internet-based mental health services risk violating Standard 5.01b. In their survey of e-therapy Web sites, Heinlen et al. (2003) found substantial gaps in ethical compliance, including (a) failure to inform consumers that the psychologist's license to provide mental health services online might be restricted by state law; (b) unsupported statements disparaging face-to-face therapies in comparison to online services; (c) descriptions of psychoeducational Web-based services that could lead consumers to believe they would receive individualized counseling, assessment, or therapeutic services; and (d) failure to clarify the boundaries of the psychologist's competence to provide services across a broad spectrum of psychological disorders.

> ☒   A psychologist developed a Web-based service for parents of children with behavioral problems at "www.parent-therapy-online.com." Parents could pay $25 to e-mail a specific question about how to help their child that was answered within 24 hours by one of eight psychologists identified on the Web site as "child experts who will provide therapeutic advice personalized to each request." In actuality, the "personal" e-mail responses provided prewritten general statements about behavioral child management techniques. In small print at the bottom of the Web page appeared the following statement: "*The information provided on this Web site is for educational purposes and does not constitute treatment.*"

(c) Psychologists claim degrees as credentials for their health services only if those degrees (1) were earned from a regionally accredited educational institution or (2) were the basis for psychology licensure by the state in which they practice.

Standard 5.01c applies only to psychologists who are claiming degrees or credentials as evidence of their competence to provide health services. Unlike Standard 5.01b, this standard is not directed at whether a psychologist actually obtained the degree but whether the degree can be claimed as a basis for offering therapy or diagnostic or other types of health services.

Psychologists may refer to only two types of degrees as evidence of education and training in the field of psychology that qualifies them as a health service provider. The first type is a degree in psychology (e.g., Ph.D., Ed.D., or Psy.D.) earned from a regionally accredited educational institution (e.g., the Commission on Higher Education of the Middle States Association of Colleges and Schools). The second type of degree is from a program in a nonaccredited institution, whose curriculum and training experiences have been approved by the state in which the psychologist practices as qualifying him or her for eligibility for licensure in psychology.

A psychologist who claims a degree as a credential for health services that does not meet the above criteria would be in violation of this standard:

> ☒ An individual licensed as a social worker in his state acquired a Ph.D. in counseling psychology from a nonaccredited university. He was unable to obtain licensure in psychology because the state in which he practices did not recognize his doctoral training as a basis for licensure in psychology. His business cards and professional letterhead included a Ph.D. after his name, the title Counseling Psychologist, and his social work licensure ID number. The letterhead did not indicate that his license was in social work and not psychology.
>
> ☒ On her personnel curriculum vitae, a psychologist claimed she had received her Ph.D. from an accredited university, when her actual degree was from an unaccredited school to which she had transferred.

5.02 Statements by Others

(a) Psychologists who engage others to create or place public statements that promote their professional practice, products, or activities retain professional responsibility for such statements.

Psychologists retain professional responsibility for false, deceptive, or fraudulent public statements by others whom they have engaged to promote their work or products. Failure to prevent or to correct such misstatements is a violation of Standard 5.02.

> ☑ A psychologist viewed the Web site of the company that was publishing a book she had just completed. She was surprised and pleased to see the company had started advertising the book as "forthcoming." She then noticed that she was wrongly listed on the Web site as Professor of Psychology at a university where she had taught as an adjunct several years ago. She called her editor at the company to notify him of

> the error and to ask him to take steps to correct the Web site. She followed up with a letter to him reiterating this request and carbon copied the chair of the psychology department at the university mentioned.
>
> ☒ A psychologist developed a program that enabled other psychologists to score a popular psychological test on their computers. The psychologist had not yet completed complementary software that would provide narrative interpretations of the scores. The marketing staff at the distribution company he contracted with to sell his product advised him that the scoring software would sell better if it was advertised as providing both scoring and interpretation. They argued that even though this was not currently true, because he was already working on the new program, eventually those who bought the original software would be able to use the complementary software for narrative interpretations. The psychologist agreed to the misleading advertisement.

(b) Psychologists do not compensate employees of press, radio, television, or other communication media in return for publicity in a news item. (See also Standard 1.01, Misuse of Psychologists' Work.)

Standard 5.02b underscores psychologists' obligations to avoid actions that might encourage others to make false or fraudulent statements about their work. This standard prohibits psychologists from paying or otherwise compensating members of the media in return for news coverage of their work. The use of the term *compensate* rather than *pay* means that psychologists who give nonmonetary gifts or pay for expensive dinners for journalists or others in the media in return for publicity in a news item may be considered in violation of this standard.

(c) A paid advertisement relating to psychologists' activities must be identified or clearly recognizable as such.

Standard 5.02c permits psychologists to run paid advertisements describing their services, publications, products, or other aspects of their work, as long as it is stated or otherwise clear to consumers that it is a paid advertisement. The standard applies to advertisements on the Internet, in print, or in other media. "Canned columns" are an example of a paid advertisement that often is presented in a way that can be deceptive to consumers. Canned columns written and paid for by psychologists are typically presented in news or advice column format intended to lead readers to believe that the psychologist has been invited or hired by the magazine or other media outlet to write the column because of his or her expertise. The "column" usually includes a description of the psychologist's services, the psychologist's picture, and contact information. Canned columns that do not include a clear statement that the column is a "paid advertisement" are in violation of this standard. In some instances, psychologists do not write the column themselves but purchase it from a writer who sells columns to psychologists nationwide. In such instances, the column must state that the psychologist is providing but has not written the column (see also Standard 5.01a, Avoidance of False or Deceptive Statements).

5.03 Descriptions of Workshops and Non-Degree-Granting Educational Programs

To the degree to which they exercise control, psychologists responsible for announcements, catalogs, brochures, or advertisements describing workshops, seminars, or other non-degree-granting educational programs ensure that they accurately describe the audience for which the program is intended, the educational objectives, the presenters, and the fees involved.

Standard 5.03 applies to workshops, seminars, and non-degree-granting educational programs that are not part of the established degree-granting education and training programs covered under Standard 7.02, Descriptions of Education and Training Programs. Psychologists who offer non-degree-granting programs are responsible for ensuring the accuracy of announcements, catalogs, brochures, or advertisements appearing in print, the Internet, or other media. Announcements must clearly specify the intended audience, educational objectives, presenters, and fees. The phrase "to the degree to which they exercise control" is included in the standard in acknowledgment that despite a psychologist's best efforts to control and monitor the process, errors or misrepresentations by others may occur during the production and distribution of materials. Psychologists should take reasonable steps to correct these errors.

☒ Registration for a 1-day workshop on projective assessment techniques given by a well-known psychologist was advertised in several psychology journals and newsletters. Individuals paid in advance to reserve a seat in the course. Registration money could be partially refunded up to 2 days prior to the workshop. Several registrants who arrived to take the workshop were surprised to learn that although they were permitted to attend, they would not be given a certificate of completion because they were not licensed psychologists. The registrants complained that the advertisement had not mentioned that a license was required to receive the certificate and asked for their money back. Stating the cancellation policy, the psychologist refused to return the fees.

☒ A psychologist offered a seminar on child abuse identification and reporting that was advertised as fulfilling the state licensing board requirement for child abuse reporting training. Attendees who later submitted their seminar completion certificate to the state board were told that the curriculum did not satisfy the state's educational requirement.

☒ A group of psychologists offered an 8-week certificate program on drug addictions counseling. Advertisements for the seminar listed the fee as $1,000. During the last week of the program, attendees were told that those who wished to obtain an official certificate documenting their participation must pay an additional $100.

Industry-Sponsored Workshops

The pharmaceutical industry has become a primary sponsor of continuing medical education because sponsors have found that it is a tool for influencing audiences to use their products (Pachter et al., 2007). Psychologists conducting industry-sponsored continuing education programs must ensure that the teaching materials are not biased toward the marketing interests of the sponsor (see also Standard 3.06, Conflict of Interest).

5.04 Media Presentations

When psychologists provide public advice or comment via print, Internet, or other electronic transmission, they take precautions to ensure that statements (1) are based on their professional knowledge, training, or experience in accord with appropriate psychological literature and practice; (2) are otherwise consistent with this Ethics Code; and (3) do not indicate that a professional relationship has been established with the recipient. (See also Standard 2.04, Bases for Scientific and Professional Judgments.)

Standard 5.04 applies to psychologists who issue public advice or comment via print, Internet, television, radio, or other media. The standard does not apply to comments made to individuals with whom psychologists have an established professional relationship, such as an Internet communication or videoconferencing with a client/patient, student, colleague, or organizational client.

Competence and Bases for Judgments. This standard prohibits psychologists from giving public advice or comment on the radio, in print media, on television, on the Internet, or other forms of communication on topics and issues that are outside the boundaries of their competence based on their education, training, supervised experience, or other accepted means of acquiring professional or scientific expertise (see Standard 2.01a, Boundaries of Competence). The standard also prohibits psychologists from giving public comment or advice that significantly deviates from or is otherwise inconsistent with established psychological literature and practice (see Standard 2.04, Bases for Scientific and Professional Judgments).

> ☒ A comparative psychologist who had spent her career specializing in language in primates appeared on several talk shows providing public advice on how parents could identify and correct child language disorders.
>
> ☒ In a television interview, a counseling psychologist advised college students to follow his 10-step cure for test anxiety. The steps included drinking green tea, taking vitamin supplements, studying in groups, and other recommendations not in accord with recent research or established counseling techniques for test anxiety.

Otherwise Consistent With the Ethics Code. Public comment or advice through the media or the Internet must be in compliance with all relevant standards of the Ethics Code.

> ☒ After speaking with a listener for 3 minutes on a live radio talk show, a psychologist stated over the air that the listener showed definite signs of obsessive-compulsive disorder. Before going to a commercial break, the psychologist asked the listener to stay on the line "for a referral to a health care professional who can help you with this serious disorder" (violation of Standards 9.01a and b, Bases for Assessments).
>
> ☒ A developmental psychologist created a Web site on which he provided critiques and recommendations for age-appropriate children's products. The Web site did not include a statement informing visitors to the site that the psychologist was on the board of directors of a company whose toys he regularly reviewed favorably (violation of Standard 3.06, Conflict of Interest).

Do Not Indicate a Professional Relationship Has Been Established. Psychologists providing public advice in response to questions over the radio, on television, on the Internet, or in published advice columns should clarify the educative versus therapeutic nature of their answers, avoid language that implies personal knowledge about the person asking the question, and take steps to avoid repeat communications with the person that may encourage the mistaken impression that a professional relationship has been established.

> ☒ A group of psychologists established a psychology advice e-mail service. The group's Web site included each participating psychologist's credentials and picture. The Web site described the service as one that provides advice for people suffering from "social anxiety." Individuals were charged by credit card for an answer to each e-mail question they submitted. The site specifically stated that the service was not therapy. However, the psychologists' answers were written in a very individualized and personal manner rather than in broad educative statements, and individuals were encouraged to identify the psychologist they would like to answer their question. There was no limit to the number of questions that could be submitted, and some clients submitted daily questions to the same psychologist over several weeks or even months (see D. E. Shapiro & Schulman, 1996, for an excellent discussion of such a case and related issues).

5.05 Testimonials

Psychologists do not solicit testimonials from current therapy clients/patients or other persons who because of their particular circumstances are vulnerable to undue influence.

Psychologists are prohibited from asking individuals who are vulnerable to undue influence to provide commercial statements testifying to the benefits of the psychologist's services. Standard 5.05 specifically prohibits solicitation of testimonials from clients/patients currently in therapy with the psychologist. Clients/patients are particularly vulnerable to exploitation by a psychologist who seeks their public testimonials because of power inequities between the therapist and client/patient, the psychological problems that brought clients/patients to therapy, the sharing of personal thoughts and feelings in therapy, and dependence on the psychologist for treatment.

> ☒   A psychologist used testimonials from current clients on a Web site advertising his Internet-based counseling services.

Parents of children with learning disabilities, who depend on a school psychologist's yearly evaluation to qualify for special education services for their children, might, because of their particular circumstances, be considered vulnerable to undue influence to offer testimonials for the psychologist. Family members in therapy with a psychologist for court-ordered treatment might also be considered vulnerable to threat or exploitation if approached to give a testimonial.

The standard does not prohibit unsolicited testimonials or the solicitation of testimonials from former clients/patients who are not vulnerable. However, psychologists should be cautious about approaching former therapy clients/patients who may be vulnerable to undue influence based on their mental status, the duration and intensity of the therapy, the circumstances of termination, the amount of time that has passed since termination, or comments that the psychologist might have made during therapy inviting the possibility of a posttermination testimonial.

5.06 In-Person Solicitation

Psychologists do not engage, directly or through agents, in uninvited in-person solicitation of business from actual or potential therapy clients/patients or other persons who, because of their particular circumstances, are vulnerable to undue influence. However, this prohibition does not preclude (1) attempting to implement appropriate collateral contacts for the purpose of benefiting an already engaged therapy client/patient or (2) providing disaster or community outreach services.

Standard 5.06 prohibits psychologists from soliciting business from individuals who, because of their particular circumstance, are vulnerable to undue influence. The standard addresses business solicitation behaviors often characterized as "ambulance chasing." Individuals who are current or potential therapy clients/patients are specifically identified as vulnerable in this standard. Others who may be vulnerable to undue influence are individuals whose loved one has just committed suicide or a person who is abusing drugs or alcohol. Psychologists are prohibited from approaching these individuals either directly or through another person to solicit business if the psychologist has not been invited by the individual or a legally authorized representative to do so.

Although not explicitly prohibited in the language of Standard 5.06, psychologists should be wary of public statements, brochures, and Web-based or other descriptions of services that are intended to exploit populations vulnerable to undue influence by generating fear and anxiety (Shead & Dobson, 2004).

> ☒ A clinical child psychologist sought to generate clients by speaking to breast cancer survivor support groups about "serious psychological disorders of childhood" that "often" emerge in children as a reaction to maternal illness.

Permitted Behaviors

The standard does not prohibit psychologists from establishing a professional relationship with persons in therapy with another professional or otherwise vulnerable to undue influence if the person approaches the psychologist for services (see also Standard 10.04, Providing Therapy to Those Served by Others).

Collateral Treatment. The standard does not preclude psychologists from approaching a family member or significant other to invite them to participate in collateral treatment to benefit a client/patient with whom a psychologist has a professional relationship.

> ☑ A psychologist treating an adult woman for bulimia, with the patient's permission, invited her husband to participate in family therapy sessions where the focus was on the woman's health. Whether the husband was currently in therapy with another professional was not an issue because the reason he had been approached was to participate in therapy where the wife was the identified patient (see also Standard 10.02a, Therapy Involving Couples or Families).

Disaster and Community Outreach. The standard also explicitly permits psychologists to approach individuals to provide disaster or community outreach services. Psychologists may offer emergency services to individuals who are distraught or otherwise vulnerable as a result of a natural or other type of disaster. Within the mental health and aging field, it is generally recognized that older adults may not spontaneously self-refer for mental health services. A variety of outreach activities have been used in public and private services for older adults that involve approaching persons who are not thinking of seeking psychological interventions, educating them about the benefits of mental health intervention, and encouraging them to seek such help. Such outreach is permissible under Standard 5.06.

HOT TOPIC

Avoiding False and Deceptive Statements in Scientific and Clinical Expert Testimony

When research and professional psychologists provide oral testimony or prepare written reports for legal proceedings conducted in the public domain, they are engaging in public statements as defined under Standard 5.01a, Avoidance of False or Deceptive Statements, of the APA Ethics Code. As articulated in Principle C: Integrity, psychologists seek to promote accuracy, honesty, and truthfulness in the science and practice of psychology. When forensically relevant statements or reports misrepresent facts through commission or omission, psychologists can be in violation of Standard 5.01a. False, deceptive, or fraudulent statements most often emerge in legal contexts when psychologists lose their objectivity as a consequence of misunderstanding the psychologist's role, conflicts of interest, or susceptibility to attorney influences. This Hot Topic identifies and suggests preventive actions to avoid these ethical pitfalls.

Navigating Relationships With Attorneys

Engagement in the legal system thrusts psychologists into dynamic relationships with attorneys whose role obligations will sometimes converge and often conflict with the ethical responsibilities of psychologists.

Understanding Distinctive Roles. The rules embedded within constitutional, civil, and criminal law ensure that justice is served by protecting the rights of each party in a dispute to control what information will be placed into evidence and debate its legal merits. The primary responsibility of attorneys is therefore to advocate on behalf of their client and ensure the party they represent has presented the best case possible before the court.

By contrast, in the legal context, the primary responsibility of psychologists serving as expert witnesses is to provide the triers of fact (e.g., the judge, jury, administrative hearing officer) with the information they need to make determinations about the legal question at hand. The primary responsibility of psychologists providing opinions to the court is therefore to advocate for the facts and not for the legal position advanced by either of the disputing parties (Melton, 1990). The objectivity necessary to advocate for the facts can be compromised when psychologists' legal opinions are influenced by pressure from the retaining attorney.

Establishing Boundaries. Prior to trial, the retaining attorney may pressure the psychologist to provide an opinion that goes beyond or is unsupported by the scientific or clinical data. Anticipating this possibility provides the psychologist with the opportunity to establish boundaries between the expert's objective role and the attorney's advocacy role (Bush et al., 2006).

Initial conversations with the retaining attorney should clarify the boundaries of competence within which the psychologist will testify (Standard 2.01f, Boundaries of Competence). Psychologists should also clarify their obligation to offer an honest opinion based on available facts (Principle C: Integrity). Shuman and Greenberg (2003) recommend the initial conversation be followed up with a retaining letter from the attorney documenting the issues on which the psychologist will be asked to testify.

Avoiding Bias in the Collection and Interpretation of Forensic Data

In the legal context, biased expert testimony can cause significant harm to the legal system and its stakeholders if it misleads the triers of fact into unfounded legal determinations (Principle A: Beneficence and Nonmaleficence; Standard 3.04, Avoiding Harm).

Inferential Bias. Data collection and interpretation biases can result in misdiagnosis, selective data collection, inaccurate and misleading expert reports, and fraudulent or deceptive statements in court (Deidan & Bush, 2002).

The following behaviors should be avoided:

- Seeking out information to confirm the litigant's argument or the psychologist's own theoretical or personal view (Bush et al., 2006; Shuman & Greenberg, 2003; Stern, 2001)
- Overreliance on diagnoses with which the psychologist is most familiar
- Over- or underattribution of behaviors to situational versus stable personal characteristics
- Preconceptions or initial impressions resistant to challenge by conflicting data
- Reliance on reconstructive memory to fill in gaps in evidence or failure to adequately record facts that arise during evidence collection (Deidan & Bush, 2002; Otto & Martindale, 2007)

Strategies to reduce the potential for such biases include the following:

- Generating alternative hypotheses (Bush et al., 2006)
- Using comprehensive batteries for forensic assessments
- Carefully recording all facts uncovered during pretrial data collection
- Examining which facts support and challenge initial impressions or preconceptions (Deidan & Bush, 2002)
- Guarding against assumptions that the attorney has provided all relevant facts and asking for pleadings and legal memorandums and competing perspectives of stakeholders in the legal case at hand (Saks & Lanyon, 2007; Shuman & Greenberg, 2003)

Resisting Requests to Alter Reports. Irrespective of the format in which the expert's opinion will be provided, psychologists are ethically required to maintain accurate records of their work for the period of time in which it may be needed to ensure the accuracy of their testimony (Standard 6.01, Documentation of Professional and Scientific Work and Maintenance of Records).

In their advocacy role, retaining attorneys may ask psychologists to modify their report in ways that bias information or opinion in favor of their client. Compliance with Standard 5.01a, Avoidance of False or Deceptive Statements, requires that psychologists deny such requests. If an attorney's suggestion represents a valid factual correction, the correction should either be presented in an amendment to the original document or be included in a clearly identified revision of the report with a written rationale for the modification (Bush et al., 2006).

Acknowledging the Limitations of Data or Conclusions. Psychologists should always anchor their scientific opinions to available empirical data and their clinical opinions to collected data. False or deceptive statements emerge in forensic testimony or reports when psychologists fail to adequately indicate limits to the certainty with which clinical data or research findings can diagnose or predict conclusions drawn about individuals (Standards 5.01a, Avoidance of False or Deceptive Statements; 9.06, Interpreting Assessment Results).

Misuse of Psychologists' Work. Attorneys will often attempt to control the nature of oral testimony to omit facts that would hurt their case or inaccurately represent the psychologist's statements to support their client's case. To take reasonable steps to correct the misrepresentation of their work, psychologists who provide expert testimony must be familiar with the judicial rules governing their ability to correct misstatements regarding their testimony (Standards 1.01, Misuse of Psychologists' Work; 2.01f, Boundaries of Competence).

For example, attorneys often attempt to limit expert's comments to "yes/no" responses. Psychologists should be aware that some jurisdictions provide expert witnesses greater leeway than other witnesses in requesting court permission to qualify their statements when they believe attorney questioning has created confusion or misrepresentation of their opinion. Another strategy for limiting attorneys' ability to misrepresent their findings is for psychologists to avoid declarative oral or written statements that do not reflect the balancing of facts that contributed to their opinion.

Maintaining Objectivity and Avoiding Bias: The Importance of Self-Evaluation

Prior to agreeing to serve as an expert witness, psychologists are encouraged to engage in the following forms of self-inquiry regarding possible biases that might lead to false or deceptive testimony (Bush et al., 2006; Fisher, 1995; Gutheil & Simon, 2004; Saks & Lanyon, 2007):

Conflicts of Interest

- Will financial interests influence my willingness to go beyond my expertise or the facts to give opinions supporting the attorney's case?

- Am I tempted to sell my testimony for monetary gains?

- Am I fearful an objective opinion will deter the attorney from hiring me in the future?

- Am I being sought because of a reputation for providing opinions consistently favoring the retaining party?

Personal and Professional Bias

- Have I already determined the nature of the testimony I will provide based on the attorney's initial description of the case?

- Am I unduly influenced by sympathy for the plaintiff or defendant?

- Does the case touch upon a personal issue?

- Will I use my testimony to advocate for a cause I believe in?

- Will moral, religious, political, or other biases intrude upon my ability to present all sides of the issue?

Multiple Relationships

- Do I have a special relationship with the attorney or the attorney's client that would impair my objectivity?

- Do I know the attorney or litigant socially?

- To what degree will these relationships place pressure on me to change my opinion if it is in conflict with the litigant's legal argument?

CHAPTER 9

Standards on Record Keeping and Fees

6. RECORD KEEPING AND FEES

6.01 Documentation of Professional and Scientific Work and Maintenance of Records

Psychologists create, and to the extent the records are under their control, maintain, disseminate, store, retain, and dispose of records and data relating to their professional and scientific work in order to (1) facilitate provision of services later by them or by other professionals, (2) allow for replication of research design and analyses, (3) meet institutional requirements, (4) ensure accuracy of billing and payments, and (5) ensure compliance with law. (See also Standard 4.01, Maintaining Confidentiality.)

In appropriately documenting and maintaining records, psychologists benefit those with whom they work (Principle A: Beneficence and Nonmaleficence) and fulfill their responsibilities to society and the specific organizations and communities in which they work (Principle B: Fidelity and Responsibility). Responsible creation and maintenance of assessment and treatment records benefit clients/patients by ensuring continuity of services provided by the individual psychologist and other qualified professionals. Scientific records provide the necessary information required for replication of research and peer, sponsor, and institutional review board (IRB) evaluation of methodological modifications that may be required. Appropriate record keeping by industrial-organizational and consulting psychologists assists organizations in maintaining and improving work performance and in ensuring compliance with relevant regulations and law. Record keeping also benefits psychologists by providing documentation of appropriate planning, implementation, evaluation, and modifications of services or research. Good record keeping will also include documentation of ethical, scientific, or practice decision making that can assist in effectively responding to ethics complaints.

Under Standard 6.01 of the American Psychological Association (APA) Ethics Code (APA, 2002b), psychologists must create, maintain, disseminate, store, retain, and dispose of records and data in a manner that enables the records to be used effectively and appropriately by the psychologist or others and to benefit those with whom the psychologist works. Steps necessary to comply with this standard will vary with the purpose of the psychological activity and applicable state and federal regulations and institutional policies. The standard applies to written reports, computer files, audio- and videotapes, and reports in any other media in which information can be created and stored. Creating or maintaining records that are disorganized, illegible to others, or have not been appropriately updated would be a violation of this standard. The phrase "to the extent the records are under their control" recognizes that psychologists may have limited or no control over records once they are appropriately released to third parties or when they are the property of an organization, company, institution, or government agency for which a psychologist works or consults (see also Standards 1.01, Misuse of Psychologists' Work; 1.03, Conflicts Between Ethics and Organizational Demands; and 3.06, Conflict of Interest).

Records for Mental Health Services

According to the Record Keeping Guidelines developed by the APA Committee on Professional Practice and Standards, Board of Professional Affairs (APA, 2007c), the level of detail and adequacy of content included in records is determined by the information necessary to "(a) provide good care, (b) assist collaborating professionals in delivery of care, (c) ensure continuity of services in the case of a psychologist's injury, disability, or death or with a change of provider; (d) provide for relevant supervision or training; (e) provide documentation required for reimbursement or required administratively under contracts or laws; (f) effectively document any decision making, especially in high-risk situations; and (g) allow the psychologist to effectively answer a legal or regulatory complaint" (p. 995).

The guidelines specify the types of information that psychologists should consider always, including in records of psychological services:

Information for the client's ongoing file

Identifying data and contact information

Fees and billing arrangements

Guardianship status, if appropriate

Informed consent/assent and any waivers of confidentiality

Mandated reporting, if relevant

Diagnosis or basis for request for services

Treatment plan (updated as appropriate)

The guidelines also recommend the type of information that should be recorded for each substantive contact with clients:

Date of service and session duration

Type of service (e.g., consultation, assessment, treatment)

Nature of professional intervention (e.g., modality)

Nature of professional contact (e.g., in-person, e-mail, phone)

Current assessment (formal or informal) of client/patient status

It may be necessary to record additional information depending on the circumstances and client needs. For example, it is often wise for practicing psychologists to note in their records unexpected contacts with clients/patients outside of the office or by phone or Internet. As described in greater detail in Chapter 6, Standard 3.05, Multiple Relationships, such records are often helpful in understanding clients'/patients' misperceptions about the therapeutic relationship or responding to ethics complaints based on misperceptions. Emergency interventions, including contacts with other professionals, family members, partners, or others to ensure adequate services or protect client/patient welfare, should also be included.

Multiple Client Records. Psychologists providing couple, family, or group therapy must be alert to issues that may arise when keeping multiple client records. For example, following marital dissolution, it may be unclear who should have access to records created during couples or family therapy. Points for consideration for multiple client records highlighted by the Record Keeping Guidelines (APA, 2007c) include (a) whether the identified client is the couple/family unit or each individual, (b) legal requirements and implications for creating separate or a single joint record, and (c) agreement of all concerned on the record-keeping policy during informed consent (see also Standards 3.10, Informed Consent; 4.01, Maintaining Confidentiality; 4.02, Discussing the Limits of Confidentiality; 10.01, Informed Consent to Therapy; 10.02, Therapy Involving Couples or Families; and 10.03, Group Therapy).

Length of Record Retention. The APA Record Keeping Guidelines (APA, 2007c) recommend that, in the absence of specific legal requirements for record retention, complete records are maintained at minimum until 7 years after the last date of service delivery for adults or until 3 years after a minor reaches the age of majority, whichever is later.

Billing and Fees. The Record Keeping Guidelines (APA, 2007c) highlight a few areas relevant to Standard 6.01 that call for special attention. First, records should include documentation of a fee and billing agreement between the psychologist and client/patient (including, when appropriate, acknowledgment of client/patient receipt of the psychologist's standard written fee policy; see Standard 6.04, Fees and

Financial Arrangements, for additional detail on fee and billing information). Second, as detailed below under Standard 6.05, Barter With Clients/Patients, barter agreements and transactions can be ethically complex and thus require careful documentation to ensure that compensation is fair to both the client/patient and psychologist. Third, psychologists need to document and justify any adjustment in the balance owed for services, especially when third parties are involved (see Standard 6.06, Accuracy in Reports to Payors and Funding Sources). Fourth, any fee collection efforts should also be recorded (see Standard 6.04e, Fees and Financial Arrangements). Psychologists providing health care–related services also need to be aware of the Department of Health and Human Services (DHHS) Transaction Rule requiring standard formatting of electronic patient records for health care claims and other purposes (see http://aspe.hhs.gov/admnsimp/).

Implications of HIPAA

Content of Records. In addition to information recommended by the Record Keeping Guidelines (APA, 2007c), the Health Insurance Portability and Accountability Act (HIPAA) of 1996 requires that records of all clinically relevant e-mail messages, including the full text of a patient's query and a psychologist's reply, should be stored in the patient's medical record. In addition, group practices need to include documentation of who is the privacy officer.

Length of Record Retention. The number of years for retention of records varies with respect to state law, federal regulations, and institutional requirements. HIPAA regulations require that policies and procedures used to comply with the Privacy Rule are documented and retained for 6 years from the date of creation or the last date in which it was in effect, whichever is later (45 CFR 164.530[j][2]). If state law establishes longer periods of record retention than HIPAA, psychologists who are covered entities must follow the state law (see "A Word About HIPAA" in the Preface to this book).

Access of Individuals to Protected Health Information. Clients/patients have the right to inspect and obtain a copy of their protected health information (PHI) records used by the psychologist to make diagnostic, treatment, and billing decisions (45 CFR 164.524). Where HIPAA regulations apply, psychologists' records must be created and stored in a manner that facilitates compliance with this and other aspects of the Privacy Rule.

Right to Amend. Clients/patients have the right to request their PHI be amended if they believe the information is incorrect (45 CFR 164.526). If a psychologist believes the amendment is justified, the amendment should be attached to the record; the psychologist should never alter the original record.

Right to an Accounting. Clients/patients have a "right to an accounting" of disclosures of PHI that entails a list of individuals or organizations to whom PHI has been disclosed in the past 6 years. Content of the accounting must include the date of the disclosure, the name of the entity or person who received the PHI and the address if known, a brief description of the PHI disclosed, and the purpose of its disclosure (45 CFR 164.528). Failure to keep an accurate record of such disclosures would be in violation of Standard 6.01.

Psychotherapy Notes. Psychotherapy or personal notes are considered a work product privilege and are immune from subpoena (Mental Health and Developmental Disabilities Confidentiality Act of 1979, ¶ 802, § 2[4]; Soisson, VandeCreek, & Knapp, 1987). Accordingly, psychotherapy notes can be disposed of at any time, unless state law provides otherwise.

HIPAA creates a separate category for "psychotherapy notes," defined as "notes recorded (in any medium) by a health care provider who is a mental health professional documenting or analyzing the contents of conversation during a private counseling session or a group, joint, or family counseling session and that are separated from the rest of the individual's medical record" (45 CFR 164.501). Patients do not have a right of access to psychotherapy notes. Psychologists may choose to provide patient access or agree to release psychotherapy notes to others with the appropriate authorization of the patient. Psychotherapy notes are exempted from HIPAA general provisions for sharing PHI for the treatment, payment, or health care operations of another entity. For example, health plan providers and other HIPAA-covered entities may *not* condition the provision of treatment, payment, enrollment in the health plan, or eligibility for benefits on a patient's authorization to have a psychologist release psychotherapy notes. For psychotherapy notes to meet HIPAA exemption criteria, psychologists *must* store the notes in a file separated from the client's/patient's other health records.

Educational Records

Psychologists working in schools need to be familiar with the Family Educational Rights and Privacy Act (FERPA) (20 U.S.C. § 1232–34 CFR Part 99; www.ed.gov/offices/OM/fpco/ferpa/index.html) to ensure compliance with Standard 6.01. Under FERPA, parents and students older than age 18 or attending college have the right to (a) inspect and review the student's education records maintained by the school, (b) request that a school correct records that they believe to be inaccurate or misleading, (c) call for a formal hearing if the school does not amend the record, and (d) place a statement with the record setting forth the parent or student views if the school still does not decide to amend the report. Records that are kept in the sole possession of the school psychologist, are used only as a personal memory aid, and are not accessible or revealed to any other person except a temporary substitute for the maker of the record are *not* considered part of a student's education record and therefore are not subject to parental or student inspection or amendment. In addition, under the Individuals with Disabilities Education Improvement Act of 2004 (Pub. L. No. 108–446, § 682[c]), schools must develop policies for the storage, retrieval, and disposal of educational records, and parents of students must be provided a statement of these policies.

Forensic Records

Psychologists conducting forensically relevant activities need to be familiar with laws governing the creation, maintenance, and disposal of records. In the legal arena, the notes, test data, testing protocols, and research protocols are governed by the rules of evidence in the court's jurisdiction. For example, with the exception of relevant client/patient privilege, the entirety of the psychologist's records created or used in a case is subject to discovery. In addition, in deposition and court testimony, psychologists are often asked when certain facts became known and, if so, by whom and in what context. Sufficiently detailed records are essential when there is an extended period between relevant interviews or data collection and hearing of a case (Committee on Legal Issues, 1996; Hess, 1998). Under Standard 6.01, forensic records must be created and maintained in a manner that facilitates their appropriate use in the legal arena (see also Standard 2.01f, Boundaries of Competence).

Documentation of Scientific Work and Maintenance of Records

Psychologists conducting research must create and maintain records in a manner that allows for replication of the research design by the psychologist or others. This includes an adequate description of recruitment procedures, documentation of informed consent, relevant demographic characteristics of participants, data collection procedures, materials or equipment, and data analysis strategies. Raw data should be stored in a form accessible to analysis or reanalysis by the psychologist or other competent professionals who seek to verify substantive claims (see Standard 8.14, Sharing Research Data for Verification).

The number of years of retention of raw data for investigators will vary with state law, federal regulations, and institutional policies. Federal regulations (Office of Management and Budget Circular A-110) and Public Health Service (PHS) Grants Policy (National Institutes of Health [NIH] Grants Policy Statement, revised March 2001) require that data generated through federal support be maintained by institutions for at least 3 years following the completion of the project and the filing of the final progress and financial reports. The number of years may be longer if a patent is involved. Specific record-keeping requirements for IRBs include maintenance of copies of the scientific proposal, the informed consent document, summaries of the project, financial reports, and reports of injuries or other serious adverse events. Authors of articles published in APA journals must have their raw data available for at least 5 years after the date of publication (APA, 2001).

Under Standard 6.01, principal investigators on federally funded grants must also create and maintain accurate records of costs associated with the research, including participant compensation, research assistant salaries, investigators' percent effort working on the grant, equipment, travel, and other supplies necessary to conduct the research. For federally funded projects, IRBs are subject to federal grants compliance and oversight. For each grant, the IRB must account for cost allocations/cost transfers, time and effort reporting, allowable grant charges, and unobligated balances (see http://grants.nih.gov/grants/compliance/compliance.htm).

6.02 Maintenance, Dissemination, and Disposal of Confidential Records of Professional and Scientific Work

(a) Psychologists maintain confidentiality in creating, storing, accessing, transferring, and disposing of records under their control, whether these are written, automated, or in any other medium. (See also Standards 4.01, Maintaining Confidentiality, and 6.01, Documentation of Professional and Scientific Work and Maintenance of Records.)

Standard 6.02 requires that psychologists protect the confidentiality of professional or scientific information in all phases of record creation, maintenance, dissemination, and disposal. The standard refers to confidential records or data in the form of written and printed materials, automated scoring reports, audio and video recordings, Internet Web sites or e-mails, company computer networks, storage on hard drives or disks, and faxes. Steps that can be taken to protect confidentiality include (a) keeping records in a secure place, (b) limiting access to staff or team members who must use the record to competently perform their duties, (c) de-identifying records using code numbers or other methods, and (d) disposing of tapes and other identifiable records when they are no longer needed and their disposal is consistent with law.

Psychologists should be careful not to assume that their staff or employees of an institution or company with which they work are familiar with confidentiality requirements or appropriate confidentiality procedures. To the extent it is under their control, they must take steps to ensure that confidential records are kept secure from staff who do not have approved access. Consider the following example of a violation of Standard 6.02a.

> ☒ A consulting psychologist was contracted to evaluate whether on-site day care centers set up at the company's offices in 10 states were fostering a positive organizational climate. The psychologist conducted taped interviews with employees to find out whether the day care centers had minimized their need to take days off from work for child care and their satisfaction with the plan. Each month, she traveled to a company's office in a different city to conduct the interviews. As she left, she usually asked one of the office secretaries to box up the tapes and UPS them to the company's main headquarters.

Implications of HIPAA. Psychologists creating or using PHI must comply with HIPAA regulations to protect the privacy rights of clients/patients. HIPAA compliance is required whenever PHI is transmitted in electronic form for health care claims, health plan premium payments, referral certification and authorization, injury reports, health care payment and remittance advice, and transfer of records to other professionals. HIPAA regulations require that client/patient authorization to transfer records of PHI to third parties should be different from and visually and organizationally separate from other permission forms, include a statement that the client/patient may revoke authorization in writing, and be signed and dated (45 CFR 164.508).

The Final Rule of the HIPAA Security Standards establishes a minimum standard for security of PHI maintained in electronic form (45 CFR 160). These standards require measures to be taken to secure this information while in the custody of entities covered by HIPAA as well as in transit between covered entities and from covered entities to others. The Final Rule includes administrative procedures, physical safeguards, technical security services, and technical mechanisms covered entities must take to safeguard the integrity, confidentiality, and availability of electronic health information pertaining to individuals. The Security Standards require covered entities to implement basic safeguards to protect electronic PHI from unauthorized access, alteration, deletion, and transmission. Implementation depends on numerous factors, including the configuration of the entity implementing it, the technology it employs, and the risks to and vulnerabilities of the information it must protect. Psychologists should be familiar with those standards that pertain to their specific practices (Department of Health and Human Services, 2003). Covered entities are also expected to keep office doors locked when no one is inside, store patient records in such a way that guests are unlikely to see PHI, and ensure for group practices that terminated employees cease to have access to files.

Practicing psychologists should remember that even if the specific files to be transmitted have never been electronically recorded by the psychologist, if any entity acting on behalf of the psychologists (e.g., a bill collection agency, a health maintenance organization) has electronically stored or transmitted PHI related to any other client/patient in the psychologist's practice, the HIPAA Privacy Rule is triggered for the entire practice. The APA Practice Directorate and the APA Insurance Trust (2002) recommend that all psychologists accepting third-party reimbursement, recording health information electronically, or employing a billing service make their confidentiality practices HIPAA compliant.

(b) If confidential information concerning recipients of psychological services is entered into databases or systems of records available to persons whose access has not been consented to by the recipient, psychologists use coding or other techniques to avoid the inclusion of personal identifiers.

Standard 6.02b draws attention to the need to take specific steps to protect confidential records when these records are stored in record systems or databases available to persons whose access has not been consented to by the recipient. To comply with this standard, practitioner and research psychologists storing data on institutional networks can use protected passwords, de-identify information, and discuss with institutional staff responsible for network maintenance and monitoring appropriate procedures for confidentiality protections. Psychologists working in group practices should be aware of and comply with HIPAA security rules governing office and other infrastructure PHI protections, including access to offices, files, and secure transmission procedures (see the section "Implications of HIPAA" under Standard 6.02a above). When applicable, psychologists should identify limitations in efforts to protect confidentiality on databases and systems of records and inform clients/patients, organizational clients, research participants, or others with whom they work about such limitations (see also Standard 4.02c, Discussing the Limits of Confidentiality).

For psychologists working in or consulting to organizations, record-keeping procedures may be governed by the legal relationship established between the psychologist and the organization. In some instances, the physical records belong to the organization and cannot be secured solely by the psychologist or leave the organization's premises. In other instances, individual consulting services, for example, the records may belong to the psychologist. In either situation, to the extent feasible, the psychologists are responsible for the appropriate documentation and maintenance of the records and must clarify to organizations their obligations under the Ethics Code if a conflict arises (see Standard 1.03, Conflicts Between Ethics and Organizational Demands).

(c) Psychologists make plans in advance to facilitate the appropriate transfer and to protect the confidentiality of records and data in the event of psychologists' withdrawal from positions or practice. (See also Standards 3.12, Interruption of Psychological Services, and 10.09, Interruption of Therapy.)

The obligation to maintain the confidentiality of professional or scientific records includes advance planning for the secure transfer of such records in the case of planned or unplanned withdrawals from a position or practice because of job termination, promotion, a new position, parental or family leave, retirement, illness, or death. Information may be transferred in person, by mail or by fax, through the Internet, or through private company networks. Psychologists planning in advance for the transfer of PHI need to be aware of the DHHS Transaction Rule requiring standard formatting of electronic patient records for health care claims and other purposes.

Psychologists planning to transfer forensically relevant records should be familiar with laws in their state governing the extent to which licensed psychologists' privilege extends to their staff (Blau, 1984). Failure to take appropriate steps to protect the confidentiality of records or data transfer would be a violation of Standard 6.02c. The following are three examples of such violations.

☒ A research psychologist who had conducted a 20-year large-scale longitudinal study retired from her faculty position. She agreed to allow the university to keep her data set for archival research by graduate students and other faculty. Among the records that she donated to the university was the coding file linking subject numbers to the names and contact information of participants.

☒ After a 2-year postdoctoral fellowship in neuropsychology at a university hospital, a psychologist prepared to leave for a new position in a different state. The day before he left, he met the new postdoctoral fellow assigned to his office space. The psychologist apologized to the new fellow about leaving his patient records in the unlocked office file cabinets. He told her that the records were important to ensure continuity of care for patients that he had assessed but that the hospital administrators had not gotten back to him about where the records should be moved. He asked the new fellow to keep them in her office or to have one of the maintenance crew move the files to a temporary place in the basement.

> ☒ A psychologist in independent practice was told by the health maintenance organization (HMO) with which he had a contract that the HMO would not extend benefits for one of the psychologist's clients unless the psychologist provided the HMO with his psychotherapy notes. Knowing that his client needed and wanted to continue therapy, the psychologist reluctantly complied without getting written authorization from the client to release the notes. A week later, he attended a professional workshop on HIPAA regulations and learned that not only is a signed client/patient authorization required to release psychotherapy notes, but also managed care companies are prohibited from conditioning treatment benefits on the patient's authorization.

6.03 Withholding Records for Nonpayment

Psychologists may not withhold records under their control that are requested and needed for a client's/patient's emergency treatment solely because payment has not been received.

Psychologists, like other professionals, have the right to be paid for their services. However, the ideal of nonmaleficence, to do no harm, articulated in Principle A: Beneficence and Nonmaleficence, is a core value of the discipline that obligates psychologists to provide informational assistance, if not doing so would jeopardize the welfare of a current or former client/patient. Standard 6.03 prohibits psychologists from withholding records needed for a client's/patient's emergency treatment solely because payment for services has not been received. The term *solely* allows the psychologist to withhold such records if disclosure is prohibited by law or, in the psychologist's judgment, release of records would cause substantial harm to the client/patient or others.

The standard does not apply to nontreatment situations, such as when parents who have not paid for a completed psychological assessment of their child request the records for an application for special educational services. Similarly, the standard does not apply to treatments that are not an emergency, such as when a therapy client/patient who has not paid for services asks a psychologist to send treatment records to a new therapist.

Emergency Treatment. The standard refers only to the provision of records for treatment and only when emergency treatment is needed. For example, a client's/patient's therapy or assessment records may be needed immediately to help other health professionals provide appropriate emergency treatment for a client/patient in an acute state of mental disorder such as a schizophrenic episode or a depression accompanied by suicidal ideation. Records may also be required to help health professionals quickly determine whether an incapacitating cognitive or language disorder is the result of an injury, medical problem, or a symptom of a previous mental disorder. Under the Ethics Code, psychologists are not required to obtain the client's/patient's consent to release information if it is requested for emergency treatment (see Standard 4.05a, Disclosures). Similarly, the HIPAA

Privacy Rule permits disclosure of PHI without patient authorization to avert a serious threat to health or safety (45 CFR 164.512[j]).

Control and Requests. For the standard to apply, two other criteria must be met. The records must be under the psychologist's control. For example, Standard 6.03 would not apply if the health care system that a psychologist works for is legally responsible for the records and the institution refuses to release the records because of nonpayment. The records must also be requested, meaning that psychologists do not have to provide such records if they simply learn that a client/patient is receiving emergency treatment.

Regulatory and Legal Caveats. The HIPAA Privacy Rule establishing the rights of clients/patients to receive their PHI records does not distinguish between emergency and nonemergency requests, nor does it consider failure to pay as a legitimate reason to refuse a patient request to release records. Thus, although ethically permissible under Standard 6.03, withholding records for nonpayment under nonemergency conditions may not be legally permissible. Psychologists should carefully review their contracts with HMOs to establish whether providers retain the right to withhold client/patient treatment records if the HMO has delayed or refused to reimburse for services.

6.04 Fees and Financial Arrangements

(a) As early as is feasible in a professional or scientific relationship, psychologists and recipients of psychological services reach an agreement specifying compensation and billing arrangements.

An individual's or organization's decision to enter into a professional or scientific relationship with a psychologist will depend in part on the costs and billing arrangements for the services. Failure to specify and agree on compensation and billing arrangements can lead to client/patient mistrust or financial exploitation. According to Standard 6.04a, psychologists providing counseling, therapy, assessment, consultation, forensic, scientific, or other services must reach an agreement about compensation and billing with the service recipient as early as is feasible in the professional or scientific relationship.

Specifying Compensation. In specifying compensation, psychologists must include a description of all reasonably anticipated costs. For forensic, organizational, or research services, this might include charges for telephone conversations; client, employee, or participant interviews; library or computer research; statistical analysis; court preparation time; travel; postage; or duplication. Psychologists arranging compensation for assessment services should provide information about fees for test administration, scoring, interpretation, and report writing. Financial agreements for therapy should include, where appropriate, discussion of (a) payment schedules, fees for therapy sessions, telephone sessions, sessions with family members or significant others, charges for consultation with other professionals and appointment cancellations, acknowledgment of third-party payor preauthorization requirements, and copayment agreements and (b) whether costs may be covered by health insurance, as well as time or cost limitations regarding third-party payors.

> ☒ A research psychologist agreed to provide expert testimony on developmental differences in the effect of divorce and stepparenting on child and adolescent development. The psychologist reached agreement with the attorney stipulating a flat fee for reviewing the case material and writing a background paper relevant to her testimony. After receiving compensation for this work, the psychologist sent the attorney a bill for duplication, computer supplies, and telephone and book purchase costs with a note saying that she would not be available to testify unless these costs were reimbursed immediately.

Billing Arrangements. Standard 6.04a requires psychologists to reach an agreement about billing arrangements as early as is feasible in the professional relationship. Psychologists must notify and reach an agreement regarding when bills will be rendered and payments expected, for example, weekly or monthly. Billing arrangements may also include agreement on a series of scheduled prepayments or compensation for different phases of the psychologist's services.

> ☑ An organizational psychologist hired by a hospital to conduct a quality improvement study set up a payment schedule tied to completion of data collection, completion of a first draft of the report, and completion of a final draft.

To avoid billing disputes that may later arise between couples or family members, psychologists conducting couples therapy or child custody assessments may wish to consider reaching an agreement in advance regarding which member of the couple or which parent will assume responsibility for payments.

Timing. The use of the phrase "as early as is feasible" permits psychologists to delay finalizing a financial arrangement to obtain additional information about the client's/patient's service needs or health care benefits. Discussion of fees in the first session may be clinically contraindicated if a new client/patient is experiencing a crisis needing immediate therapeutic attention. In such situations, agreement on compensation and billing must be finalized as soon as all information is available or the crisis has subsided (see also Standard 10.01a, Informed Consent to Therapy).

> ☑ A series of consultations with different company executives was required before a psychologist could develop a comprehensive plan for and pricing of services required.

☑ A psychologist was aware that a new patient's HMO frequently failed to provide timely feedback about the extent and limits of patient health care benefits. The psychologist mentioned the possibility of this occurring during the initial consultation with the patient and discussed delaying additional sessions until the extent of coverage could be clarified.

☑ At his first session with a psychologist for treatment for alcoholism, the client was obviously intoxicated, evidencing speech impairment and a lack of coherence in his remarks. The psychologist addressed clinical issues with the client relevant to the immediate situation and made an appointment with him to discuss fees and other issues regarding therapy at a time when he would be sober.

Contingent Fees. A contingent fee is typically defined as a fee to be paid only in the event of a future occurrence. Psychologists should avoid contingent fees that have the potential to impair objectivity and unduly influence their methods, activities, or reports (see Standard 3.06, Conflict of Interest). In forensic contexts, psychologists should avoid accepting contingent fees when the services delivered involve offering evidence to a court or administrative body or affirmations or representations intended to be helpful to a court or to be relied upon by third parties. Other promises of future payment that might be considered contingent fees are those that are promised dependent on the outcome of the legal matter at hand, such as future proceeds or settlement benefits (Committee on the Revision of the Specialty Guidelines for Forensic Psychology, 2008).

(b) Psychologists' fee practices are consistent with law.

This standard specifically requires psychologists' activities to be consistent with relevant laws. To comply with Standard 6.04b, psychologists must be familiar with and develop fee practices compatible with local, state, and federal laws governing fee practices, including legal contracts with managed care organizations. Health care fraud or the submission of false claims is open to legal censure and actions, which can result in costly fines or imprisonment. It includes falsifying costs of services, intentionally overdiagnosing mental health disorders, or omitting information that might lead to denial of benefits. The following are examples of fee practices violating this standard:

☒ A managed care organization agreed to pay a psychologist 80% of his standard $100 hourly fee. The psychologist typically waived the $20 copayment for patients insured by this HMO. The HMO eventually accused the psychologist of insurance fraud, noting that in reality, his standard hourly fee for their insureds had become $80.

☒ A single mother who had a minimum-wage job sought treatment for depression. She informed the psychologist that because of her limited funds, she had purchased health insurance for her 3-year-old daughter but not for herself. The psychologist reasoned that her mental health would affect her child's well-being and told her he would be willing to bill the insurance company under the daughter's policy.

> ☒ A client's health insurer did not cover mental health services for emotional problems associated with bereavement over the death of a spouse. The psychologist gave the client a diagnosis of major depressive disorder when she submitted the insurance form to gain coverage for sessions.
>
> ☒ A group of psychologists started a mental health referral service. They charged psychologists to whom they referred patients a first-time fee for each referral and a fee for each subsequent session based on the patient's monthly bill. This method of reimbursement violated their state laws prohibiting kickbacks and fee splitting.
>
> ☒ The Medicaid system in the state in which a psychologist worked required professionals to have a preliminary meeting with a child to provide an initial diagnostic report that would then be used to request approval for a full battery of psychological testing. The psychologist routinely wrote the preliminary report without interviewing children to limit the loss of school time and to shorten the approval period.
>
> ☒ A psychologist charged a first-time fee when a client asked for a list of individuals to whom the psychologist had released the client's PHI over the past 2 years. The psychologist was unaware that under HIPAA, each year clients/patients have the right to receive one free accounting of all disclosures of PHI information made within the previous 6 years.

(c) Psychologists do not misrepresent their fees.

This standard requires that psychologists provide clients/patients, organizational clients, and others who will be charged for services an accurate statement of the costs of the services that will be offered. For example, under Standard 6.04c, psychologists are prohibited from the following:

> ☒ Listing in advertisements, brochures, or other public representations fees lower than what the psychologist actually charges (see also Standards 5.01a, Avoidance of False or Deceptive Statements, and 5.02, Statements by Others)
>
> ☒ Adding unnecessary tests to an assessment battery to raise the cost of services after reaching an agreement about fees with the client/patient
>
> ☒ Failing to disclose expectable costs of secretarial assistance or time devoted to telephone conversations, library reference work, or travel during fee negotiations for consulting or forensic work
>
> ☒ Using "bait-and-switch" tactics, such as offering low rates to lure a client/patient into therapy, only to raise the rates after a few sessions
>
> ☒ Inflating reports of hourly fees for noninsured patients to obtain a higher rate for covered services when submitting a provider application to an HMO

(d) If limitations to services can be anticipated because of limitations in financing, this is discussed with the recipient of services as early as is feasible. (See also Standards 10.09, Interruption of Therapy, and 10.10, Terminating Therapy.)

In some instances, financial limitations in providing services may be anticipated at the beginning or during the course of a professional or scientific relationship. This most frequently occurs when HMOs readily provide health care professionals with their policies on the type of mental health services and number of sessions that are covered by a client's/patient's health plan. When, in a psychologist's professional judgment, clients/patients will require more therapy than their health plan covers, the psychologist must discuss this as early as is feasible in the professional relationship. Such discussion enables clients/patients to decide if they want to begin the treatment under the HMO's limitations and provides the psychologist the opportunity to inform clients/patients about other financial arrangements that can be made to ensure continued care. Alternative financial arrangements can include reduced fees, deferred payment, limited sessions, or referral to lower cost services.

> ☒ A psychologist in independent practice had an initial consultation with a patient who appeared to be suffering from obsessive-compulsive disorder. The psychologist was aware that short-term treatments for this disorder have not proven effective. However, the patient's HMO would approve only 10 sessions. The psychologist told the patient she was confident she could convince the HMO to extend payments after 10 sessions and recommended they begin treatment. After 10 sessions, the HMO refused approval for additional sessions, and the patient could not afford additional treatment on his own.

Standard 6.04d also applies to instances when, during the course of a contractual agreement, organizational, consulting, forensic, or research psychologists become aware that the actual costs of a project will exceed the agreed on costs. As soon as this becomes apparent, psychologists must discuss the limitations with the parties with whom they are contracted.

> ☑ A consulting psychologist was aware that the hospital that hired him to conduct a quality assurance study had a limited budget. His original proposal for the study was well within this budget. As the study was getting started, the hospital became involved in a lawsuit that required in-depth evaluation of practices that were only of marginal interest in the original quality assurance study. The psychologist quickly estimated the additional costs of examining these practices in depth and set up a meeting to discuss limitations of the original proposal and its costs to handle the hospital's sudden needs.

(e) If the recipient of services does not pay for services as agreed, and if psychologists intend to use collection agencies or legal measures to collect the fees, psychologists first inform the person that such measures will be taken and provide that person an opportunity to make prompt payment. (See also Standards 4.05, Disclosures; 6.03, Withholding Records for Nonpayment; and 10.01, Informed Consent to Therapy.)

Psychologists are permitted to use collection agencies or other legal measures to obtain compensation when the recipient of services has not made agreed on payments. Before using such services, under Standard 6.04e, psychologists must inform the client/patient or other service recipient that such measures will be taken and provide that person an opportunity to make prompt payment. The definition of prompt payment should be reasonable but need not extend beyond a month depending on the length of time that payments have been delinquent. As a rule of thumb, most businesses turn unpaid bills over to a collection agency after 60 to 90 days.

> ☑ During informed consent, a psychologist always informed clients/patients that his fee policy was to be paid in full for services on a bimonthly basis, that bill collection procedures would be initiated when clients/patients reached an accumulated debt of the cost of 6 sessions, and that a letter alerting patients about billing concerns would be mailed to them if billing accumulated at 4 weeks to give them time to pay the bill.

Standard 6.04e applies to psychologists providing therapy, assessment, consultation, forensic, and other services when the service recipient is an individual, couple, or family. The standard does not apply when psychologists choose to use a collection agency or legal measures to collect unpaid fees from attorneys, companies, organizations, or institutions.

Implications of HIPAA. Several HIPAA regulations are relevant to Standard 6.04e. First, HIPAA permits covered entities to use and disclose PHI to carry out treatment, payment, or health care operations without specific authorization from the patient (45 CFR 164.506). Although specific requirements regarding consent were removed from the final HIPAA Privacy Rule, clients/patients must be aware of the covered entity's disclosure policies. Thus, covered entities who want the option of using collection agencies for nonpayment for health services must include this information in a Notice of Privacy Practices given to the client/patient at the onset of services (45 CFR 164.520). Psychologists should also include this information in their informed consent procedures (see Standards 4.02, Discussing the Limits of Confidentiality; 9.03, Informed Consent in Assessments; and 10.01, Informed Consent to Therapy). Psychologists who are HIPAA-covered entities should be aware that the Notice of Privacy Practices must be a separate document from the consent materials used for assessment or therapy. The APA Insurance Trust and APA Practice Directorate have available for purchase model Notice of Privacy Practices forms (see www.apait.org/hipaa).

Collection agencies hired by a psychologist may be considered a "business associate" under HIPAA (45 CFR 160.103). A business associate is an entity who acts on behalf of a covered entity but not as an employee of the covered entity. An arrangement with a business associate must ensure that the business associate, on behalf of the covered entity, agrees to safeguard the use and disclosure of PHI in ways that are HIPAA compliant (45 CFR 164.504[e]).

What to Disclose to Collection Agencies. HIPAA's "minimum necessary" standard (45 CFR 164.502[b]), as well as Standard 4.01, Maintaining Confidentiality, in the APA Ethics Code can be interpreted as requiring psychologists to limit the information provided to collection agencies to the minimum necessary to accomplish the intended purpose. Information to such agencies should be limited to (a) the client's/patient's name, (b) the dollar amount of the fee that is overdue, (c) the date of services for which the unpaid fee was billed, and (d) the client's/patient's address, telephone number, and other relevant contact information. Psychologists should never reveal a client's/patient's diagnosis or reason for seeking services. In most instances, psychologists do not need to mention the type of services provided (e.g., therapy) and can simply inform the collection agency that the overdue bill is for "services provided."

> ☒ A patient who had terminated therapy with a psychologist had failed to pay for sessions during the last 2 months of treatment. After sending the former patient several notices requesting payment and the psychologist's intention to use a collection agency if payment was not received, the psychologist turned the matter over to an agency. During the course of treatment, the psychologist had observed signs of sociopathy in the patient. Concerned that individuals at the collection agency might place themselves in danger if they angered the patient, the psychologist informed the head of the collection agency of the diagnostic reasons for these concerns.

6.05 Barter With Clients/Patients

Barter is the acceptance of goods, services, or other nonmonetary remuneration from clients/patients in return for psychological services. Psychologists may barter only if (1) it is not clinically contraindicated, and (2) the resulting arrangement is not exploitative. (See also Standards 3.05, Multiple Relationships, and 6.04, Fees and Financial Arrangements.)

This standard applies when psychologists accept from clients/patients nonmonetary remuneration for services. The issue of bartering often emerges in response to a client's/patient's financial limitations or lack of affordable health insurance. Providing services in return for bartered goods is ethically permissible in situations when to not do so would deprive clients/patients of needed services or run counter to community economic or cultural practices. Although barter is not a per se violation of the Ethics Code, psychologists need to be cautious about accepting bartered goods or services from clients/patients in lieu of monetary payments because such arrangements have an inherent potential for client/patient harm, exploitation, and unethical multiple relationships (Standard 3.05a, Multiple Relationships). For example, it is often difficult to determine the extent to which a bartered good is equivalent in price to the dollar amount of a psychologist's fee, running the risk that clients/patients will be exploited or the psychologist underpaid. Bartering clerical or other (e.g., house painting, babysitting) services for psychological services risks creating potentially harmful multiple relationships resulting from interactions with the client/patient outside of a professional role or loss of professional objectivity in reaction to the quality of the client/patient bartered services.

Standard 6.05 specifically prohibits barter with clients/patients when it is clinically contraindicated or exploitative. The following are an example of a potential violation of this standard and an example of ethically permissible barter.

☒ A psychologist in independent practice in a wealthy suburban community saw clients in an office attached to her home. One of her clients, a landscaper, noticed that her driveway and landscaping in front of her home were in serious disrepair. He suggested that instead of paying fees for 2 months, he would landscape her home. Although the cost of the landscaping would be greater than the psychologist's fees during this period, the psychologist agreed. The client was unable to complete the job in the 2-month period, leading to increased tension during the therapy sessions.

☑ A school psychologist worked 2 days a week at an isolated Alaskan Native fishing community providing parent and teacher consultations and behavior therapy for children diagnosed with attention deficit hyperactivity disorder and other learning problems. During the year, an oil spill created serious economic consequences for the village. It was estimated that it would take 2 months for normal fishing to resume. The tribal leader, on behalf of the parents and school, asked the psychologist if she would be willing to take free room, board, office space, and travel to the village donated by the tribe equivalent to her fees during this period. The psychologist agreed and set up a time-limited remuneration contract specifying the equivalent monetary value of the services. The psychologist reasoned that barter in this case would be ethically permissible because the barter did not directly affect her therapeutic relationships with the children or the parents or teachers with whom she consulted, and the exchange was a fair rate that was not exploitative. In addition, the psychologist's agreement to barter demonstrated her recognition and respect for the efforts and importance the tribe attributed to her services.

6.06 Accuracy in Reports to Payors and Funding Sources

In their reports to payors for services or sources of research funding, psychologists take reasonable steps to ensure the accurate reporting of the nature of the service provided or research conducted, the fees, charges, or payments, and where applicable, the identity of the provider, the findings, and the diagnosis. (See also Standards 4.01, Maintaining Confidentiality; 4.04, Minimizing Intrusions on Privacy; and 4.05, Disclosures.)

This standard requires accuracy in reports to payors and funding sources and reflects the values of honesty and truthfulness articulated in Principle C: Integrity. The standard applies when psychologists bill insurance companies for client/patient therapy or assessments, charge companies for consulting fees or forensic clients for services, or document grant-related research expenses. The phrase "take reasonable steps" recognizes that in some instances, psychologists may have limited control over financial reports sent to third-party payors (i.e., psychologists working in group practices or in health delivery systems) or to funding sources (i.e., research psychologists working in academic institutions through which reports to external funders must be made).

Research and Industrial-Organizational and Forensic Services

Psychologists receiving research support from their institution, private foundations, or federal programs must provide accurate reports of charges for and the research-related purpose of equipment and supplies, travel, and payments to research participants, investigators, and research assistants. Psychologists billing companies or forensic clients for services should provide an accurate accounting of the number of hours worked on the particular project, the nature of and work product produced during those hours, and any other legitimate expenses (i.e., additional staff, travel, duplication or postage costs) associated with the work contracted for.

Therapy

Accurate Diagnosis. Psychologists conducting therapy must provide an accurate diagnosis to third-party payors. Psychologists who provide an incorrect diagnosis to obtain reimbursement from a client's/patient's health plan would be in violation of this standard. In addition, such practices would represent insurance fraud and violation of Standard 6.04b, Fees and Financial Arrangements.

Billing for Missed Appointments. Some psychologists have a policy of charging for sessions missed when a client/patient cancels a therapy appointment. Health insurers will not reimburse for these charges because no mental health services were provided. In their report to third-party payors, psychologists must clearly identify sessions for which charges are for a client/patient cancellation. Psychologists must also make any missed-appointment policies clear to clients/patients at the outset of the professional relationship (Standards 6.04a, Fees and Financial Arrangements, and 10.01, Informed Consent to Therapy).

Accurate Representation of Billing Practices. Some HMOs calculate reimbursement for provider services on a percentage of the psychologist's fee scale. Psychologists must provide these organizations with an accurate representation of their billing practices for all clients/patients for the period requested by the HMO, including use of a sliding-fee scale if relevant. In some instances, licensed psychologists may supervise therapy or assessments conducted by unlicensed trainees or employees. When reimbursement for such therapy or assessment is sought from third-party payors, the licensed psychologist must clearly identify the actual provider of the services.

6.07 Referrals and Fees

When psychologists pay, receive payment from, or divide fees with another professional, other than in an employer-employee relationship, the payment to each is based on the services provided (clinical, consultative, administrative, or other) and is not based on the referral itself. (See also Standard 3.09, Cooperation With Other Professionals.)

One reason psychologists are sued is for improper referral (Bennett et al., 2006). This standard is meant to ensure that client/patient referrals among professionals are based on the expertise of the professional to whom the referral is being made, as well as the appropriateness of the service for the client/patient, and not on the basis of the referral itself. Standard 6.07 prohibits psychologists from charging other professionals for client/patient referrals or, conversely, from paying another professional for a referral. Such payments place psychologists in a potential conflict of interest if the referral is based on the financial remuneration rather than on the needs of the client/patient (see Standard 3.06, Conflict of Interest).

Standard 6.07 is also meant to ensure that fees charged to clients/patients reflect the services provided. A psychologist may divide fees with another professional only if both have contributed to the service.

> ☑ A clinical geropsychologist regularly consulted with a neurologist when conducting cognitive assessments of patients with Parkinson's disease and other neurological disorders. The patient fee included the amount of money the psychologist paid the neurologist for the consultation. These billing arrangements were described to the patient or his or her legal guardian in advance, and the psychologist accurately described the arrangement in billing statements to patients and third-party payors (see Standards 6.06, Accuracy in Reports to Payors and Funding Sources; 9.03, Informed Consent in Assessments; and 10.01, Informed Consent to Therapy).

Referral Services. The standard does not prohibit psychologists who are members of a psychotherapy referral service from paying a percentage of a referred client's/patient's fee to support the administrative costs of the service, including the intake interview, as long as (a) the service follows a policy of making referrals only to those members who have expertise appropriate to a client's/patient's treatment needs, and (b) the costs of the administrative and professional services are spread over the membership so that no individual psychologist is treated as a preferred referral solely because of his or her financial contribution to the service. However, psychologists need to be familiar with their state regulations regarding kickbacks and fee splitting to ensure these activities are consistent with law.

Other Permissible Payments. The standard does not prohibit psychologists from (a) charging another psychologist payment for office space, (b) paying professionals who are employees a percentage of a client/patient fee, (c) paying an institution for referrals, or (d) having membership in an HMO (Canter et al., 1994).

HOT TOPIC

Managing the Ethics of Managed Care

The primary function of HMOs and other forms of managed health care, such as managed care organizations (MCOs), preferred provider organizations (PPOs), Medicare, and Medicaid, is to control health care costs while maintaining high-quality care. HMOs seek to accomplish this by (a) identifying which health conditions will qualify for benefits, (b) determining the manner and frequency in which services will be provided, (c) monitoring their delivery, and (d) regulating distribution of monetary reimbursement. This is accomplished through forming contractual relationships among insurers, providers, and clients/patients.

Ideally managed mental health should enhance accountability, treatment effectiveness, and quality assurance. However, even when conducted properly, managed care plans raise a unique set of ethical challenges for psychologists. This Hot Topic section highlights ethical pitfalls related to fees and financial arrangements under managed care.

Payment for Services

Practicing psychologists have different payment relationships with managed care organizations and third-party insurers. Some psychologists contract directly with an HMO and receive referrals from that company. Others bill the HMO directly or bill the client/patient directly while providing the information necessary for the clients/patients to receive reimbursement from the insurer. Irrespective of payment arrangements, psychologists are responsible for fact finding about and communicating to clients/patients the nature of their HMO coverage.

As soon as feasible, psychologists should inform clients/patients about the following (Acuff et al., 1999; Standards 6.04, Fees and Financial Arrangements; 9.03, Informed Consent in Assessments; and 10.01, Informed Consent to Therapy):

- The HMO's provisions related to the number of authorized sessions
- The method and timing of utilization review
- The nature of the information required by the HMO to authorize services
- The amount of reimbursement provided
- The patient's share of any expenses (copayment or deduction)
- The services that are covered or excluded
- The responsibility for payment if the HMO determines that a particular service is not covered under the patient's plan

When a delay in the HMO determination regarding coverage and length of care presents a problem for establishing a therapeutic relationship, psychologists should consider and discuss with clients/patients delaying future sessions until benefits are determined.

Perverse Incentives

Capitation is a specific cost containment model adopted by a number of HMOs and government-sponsored health plans that sets outpatient mental health benefits at a certain fixed price per client/patient. Capitation guarantees a provider with a fixed (capitated) amount of dollars for each patient, irrespective of disorder or number of sessions. It is intended to incentivize practitioners to provide the most cost-effective treatment by providing briefer sessions for clients/patients with less severe disorders to allow for more sessions for individuals with severe disorders.

While capitation offers psychologists greater flexibility in determining treatment modality and frequency of sessions, it also establishes a financial incentive to keep sessions for all clients/patients to a minimum to maximize profits. Capitation thus runs the risk of becoming a "perverse incentive" (Haas & Cummings, 1991) that places psychologists in a conflict of interest between patient care and their financial gain (see Standard 3.06, Conflict of Interest). To avoid unintentionally downgrading services for financial gain under capitation, Acuff et al. (1999) recommend psychologists develop an internal monitoring system for one's practice to compare the length of care for patients in the capitated plans with those who are in fee-for-service or other forms of coverage.

Diagnosing for Dollars

The American Psychiatric Association's (2000) *Diagnostic and Statistical Manual of Mental Disorders* (*DSM*) is the most widely used system for classifying mental health disorders in the United States (Seligman, 1999). HMOs use the *DSM* classifications to determine criteria for coverage, length of treatment, and treatment outcomes. They often deny insurance reimbursement for certain *DSM* classifications that are common among clients/patients served by psychologists, including adjustment disorders, diagnostic codes that are exclusive to *DSM* Axis II (Personality Disorders) and *DSM* V codes (Relational Problems and Other Conditions That May Be a Focus of Clinical Attention) (Braun & Cox, 2005).

Patients with diagnoses not covered by their HMO may not be able to pay for out-of-pocket costs. In response, some psychologists may be tempted to "upcode" (overdiagnose) a disorder or exaggerate or exclude relevant client symptoms to establish a diagnosis that meets an HMO's benefits criteria. Upcoding also occurs when a psychologist conducting couples or family counseling services not covered by an HMO provides a false diagnosis for one spouse to obtain individual benefits to cover the joint counseling. Wylie (1995) labeled these practices as *diagnosing for dollars*, and Rappo (2002) noted that this term adequately describes diagnoses aimed at managing health costs rather than managing care.

Legal and Ethical Implications. "Upcoding" and other false diagnoses are illegal and unethical. Overdiagnosing a client/patient to receive health care benefits is insurance fraud and thus a violation of Standard 6.04, Fees and Financial Arrangements. It is also inconsistent with Principle C: Integrity, under which psychologists do not engage in fraud, subterfuge, or intentional misrepresentation of fact. Moreover, it violates Standard 3.06, Conflict of Interest, by allowing personal financial interests to interfere with psychologists' objectivity.

Psychologists suspected of "upcoding" can be investigated and prosecuted under the False Claims Amendments Act of 1986 (U.S. Code 31, Chapter 37, Subchapter III), which permits clients/patients to bring cases against practitioners on behalf of the government for which a practitioner's claim of ignorance is an insufficient defense (see Braun & Cox, 2005). Psychologists found guilty of insurance fraud will most likely lose their state license to practice, be required to pay substantial monetary penalties, and, in the case of criminal charges based on defrauding Medicare or Medicaid, may spend time in prison.

Distributive Justice. Some psychologists defend overdiagnosis as an ethical choice that places the best interests of the client over the "unjust" criteria used by health care management organizations to distribute health care. This defense rests on the fallacious assumption that health care resources are unlimited. While it is beyond the scope of this book to address political and economic influences on the availability and costs of health care, health resources are finite. Therefore, when psychologists upcode a client's/patient's diagnosis to receive reimbursement for services, they are further limiting the resources available for individuals who actually have more serious disorders and, in the long run, potentially contributing to a rise in insurance costs to cover the number of clients/patients who are meeting diagnostic criteria (Principle D, Justice).

Client/Patient Harm. Upcoding a diagnosis to gain health care benefits can lead to multiple foreseeable harms (Principle A: Beneficence and Nonmaleficence; Standard 3.04, Avoiding Harm). First, the exaggerated diagnosis becomes a permanent part of the client's/patient's health record and potentially could be categorized as a "pre-existing condition" that will form the basis of insurance denial or increased costs for the client/patient in the future. Second, a false diagnosis can lead to inappropriate treatment decisions by the HMO or future care providers that are iatrogenic for the client/patient and outside the psychologist's control. Overdiagnoses can also create social stigma and negatively affect clients'/patients' assessment of their psychological well-being and their responsiveness to therapy or contribute to a harmful self-fulfilling prophecy.

Colluding With Clients/Patients in Upcoding. Some psychologists erroneously believe that they should involve clients in decisions regarding which diagnosis to submit to their health care insurer. Such actions compromise the psychologist-client/patient relationship. First, it represents an abdication of the psychologist's fiduciary responsibility to arrive at a diagnosis and treatment plan that accurately reflects the client's/patient's psychological problems (Principle B: Fidelity and Responsibility). It can thus set the stage for clients/patients to lose faith in or mistrust the psychologist's intent and ability to provide the best standard of care. Second, it communicates to the client/patient that the psychologist believes deception, false claims, and lies are acceptable forms of achieving goals, a message inconsistent with the aims of therapy (Principle C, Integrity).

CHAPTER 10

Standards on Education and Training

7. EDUCATION AND TRAINING

7.01 Design of Education and Training Programs

Psychologists responsible for education and training programs take reasonable steps to ensure that the programs are designed to provide the appropriate knowledge and proper experiences, and to meet the requirements for licensure, certification, or other goals for which claims are made by the program. (See also Standard 5.03, Descriptions of Workshops and Non-Degree-Granting Educational Programs.)

Psychologists responsible for education and training programs have an obligation to establish relationships of loyalty and trust with their institutions, students, and members of society who rely on academic institutions to provide the knowledge, skills, and career opportunities claimed by the specific degree program (Principle B, Fidelity and Responsibility). Psychologists responsible for administering academic programs must ensure that course requirements meet recognized standards in the relevant field.

> ☑ Department chairs and other faculty responsible for undergraduate curricula development need to ensure that course requirements expose undergraduate psychology majors, minors, and individuals taking survey courses to the knowledge and skills considered fundamental to the discipline.

> ☑ Chairs or directors of doctoral programs claiming to produce graduates competent to conduct psychological research need to ensure that students receive education and training in the theoretical, methodological, and statistical skills required to competently conduct psychological science in the specific fields emphasized by the program.
>
> ☑ Psychologists responsible for professional degree programs need to ensure that course requirements and field experiences meet those required by potential employers, relevant state or professional organizations for program accreditation, internship placements where relevant, and applicable individual licensure and credentialing bodies.
>
> ☑ Psychologists administering internship programs must ensure that supervisory and training experiences meet the standards of the specific areas of psychological practice claimed, appropriate state and professional accreditation criteria, and state licensing board requirements.

The term *reasonable steps* reflects recognition that despite a program administrator's best efforts, there may be periods during which curriculum adjustments must be made in reaction to changes in faculty composition, departmental reorganizations, institutional demands, modifications in accreditation or licensure regulations, or evolving disciplinary standards.

7.02 Descriptions of Education and Training Programs

Psychologists responsible for education and training programs take reasonable steps to ensure that there is a current and accurate description of the program content (including participation in required course- or program-related counseling, psychotherapy, experiential groups, consulting projects, or community service), training goals and objectives, stipends and benefits, and requirements that must be met for satisfactory completion of the program. This information must be made readily available to all interested parties.

Department and program chairs and psychologists responsible for internship training programs must also ensure that prospective and current students have an accurate description of the nature of the academic and training programs to which they may apply or have been admitted. This standard of the American Psychological Association (APA) Ethics Code (APA, 2002b) requires psychologists responsible for these programs to keep program descriptions up-to-date regarding (a) the required coursework and field experiences, (b) the educational and career objectives supported by the program, (c) the current faculty or supervisory staff, (d) currently offered courses, and (e) the dollar amount of available student stipends and benefits, the process of applying for these, and the obligations incurred by students, interns, or postdoctoral fellows who receive stipends or benefits.

Standard 7.02 specifically obligates teaching psychologists to ensure that prospective and current students, externs, or interns are aware of program requirements to participate in personal psychotherapy or counseling, experiential groups, or any other courses or activities that require them to reveal personal thoughts or feelings. Many program descriptions now appear on university or institutional Web sites. Psychologists need to ensure to the extent possible that these Web sites are appropriately updated. The term *reasonable steps* recognizes that efforts to ensure up-to-date information may be constrained by publication schedules for course catalogues, webmasters not directly under the auspices of the department or program, and other institutional functions over which psychologists may have limited control.

> ☒ A psychology graduate department described itself as offering an industrial-organizational track that included paid summer placements at companies in the city in which the university is located. The required curriculum included only one class in industrial-organizational psychology taught by an adjunct professor. Other required courses for the industrial-organizational track consisted of traditional intelligence and personality test administration classes, test construction, and statistics courses offered by faculty in the department's clinical and psychometric programs. For the past 2 years, the department had been able to place only one or two students in paid summer internships.

7.03 Accuracy in Teaching

(a) Psychologists take reasonable steps to ensure that course syllabi are accurate regarding the subject matter to be covered, bases for evaluating progress, and the nature of course experiences. This standard does not preclude an instructor from modifying course content or requirements when the instructor considers it pedagogically necessary or desirable, so long as students are made aware of these modifications in a manner that enables them to fulfill course requirements. (See also Standard 5.01, Avoidance of False or Deceptive Statements.

Standard 7.03a requires that teaching psychologists provide students with accurate and timely information regarding course content; required and recommended readings; exams, required papers, or other forms of evaluation; and extra-classroom experiences, if required. Psychologists who provide their syllabi via the Internet or who require students to use Web-based references need to keep these Web sites accurate and appropriately updated.

Modifying Course Content or Requirements. This standard also recognizes that syllabi may sometimes include an unintentional error, required readings may become unavailable, changes in institutional scheduling sometimes create conflicts in dates set for exams, and many times psychologists have valid pedagogical reasons for changing course content or requirements at the beginning or middle of a semester.

For example, a professor may find that assigned readings are too difficult or not sufficiently advanced for the academic level of students in the class. In such instances, it would be appropriate for professors to modify course reading requirements as long as materials are available to students and they are given sufficient time to obtain and read them. Similarly, in response to constraints imposed by publishers, bookstores, other professors, or the institution, psychologists may rightly need to modify required texts or exam schedules.

Modifications to course content or requirements do not violate this standard as long as students are made aware of such modifications in a clear and timely manner that enables them to fulfill course requirements without undue hardship. However, a professor who has neither discussed nor specified how students will be evaluated until the last week of class or one who fails to update an old syllabus that does not reflect the current content of the course would be in violation of this standard.

☑ In his first year of teaching, an assistant professor prepared a syllabus for an undergraduate developmental psychology course that drew largely on required readings from books by well-known developmental theorists. He carefully planned weekly quizzes, a midterm exam, and a term paper requiring a critique of several journal articles. Students performed very poorly on the first two quizzes and did not seem to be involved in class discussions. The professor learned that for reasons unknown to the department chair, the dean's office had assigned this class as a "nonmajor" section. The students were therefore not as prepared as had been anticipated because introductory psychology was not a prerequisite for enrollment for nonpsychology majors. The psychologist decided to modify the curriculum to ensure that students received a basic foundation in developmental psychology. He rush-ordered a basic developmental psychology text, extended the date of the midterm, and changed the topic of the term paper to a review of sections of the originally assigned books. He distributed a revised syllabus detailing the changes and gave the students the option of using the first two quizzes as extra credit.

(b) When engaged in teaching or training, psychologists present psychological information accurately. (See also Standard 2.03, Maintaining Competence.)

Standards prescribing the nature of information that teachers should provide raise legitimate concerns about academic freedom. At the same time, in many ways, teaching is a "process of persuasion" where instructors are in the unique socially sanctioned and desired role of systematically influencing the knowledge base and belief systems of students (Friedrich & Douglass, 1998). Standard 7.03b reflects the pedagogical obligation of psychologists to share with students their scholarly judgment and expertise along with the right of students to receive an accurate representation of the subject matter enabling them to evaluate where a professor's views fit within the larger discipline.

The narrowness or breadth of information required to fulfill this standard will depend on the nature of the course. For example, a psychologist who presented readings and lectures only on psychodynamic theories of personality would be presenting accurate information in a course by that name but inaccurate information if teaching a general survey course on theories of personality. A professor who was teaching the same material for 20 years when such material was considered obsolete in terms of recognized standards of the discipline would be providing students inaccurate information about the current state of the subject matter.

7.04 Student Disclosure of Personal Information

Psychologists do not require students or supervisees to disclose personal information in course- or program-related activities, either orally or in writing, regarding sexual history, history of abuse and neglect, psychological treatment, and relationships with parents, peers, and spouses or significant others except if (1) the program or training facility has clearly identified this requirement in its admissions and program materials or (2) the information is necessary to evaluate or obtain assistance for students whose personal problems could reasonably be judged to be preventing them from performing their training- or professionally related activities in a competent manner or posing a threat to the students or others.

This standard requires psychologists to respect the privacy rights of students and supervisees. In many instances, information about students' or supervisees' sexual history, personal experience of abuse or neglect, whether they have or are currently receiving psychotherapy, and their relationships with relatives, friends, or significant others is outside the legitimate boundaries of academic or supervisory program inquiry.

With two exceptions, Standard 7.04 prohibits psychologists from requiring students or supervisees to disclose such information:

Clear Identification of Requirements. Teaching and supervisory psychologists may require disclosure of information about sexual experiences, history of abuse, psychological treatment, or relationships with significant others only if the admissions and program materials have clearly identified that students or supervisees will be expected to reveal such information if admitted into the program. The requirement for advance notification includes programs that explore countertransference reactions during supervisory sessions, if questions about such reactions will tap into any of the categories listed above. Clear and advance notification about the types of disclosures that programs require will allow potential students to elect not to apply to a program if they find such a requirement intrusive or otherwise discomforting.

Interference With Academic Performance or Self-Harm or Other Harm. The standard also recognizes that there are times when students' personal problems may interfere with their ability to competently perform professionally related activities or pose a threat of self-harm or harm to others. In such instances, psychologists are permitted to require students or supervisees to disclose the personal information necessary to help evaluate the nature of the problem, to obtain assistance for the student or supervisee, or to protect others' welfare.

☑ A psychologist supervising a third-year clinical student's work at the university coun-seling center was growing increasingly concerned about the sexual nature of verbal exchanges the student reported having with one of her undergraduate clients. The psychologist also suspected from one of the student's comments that she had been meeting with the client outside of the counseling sessions. Concerned that the student might be in violation of Standards 3.05, Multiple Relationships, or 10.05, Sexual Intimacies With Current Therapy Clients/Patients, the supervisor asked the student whether she had been seeing the client socially. When she responded yes, the psychologist probed further to find out if she was having a romantic relationship with the client.

☒ A student came to see a professor during office hours to discuss his poor grade on the midterm exam in a graduate course on human sexuality. The professor asked the student if he might be doing poorly in the course because of anxieties about his own sexuality.

7.05 Mandatory Individual or Group Therapy

(a) When individual or group therapy is a program or course requirement, psychologists respon-sible for that program allow students in undergraduate and graduate programs the option of selecting such therapy from practitioners unaffiliated with the program. (See also Standard 7.02, Descriptions of Education and Training Programs.)

Standard 7.05a addresses the privacy rights of psychology students enrolled in programs that require individual or group psychotherapy. During the commenting period for the revision of the 2002 APA Ethics Code, a number of graduate students raised concerns about revealing personal information (a) in the presence of other students in required group therapy or experiential courses and (b) to therapists in required individual psychotherapy, if the therapist was closely affiliated with their graduate program. In response to these concerns, this standard requires programs that have such requirements to allow students to select a therapist unaffiliated with the program.

Standard 7.05a does not prevent programs from instituting a screening and approval process for practitioners outside the program whom students may see for required psychotherapy. It is sound policy for programs to ensure that required individual or group therapy is conducted by a qualified mental health professional. In addition, in some programs, the therapeutic experience may be seen as one facet of training about a particular form of psychotherapy, and the program is entitled to require students to select a private therapist who conducts treatment consistent with the program's training goals.

Postdoctoral Training. This standard does not apply to postdoctoral programs, such as postgraduate psychoanalytic programs, that require a training analysis with a member of the faculty. These advanced programs are optional for individuals who seek specialized training beyond a graduate degree in psychology, and unlike such requirements at the graduate level, a decision not to enroll in such programs because of therapy requirements does not restrict opportunities to pursue a career in professional psychology.

(b) Faculty who are or are likely to be responsible for evaluating students' academic performance do not themselves provide that therapy. (See also Standard 3.05, Multiple Relationships.)

This standard is designed to protect the integrity and fairness of evaluations of student academic performance. Whereas Standard 7.05a protects a student's right to keep personal information private from program-affiliated practitioners, Standard 7.05b protects the student from grading or performance evaluation biases that might arise if a faculty member who serves as the student's psychotherapist is also involved in judging his or her academic performance. This standard pertains not only to faculty who might teach a course in which a student who is in therapy with them might enroll but also to faculty who may be involved in decisions regarding passing or failing of comprehensive exams, advancement from master's-level to doctoral-level status, training supervision, and dissertation committees. As indicated by the cross-reference to Standard 3.05, Multiple Relationships, serving in the dual roles of therapist and academic evaluator can impair the therapist's objectivity when knowledge gained from one role is applied to the other, or it can undermine treatment effectiveness when students are afraid to reveal personal information that might negatively affect their academic evaluations.

> ☒ A clinical psychology program that required first-year graduate students to receive 1 year of individual psychotherapy had a referral list of 20 "approved" independent practitioners in the area that students could select as their therapist. The program often drew on these same practitioners to teach required courses as adjunct professors when regular faculty were on sabbatical.

7.06 Assessing Student and Supervisee Performance

(a) In academic and supervisory relationships, psychologists establish a timely and specific process for providing feedback to students and supervisees. Information regarding the process is provided to the student at the beginning of supervision.

Psychologists establish academic and supervisory relationships of trust with students and supervisees based on fair processes of evaluation that provide students and supervisees with the opportunity to learn from positive and negative feedback of their work. Under Standard 7.06a, psychologists must inform students and supervisees (a) when and how often they will be evaluated, (b) the basis for evaluation (e.g., performance on exams, attendance, summaries of client/patient sessions, administration and interpretation of psychological assessments), and (c) the timing and manner in which feedback will be provided.

☒ A psychology professor teaching a graduate course in statistics used a midterm and final exam to evaluate students. The professor delayed returning the midterm, telling the students they should not worry because most of them would do very well. When she returned the graded midterms during the last week of class, students were shocked to discover that most had received Cs and Ds on the exam. Many felt the delay caused them to miss opportunities to learn what aspects of course material they had misunderstood and to adequately prepare for the final.

Providing specific information about student evaluation at the beginning of the process is especially important for the supervision of clinical work, psychological assessment, or research because these supervisory activities are often less uniformly structured than classroom teaching.

☒ A student in a Ph.D. program in school psychology had a second-year externship in a residential school for students with severe emotional disorders. The school psychologist serving as her on-site supervisor relied on "countertransference" techniques to train his externs. Each time the student asked her supervisor for specific information on how her work with student clients would be evaluated, the supervisor would shift the discussion to how the extern's personal reactions to her clients was causing her anxiety about the evaluation of her performance. The extern felt increasingly frustrated and anxious about the lack of specific feedback. At the end of the year, the supervisor gave her a poor evaluation, stating that the student's anxieties interfered with her ability to take direction.

(b) Psychologists evaluate students and supervisees on the basis of their actual performance on relevant and established program requirements.

Fairness and justice require that academic and supervisory evaluations should never be based on student personal characteristics that have not been observed to affect their performance or that are outside the established bounds of program requirements.

☒ A psychologist learned from a member of the clinic staff that one of her supervisees had expressed harsh, racially prejudiced attitudes at a staff party. Over the course of the supervisory period, there was no evidence that the supervisee treated clients in a racially biased manner. However, in the final written evaluation, the psychologist reported that the supervisee appeared to have difficulty working with clients from other racial backgrounds.

Additional discussion regarding psychologists' ethical responsibilities during supervision can be found in the Hot Topic, "Ethical Supervision of Trainees," at the end of this chapter.

7.07 Sexual Relationships With Students and Supervisees

Psychologists do not engage in sexual relationships with students or supervisees who are in their department, agency, or training center or over whom psychologists have or are likely to have evaluative authority. (See also Standard 3.05, Multiple Relationships.)

Sexual relationships with students or supervisees are specifically prohibited by Standard 7.07. The student-professor/supervisor role is inherently asymmetrical in terms of power. Teachers and supervisors have the power to affect student careers through grading, research and professional opportunities, letters of recommendation, scholarships and stipends, and reputation among other faculty or staff. Using this power to coerce or otherwise unduly influence a student to enter a sexual relationship is exploitative (Standard 3.08, Exploitative Relationships). The prohibition against sex with students and supervisees applies not only to those over whom the psychologist has evaluative or direct authority but also to anyone who is a student or supervisee in the psychologist's department, agency, or training center or over whom they might be likely to have evaluative authority while the student is in the program or supervised setting.

Sexual relationships with students and supervisees are a specific example of an unethical multiple relationship (Standard 3.05, Multiple Relationships). When psychologists enter into a sexual relationship with a student or supervisee, their ability to judge the student's/supervisee's academic, professional, or scientific performance objectively is impaired. In addition, when other students learn about such relationships, it can jeopardize the psychologist's ability to maintain an impression of professional impartiality and provides students with a model of unethical conduct that jeopardizes the psychologist's effectiveness as a teacher or supervisor. Such relationships also risk compromising psychologists' ability to exert appropriate authority or evaluations regarding the student/supervisee and others with whom they work if the sexual partner can manipulate the psychologist through threats of exposure or complaints of misconduct.

In many psychology programs, graduate students serve as teaching or research assistants charged with evaluating undergraduate or graduate students' academic performance or supervising their research projects. Standard 7.07 applies to sexual relationships between graduate assistants and students when assistants are either student members of the American Psychology Association or their department has adopted the APA Ethics Code in its policies and procedures.

HOT TOPIC

Ethical Supervision of Trainees

Supervision is a primary means by which students in professional psychology programs acquire and develop skills needed to provide effective and ethical mental health services (Romans, Boswell, Carlozzi, & Ferguson, 1995). Competent and ethical supervision provides a foundation for the attitudes, skills, and commitment supervisees will need to know what is right and the motivation for self-evaluation and lifelong learning necessary to do what is right throughout their careers.

Supervisors have a fiduciary obligation to their supervisees, the clients/patients under the supervisees' care, and the public. They must nurture the supervisees' professional skills and attitudes, ensure that supervisees' clients/patients are provided appropriate mental health treatment, and serve as gatekeepers who take appropriate actions to prevent supervisees not able to demonstrate the needed professional competence from entering the profession and practicing independently (Barnett, Cornish, Goodyear, & Lichtenberg, 2007; Bernard & Goodyear, 2004). The goal of this Hot Topic is to describe the competencies needed to provide effective and ethical supervision, desired outcomes on which to fairly evaluate supervisee performance, and how trainees can contribute to their supervisory experience.

Competencies for Effective Supervision

Competencies for effective supervision include professional knowledge and expertise and the interpersonal skills necessary to create a trusting supervisory alliance (Falender et al., 2004; Standard 2.01, Boundaries of Competence).

Professional Knowledge and Expertise. Supervisors must have the necessary clinical knowledge and expertise to identify client mental health needs within a diversity-sensitive context, guide supervisees in client-appropriate treatment techniques, and recognize when clients are not responding to supervisee interventions. They must also be familiar with academic credit or credentialing supervision requirements, on-site institutional policies, and relevant laws as well as appropriate risk management strategies.

Finally, supervisors must fully integrate into the supervisory process the profession's ethical values and standards (Barnett et al., 2007; Gottlieb et al., 2007). This includes

- Discussion of informed consent, confidentiality and disclosure decisions, avoidance of harmful multiple relationships, attention to personal problems or biases that may interfere with treatment efficacy
- Consistent monitoring of and feedback on supervisee ethical practices
- Preparing students for orderly and appropriate resolution of client responsibility when the training rotation ends
- Maintaining appropriate boundaries and avoiding exploitative or harmful multiple relationships

Interpersonal Competencies. The supervisory context should encourage open discussion of treatment challenges and attempts to try new strategies by providing constructive feedback in a manner that minimizes trainee anxiety and decreased feelings of self-efficacy (Barnett et al., 2007; Daniels & Larson, 2001). At the same time, supervisors cannot shy away from providing negative feedback when it is necessary to ensure that clients are receiving adequate care and that their evaluations of supervisee clinical acumen is objective and in accord with the standards of the profession.

Structuring the Supervisory Process

Structuring the supervisory process requires the ability to tailor training to the supervisee's level of competence, identify appropriate outcome measures for evaluation, and present clear standards for assessment.

Identifying Supervisee's Competencies. The goals and desired outcomes of a training experience need to be tailored to the supervisee's current competencies in relation to client needs and institutional requirements. To meet obligations to trainees and the trainees' clients, supervisors need to evaluate each supervisee's developing competence and the clinical responsibilities with which he or she can be entrusted (Falender & Shafranske, 2007; Standard 2.05, Delegation of Work to Others).

Identifying Appropriate Training Outcomes. Evaluations must be based on the supervisee's actual performance on relevant and established requirements (Standard 7.06, Assessing Student and Supervisee Performance). Falender and Shafranske (2007) identify the following abilities by which the trainee's professional growth can be evaluated:

- Apply clinical knowledge and skills in a consistent fashion and incorporate new knowledge into existing competencies
- Deal with increased confusions and varied situational aspects that shape clinical work
- Respond to constructive feedback
- Carry out recommendations to ensure adequate client care
- Use problem-solving and clinical reasoning skills appropriate to specific clinical tasks and ethical challenges
- Master technical and facilitative variables appropriate to the students' stage of training

Feedback and Evaluation. Standard 7.06 also requires that supervisors establish a timely and specific process for providing feedback to supervisees and explain the process to trainees at the beginning of supervision. This includes delineating setting-specific competencies the supervisee must attain for successful completion of the supervised interval (Falender & Shafranske, 2007).

Meaningful evaluations, scheduled at predetermined intervals, provide trainees with adequate time to improve their skills and the supervisor opportunity to evaluate the trainee's responsiveness to constructive feedback. When supervisees are unresponsive, fail to demonstrate needed competence, or exhibit impaired professional competence as a result of personal problems, these issues should be addressed in supervision and the trainee provided reasonable opportunities for remediation or intervention. When necessary, the supervisor must act to prevent inappropriate actions resulting in poor-quality client care, violation of ethical standards, or harm to the institution through the supervisee's violation of policy or law. When appropriate, supervisors should inform their institution or the students' academic program and provide a written report documenting the reasons for their concerns (see Gizara & Forest, 2004).

Enhancing the Supervisory Experience

The quality of clinical supervision will significantly affect students' development as competent and ethical practitioners.

Externships and internships in professional psychology programs are often off-site and supervised by non-faculty members. When applying for training at these sites, students should obtain the following information:

- Has the graduate program and externship training site entered into a formal relationship that includes articulation of specific training goals and standards, open communication between program faculty and on-site supervisors, and a system of formalized feedback from students regarding the quality of the training experience?
- Who in their graduate program or externship or internship site can students go to if they have a problem with an off-site supervisor? Is there a formal complaint process?
- If a supervisor is providing inadequate training, will the department or training site assist the student in obtaining the necessary clinical experience and supervision?

Competent practice in professional psychology requires an understanding of and adherence to ethical standards, institutional policy, and law. Supervisees should be provided copies of the relevant agency policies and procedural manuals, including mandatory and discretionary reporting policies and steps to be taken in case of an emergency. Supervisees should also be made aware of the nature of routine institutional intake procedures and their own responsibilities regarding obtaining informed consent and communicating to clients/patients information regarding Health Insurance Portability and Accountability Act policies, confidentiality policies, the fact that they are in training, and the name and contact information of their supervisor (10.01, Informed Consent to Therapy).

Self-reflection and the motivation to improve one's clinical knowledge and skills are fundamental to good practice. Supervisees should take an active role in constructing a meaningful learning experience. To help their supervisors in establishing appropriate training experiences and evaluation criteria, supervisees should be encouraged to be frank when asked to discuss their current level of clinical competence and training goals and to continue throughout the training experience to ask for additional or more focused training in a specific area of clinical concern, including asking the supervisor about APA Ethics Code requirements and how they relate to current treatment issues.

CHAPTER 11

Standards on Research and Publication

8. RESEARCH AND PUBLICATION

8.01 Institutional Approval

When institutional approval is required, psychologists provide accurate information about their research proposals and obtain approval prior to conducting the research. They conduct the research in accordance with the approved research protocol.

The Code of Federal Regulations Title 45–Part 46 Protection of Human Subjects (www.nihtraining.com/ohsrsite/guidelines/45cfr46.html) mandating institutional review of research emerged in response to abuse of research participants internationally (the Nuremberg Code, 1949) and in the United States, particularly to the 1972 public disclosure of the 30-year government-supported Tuskegee Syphilis Study, in which 300 Black rural men were left untreated for diagnosed syphilis even after effective antibiotics became available (Jones, 1993). Institutional review boards (IRBs) are charged with ensuring that investigators protect the rights and welfare of research participants. Specific IRB requirements reflect three general moral principles that are incorporated more broadly into the APA Ethics Code: see Principles A: Beneficence and Nonmaleficence, D: Justice, and E: Respect for People's Rights and Dignity. The ideals reflected in the principle of beneficence require IRBs to ensure that research is designed to maximize benefits for science, humanity, and research participants and to avoid or minimize risk or harm. Applied to the research context, the moral principle of justice means that IRBs must ensure that investigators equitably select participants and that the potential benefits and costs of research participation are fairly distributed among persons and diverse groups. The moral principle of respect for personhood requires IRBs to ensure that informed consent and confidentiality procedures protect the autonomy and privacy rights of participants.

Standard 8.01 of the American Psychological Association (APA) Ethics Code (APA, 2002b) has four basic requirements. First, psychologists must know if and from whom institutional approval is required. All institutions receiving federal funding for biomedical or behavioral research are required to establish IRBs to protect the rights and safety of research participants. Institutions must also follow federal, state, and local laws requiring the review and regulation of research involving animal subjects. In addition, many social welfare agencies, health care facilities, schools, correctional facilities, businesses, and other public and private organizations have their own internal review requirements for research. Federal guidelines list activities that are exempt from institutional review; however, the exempt status of any specific project must be approved by an institution's IRB (Department of Health and Human Services [DHHS], 2005). Depending on institutional policy, psychology laboratory course experiments may not require review.

The remaining three requirements within the standard are that applications for institutional review must be accurate, approval must be obtained before the research is conducted, and research procedures must follow the approved protocol. Failure to meet any of these conditions violates this standard. It is not unusual for methods to be modified during different phases of research. Any changes in participant informed consent language or procedures, compensation, confidentiality protections, or methods that increase human or animal participant risk or safety should be resubmitted for institutional approval prior to implementation. Psychologists should consult the appropriate IRB about the need to provide an informative memo or to resubmit proposals for minor changes unrelated to participant protections or welfare. Readers may wish to refer to the Hot Topic at the end of this chapter, "Submitting Successful IRB Proposals."

Implications of HIPAA. Investigators conducting program evaluation or archival research involving "protected (identifiable) health information" (PHI) as defined under the new Health Insurance Portability and Accountability Act of 1996 (HIPAA; 45 CFR 160–164) should be aware that institutions, health plans, or providers who have obtained the information in many instances must have a waiver from either an IRB or a "privacy board" before they may provide such information to an investigator without specific written patient authorization. The next section provides an expanded discussion of HIPAA as it relates to informed consent to research. Readers may also refer to the section "A Word About HIPAA" in the Preface of this book.

8.02 Informed Consent to Research

(a) When obtaining informed consent as required in Standard 3.10, Informed Consent, psychologists inform participants about (1) the purpose of the research, expected duration, and procedures; (2) their right to decline to participate and to withdraw from the research once participation has begun; (3) the foreseeable consequences of declining or withdrawing; (4) reasonably foreseeable factors that may be expected to influence their willingness to participate such as potential risks, discomfort, or adverse effects; (5) any prospective research benefits; (6) limits of confidentiality; (7) incentives for participation; and (8) whom to contact for questions about the research and research participants' rights. They provide opportunity for the prospective participants to ask questions and receive answers. (See also Standards 8.03, Informed Consent for Recording Voices and Images in Research; 8.05, Dispensing With Informed Consent for Research; and 8.07, Deception in Research.)

Ensuring Consent Is Informed, Rational, and Voluntary

Within the context of research, informed consent requirements reflect Principle E: Respect for People's Rights and Dignity by ensuring that individuals' decision to participate is informed, voluntary, and rational. To comply with this standard, psychologists must obtain and document written or oral consent in the manner set forth in Standard 3.10, Informed Consent. The informed component of consent requires that individuals are provided all the pertinent information needed to make a reasoned choice about whether they wish to participate in a study. This includes providing information in a language and at a language level understood by prospective participants and, where applicable, their legally authorized representative. When obtaining guardian permission and participant assent for research involving populations that do not speak English or for whom English is a second language, psychologists should be alert to the possibility that prospective participants and their legal guardians may have different language preferences and proficiencies (Council of National Psychological Associations for the Advancement of Ethnic Minority Interests, 2000; Fisher et al., 2002).

> ☑ A psychologist sought to obtain parental permission for a study on perceived racial/ethnic discrimination among high school students. The high school from which students would be recruited served a large proportion of families who had emigrated from Vietnam. While all the students spoke English at school, the psychologist created parent permission and child assent forms written in English on one side and Vietnamese on the other side.

Describing the Nature of Participation. Prospective participants and, when appropriate, their legal guardians must be given information and the opportunity to ask questions about the purpose, duration, procedures, foreseeable risks, potential benefits, and compensation involved in participation that is sufficient to make an informed decision. The Office for Human Subjects Protections (http://www.hhs.gov/ohrp/faq.html) has interpreted federal regulations as prohibiting investigators from describing participant compensation as a benefit when obtaining informed consent (see Standard 8.06, Offering Inducements for Research Participation).

Persons With Questionable Capacity to Consent. The rational component of informed consent requires that prospective participants are able to understand the information presented. Psychologists often conduct research involving adult populations with questionable consent capacity. The rational decision-making capacity of active drug users, for example, will vary with their state of intoxication or withdrawal (Fisher, 2004; Jeste & Saks, 2006). The consent capacity of adults with schizophrenia and related disorders is often transient depending on whether they are in an acute stage, remission, or responding positively or negatively to medication. Elder adults or individuals with Alzheimer's may also have fluctuating or decreasing ability to understand consent information. When consent capacity of a participant population is known to be questionable, psychologists should use available assessment techniques to determine the ability of prospective participants to understand the nature of and their rights in research (see, e.g., Carpenter et al., 2000; Fisher et al., 2006; Hot Topic, "Goodness-of-Fit Ethics for Informed Consent Involving Adults With Impaired Decisional Capacity," Chapter 6).

As required in Standard 3.10b, Informed Consent, psychologists must (a) provide appropriate explanations and obtain assent for research participation from persons legally incapable of informed consent, such as children or adults with severely impaired cognitive capacities, and (b) obtain appropriate permission from a legally authorized person, if such substitute consent is permitted or required by law. Under federal regulations, passive consent procedures (sending guardians forms asking for a response only if they do *not* wish their child to participate in the research) are not an ethical substitute for guardian permission. Psychologists who do not obtain the active affirmative permission of guardians violate this standard except when the research meets the conditions for Standard 8.05, Dispensing With Informed Consent for Research, or when an IRB waives the requirement for guardian permission under federal regulation 45 CFR 46.116d and 46.408c (see also this chapter's Hot Topic: "Submitting Successful IRB Proposals"). Research psychologists conducting longitudinal studies with minors should also consider re-consent procedures appropriate to children's changing consent maturity.

☑ A psychologist was conducting a study on language skills involving adults with mild levels of mental retardation and developmental disabilities (MR/DD) living in community group residences. Some of the prospective participants had a parent or sibling who was their legal guardian. The psychologist obtained signed permission from all legal guardians followed by the signed assent of individuals who wished to participate. Other prospective participants had maintained the legal right to consent to decisions affecting their lives, but such decisions were often made in collaboration with residence staff and family. The psychologist obtained signed consent from all adults with MR/DD who had the legal right to consent. Letters describing the study also were sent in advance to the family members with whom these individuals relied on for decision making. In all situations, the psychologist did not attempt to obtain consent from a prospective participant until after a resident staff member had confirmed that the individual wanted to be approached.

The Voluntary Nature of Participation. Consent procedures must directly inform participants they will not be penalized for declining or withdrawing from participation, especially when the prospective participant has reason to believe that dissent may result in adverse consequences (see Standards 8.02b, Informed Consent to Research, and 8.04, Client/Patient, Student, and Subordinate Research Participants). Institutional populations are particularly vulnerable to involuntary participation in research. Prisoners and youth held for brief periods in detention centers, for example, are highly vulnerable because of their restricted autonomy and liberty, often compounded by their low socioeconomic status, poor education, and poor health (Gostin, 2007). Incarcerated persons have few expectations regarding privacy protections and may view research participation as a means of seeking favor with or avoiding punishment from prison or detention guards or officials (see also Standard 3.08, Exploitative Relationships; DHHS, 2005, Subpart C).

The conditions under which individuals will qualify for full compensation for participation or continuation of experimental interventions if they withdraw from the study must also be fully described (see Standard 8.06, Offering Inducements for Research Participation).

> ☒ A neuropsychologist designed a study of brain activity during sleep that required participants to stay overnight at the research laboratory for 3 consecutive days. The informed consent explained that participants could withdraw at any time and would be compensated $100 a night for a total of $300. When several participants chose to withdraw from the study after the first night, they were shocked to learn that the psychologist's policy was to only compensate individuals who had participated all 3 nights. The psychologist justified his decision on the basis that 1 or 2 nights' data could not be used to statistically test study hypotheses.

Confidentiality. Disclosure of confidential information can result in criminal or civil liability or financial or social damage. Informed consent procedures must provide a clear explanation of the extent and limits of confidentiality, including (a) whether investigators must comply with reporting requirements such as mandated child abuse reporting, elder abuse, or duty-to-warn laws; (b) the investigator's confidentiality and disclosure policy for responses indicating that a participant or another person is in immediate danger or otherwise at a high level of risk; or (c) if the method of data collection itself may limit the extent of confidentiality protections, as may be the case when research is conducted via the Internet (see discussions of confidentiality in research in Chapter 7 under Standards 4.01, Maintaining Confidentiality; 4.02, Discussing the Limits of Confidentiality; and 4.05, Disclosures). Investigators conducting research in schools or studies involving children or adults with questionable consent capacities should familiarize themselves with evolving federal and state laws governing guardians' rights of access to health- or school-related records created, used, or disclosed by a researcher (e.g., HIPAA, the Protection of Pupil Rights Amendment [PPRA]; see below) and disclose such information to guardians and children during informed consent.

☒ A psychologist began conducting a survey study on marital conflict over the Internet. She posted an explanation of the study on a university Web site. Those who wished to participate were asked to copy and then paste the questions and answers into an e-mail response back to the psychologist. The Web site claimed that participant responses were anonymous and thus there were no risks to confidentiality. However, this was not true since the responses were embedded in the e-mail and thus linked to respondents' identifying e-mail addresses. The psychologist did not realize her error until too late, when she discovered that her research assistants had identified a faculty member as one of the respondents as they were coding the data.

The Certificate of Confidentiality. The Public Health Service Act of 1946 permits investigators to apply for a Certificate of Confidentiality issued by the National Institutes of Health (NIH) and other Department of Health and Human Services (DHHS) agencies. The certificate protects investigators from being forced or compelled by law enforcement or subpoena to disclose personally identifiable research information that could place participants in legal jeopardy or damage their financial standing, employability, insurability, or reputation (see www.hhs.gov/ohrp/humansubjects/guidance/certconf.htm). The certificate does not protect investigators from being compelled by law to release confidential information related to suspected child abuse or preclude investigators from voluntarily disclosing confidential information. If investigators who have acquired a certificate intend to make certain voluntary disclosures to protect the research participant or others from harm (see Standard 4.05, Disclosures), the consent form should detail both the certificate protections and the investigator's disclosure legal and ethical responsibilities.

☒ The consent form used by a psychologist conducting a yearlong community-based study on adolescent membership in urban gangs included a statement that a Certificate of Confidentiality had been obtained that protected the psychologist from being compelled by law enforcement to reveal information regarding illegal drug activities of participants. The consent form did not specify that the psychologist would voluntarily disclose confidential information to protect participants or others from harm. During the course of the study, the psychologist informed local police when he learned during an interview that several participants were planning to set fire to a school playground over the weekend. While some participants were grateful the fire was prevented, they all felt the psychologist had violated the informed consent agreement and refused to continue participation in the study.

Tribal and International Research and the Role of Others in the Consent Process. When conducting cross-cultural research involving American Indian and Alaskan Native communities or villages in countries outside the United States, cultural traditions sometimes require investigators to obtain permission from a tribal leader or village council before they can approach individual community members (Mohatt & Thomas, 2006; National Bioethics Advisory Committee [NBAC], 2001; Noe et al., 2006). In other cultures, an investigator may be required to obtain permission from a woman's husband, father, or other male relative before she can be approached for research participation. Obtaining tribal leaders' or a family member's permission to recruit individuals for research participation should not be confused with or compromise individual consent. Investigators gaining community permission should approach each individual member and implement consent procedures that ensure that agreement to participate is informed, rational, and voluntary. Research should not be conducted in communities where the political structure or power imbalances based on gender compromise the voluntary requirement of consent by placing pressure on individuals to participate (see also NBAC, 2001; Standard 3.08, Exploitative Relationships; Chapter 3, this volume).

In international mental health research, the investigator and participant community may differ in their concepts of physical, informational, and decisional privacy (Goldman & Choy, 2001). In some communities with less rigid building structures and cultural values emphasizing community openness and family interdependence, participants may question the motives of an investigator who attempts to protect privacy by conducting research interviews in a secluded area and in the absence of family members (Monshi & Zieglmayer, 2004). In cross-cultural research, therefore, it is important to determine how the participant population defines and values privacy, design confidentiality procedures to reflect these values, and clarify during informed consent how confidentiality safeguards have been selected to respect community values and fulfill investigators' ethical responsibilities.

Informed Consent for Qualitative Research. The open-ended nature of ethnographic, phenomenological, and participant observation studies can make it difficult to anticipate the exact nature of information that may be gained through participant-investigator interactions. The focus on discovering emergent themes in qualitative research means that investigators do not always know beforehand privacy and confidentiality issues that may emerge during the course of research (Fisher, 2004). Investigators should alert the prospective participant to this possibility during informed consent, monitor verbal or behavioral information during the course of the study, and remind the participant about confidentiality protections and limitations when unexpected subjects emerge. If a new direction of inquiry emerges that might be in conflict with participants' confidentiality expectations, this should be identified and the participant given the opportunity to re-consent. In field studies involving drug use or other illegal behaviors, an agreement can be reached during informed consent about which activities will and will not be asked or witnessed (Singer et al., 2000).

Implications of HIPAA

Under HIPAA, PHI is defined as any information transmitted or maintained in any form or medium relating to the past, present, or future physical or mental health condition; provision of care; or payment for provision of care for an individual that either identifies or can be used to identify the individual.

HIPAA requires that all providers who are covered entities under HIPAA (a health plan, a health care clearinghouse, or a health care provider who transmits any health information in electronic form relevant to carry out financial or administrative activities related to health care) comply with the regulations (45 CFR 160.102). Whether or not an individual investigator is providing the service or is a health care provider, if the research is conducted in an organized system of health care or implemented by a provider, HIPAA will apply (see www.hhs.gov/ocr/hipaa/finalreg.html and discussions of the implications of HIPAA for confidentiality in research in Chapter 7 under Standards 4.01, Maintaining Confidentiality, and 4.02a, Discussing the Limits of Confidentiality).

Authorization to Use PHI for Research. HIPAA requires that in order for a covered entity to create, use, or disclose PHI for research purposes, the covered entity must receive a signed authorization from the prospective participant or a legal guardian limited to the specific research project (45 CFR 164.508[c]). Research is one of the few activities for which HIPAA permits authorization for the use or disclosure of PHI to be combined with informed consent information and other types of written permission for the same research (45 CFR 164.508[b][3][i]). Under HIPAA, a valid authorization must contain the following:

- A description of the information to be used or disclosed written in clear language
- Specific identification of the person(s) who will be involved in the request for, use, and disclosure of PHI
- A description of each purpose of the requested use or disclosure
- An expiration date
- Signature and date of signature
- A statement regarding the individual's right to revoke the authorization in writing
- Exceptions to the right to revocation (e.g., if the PHI already has been obtained and used on the basis of the original authorization, the investigator may maintain data analyses based on the information, although no additional information may be used or disclosed following revocation)
- The consequences to the individual of a refusal to sign the authorization. Research is one of the few conditions in which HIPAA permits treatment to be conditioned upon authorization (45 CFR 164.508[b][4][i]).
- The participant must receive a copy of the authorization.

The HIPAA Transition Provision. So as not to unnecessarily impede research, HIPAA has a transition provision that permits the use of PHI obtained with appropriate IRB-approved informed consent prior to the April 14, 2003, compliance date. However, individuals who are participating in longitudinal studies must be re-consented with appropriate HIPAA authorization if they are retested or otherwise reinvolved in the research after that date (45 CFR 164.532).

Health Records Research. HIPAA is also relevant for research psychologists conducting records research on PHI collected by social services agencies, hospitals, or other health or service provider institutions. With some exceptions, covered entities can allow investigators access to PHI only if the covered entity obtains authorization by the client/patient or a legally authorized representative to release PHI for the specific research purposes and to the specific investigator or investigative team. Whenever a covered entity releases PHI to an investigator, the covered entity is required to disclose only the "minimum necessary" to reasonably achieve the purpose of the disclosure (45 CFR 164.514[3]). Under the HIPAA Privacy Rule, covered entities are permitted to use and disclose PHI for research without a client's/patient's authorization under specific conditions described below in the discussion of Standard 8.05, Dispensing With Informed Consent for Research.

Parental Consent in School-Based Research

Implications of PPRA for U.S. Department of Education–Funded Research. The Protection of Pupil Rights Amendment (PPRA) of 2004 (www.ed.gov/offices/OM/fpco/ppra/index.html) seeks to ensure that certain instructional materials used in connection with a federally funded survey, analysis, or evaluation of students are available for inspection by parents and that written parental consent is obtained before minor students participate in such research. The types of materials to which PPRA applies include the following:

1. Political affiliations

2. Mental and psychological problems potentially embarrassing to the student and his or her family

3. Sexual behaviors and attitudes

4. Illegal, antisocial, self-incriminating, and demeaning behaviors

5. Critical appraisals of other individuals with whom respondents have close family relationships

6. Legally recognized privileged or analogous relationships, such as those of lawyers, physicians, and ministers

7. Income (other than that required by law to determine eligibility for participation in a program or for receiving financial assistance under such programs)

Evolving Law. Psychologists conducting research in the schools should also stay up-to-date on the implementation of the Hutchinson Amendment to the Reauthorization of the Elementary and Secondary Education Act of 1965 (ESEA) directing state and local education agencies that receive funds under ESEA to develop guidelines to protect student privacy in dealings with public and private entities that are not schools.

(b) Psychologists conducting intervention research involving the use of experimental treatments clarify to participants at the outset of the research (1) the experimental nature of the treatment;

(2) the services that will or will not be available to the control group(s) if appropriate; (3) the means by which assignment to treatment and control groups will be made; (4) available treatment alternatives if an individual does not wish to participate in the research or wishes to withdraw once a study has begun; and (5) compensation for or monetary costs of participating including, if appropriate, whether reimbursement from the participant or a third-party payor will be sought. (See also Standard 8.02a, Informed Consent to Research.)

This standard governs research on behavioral, psychosocial, biomedical, psychopharmacological, or other interventions involving individuals, families, groups, or communities.

Addressing the "Therapeutic Misconception." Appelbaum, Roth, and Lidz (1982) coined the term *therapeutic misconception* to describe two common but incorrect beliefs held by participants regarding randomized clinical trials (RCTs): (a) that their individualized needs will be taken into account in condition assignment and (b) there is a high probability that they will benefit from research participation (see also Appelbaum, Lidz, & Grisso, 2004). These misconceptions may be compounded by therapeutic mistrust in underserved or marginalized populations (Fisher et al., 2008).

Standard 8.02b requires that psychologists address such potential misconceptions during informed consent. The first provision, clarifying the experimental nature of the treatment, requires that informed consent procedures address the general misconception that "experimental" treatment means "better" treatment with known direct benefits for participants. The primary goal of intervention research is to provide generalizable information on whether a particular type of intervention is successful. Depending on the stage of research, an untested experimental treatment may place participants at greater risk than a no-treatment or treatment-as-usual condition. Most important, psychologists must take reasonable steps to communicate to prospective participants that the purpose of conducting treatment research is to determine whether a treatment works or how it works in comparison to another treatment.

This standard does not prevent psychologists from describing direct benefits that may be derived from participation, such as (a) access to new experimental treatments not yet available for general use, (b) receipt of the experimental treatment if it proves effective during or following the conclusion of the study, (c) comprehensive psychological assessment and monitoring, (d) treatment referrals, or (e) upon participant-signed authorization, forwarding a summary of the participant's response to the treatment conditions to a qualified mental health professional.

☑ A team of developmental psychologists designed an innovative intervention study to determine whether integrating readings on alcohol use and abuse into 10th-grade English and biology classes would yield more effective drinking reduction results than the 2-week section on substance abuse currently taught in the 10th-grade health course. The district superintendent gave the investigators permission to randomly assign the 10 district schools to either the new or existing curriculum condition.

Students in both conditions whose parents gave signed permission and who assented would be surveyed through 12th grade to compare the short- and long-term effectiveness of the programs on student alcohol attitudes and use. Prior to initiating the study, discussions with parent groups indicated concern that students in the control schools would be deprived of an effective intervention. On the basis of this information, the investigators worked with parent groups to ensure that the language of the parental permission and assent forms clarified that the study was being conducted because at this time it was unknown whether one curriculum-based approach would be more effective than the other in reducing high school drinking. In addition, the psychologists agreed to offer a yearly talk about adolescent drinking to each school's parent organization and provide a report on the results of the study to both school administrators and parents (see also Standard 8.08, Debriefing).

Explanation About Control Groups and Methods of Assignment to Treatment Conditions. The principles of good scientific design often require investigators to (a) assign some participants to control group conditions as a point of comparison for the experimental treatment (between-group designs) or (b) vary the treatment and control conditions for individual participants (within-group designs). Control conditions may consist of participants receiving different levels of the investigational intervention, a treatment of documented effectiveness, currently available services (treatment as usual), a placebo, or no treatment. Provisions 2 and 3 of Standard 8.02b require that informed consent adequately describes the nature, potential risks, and probable benefits of control group assignment as well as how assignment to experimental and control group conditions will be made. When appropriate, the nature of random assignment should be explained in language that can be understood by individuals unfamiliar with the scientific method. Informed consent for studies using single- or double-blind procedures should describe the extent to which participants and members of the treatment and research teams will know which group the participant has been assigned to and steps that will be taken to determine if and how the blind will be broken.

☑ Prescribing psychologists at a medical school received IRB approval to assess the treatment efficacy of a medication for developmentally disabled (MR/DD) children with comorbid aggressive behavioral disorder. The medication was approved by the Food and Drug Administration (FDA) for treatment with developmentally disabled adults. Only children who had failed to respond to currently prescribed pediatric medications were to be recruited. Although no long-lasting negative effects of the medication had been observed in adult studies, there was some controversy in the literature about whether animal studies demonstrating some negative effects were applicable to humans. To ensure that parents were fully informed, permission forms described the adult and animal results and stated that based on animal studies, there was some unknown risk that the drug could cause neurological damage in participating children. To avoid inadvertently implying to these parents that the animal data suggested that the medication was therefore a powerfully effective drug, the consent form also clarified that the study was being conducted because there was as yet no empirical evidence indicating that the medication would be more effective than currently used medications for children with MR/DD and aggressive disorder.

The design required that each child would be given 2 weeks each of five experimental conditions (placebo, three different dosages of the experimental medication, and one dosage of the child's current medication). Parental permission forms explained how the order of these conditions would be randomly assigned for each child and that neither the parents nor the psychologist directly involved in the child's behavioral assessments would know which type of treatment the child was receiving during any 2-week period. The permission form further explained that the treating psychologist would be carefully monitoring the child's behavior and that if either the psychologist or the parent became concerned that the child's mental health was significantly deteriorating in ways that placed the child or others in danger, the "blind" would be broken, the child withdrawn from the study, and appropriate treatment provided. Parents were also informed that at the end of the child's study participation, the investigators would prepare a summary letter for the parent and, with signed parental authorization, send the child's primary mental health provider the child's diagnosis, a summary of the nature of the treatment conditions, observed behavioral changes in reaction to the different experimental conditions, and any recommendations for treatment that emerged from the child's responses to different conditions (adapted from Fisher, Hoagwood, & Jensen, 1996).

The Right to Refuse Participation Without Penalty. Provision 4 addresses the need to ensure that research participation is voluntary. Individuals who apply for or who already receive nonexperimental services at the study site may fear that failure to participate will result in deterioration or removal of existing services (see also Standard 8.04, Client/Patient, Student, and Subordinate Research Participants). Informed consent procedures must ensure clients/patients currently receiving services that dissent will not disrupt their ongoing treatment and inform individuals new to the treatment facility of available alternative services. This standard does not require psychologists to describe or provide treatment alternatives when they are not otherwise available.

Costs and Compensation. The cost of treatments provided in intervention research may be provided at no cost to the participant through federal or private funding of the research, charged to the participant, or billed through a participant's health plan. Understanding the financial costs and the extent to which third-party payors will be aware of diagnoses and services received during a research study is essential for informed decision making. In some cases, participants may be provided monetary compensation for participation. Provision 5 requires that prospective participants are given sufficient information about the nature of such financial arrangements to make an informed decision about participation (see also Standard 6.04, Fees and Financial Arrangements).

Implications of HIPAA. Psychologists creating, using, or disclosing PHI during the conduct of research evaluating health interventions such as different therapeutic techniques will have to comply with HIPAA regulations under almost all circumstances. For specific discussion of the relevance of HIPAA to such research, see "A Word About HIPAA" in the Preface of this book; see also discussions in other chapters of Standards 3.10, Informed Consent; 4.01, Maintaining Confidentiality; 4.02, Discussing the Limits of Confidentiality; 8.02a, Informed Consent to Research; 9.03, Informed Consent in Assessments; 10.01, Informed Consent to Therapy; and other sections in this book identified by the HIPAA icon.

8.03 Informed Consent for Recording Voices and Images in Research

Psychologists obtain informed consent from research participants prior to recording their voices or images for data collection unless (1) the research consists solely of naturalistic observations in public places, and it is not anticipated that the recording will be used in a manner that could cause personal identification or harm, or (2) the research design includes deception, and consent for the use of the recording is obtained during debriefing. (See also Standard 8.07, Deception in Research.)

Psychologists must obtain informed consent to electronically record research participation before beginning data collection. Stored auditory and visual records pose a greater risk of personal identification over time than other data formats, and therefore consent procedures must allow persons to evaluate the personal consequences of such risks prior to research participation. Restricting data access to the research team best protects personal identification. If recordings will also be used for training purposes or presentation at professional meetings, consent must be obtained specifically for these purposes unless image scrambling, voice distortion, or other identity-masking techniques can ensure adequate disguise (see also Standard 4.07, Use of Confidential Information for Didactic or Other Purposes).

The inclusion of the phrase "prior to recording their voices or images for data collection" allows investigators to record the consent procedure itself for documentation or other legitimate purposes as long as participant permission is obtained in advance and recording ceases if the individual refuses participation.

> ☑ A research team was conducting a study on neurological functioning in community-dwelling adult intravenous drug users. The researchers planned to screen for sobriety prior to obtaining informed consent, and as part of street recruitment, individuals were informed that participation required them to be sober when they arrived at the testing site. The investigators realized that some consent-relevant cognitive impairments might be detected only by neurological tests administered as part of the study. With approval from the IRB, the investigators decided to tape-record the informed consent procedures so that they could incorporate the neurological test results in an analysis of participants' consent understanding with the goal of developing ways of improving the consent process for this population. At the beginning of the consent conference, investigators explained to each prospective participant that they were going to describe the study so the individual could decide if he or she wanted to participate and asked the participants questions to make sure they understood the consent information. They then asked for permission to tape-record responses to the consent procedure, underscoring that participants who refused to have the consent conference recorded would still be eligible for participation in the study. Only the consent conferences of individuals who gave permission were recorded.

Exceptions. Investigators may record the voices and images of persons without their consent if (a) observations occur in a public setting in which one would have no reasonable expectation of privacy, for example, a public park, a hotel lobby, or a street corner; (b) procedures do not disturb or manipulate the natural surroundings; and (c) protections are in place to guard against personal identification and harm, especially when the behaviors observed place participants at legal or social risk, for example, vandalism. Investigators conducting deception research that meets the requirements of Standard 8.07, Deception in Research, can receive approval from their IRB to waive the requirement to obtain consent for recording prior to data collection, but they must seek permission to use recordings for data analysis from participants during debriefing. Recordings must be destroyed if the participant declines permission.

8.04 Client/Patient, Student, and Subordinate Research Participants

(a) When psychologists conduct research with clients/patients, students, or subordinates as participants, psychologists take steps to protect the prospective participants from adverse consequences of declining or withdrawing from participation.

Clients/patients, students, employees, prisoners, or other institutionalized persons may not feel free to decline or withdraw participation in a study conducted by a psychologist serving as their treatment provider, professor, supervisor, employer, or member of the institutional staff. Standard 8.04a requires psychologists to take specific steps to ensure that (a) refusal to participate does not result in a reduction in the amount or quality of services, lowered grades, poor job performance evaluations, or loss of institutional privileges, and (b) prospective participants are aware of these protections during recruitment and throughout the course of research (see 8.02, Informed Consent to Research). When power differentials inherent in an existing professional relationship are apparent (such as when the investigator is also the student's professor or a participant's service provider), psychologists should refrain from conducting the informed consent process and any research procedures involving direct contact with the individual (see also Standard 3.05, Multiple Relationships). In some settings, it may be desirable to appoint a participant advocate to (a) explain to prospective participants the purpose of the study, the role of the investigator, and protections against adverse consequences of nonparticipation; (b) determine if vulnerable persons wish to be approached by the research team to give informed consent; and (c) monitor the continued voluntariness of participation.

☑ A graduate student member of the APA received permission to collect data for her doctoral dissertation at her internship site. The methodology included individual interviews with patients at the veterans hospital where she interned. The graduate student restricted her recruitment to hospital patients who were not in the section in which she worked. In addition, she hired and trained a research assistant to recruit participants and obtain informed consent.

(b) When research participation is a course requirement or an opportunity for extra credit, the prospective participant is given the choice of equitable alternative activities.

In many colleges and universities, psychology instructors require or give extra course credit for undergraduate student participation in research. The pedagogical rationale for required research participation is to provide direct experience with the process of research. Yet the requirement can be coercive to students who do not want to be involved in experimental procedures. In addition, psychology faculty and graduate students conducting research at the university benefit from a yearly "subject pool" of prospective participants, creating the potential for student exploitation (Standards 3.06, Conflict of Interest, and 3.08, Exploitative Relationships). Standard 8.04b addresses these concerns by requiring that psychologists offer students pedagogical alternatives equivalent in time and effort to research participation, such as watching a video on a research topic, summarizing an article on research techniques, or assisting with the conduct of an experiment.

☒ A psychology department instituted a 2-hour research participation requirement for all students enrolled in introductory psychology classes. Students who did not wish to participate in the research had to set up a meeting to explain their objection to the instructor and write a 10-page paper on a research topic approved by the professor. In anonymous course evaluations, many students said they had participated in the required research because they were afraid they would get a bad grade in the course if the professor knew they did not want to participate in the subject pool or because they believed it would take more than 2 hours to complete a 10-page paper.

8.05 Dispensing With Informed Consent for Research

Psychologists may dispense with informed consent only (1) where research would not reasonably be assumed to create distress or harm and involves (a) the study of normal educational practices, curricula, or classroom management methods conducted in educational settings; (b) only anonymous questionnaires, naturalistic observations, or archival research for which disclosure of responses would not place participants at risk of criminal or civil liability or damage their financial standing, employability, or reputation, and confidentiality is protected; or (c) the study of factors related to job or organization effectiveness conducted in organizational settings for which there is no risk to participants' employability, and confidentiality is protected or (2) where otherwise permitted by law or federal or institutional regulations.

This standard restricts dispensing with informed consent for research to three well-defined conditions—all of which are predicated on the condition that the research will not create distress or harm. Criteria (a) and (b) of the standard is consistent with the criteria for research that is exempt from IRB review under federal regulations 45 CFR 46.101 (b)(1). Psychologists should remember that the determination of whether a study meets the criteria for dispensing with informed consent or exempt status is the responsibility of the IRB and not the individual investigator. This is particularly true for the still controversial status of quality improvement/quality assurance research (Miller & Emanuel, 2008). Therefore, when working in an institution with an IRB, investigators designing research that meets the criteria of Standard 8.05 must still obtain appropriate institutional approval for such waivers (Standard 8.01, Institutional Approval; see also the Hot Topic, "Submitting Successful IRB Proposals," at the end of this chapter).

Research Conducted in Schools

Ethical justification for waiving the informed consent requirement for specific types of research conducted in educational settings is predicated on the right and responsibility of educational institutions to evaluate their own programs, practices, and policies to improve services as long as the research procedures themselves do not create distress or harm. Studies of normal educational practices that do not require informed consent include comparisons of different instructional methods and classroom management techniques or evaluation of educational placements.

In elementary and secondary school settings, dispensing with informed consent is a waiver of guardian permission for research involving persons who are legally incapable of consent. Irrespective of whether the type of research conducted meets the criteria for waiving parental permission under this standard, psychologists should consider state and federal laws and parental expectations regarding parental involvement in children's participation in normal educational practices before deciding whether to dispense with parental permission or student assent. Psychologists conducting program evaluation in the schools should also be familiar with the Family Educational Rights and Privacy Act (FERPA) and other federal regulations that may require parental access to their child's school records irrespective of whether parental permission for the evaluation was required or obtained.

Permission to dispense with informed consent for research in educational settings does not apply to studies designed to describe or test hypotheses regarding the relationship between student personality traits or mental health disorders and school performance (e.g., gender differences in math anxiety and its relationship to scores on a math achievement test). The assessment of such personal characteristics is not a part of normal educational practice and could constitute an invasion of privacy. In addition, some investigator-initiated school-based programs, such as drug prevention programs, may not be considered a normal educational practice or part of the school curricula and thus would not meet the Standard 8.05 criteria for waiver of parental permission or child/adolescent assent or consent. Investigators conducting such studies must either follow the consent requirements outlined in Standards 3.10, Informed Consent, and 8.02a, Informed Consent to Research, or obtain a waiver of parental permission from their IRB in compliance with Part 2 of this standard.

> ☒ A developmental psychologist received permission from a local school district to design and test a conflict resolution program for fifth and sixth graders. The school permitted her to offer the program during regularly scheduled health classes. Half of the classes served as controls. The success of the program was evaluated by comparing baseline and postprogram responses of children to questions about their conflicts with peers, siblings, and parents. Without consulting with her IRB, the psychologist told the school superintendent that parental permission would not be required for this type of research.

Anonymous, Naturalistic, or Archival Research

Informed consent is not required for investigations using anonymous questionnaires, naturalistic observations, or archival research when (a) confidentiality is protected; (b) disclosure of responses would not place participants at legal, financial, or social risk; and (c) the research methods would not reasonably be expected to cause distress or harm. The phrase "for which disclosure of responses would not place participants at risk" refers to both the certitude that participants could never be identified and the nature of data collected. Thus, unless anonymity can be ensured, psychologists should avoid dispensing with informed consent when personal information collected would create participant distress or involve criminal activity, substance abuse, or other activities that, if known, would place the participant at risk. Psychologists using archival data that include PHI as defined by HIPAA should refer to the section below detailing the specific criteria for waiving the requirement for client/patient authorization for use and disclosure of data from their records.

When research is conducted through the mail or on the Internet and adequate protections are put in place to ensure that participants' responses are anonymous (e.g., postmarks will not reveal participants' home addresses, Web-based responses cannot be linked to identifying information), informed consent information must be provided at the beginning of the survey, in the same detail required by Standards 3.10, Informed Consent, and 8.02, Informed Consent to Research. However, documentation of consent (e.g., name and signature confirming agreement) is not required because (a) completing the survey, mailing it to the investigator, or submitting it via the Internet is considered evidence of voluntary consent, and (b) requiring identifying documentation would compromise participant anonymity.

☑ An anonymous survey on attitudes toward caretaking of ill elderly household members included (a) a brief questionnaire asking for general demographic information such as gender, age, and ethnicity of household members and (b) health-related information such as whether there was an ill elderly person living in the household, which family member did or would take care of an elder family member if he or she was ill, how the respondents rated the adequacy of their health insurance plan for elder care, and several questions tapping who the respondent thought should be most responsible for elder care, for example, spouses, adult children, private nursing homes, or government-run hospitals. The survey was mailed to 10,000 randomly selected households in a large metropolitan area where respondents could not reasonably be expected to be identified by their answers or ZIP code. No names were on the survey, and the mailed packet included a self-addressed stamped envelope. The IRB agreed that informed consent was not required, but that the investigators should include a statement explaining the purpose, anonymous nature of the study, and their contact information.

Unique or Small Communities. Investigators should also consider whether the uniqueness of the population studied (e.g., individuals from small and geographically restricted ethnocultural communities; persons with rare genetic, medical, or psychological disorders) increases the probability that anonymous, naturalistic, or archival procedures may not be sufficient to safeguard identification of participants or their immediate community (Fisher et al., 2002).

☒ A health psychologist decided to conduct a naturalistic observation of the interactions among health care providers and patients in the emergency room of a small hospital in an isolated Appalachian town. He would sit in the back of the room on Saturday nights when the emergency room was most crowded. He dressed in such a way as to ensure that he would not be recognized from week to week. The psychologist took detailed notes on how specific doctors responded to the patients. He published an article highly critical of some of the interactions he had observed. Although the psychologist used pseudonyms for the hospital and the doctors, the unique location of the hospital, the medical events reported, and the detailed descriptions of the treatment staff made them readily identifiable. Following the publication, several members of the treatment staff were sued for malpractice.

Naturalistic Observation on the Internet. Studies of individual responses in chat rooms and on listservs may be considered naturalistic observation if the users have no reasonable expectation of privacy and the investigator is not manipulating the discussion to test or elicit particular responses. Under Standard 8.05, psychologists may dispense with informed consent under these situations if protections are in place to guard against personal identification and harm.

Studies of Job or Organization Effectiveness

Subpart 1c recognizes the right and responsibility of organizations to draw on the research expertise of psychologists to investigate factors related to job or organization effectiveness as long as (a) research participation does not pose a direct risk to an individual's current employment status, (b) confidentiality is adequately protected, and (c) the research procedures themselves would not be expected to create distress or harm. This standard is meant to apply to dispensing with informed consent to research directly linked to a specific organization's needs and not to studies designed to test general hypotheses regarding organizational effectiveness.

The phrase "not reasonably be assumed to create distress or harm" highlights the fact that in most circumstances, it would be ethically inappropriate to dispense with informed consent for organizational effectiveness studies using measures of psychopathology or biological data because assessment of mental health or physiological responses without consent can violate an individual's right to privacy of information not directly related to job performance and be experienced as personally intrusive and distressful.

> ☑ An industrial-organizational psychologist collected criterion-related validation data on a test designed to select sales personnel by administering the test to all job incumbents. The incumbents were informed that their test performance would be kept confidential and would not affect employment status. To match the test data on measures of job performance (sales volume and supervisor performance ratings), the psychologist needed to collect identifying information on the test form. The psychologist maintained several levels of security on the test materials and associated database. As soon as the predictor test and performance criterion data were matched, all identifying information was stripped from both the hard-copy test materials and electronic database. No information collected for purposes of the validation was released to anyone in the organization, and there were no consequences for those incumbents who performed poorly on the experimental test.

Where Otherwise Permitted by Law or Federal or Institutional Regulations

Part 2 of this standard permits psychologists to dispense with informed consent for reasons not included in Part 1 where consent waiver is permitted by law or federal or institutional regulations. In such instances, researchers bear the burden of demonstrating that such conditions are met.

HIPAA Requirements for Use of PHI for Research Without Client/Patient Authorization. Under HIPAA federal regulations, PHI may be used for research purposes without client/patient authorization if the covered entity who is being asked to disclose the PHI receives written documentation that waiver of patient authorization has been approved by an IRB in conformance with federal guidelines, and if

- the use or disclosure of PHI involves no more than minimal risk to the individuals;

- the alteration or waiver will not adversely affect the privacy rights and the welfare of the individuals;

- the research could not practicably be conducted without the alteration or waiver;

- the research could not practicably be conducted without access to and use of the PHI;

- the privacy risks to individuals whose PHI is to be used or disclosed are reasonable in relation to the anticipated benefits, if any, to the individuals and the importance of the knowledge that may reasonably be expected to result from the research;

- there is an adequate plan to protect the identifiers from improper use and disclosure;

- there is an adequate plan to destroy the identifiers at the earliest opportunity consistent with conduct of the research, unless there is a health or research justification for retaining the identifiers or such retention is otherwise required by law; and

- there are adequate written assurances that the PHI will not be reused or disclosed to any other person or entity, except as required by law, for authorized oversight of the research project or for other research for which the use or disclosure of PHI would be permitted by the subpart (rules for research are under 45 CFR 164.501, 164.508[f], 164.512[i]).

Covered entities may also waive the requirement for client/patient authorization for the use and disclosure of their PHI for research under the following conditions (45 CFR 164.512[i]):

- Information is *de-identified* by the covered entity (de-identification has specific requirements under HIPAA; see 45 CFR 164.514). If de-identified information is later re-identified by the covered entity, a client/patient authorization is required.

- The researcher is reviewing the PHI for the sole purpose of preparing a research protocol, or for similar purposes *preparatory to research,* the information is necessary for the research purposes, and the PHI is not removed from the covered entity's premises.

- Research is on *decedent's information,* and the researcher provides the covered entity with representation that the use or disclosure sought is solely for research on the PHI of the decedents, the death is documented, and the PHI is necessary for the research.

- Disclosure is restricted to a *limited data set* (as specifically defined by HIPAA 45 CFR 164.513[e][2]) and the investigator enters into a "data use agreement" with the covered entity.

- The investigator signs a *business associate contract* with a covered entity to use PHI to conduct data analysis or quality assurance or other activities on behalf of the covered entity and to comply with all HIPAA regulations (45 CFR 160.103 and 164.504[e][1]).

8.06 Offering Inducements for Research Participation

(a) Psychologists make reasonable efforts to avoid offering excessive or inappropriate financial or other inducements for research participation when such inducements are likely to coerce participation.

Selecting noncoercive compensation for research participation helps ensure that participation is voluntary, that research burdens are not borne unequally by economically disadvantaged populations, and that these populations are not deprived (based on inability to afford to participate in the study) of knowledge generated by research that can be applied to enhance their well-being (Principle D: Justice). Compensation for effort, time, and inconvenience of research is permitted if inducements do not encourage individuals to lie or conceal information that would disqualify them from the research or lure them into procedures they would otherwise choose to avoid. As noted in the discussion of Standard 8.02, Informed Consent to Research, the Office for Human Subjects Protections (http://www.hhs.gov/ohrp/faq.html) has interpreted federal regulations as prohibiting investigators from describing participant compensation as a benefit when obtaining informed consent (see Standard 8.06, Offering Inducements for Research Participation).

Standard 8.06 recognizes that some inducement is often necessary to ensure a sufficiently large and representative sample and that it is possible for investigators to distinguish between "due" and "undue" inducements (Dickert & Grady, 1999; Macklin, 1981). Some institutions adopt a standard compensation rate for all research participation. Others have defined noncoercive financial inducements as the amount of money a normal, healthy volunteer would lose in work and travel time or by fair market value for the work involved. Different economic and cultural circumstances may lead to varying perceptions of a cash inducement as fair or coercive. At the same time, fairness and justice entitle all persons to equal compensation for equal levels of participation in a particular research project (Principle D: Justice). Consulting with members of the population who will be recruited for research participation about different types of research compensation can help investigators and their IRBs determine the extent to which cash or nonmonetary compensation is fair or coercive (Fisher, 2003a).

☑ A health psychologist was studying the relationship between acculturation, stress, health knowledge and attitudes, and asthma among students in a large school district. Students who participated would spend an hour in focus group discussion and 30 minutes responding to focus group questions. Prestudy interviews with parents, teachers, and students indicated that compensation of $15 would be considered fair and noncoercive for the time students would give to the study. However, representatives from two schools in crime-ridden neighborhoods expressed concern that cash payments would place students in danger as they left the study. The psychologist and representatives agreed that offering a $15 popular school sweatshirt instead of cash would be equitable and safety-sensitive compensation for research participation.

☑ Community psychologists wanted to study the effectiveness of a needle exchange program for intravenous drug users in the community. While the investigators' preliminary community interviews suggested that $30 was a fair and noncoercive compensation for research participation, the psychologists were concerned that providing participants with cash payment might be used by participants to purchase illegal drugs, encourage them to maintain their drug habits, or distort the evaluation of drug use dangers. They obtained IRB approval to compensate participants with $30 coupons to a local food market. The investigators were surprised to learn that many participants did not usually purchase food at that market, were selling their coupons for less cash than they were worth, and perceived the investigators' efforts as paternalistic and disrespectful of participant judgment and autonomy. The psychologists began to collect data on the participants' reactions to the coupons, which they then presented to the IRB as justification to switch to cash payments. The IRB's community representative strongly supported the investigators' request, and it received IRB approval.

(b) When offering professional services as an inducement for research participation, psychologists clarify the nature of the services, as well as the risks, obligations, and limitations. (See also Standard 6.05, Barter With Clients/Patients.)

Providing psychological services as compensation for research participation is ethical when participants are fully aware of (a) the nature and risks of services (e.g., the type of treatment, the type of provider, risks to confidentiality), (b) the personal and financial obligations and time commitment involved in receiving the services, and (3) limitations of the type and in the length of services provided (see also Standards 6.04, Fees and Financial Arrangements; 6.05, Barter With Clients/Patients; and 10.01, Informed Consent to Therapy). Linking involvement in nontherapeutic research with treatment that immediately follows may encourage participants with mental health problems to engage or continue in treatment. However, psychologists should take special steps to ensure that offering such services does not compromise the voluntary nature of research participation of individuals who do not have access to adequate health care and social services (Fisher, 2004; Oransky, Fisher, Mahadevan, & Singer, in press).

8.07 Deception in Research

(a) Psychologists do not conduct a study involving deception unless they have determined that the use of deceptive techniques is justified by the study's significant prospective scientific, educational, or applied value and that effective nondeceptive alternative procedures are not feasible.

Deceptive techniques intentionally withhold information or misinform participants about the purpose of the study, the experimental procedures or equipment, or the roles of research team members (Sieber, 1982). Under Principle C: Integrity, deception should be avoided unless it is necessary to maximize benefits and minimize harms. Deception research may produce benefits unavailable through alternative methods by keeping participants naive about the purpose and procedures of a study, thereby increasing methodological realism and spontaneous response to experimental manipulation. However, these advantages may not be actualized if participants are predisposed to be suspicious of psychology experiments or are actively engaged in hypotheses regarding an experiment's true purpose (Fisher & Fyrberg, 1994).

The "Consent Paradox." By its very nature, informed consent for participation in a deception study creates a moral paradox by compromising an individual's ability to make a fully informed decision about research participation (Fisher, 2005; Principle E: Respect for People's Rights and Dignity). The ethical imperative for informed consent to research participation arose following the revelation of Nazi medical science atrocities revealed during the Nuremberg trials. The Nuremberg Code (1949) codified the international community's distrust in scientists' motivation to make decisions that would serve the best interests of participants, and informed consent of the participant rather than morally responsible decisions by scientists came to be seen as the primary means of protecting participant autonomy and welfare.

Informed consent to a deception study reflects the moral ambiguity continuing to surround respect for participant autonomy inherent in professional ethics codes and federal regulations. During the consent process, investigators conducting deception research intentionally give participants false information about the purpose and nature of the study. Individuals providing an affirmative response to participate are therefore erroneously led to believe they have autonomy to decide about the type of experimental procedures they are willing to be exposed to, when in fact they do not and thus have no decisional control over these experiences or the potential discomfort that may arise at the end of the study when they are debriefed about the deception (Standards 8.07c, Deception in Research, and 8.08, Debriefing). It is for these reasons that Standard 8.07 requires that deception research meet more stringent criteria for implementation than nondeceptive studies.

Scientific and Social Justification. Under Standard 8.07a, deception studies are ethically justified only if psychologists demonstrate that (a) prospective benefits to science or society significantly outweigh violating participants' right to determine whether they want to be involved in the type of experimental procedures for which they are recruited, and (b) nondeceptive alternative procedures do not offer sufficient scientific controls to test the hypothesis under investigation. Some alternative methodologies that can be considered include naturalistic observation, field or game simulations, role-playing, or experimental methods. Failure to use scientifically valid nondeceptive alternative methods simply because of inconvenience or financial cost may be a violation of this standard under some circumstances.

(b) Psychologists do not deceive prospective participants about research that is reasonably expected to cause physical pain or severe emotional distress.

Even if deceptive techniques have significant scientific, educational, or social value and effective nondeceptive alternatives are not feasible, thus meeting the criteria of Standard 8.07a, Standard 8.07b prohibits withholding or misleading prospective participants about procedures causing physical pain or severe emotional distress. The prohibitions in this standard are absolute and do not depend on the duration of physical pain or whether severe emotional harm can be alleviated during debriefing procedures.

> ☒ Following the September 11, 2001, attacks on the United States, a social psychologist at a university in New York City decided to study ways in which three types of warning systems would positively or negatively affect crowd behavior in response to a perceived terrorist attack. The psychologist had confederates enter nine classrooms and use of one of three types of warning systems instructing students in evacuation procedures for a "suspected bomb that might be planted in the building by a terrorist group." Many students started crying or screaming, some called their parents on cell phones to say goodbye, and two students fainted during the exercise.

(c) Psychologists explain any deception that is an integral feature of the design and conduct of an experiment to participants as early as is feasible, preferably at the conclusion of their participation, but no later than at the conclusion of the data collection, and permit participants to withdraw their data. (See also Standard 8.08, Debriefing.)

When deception is used, individuals must be informed about a study's deceptive aspects as soon as possible, preferably at the end of their participation. This procedure is often called dehoaxing. In some instances, participants may find revelations about the deception and true purpose of the study to be educative; in other cases, there may be transient or longer term discomfort or distress arising from perceptions of invasion of privacy or loss of self-esteem and negative reactions to being observed or induced to commit what the participant may perceive as embarrassing or reprehensible acts (Baumrind, 1985; Fisher & Fyrberg, 1994). The design of dehoaxing procedures must be sensitive to individual differences in participant reactions (see Standard 8.08, Debriefing).

There may be situations in which explaining the deception can compromise the methodological validity of the research involving future participants, for example, if research is conducted in a small university where students are likely to speak with one another about their experiences. In such circumstances, dehoaxing may be delayed until data collection is completed. Psychologists must also take reasonable steps to alleviate psychological harm resulting from dehoaxing and may withhold information about deceptive procedures to protect the participant from harm (see Standard 8.08b and 8.08c, Debriefing).

Data Withdrawal. Psychologists must permit participants to withdraw their data after learning about the deception. Although the standard stops short of requiring psychologists to ask participants if they want to withdraw their data, dehoaxing procedures should not preclude participants from making such a request. Giving individuals an opportunity to withdraw data should not be interpreted as implying their "deferred" consent to the deception—informed consent can only be obtained prospectively (Office for Protection From Research Risks, 1993).

8.08 Debriefing

(a) Psychologists provide a prompt opportunity for participants to obtain appropriate information about the nature, results, and conclusions of the research, and they take reasonable steps to correct any misconceptions that participants may have of which the psychologists are aware.

To protect methodological validity, informed consent procedures often do not include the hypothesis or other information about the research that would not be expected to affect willingness to participate but might bias participant responding. Debriefing procedures provide participants the opportunity to be informed about such undisclosed information and to ask questions about the research. Standard 8.08a requires that psychologists take reasonable steps to correct any misconceptions about the research of which they are aware. The use of the terms *reasonable* and *aware* in this standard reflect the fact that despite the best efforts of a psychologist, some participants may continue to hold misimpressions about the research or may not share these misperceptions with the investigator. As part of debriefing, psychologists should make a summary of the results of the research available to participants. Because data analysis and interpretation of results typically occur after data collection is completed, psychologists can make summaries available through mailings to participants, newsletters to the site at which the research occurred, Web site postings, or other mechanisms that do not incur unreasonable expense.

(b) If scientific or humane values justify delaying or withholding this information, psychologists take reasonable measures to reduce the risk of harm.

There may be humane justification for withholding information about the nature, results, and conclusions of research. For example, individuals participating in deception research may experience loss of self-esteem or other negative psychological reactions if told they committed a social or moral breach of which they were not aware or which they did not know others had observed. In other situations, child participants may not have the recursive thinking skills to understand the rationale behind the research and feel confused upon debriefing or, in the case of deception research, may feel embarrassed or betrayed. In such circumstances, the study should be explained to the children's guardians.

☑ Investigators working with inpatient boys diagnosed with conduct disorder designed an analog task that could distinguish between the children's use of instrumental and hostile aggression. The task was a computer game in which the boys played against an unseen "boy" (in actuality, formatted responses programmed by the investigators) in an adjacent room. According to the rules of the game, opponents could block each other's game (instrumental aggression) or send a noxious, but not harmful, noise through the computer headsets (hostile aggression). The investigators believed that these deceptive conditions were safer for the participants than alternative methodologies that manipulated or observed aggression in actual competitive situations. Parents thought the research was important but voiced concern that if the boys were told about the deception, they would lose trust in the staff at the facility. The investigators agreed. To minimize any distress that might emerge during the computer game, the boys could not see their scores during the game, and when the game was over, all boys were told they had won (adapted from Fisher, Hoagwood, & Jensen, 1996).

(c) When psychologists become aware that research procedures have harmed a participant, they take reasonable steps to minimize the harm.

Consistent with Principle A: Beneficence and Nonmaleficence, psychologists must try to alleviate psychological distress or harm that they are aware has arisen from research participation. Psychologists may not always be able to anticipate participant stress reactions in response to debriefing. In such cases, psychologists might alleviate distress by explaining participant responses within the context of normative behavior if appropriate. In other situations, such as research involving genetic screening for predisposition for a serious medical or mental health disorder, psychologists may anticipate postexperimental stress if debriefing includes information concerning personal health vulnerabilities and should be prepared to provide referrals for appropriate counseling services.

☑ In a study to examine psychosocial factors contributing to the spread of the HIV/AIDS virus among intravenous drug users (IDUs), participants (a) answered questions about their drug use, needle sharing, sexual history, and sexual practices; (b) responded to standardized psychological assessments; and (c) had their blood tested for the HIV virus, hepatitis C, and other sexually transmitted diseases. The results of these blood tests were provided to participants during debriefing. The investigators developed two types of debriefing procedures. Aware that telling IDUs that they had tested negative for sexually transmitted diseases might lead them to falsely assume they were "AIDS safe," debriefing for these participants included counseling on continued risk of infection and risk reduction practices. Debriefing for participants who tested positive for any of the diseases included counseling on availability of current treatments, risk reduction practices, and referrals to appropriate health care providers.

8.09 Humane Care and Use of Animals in Research

The goal of animal research can be to understand and improve the lives of the species studied. More frequently, however, the use of animals in psychological research is aimed at increased understanding of the human condition. This raises ethically complex questions, especially when methods will cause animals discomfort or pain. Society has yet to reach consensus on whether animals have the right not to be harmed by virtue of the fact that they have inherent (not just conditional) value, whether humans as moral agents have an obligation to treat all life with dignity, or what role animals' relative lack of self-awareness and limited cognitive capacities to anticipate pain and distress or consequences makes them more or less vulnerable to research participation (C. Cohen, 1986; Gluck, Bell, & Pearson-Bish, 2003; Regan, 1983).

The use of animals in research enables the control and manipulation of environmental, biological, and genetic factors leading to scientific discoveries producing tangible benefits for humans and animals not possible otherwise. However, drawing on Principle A: Beneficence and Nonmaleficence, the benefits of animal research never justify inhumane treatment. Psychologists conducting research involving animal subjects have a moral obligation to protect the animal subjects' welfare. The inclusion of the phrase "humane care" in the title chosen for Standard 8.09 reflects the fact that Standards 8.09a–g represent conditions that must be met to ensure care and use of animals in research is humane.

(a) Psychologists acquire, care for, use, and dispose of animals in compliance with current federal, state, and local laws and regulations, and with professional standards.

The federal government, through the Health Research Extension Act of 1985 (Public Law 99–158), regulates the humane care and protection of animals used in research. The NIH, through the Office of Laboratory Animal Welfare, administers programs and provides guidance to institutions that must comply with the policy. Among the regulations is the requirement that all institutions covered by the act have an Institutional Animal Care and Use Committee (IACUC) to approve and monitor the ethical acquisition, care, use, and disposal of animals in research. The U.S. Department of Agriculture requires the planned and unscheduled inspections of animal research facilities twice a year to ensure that animal housing and research procedures are safe, sanitary, and appropriate for the particular environmental and nutritional needs of the species. In addition, animals not bred in the psychologist's laboratory must be acquired lawfully and with appropriate permits. State and local governments also have regulations regarding housing standards, veterinary care and inspection, research procedures, and disposal.

Animal research practices must also be in compliance with the Guidelines for Ethical Conduct in the Care and Use of Animals developed by the APA Committee on Animal Research and Ethics (CARE, 1996) (see www.apa.org/science/anguide .html). Other organizations such as the American Association for Laboratory Animal Science, the American Association for the Accreditation of Laboratory Animal Care, and the National Association for Biomedical Research have comprehensive rules for the conduct of animal research. Psychologists conducting research with animals must adhere to all relevant regulations and guidelines. The APA requires members working outside the United States to follow all applicable laws and regulations of the country in which the research is conducted.

(b) Psychologists trained in research methods and experienced in the care of laboratory animals supervise all procedures involving animals and are responsible for ensuring appropriate consideration of their comfort, health, and humane treatment.

This standard requires that psychologists conducting animal research have appropriate training and carefully supervise all personnel involved in the acquisition, care, research procedures, and disposal of animal subjects. Competencies include education, training, or experience with relevant animal research models; behavioral and surgical techniques; and knowledge of species-specific behavioral, social, and medical requirements. Psychologists conducting animal field research should have sufficient knowledge of the ecosystems they will observe to minimize harm to the natural behaviors and environment of the animal population under investigation and other plant and animal life.

(c) Psychologists ensure that all individuals under their supervision who are using animals have received instruction in research methods and in the care, maintenance, and handling of the species being used, to the extent appropriate to their role. (See also Standard 2.05, Delegation of Work to Others.)

Psychologists must ensure that all personnel involved in the housing, care, experimental methods, or disposal of animal research subjects are competent to fulfill these duties in a way that ensures animals are treated humanely and appropriately (see also Standard 2.05, Delegation of Work to Others). A wide range of animal species is used in research, and each species has its own unique housing, nutrition, medical, and psychological needs. Psychologists must make sure that individuals to whom animal care is delegated are sufficiently knowledgeable about the species and the duties they must perform through prior education, training by the psychologist, or close supervision.

> ☒ A psychologist who conducted research on aggressive behavior in male rats hired a research assistant to clean each animal's housing. Rather than provide direct supervision, the psychologist told the assistant to begin work and to feel free to ask the psychologists any questions that arose. To facilitate cleaning, the assistant decided to take three of the animals out of their separate housings and place them in a larger empty glass enclosure. The animals immediately began to fight with each other, incurring several injuries.

(d) Psychologists make reasonable efforts to minimize the discomfort, infection, illness, and pain of animal subjects.

Species-appropriate housing, sanitary conditions, feeding, regular veterinary checkups, and development and monitoring of safety conditions during active experimentation should be implemented to protect the health and welfare of animal research subjects. Psychologists and their staff should be alert and competent to detect signs of illness or injury in animal subjects and be able to obtain the immediate and appropriate treatment. When alternative experimental procedures are available, psychologists should select the one that will produce the minimum amount of animal discomfort. The APA Guidelines for Ethical Conduct in the Care and Use of Animals also recommends that, whenever possible, psychologists should try to provide care and housing that can enrich the psychological well-being of the animal subject.

> ☑ A psychologist studying cognition in pigeons presented various landmarks and observed the pigeons' use of these cues. During initial testing, the psychologist unexpectedly found that some arrangements caused confusion, resulting in minor injuries when several pigeons flew into the landmarks. The psychologist modified these arrangements to protect the animals' safety.

(e) Psychologists use a procedure subjecting animals to pain, stress, or privation only when an alternative procedure is unavailable and the goal is justified by its prospective scientific, educational, or applied value.

Exposing animals to experimentally induced pain or suffering is not ethically justified unless the psychologist can demonstrate that the knowledge produced from experimentation has the clear potential to substantially contribute to science, to teaching about animal behavior or research techniques, or to benefit other animals or humans. Animals should never be subjected to pain, physical or psychological stress, or food deprivation if alternative procedures have equal pedagogical value or can adequately test the research question. When aversive procedures cannot be avoided, psychologists must select the minimal level of pain, stress, or privation necessary to achieve the goals of the research.

> ☒   An introductory psychology laboratory instructor decided to demonstrate to the class how the phenomenon of learned helplessness is experimentally tested. The demonstration included placing laboratory rats in a cage with an electrified grid and preventing them from escaping when a painful shock was distributed through the grid.

(f) Psychologists perform surgical procedures under appropriate anesthesia and follow techniques to avoid infection and minimize pain during and after surgery.

Research requiring surgery must be conducted by appropriately trained psychologists or other competent personnel using methods that minimize risks of infection and pain. Unless there is a legitimate scientific or medical reason to do otherwise, animals must be anesthetized throughout the surgical procedure. Psychologists are responsible for monitoring postoperative care of research animals using appropriate medications to minimize discomfort and avoid infection. Exposing animals to multiple surgeries as a matter of convenience or to minimize cost is unethical.

> ☑   Researchers designed a study with rhesus monkeys to test the reinforcing effects of three commonly abused drugs. To enable the animals to reinforce their behavior with the drugs, a catheter was implanted in a jugular vein. The procedure was conducted under effective anesthesia and aseptic conditions. Monkeys were treated postoperatively with antibiotics for 10 days and with an analgesic for 3 days. Testing was not begun until it was determined that the monkey was in good postoperative health. The investigators also determined that using a within-subjects design could minimize the number of monkeys needed to adequately test the reinforcing properties of the drugs. After the experiment, the catheters were removed under the same careful anesthesia and aseptic conditions, and each monkey was given appropriate postoperative care.

(g) When it is appropriate that an animal's life be terminated, psychologists proceed rapidly, with an effort to minimize pain and in accordance with accepted procedures.

Humane or scientific considerations may necessitate terminating the life of animal research subjects when experimental procedures create chronic pain or discomfort that cannot be alleviated through medication or other remedies. Participation sometimes renders an animal unsuitable for future research and returning it to the wild or giving it a home outside the laboratory is not safe or possible. Other times, autopsies are necessary to validate the efficacy of the surgical technique or to understand physiological processes and structures related to the psychological phenomenon under investigation. When termination is necessary, psychologists must use procedures that are humane, immediate, and appropriate for the species. According to the APA Guidelines for Ethical Conduct in the Care and Use of Animals, termination procedures should be in accordance with procedures of the latest version of the American Veterinary Medical Association Panel on Euthanasia, and disposal of euthanized animals should be consistent with law.

8.10 Reporting Research Results

(a) Psychologists do not fabricate data. (See also Standard 5.01a, Avoidance of False or Deceptive Statements.)

Principle C: Integrity underscores the centrality of accuracy, honesty, and truthfulness in the conduct of science. Fraud in research is one of the most serious forms of scientific misconduct because it disrupts the scientific process, dilutes community confidence in the integrity of science, and can lead to misinformed interventions and policies. Psychologists do not falsify, make up, alter, or distort the responses of human participants or animal subjects or the results of data analysis. This standard is not limited to published reports and applies to the fabrication of data in journal entries or intentional manipulation of the data collection process itself that would lead to a false report. See Standard 5.01, Avoidance of False or Deceptive Statements, for additional prohibitions against publishing or presenting research findings psychologists know are false.

> ☒   After conducting planned statistical analyses of the data, a psychologist realized that if the data from just 4 of the 30 participants were eliminated, the statistical analyses would yield significance. The characteristics of these 4 participants met all the original inclusion criteria for the study, and there was no deviation in the administration of testing procedures for these individuals. Reasoning that there must be some undetected characteristic responsible for these participants' outlier responses, the psychologist decided to eliminate their data from the analysis. Because there were no criteria other than their responses on which to exclude them, the psychologist decided not to report their elimination in a manuscript submitted for publication.

(b) If psychologists discover significant errors in their published data, they take reasonable steps to correct such errors in a correction, retraction, erratum, or other appropriate publication means.

The research design, measurement tools, and analytic strategies selected by an investigator may lead to erroneous conclusions based on honest differences in interpretation, chance responding, or extraneous influences that are revealed only when new techniques are used to examine the hypothesis tested. Erroneous conclusions about natural phenomena based on methodologically sound research designs are themselves a natural part of the scientific process and are not unethical. A cornerstone of scientific progress is the process of self-correction in which the validity of results obtained in a single experiment can be confirmed or refuted following replication by others within the scientific community. Accurate reporting of research is essential to this process because it enables others to critique, replicate, dispute, and expand on the methods and interpretations reported.

The purpose of this standard is to safeguard the self-correction process by requiring that psychologists take steps to correct errors in published reports that compromise the readers' ability to replicate the research design or interpret the results because the methodology, data, or statistical analysis was incorrectly described. Informing the journal editor or publisher about the error and requesting a published correction can comply with this standard. The use of the term *reasonable steps* recognizes that investigators have limited control over editors or publishers who refuse to publish corrections.

> ☑ Following the publication of an article, a psychologist realized that the *F* values and probability levels in one of the tables had been wrongly transcribed. The psychologist wrote to the editor of the journal requesting that an addendum be published briefly describing the error and informing readers they can obtain the corrected table from the author. The psychologist also placed an addendum page onto all reprints distributed to other investigators.

8.11 Plagiarism

Psychologists do not present portions of another's work or data as their own, even if the other work or data source is cited occasionally.

Plagiarism is the representation of another person's ideas or words without appropriate credit. Plagiarism is inconsistent with Principle C: Integrity since it deceives readers into believing that the words and ideas of others are original to the author. A common misconception is that plagiarism is limited to word-for-word replication or paraphrasing of another's written work without appropriate citation. Whereas this form of plagiarism is clearly prohibited, violation of this standard also occurs when a psychologist knowingly presents throughout a publication or formal report another's ideas as his or her own, citing the work from which it was drawn in a manner intended to obscure the original author's contribution. (See Standard 5.01, Avoidance of False or Deceptive Statements, for situations in which a psychologist may be in violation of the Ethics Code for appropriating the work of others outside the research or publication context.)

☒ In a manuscript submitted for publication, a psychologist used the organization, heading formats, and arguments presented by authors in an article published in an obscure journal. The psychologist cited the original article once in the opening paragraph of the manuscript. Two paragraphs duplicated word-for-word sentences in the original article—and many of the original article's paragraphs were paraphrased. The psychologist added five new references that appeared after the original article was published.

8.12 Publication Credit

(a) Psychologists take responsibility and credit, including authorship credit, only for work they have actually performed or to which they have substantially contributed. (See also Standard 8.12b, Publication Credit.)

This standard prohibits psychologists from taking credit for research they did not directly perform or for which they did not make a substantial intellectual contribution. Substantial intellectual contributions include formulating the hypothesis, developing the experimental design, selecting the analytic procedures, interpreting the data, writing the first draft of the article, or providing important intellectual revisions to the manuscript content (APA, 2001). According to this standard, any psychologist listed as an author must take responsibility for the content of the publication. This means that all coauthors must review the final draft of a manuscript before it is submitted for publication. In recent years, many scientific journals have required that all authors of a submitted manuscript sign a statement confirming that they contributed to the research and reviewed the written content of the paper.

☒ A junior faculty member asked a nationally recognized senior research psychologist to collaborate on an article based on data that the junior faculty member had collected. The junior member thought that including the accomplished researcher as an author would improve the chances of the manuscript being accepted for publication. The senior psychologist agreed to have his name included and told the junior faculty member that after hearing a description of the writing plan, he would not have to read the manuscript before it was submitted for publication.

☒ A research psychologist agreed to conduct a study funded by a pharmaceutical firm to test the comparative efficacy of two psychoactive drugs. The psychologist sent the collected data to the sponsor for statistical analyses. After the data were analyzed, the sponsor offered to ghost-write the article and permitted the psychologist to submit it to a journal as sole author (see also Standard 3.06, Conflict of Interest; Pachter et al., 2007).

(b) Principal authorship and other publication credits accurately reflect the relative scientific or professional contributions of the individuals involved, regardless of their relative status. Mere possession of an institutional position, such as department chair, does not justify authorship credit. Minor contributions to the research or to the writing for publications are acknowledged appropriately, such as in footnotes or in an introductory statement.

Principal authorship must reflect the extent to which each individual contributed to the origination of the research problem, the research design, interpretation of results, and drafting of the manuscript. In addition to underscoring the importance of the relative contribution as the determining factor for authorship credit, the wording of this standard is intended to protect students and junior faculty or research associates from exploitation by professors, supervisors, or senior administrators who might demand principal authorship based simply on the status of their position. The standard also requires that minor contributions not constituting authorship be acknowledged. Minor contributions include supportive functions such as designing or building the apparatus, suggesting or advising about the statistical analysis, collecting or entering the data, modifying or structuring a computer program, and recruiting participants or obtaining animals (APA, 2001).

> ☑ A psychologist was the director of a large research center where postdoctoral students were encouraged to apply for young investigator awards listing the director as mentor. The psychologist always commented on drafts of manuscripts that the highly competent postdoctoral students submitted for publication but had a policy of being included as an author only if she directly contributed to the design, implementation, analysis, data interpretation, or writing.

(c) Except under exceptional circumstances, a student is listed as principal author on any multiple authored article that is substantially based on the student's doctoral dissertation. Faculty advisors discuss publication credit with students as early as feasible and throughout the research and publication process as appropriate. (See also Standard 8.12b, Publication Credit.)

This standard recognizes that doctoral work is expected to represent an independent and original contribution devised and conducted largely by the student. Consequently, doctoral students should receive principal authorship on publications substantially based on their dissertation. The rare exception to this standard might occur when a student's doctoral dissertation is published in monograph form as part of a collection of studies by other researchers that cumulatively substantiates a phenomenon or supports or refutes a hypothesis.

Whether students merit principal authorship on master's-level or other predoctoral research will depend on their specific contributions to the research. When a student makes the primary contribution to a study, Standard 8.12b requires that she or he should be listed as first author. Some students conducting master's and undergraduate honors research theses choose to work within an apprenticeship model distinctly different from the independent work model of the dissertation (Fine & Kurdek, 1993; Fisher & Younggren, 1997). For students who are only beginning to acquire the theoretical, methodological, statistical, and writing skills necessary to make a primary scientific contribution, the apprenticeship model provides the opportunity to learn these skills through collaboration on a faculty-originated project. In such cases, authorship should be determined by the relative contributions of student and faculty member to the project.

Standard 8.12c affords additional student protections by requiring that faculty advisers discuss publication credit with students as early as is feasible to provide students an opportunity to evaluate their skills and select the best mentoring experience (apprenticeship vs. independent scholar model) to meet their training needs and expectations for publication credit. Recognizing that research collaboration is a dynamic process in which relative contribution can change over time, research mentors should discuss with students any such changes they observe or anticipate that would affect publication credit at the point at which they emerge. For all student-faculty research collaborations, assignment of principal authorship must follow the rule of relative scientific contribution established in Standard 8.12b.

8.13 Duplicate Publication of Data

Psychologists do not publish, as original data, data that have been previously published. This does not preclude republishing data when they are accompanied by proper acknowledgment.

Scientific knowledge is based on cumulative evidence of the reliability of observations and relationships among variables tested over time and in different experimental contexts. When psychologists present the same data in different publications without proper acknowledgment, they jeopardize the evolution of scientific knowledge by giving the erroneous impression that replication of results has occurred (see Principles B: Fidelity and Responsibility and C: Integrity). Duplicate publication of data without appropriate citation can jeopardize the validity of meta-analyses that shed light on a problem through a statistical synthesis of the data from a set of independent but comparable studies examining the problem. Publishing original data in more than one source without proper attribution also misrepresents the amount of experimental work the author has actually conducted and, in some instances, may result in violation of copyright law. Standard 8.13 does not prohibit psychologists from publishing the same data in different journals for the purpose of reaching different audiences as long as proper citations of the original publication source are provided and psychologists have confirmed that such publication does not violate the original publisher's copyright.

The extent to which posting a manuscript on a psychologist's or his or her employer's Web site in manuscript form submitted, accepted, or published by a journal will depend on the journal's policy for such posting and whether the relationship of the posted document to prepublished or published materials is clearly posted along with the manuscript. For example, APA Publications frequently updates its Internet posting policies at www.apa.org/journals/authors/posting .html. In the most recent policy (APA, 2006),

1. Authors can post unpublished papers on a Web site prior to submission as long as they are clearly labeled as unpublished.

2. Editors are advised of the Web site posting when the manuscript is submitted for review.

3. Manuscripts of accepted articles can be posted in word-processing form, provided they carry an APA copyright notice and link to the journal home page, as well as include the following statement: "This article may not exactly replicate the final version published in the APA journal. It is not the copy of record."

4. The manuscript cannot be archived with any non-APA repositories.

5. The APA-published version does not appear in a scanned or otherwise copyrighted form.

Publishing multiple or piecemeal reports of different aspects of a single research project may be unethical without a reasonable theoretical, methodological, or practical justification for doing so. In such cases, investigators should inform the editor of the publication where the manuscript was submitted about their plans for publishing different parts of the study. Usually, Standard 8.13 does not preclude publication of full-length reports of materials published as conference abstracts or manuscripts with limited circulation (e.g., U.S. dissertations or internal agency reports; see APA, 2006). Exceptions occur when conference proceedings are published as full-length presentations in a volume that has an ISBN.

The NIH Public Access Policy. The NIH Public Access Policy, implementing Division G, Title II, Section 218 of PL 110–161 (Consolidated Appropriations Act, 2008), was developed to ensure that published results based on NIH-funded research are available to the public (http://publicaccess.nih.gov/index.htm). It requires that as of April 7, 2008, investigators submit the accepted version of a peer-reviewed manuscript arising from NIH funds to the PubMed Central (www.pubmedcentral .nih.gov/). To comply with the policy, investigators must

• Make sure that any copyright transfer allows the final peer-reviewed manuscripts to be submitted to NIH in accordance with the policy. Journals that have agreed to do this automatically are listed at http://publicaccess.nih.gov/submit_ process_journals.htm. For those journals not listed, the author must inform the journal that the final peer-reviewed manuscript is subject to the Public Access Policy when submitting it for publication.

• Submit the final draft of the accepted peer-reviewed manuscript to NIH.

• When citing their NIH-funded papers in NIH applications, proposals, or progress reports, investigators must include the PubMed Central reference number for each article (effective May 25, 2008).

8.14 Sharing Research Data for Verification

(a) After research results are published, psychologists do not withhold the data on which their conclusions are based from other competent professionals who seek to verify the substantive claims through reanalysis and who intend to use such data only for that purpose, provided that the confidentiality of the participants can be protected and unless legal rights concerning proprietary data preclude their release. This does not preclude psychologists from requiring that such individuals or groups be responsible for costs associated with the provision of such information.

The self-correcting nature of science requires investigators to share research data for the purpose of replication and reanalysis. Such openness protects the integrity of science through independent validation of data coding, analysis, and interpretation and reflects awareness of their responsibilities to the scientific community and the public (Principle B: Fidelity and Responsibility).

Psychologists should follow appropriate guidelines for retention of data (see also Standard 6.01, Documentation of Professional and Scientific Work and Maintenance of Records). For example, authors of articles published in APA journals are required to have their raw data available for at least 5 years after the date of publication (APA, 2001).

The term *competent professionals,* as used in this standard, limits the obligation to provide data to individuals competent in the research methods and data-analytic techniques necessary to substantiate claims through reanalysis. Psychologists are not required to share data with individuals for purposes of developing and testing new theories or other goals beyond reanalysis and verification of data. The standard recognizes there may be legitimate ethical, legal, and financial barriers to data sharing. In some instances, it may be impossible to de-identify data to adequately protect the confidentiality rights of those who participated in the research. In other instances, a third party who is not a psychologist may own the proprietary rights to the data. To avoid subjecting investigators to financial hardship or harassment, the standard permits psychologists to require that costs of the exchange be borne by the requesting party.

(b) Psychologists who request data from other psychologists to verify the substantive claims through reanalysis may use shared data only for the declared purpose. Requesting psychologists obtain prior written agreement for all other uses of the data.

This standard protects the intellectual property rights of the owner of the data by prohibiting the requesting psychologist from piggybacking on the work of another by using the data for any purpose other than reanalysis or to verify substantive claims. The data cannot be used to test related or peripheral hypotheses or to develop new research or analytic techniques unless the psychologist obtains prior written agreement.

> ☒ On the basis of a written request, a psychologist received data from another psychologist to verify through inspection of the data and reanalysis the interpretation of findings stated in a recent publication. After receiving the data, the psychologist realized that there were several additional hypotheses that could be tested with the data set. The psychologist quickly developed an analytic plan and got together a team of graduate students to implement the plan in time to submit the analysis of new hypotheses for presentation at an upcoming professional meeting.

8.15 Reviewers

Psychologists who review material submitted for presentation, publication, grant, or research proposal review respect the confidentiality of and the proprietary rights in such information of those who submitted it.

Research psychologists have an obligation to establish relationships of trust and are aware of their responsibilities to other investigators and the scientific community (Principle B: Fidelity and Responsibility). Psychologists are prohibited from using privileged and proprietary information obtained through confidential review of research materials, including the review of grant applications and papers submitted for publication or presentation at professional meetings. This standard protects the intellectual property rights of individuals who describe their theories, research designs, and data in unpublished materials from use by others who obtain this information during the peer review process. If for reasons of expertise or training reviewers wish to have a colleague or graduate student review the material, they must first obtain prior permission of the grants program officer, journal editor, or meeting chair. Reviewed materials should be returned or destroyed following completion of the review.

> ☒ A research psychologist on an NIH special emphasis panel was primary reviewer on an RO1 grant application addressing a conceptual problem the psychologist had been tackling in her own lab. The psychologist wrote a critical review of the proposal and argued strongly for a score in the unfundable range. Several months later, the principal investigator of the RO1 application was distressed to learn that the psychologist had begun a series of studies almost identical to those in the rejected proposal (see also Standard 3.06, Conflict of Interest).

HOT TOPIC

Submitting Successful Institutional Review Board (IRB) Proposals

The responsible conduct of psychological research depends on ethically informed planning by psychologists and careful review by federally mandated institutional review boards (IRBs). Public Law 93–348, National Research Act of 1974 (see www.ucop.edu/raohome/certs/93-348.html), mandates that universities receiving federal funding for biomedical or behavioral research must establish an IRB. Codified at Title 45, Part 46 of the Code of Federal Regulations, IRBs must ensure that federal regulations are met and that research participants' rights and welfare are protected (www.hhs.gov/ohrp/humansubjects/guidance/45cfr46.htm). Institutions with IRBs found to be in noncompliance with regulations can lose federal funding for both their research and student programs. The diversity of expertise and wide latitude in decision making given to individual IRBs under federal regulations can be intimidating to psychologists who must gain IRB approval before conducting their research (Standard 8.01, Institutional Approval; De Vries, DeBruin, & Goodgame, 2004; DuBois, 2006; Eissenberg et al., 2004). As a first step in developing IRB applications, psychologists should familiarize themselves with federal regulations and the Office of Human Research Protection's "Frequently Asked Questions" sites (www.hhs.gov/ohrp/faq.html). This special section highlights additional ways to make the IRB submission process less daunting and increase the probability of successful review.

Provide a Scientific Justification for the Research

A common error in IRB submissions is omitting explanation of the scientific justification for the study based on the erroneous assumption that IRBs are not responsible for evaluating scientific merit. While IRBs should never take on the role of a scientific peer review panel, they are obligated to evaluate the balance of potential research benefits to risks. Since a study that lacks methodological validity cannot provide scientific or social benefits, a research protocol, which poses even minimal risk, may not be approved if an IRB has no evidence that the design has scientific merit. Psychologists can facilitate approval of their protocols by including in their IRB applications brief explanations of the scientific rationale for their selection of research questions, methods, and participant populations.

Justify Requests for Expedited Review

Under expedited review procedures, protocol evaluation may be carried out by the IRB chairperson or designee in lieu of full board review if the research involves no more than minimal risk or consists of only minor changes to previously approved research (45 CFR 46.110). Federal regulations' define "minimal risk" as "the probability and magnitude of harm or discomfort anticipated in the research are not greater in and of themselves than those ordinarily encountered in daily life or during the performance of routine physical or psychological examinations or tests" (45 CFR 46.102(i)). While many psychological studies meet the minimal risk criteria, IRBs often overestimate social behavioral research risk and thus fail to expedite protocols that meet the federal criteria (National Research Council [NRC], 2003). One reason is that federal guidance on expedited categories is short on examples of social behavioral research (see www.hhs.gov/ohrp/humansubjects/guidance/expedited98.htm).

Expanding Exemplars of Minimal Risk. To address this problem, the NRC (2003) has provided an expanded list of "minimal risk" research exemplars for research involving adults. Similarly, the Institute of Medicine's (IOM's) Committee on the Ethical Conduct of Clinical Research Involving Children (Field & Behrman, 2004) and the DHHS Secretary's Advisory Committee for Human Research Protections (SACHRP; Fisher, Kornetsky, & Prentice, 2007) have addressed the issue of expedited review of research involving children by broadening the range of "minimal risk" exemplars to the "well-child" medical and mental health visit. For example, a central objective of the history component of routine pediatric medical and psychological examinations is to identify age-appropriate health and mental health risks such as poor diet, parent-child relationships, signs of anxiety or depression, and risks associated with sexual behavior, drug and alcohol use, and other health-compromising behaviors—topics of research that IRBs often mistakenly assume automatically categorize child and adolescent research as greater than minimal risk. To facilitate expedited review of new IRB applications, psychologists should carefully document their rationale for why the research is minimal risk, citing these federal committees' conclusions as supportive documents.

Confidentiality and Minimal Risk. Psychologists conducting studies involving vulnerable populations such as illicit drug users often find that IRBs deny expedited review for protocols involving these populations because they erroneously view confidentiality risks as precluding such review. In fact, under federal regulations, IRBs can consider protocols involving vulnerable groups that provide sufficient confidentiality protections as meeting the minimal risk criteria. To correct this misconception, in their IRB applications, psychologists can cite Part (C) of the "Categories of Research That May Be Reviewed by the Institutional Review Board (IRB) Through Expedited Review" (63 FR 60364-60367, November 9, 1998; www.hhs.gov/ohrp/humansubjects/guidance/expedited98 .htm), which states that while expedited review may not be used where identification of research participants or their responses "would reasonably place them at risk of criminal or civil liability or be damaging to the subjects' financial standing, employability, insurability, reputation, or be stigmatizing," protocols can be expedited if "*reasonable and appropriate protections will be implemented so that risks related to invasion of privacy and breach of confidentiality are no greater than minimal*" (www.hhs.gov/ohrp/humansubjects/guidance/expedited98.htm).

Demonstrate the Adequacy of Consent Procedures for Adults With Questionable Capacity to Consent

At present, no specific federal regulations govern research involving adults with schizophrenia, developmental disabilities, dementia, or other disorders characterized by permanent or transient cognitive impairments. However, the NIH has developed an interim list of points to consider (http://grants2.nih.gov/grants/policy/questionablecapacity.htm; see also Standard 3.10b, Informed Consent). To facilitate IRB review, psychologists should show evidence that their consent procedures are (a) sensitive to differing and fluctuating levels of capacity, (b) tailored to the specific research context, (c) timed to avoid periods of heightened vulnerability, and (d) repeated when studies are longitudinal. IRB applications should also include legal, psychological, and ethical criteria for determining consent capacity and decisions regarding when and from whom surrogate consent will be sought and how the voluntary nature of participant assent will be obtained and protected (see Appelbaum, Grisso, Frank, O'Donnell, & Kupfer, 1999; Carpenter et al., 2000; Fisher, 2002a; Fisher et al., 2006; Standard 3.10b, Informed Consent; Hot Topic "Goodness-of-Fit Ethics for Informed Consent Involving Adults With Impaired Decisional Capacity," Chapter 6).

Refer to Appropriate Federal Regulations and State Law When Requesting Waiver of Guardian Permission for Research Involving Children

Standard 3.10b, Informed Consent, and federal regulation 45 CFR 46.408b require guardian permission for research involving children. Exceptions outlined in 45 CFR 46.402a include emancipated or mature minors who have assumed adult responsibilities such as self-support, marriage, or procreation or who, according to state law, may be treated as an adult for certain purposes (e.g., treatment for venereal disease, drug abuse, emotional disorders). When the research involves no more than minimal risk to participants, guardian permission may also be waived if the research will not adversely affect participant rights and welfare, could not practicably be carried out without the waiver, and participants are provided with additional pertinent information after participation (45 CFR 46 116.d; see also Standard 8.08, Debriefing). Under 45 CF 46.408c, an IRB may also waive guardian permission when there is serious doubt as to whether the parents' interests adequately reflect the teenager's interests (e.g., research on child abuse or neglect, genetic testing of the healthy sibling of a child with a mental disorder) or when parental consent cannot reasonably be obtained (e.g., research on runaway youth). Requests to IRBs to waive guardian permission should thus include, when relevant, (a) state laws on emancipated and mature minor status, (b) justification of minimal risk status of research, (c) why guardian consent will not be in the child's best interest or is unavailable, and (d) how an independent participant advocate will be appointed, verify youths' understanding of procedures, support their participation preferences, and assess reactions to planned procedures (Fisher, Hoagwood, & Jensen, 1996).

Justify the Selection of Intervention and Control Group Conditions

The ethics of intervention research requires equipoise—genuine uncertainty on the part of the scientific community regarding the comparative therapeutic merits of each arm in a clinical trial (see, e.g., http://placebo.nih.gov). IRBs generally will not approve research if either a treatment or control condition has been empirically substantiated as inferior (see also Standard 3.04, Avoiding Harm). This does not exclude psychologists from conducting studies that seek to test new treatments for nonresponders to empirically validated interventions, to improve upon existing treatments, to study the practical effectiveness of interventions validated under highly controlled conditions, or to study the generalizability of validated treatments to unstudied populations. IRBs do expect investigators to provide evidence why they believe (a) participants placed in a control group will not be deprived of an available treatment with empirically validated effectiveness, and (b) individuals assigned to the experimental intervention will not be exposed to greater risk than if they had been assigned to a control or standard treatment condition.

Successful IRB proposals for treatment research will also include (a) informed consent protocols that adequately describe the experimental nature of the treatments, random assignment, and alternatives to participation (see Standard 8.02b, Informed Consent to Research); (b) steps to ensure that participation is voluntary (see Standards 3.08, Exploitative Relationships, and 8.04, Client/Patient, Student, and Subordinate Research Participants); (c) absence of conflict of interest in the role of the clinical researcher versus the treating clinician (see Standards 3.05, Multiple Relationships, and 3.06, Conflict of Interest); and (d) a data safety monitoring plan to detect anticipated or unanticipated adverse events during and, when appropriate, following study participation (see http://grants.nih.gov/grants/policy/hs/data_safety.htm).

CHAPTER 12

Standards on Assessment

9. ASSESSMENT

9.01 Bases for Assessments

(a) Psychologists base the opinions contained in their recommendations, reports, and diagnostic or evaluative statements, including forensic testimony, on information and techniques sufficient to substantiate their findings. (See also Standard 2.04, Bases for Scientific and Professional Judgments.)

Psychological assessment serves the public good by providing information to guide decisions affecting the well-being of individuals, families, groups, organizations, and institutions. Psychologists who draw their conclusions on information and techniques based in the scientific and professional knowledge of the discipline are uniquely qualified to interpret the results of psychological assessments in ways that merit the public trust. However, the public and the profession are harmed when psychologists provide opinions unsubstantiated by information obtained or drawn from data gathered through improper assessment techniques (Principle A: Beneficence and Nonmaleficence and Principle B: Fidelity and Responsibility). Standard 9.01a of the American Psychological Association (APA) Ethics Code (APA, 2002b) prohibits psychologists from providing written or oral opinions that cannot be sufficiently substantiated by the information obtained or the techniques employed.

The standard is broadly worded to apply to all written and oral professional opinions irrespective of information recipient, setting, or type of assessment.

Information Recipient. The standard prohibits unfounded professional opinions offered to, among others, (a) individual clients/patients or their representatives; (b) other professionals; (c) third-party payors; (d) administrative and professional staff at schools, hospitals, and other institutions; (e) businesses, agencies, and other organizations; (f) the courts; (g) the military or other governing legal authorities; and (h) callers to talk-radio programs or those interacting with psychologists through other media.

Setting. Standard 9.01a applies to (a) diagnostic opinions offered orally in the office of a private practitioner; (b) written reports provided to clients/patients, other practitioners, or third-party payors through the mail, the Internet, or other forms of electronic transmission; (c) testimony provided in the courts; and (d) opinions about an individual's mental health offered over the Internet, radio, television, or other electronic media.

Types of Assessment. The standard pertains to all unfounded opinions claiming to be based on any form of evaluation, including but not limited to (a) standardized psychological, educational, or neuropsychological tests; (b) diagnostic information gained through clinical interviews; (c) collateral data obtained through discussions with family members, teachers, employee supervisors, or other informants; (d) observational techniques; or (e) brief discussion or correspondence with an individual via radio, television, telephone, or the Internet.

Violations of this standard are often related to failure to comply with other standards, including Standards 2.04, Bases for Scientific and Professional Judgments; 9.01b, Bases for Assessments; and 9.02b, Use of Assessments. The following are examples of opinions based on insufficient information or techniques that would be considered violations under this standard:

☒ Testifying on the validity of a child abuse allegation based on the results of an idiosyncratic, improperly constructed parent checklist of child behaviors

☒ Diagnosing an adult with impaired decisional capacity as developmentally disabled without taking a developmental history

☒ Providing preemployment recommendations on the basis of a personality test with no proven relationship to job performance

☒ Submitting a diagnosis of neurological impairment to a health insurance company based solely on information derived during therapy sessions

☒ Informing parents that their preschooler is autistic on the basis of a single observational session

☒ Recommending a child for special education placement solely on the basis of scores on a standardized intelligence test

☒ Offering a diagnosis of posttraumatic stress disorder based on a 5-minute discussion with a listener to a radio program hosted by the psychologist

☒ Prescribing a psychotropic medication to an elderly patient complaining of memory lapses without conducting a neuropsychological assessment

Psychologists who knowingly provide unsubstantiated opinions in forensic, school, or insurance reports fail to live up to the ideals of Principle C: Integrity and may also find themselves in violation of Standard 5.01, Avoidance of False or Deceptive Statements (see Hot Topic "Avoiding False and Deceptive Statements in Scientific and Clinical Expert Testimony," Chapter 8).

(b) Except as noted in 9.01c, psychologists provide opinions of the psychological characteristics of individuals only after they have conducted an examination of the individuals adequate to support their statements or conclusions. When, despite reasonable efforts, such an examination is not practical, psychologists document the efforts they made and the result of those efforts, clarify the probable impact of their limited information on the reliability and validity of their opinions, and appropriately limit the nature and extent of their conclusions or recommendations. (See also Standards 2.01, Boundaries of Competence, and 9.06, Interpreting Assessment Results.)

Standard 9.01b specifically addresses the importance of in-person evaluations of individuals about whom psychologists will offer a professional opinion. Under this standard, with few exceptions, psychologists must conduct individual examinations sufficient to obtain personal verification of information on which to base their professional opinions and refrain from providing opinions about the psychological characteristics of an individual if they themselves have not conducted an examination of the individual adequate to support their statements or conclusions.

> ☒ A psychologist testified about a parent's psychological fitness for visitation rights, drawing his opinion solely from comments made by the child and divorced spouse in the absence of an individual examination of the parent.
>
> ☒ A psychologist contracted by an insurance company to evaluate an individual's mental health as part of a current disability claim provided an opinion based solely on job performance evaluations written by the insured's immediate supervisors and diagnostic information collected by another psychologist prior to the incident cited in the claim.
>
> ☒ A psychologist working in a correctional facility who was asked to recommend whether a prison guard's mental status was a risk to prisoner protections did not personally examine the guard but instead gave an opinion based on reports by facility administrators, staff, and prisoners.

Standard 9.01b also recognizes that in some cases, a personal examination may not be possible. For example, an individual involved in a child custody suit, a disability claim, or performance evaluation may refuse or, because of relocation or other reasons, be unavailable for a personal examination. The standard requires that psychologists make "reasonable efforts" to conduct a personal examination. Efforts that would not be considered reasonable in the prevailing professional judgment of psychologists engaged in similar activities would be considered a violation of this standard. Consider the following two examples of potential violations:

> ☒ A psychologist was contracted by a prison to evaluate the job potential of guards hired for a probationary period. Without conducting an individual interview, the psychologist wrote a report concluding that one job candidate's emotional instability made him ineligible for full-time employment. The psychologist justified the lack of a personal examination on the fact that several coworkers claimed the guard was too dangerous to interview.
>
> ☒ A psychologist hired by the attorney of a husband engaged in a custody suit provided court testimony on the wife's parenting inadequacies without having interviewed her personally. The psychologist claimed the wife did not respond to the psychologist's letter requesting the interview. On cross-examination, it was revealed that the letter written by the psychologist included the following language seemingly designed to discourage agreement to be examined: "I have reason to believe from interviews with your spouse and an examination of your children that you are responsible for the children's current mental health problems and would like to conduct an examination to confirm or dispute these assumptions."

When, despite reasonable efforts, a personal interview is not feasible, under Standard 9.01b, psychologists in their written or oral opinions must document and explain the results of their efforts, clarify the probable impact that the failure to personally examine an individual may have on the reliability and validity of their opinions, and appropriately limit their conclusions or recommendations to information they can personally verify. For example:

> ☑ A court-appointed psychologist attempted to contact the biological parent of a child currently in foster care to make recommendations regarding parental visitation. The parent was no longer at the last known residence and had not left a forwarding address. In testimony, the psychologist described the current mental health status of the child, the child's statements regarding the biological parent, and the observed relationship between the child and foster parents. In referring to the biological parent, the psychologist informed the court of efforts to contact the parent, described how failure to interview the parent limited any conclusions that could be drawn regarding the parent's psychological characteristics and parenting competence, and clarified that recommendations regarding visitation were based on the child's attitudes, mental health, and foster care arrangements.

(c) When psychologists conduct a record review or provide consultation or supervision and an individual examination is not warranted or necessary for the opinion, psychologists explain this and the sources of information on which they based their conclusions and recommendations.

This standard applies to those assessment-related activities for which an individual examination is not warranted or necessary for the psychological opinion. Such activities include record or file reviews where psychologists are called on to review preexisting records and reports to assist or evaluate decisions made by schools, courts, health insurance companies, organizations, or other psychologists they supervise or with whom they consult. Record reviews can be performed to (a) determine whether a previously conducted assessment was appropriate or sufficient; (b) evaluate the appropriateness of treatment, placement, employment, or the continuation of benefits based on the previously gathered information and reports; (c) adjudicate a disability or professional liability claim based on existing records; or (d) resolve conflicts over the applicability of records to interpretations of federal and state laws in administrative law or due process hearings (Hadjistavropoulos & Bieling, 2001; Krivacska & Margolis, 1995).

According to Standard 9.01c, psychologists who provide such services must clarify to the appropriate parties the source of the information on which the opinion is based and why an individual interview conducted by the psychologist is not necessary for the opinion.

Simply complying with this standard may not be sufficient for psychologists who are in supervisory roles that carry legal responsibility for the conduct of assessments by unlicensed supervisees or employees. In many of those instances, psychologists may be directly responsible for ensuring that individuals are qualified to conduct the assessments and do so competently (see Standard 2.05, Delegation of Work to Others).

Review of Data From Surreptitious Investigative Recording. There are instances when forensic psychologists may be asked to evaluate past mental states from audio or video recordings of a defendant's behavior at the time of the alleged offense or surreptitious recordings of a plaintiff's behavior in a personal injury, insurance disability, or divorce case (Denney & Wynkoop, 2000). Before agreeing to review such recordings, psychologists should make sure that the surveillance information was obtained legally at the time it was recorded, that the party requesting the psychologist's evaluation has the legal right to share such information, and that inadmissibility of such information will not compromise the psychologist's findings. Psychologists should also take reasonable steps to ascertain that they have been provided with all legally available recordings and other available information relevant to the forensic opinion. The psychologist's oral testimony or written report should clarify the source of the information and why an individual examination is not warranted or necessary for the type of evaluation requested.

9.02 Use of Assessments

(a) Psychologists administer, adapt, score, interpret, or use assessment techniques, interviews, tests, or instruments in a manner and for purposes that are appropriate in light of the research on or evidence of the usefulness and proper application of the techniques.

The appropriate use of psychological assessments can benefit individuals, families, organizations, and society by providing information on which educational placements, mental health treatments, health insurance coverage, employee selection, job placement, workers' compensation, program development, legal decisions, and government policies can be based. The inappropriate use of assessments can lead to harmful diagnostic, educational, institutional, legal, and social policy decisions based on inaccurate and misleading information.

Standard 9.02a is concerned with the proper selection, interpretation, scoring, and administration of assessments. It refers to the full range of assessment techniques used by psychologists, including interviews and standardized tests administered in person, through the Internet, or other media. According to this standard, ethical justification for the use of assessments is determined by research on or evidence supporting the purpose for which the test is administered, the method of administration, and interpretation of scores. To comply with the standard, psychologists should be familiar with the data and other information provided in test manuals detailing (a) theoretical and empirical support for test use for specific purposes and populations, (b) administration procedures, and (c) how test scores are to be calculated and interpreted. Psychologists should also keep apprised of ongoing research or evidence of a test's usefulness or obsolescence over time (see also Standards 2.03, Maintaining Competence; 2.04, Bases for Scientific and Professional Judgments; and 9.08b, Obsolete Tests and Outdated Test Results).

Internet-Mediated Assessments. Psychologists administering assessments via the Internet need to remain up-to-date on research demonstrating their validity or lack thereof for use in this media (Standard 2.03, Maintaining Competence). Verification of the examinee's age, gender, and honesty of disclosures is important to the assessment's validity and reliability (Alleman, 2002). Some assessments developed for in-person administration require verbal, auditory, or kinesthetic clues for accurate diagnosis (Barak & English, 2002). When assessments have not been validated for use of the Internet, psychologists should make every effort to conduct an in-person evaluation. When this is not possible, psychologists should select instruments that research or other evidence indicates are most appropriate for this media, implement when possible information-gathering techniques that can best approximate in-person settings (e.g., video and auditory interactive technology), and acknowledge limitations of the assessment in interpretations of the data (Standard 9.06, Interpreting Assessment Results).

Violations of Standard 9.02a occur when psychologists use assessments in a manner or for a purpose that is not supported by evidence in the field (see also this chapter's Hot Topic on "The Use of Assessments in Expert Testimony: Implications of Case Law and the Federal Rules of Evidence").

☒ A psychologist contracted to conduct employment testing for an organization administered a series of personality inventories with little or no validity evidence supporting the link between scores on the inventories and actual job performance.

☒ A counseling psychologist working with an isolated rural community administered a series of tests over the Internet without previously establishing whether the Internet-mediated scores measure the same construct as scores from the paper-and-pencil version (Buchanan, 2002).

☒ A school psychologist working under pressure to meet the school system's quotas for weekly testing gave the same battery of tests to all students irrespective of their grade level or presenting problem.

☒ A neuropsychologist conducted a forensic examination of a prisoner in a room occupied by other prisoners, thereby compromising the validity of score interpretation based on norms established under standardized distraction-free testing environments.

Test administration for individuals with disabilities may require modifications and adaptations in testing administration to minimize the effect of test taker characteristics incidental to the purpose of the assessment. Standard 9.02a permits departure from a standard administration protocol if the method of test adaptation can be justified by research or other evidence. For example, converting a written test to Braille for a blind individual, physically assisting a client with cerebral palsy to circle items on a written test, or providing breaks for an individual with a disability associated with frequent fatigue is acceptable if the particular disability is not associated with the construct to be measured by the test and there are professional or scientific reasons to assume that such modifications will not affect the validity of the test (American Educational Research Association [AERA], APA, & National Council on Measurement in Education [NCME], 1999). Such accommodations are not appropriate if the disability is directly related to the abilities or characteristics that the test is designed to measure. Federal regulations relevant to the assessment of individuals with disabilities include the Individuals with Disabilities Education Improvement Act of 2004 (IDEA; http://idea.ed.gov/), Section 5.04 of the Rehabilitation Act of 1973 (http://www.hhs.gov/ocr/504.html), and the Americans with Disabilities Act of 1990 (ADA; www.ada.gov).

Presence of Third Parties to Assessments

Standard 9.02a requires that psychologists administer tests in a manner consistent with procedures and testing contexts used in the development and validation of the instruments. Many psychological assessment instruments and procedures are validated under administration conditions limited to the presence of the psychologist and testee. In rare instances, psychologists may judge it necessary to include third parties to control the behavior of difficult examinees (e.g., parents of young children, hospital staff for psychiatric patients with a recent history of violence). In such situations, psychologists should select assessment instruments that are least likely to lend themselves to distortion based on the presence of a third party and include in their interpretations of test results the implications of such violations of standardized testing conditions.

Psychologists providing expert forensic consultations in relation to a criminal case, tort litigation, insurance benefits, or workers' compensation claims may find that state law, institutional policy, or a judge's ruling mandating the presence of a third party during forensic assessment can compromise the assessment validity of tests when third parties are present. For example, in neuropsychological assessments related to workers' compensation cases, the presence of the plaintiff's legal counsel, family members, or company representatives may distort the testing process or render test scores and interpretations invalid if the third party influences the test taker's motivation, behavior, or psychologist-testee rapport (American Academy of Clinical Neuropsychology, 2001). The use of data from such assessments may be unfair to individuals if it leads to invalid test administration or misleading interpretations of the testee's responses (Principle D: Justice and Standards 1.01, Misuse of Psychologists' Work; 1.02, Conflicts Between Ethics and Law, Regulations, or Other Governing Legal Authority; and 9.06, Interpreting Assessment Results). When there is no legal flexibility in denying third-party presence during an assessment, psychologists should select tests and procedures found to be least susceptible to distortion under these conditions and ensure that their written reports highlight the unique circumstances of the assessment and the limitations in interpretation.

Trainees and Interpreters as Third Parties. Third parties may observe evaluations for training purposes or serve as interpreters when translation is necessary to ensure accuracy and fairness of assessments (Standard 9.02c, Use of Assessments). In such instances, psychologists must select procedures that research or other evidence has demonstrated can be applied appropriately under these circumstances, ensure that trainees and interpreters are trained adequately to minimize threats to the proper test administration, and include in their reports any limitations on conclusions presented by the presence of the third parties (Standards 2.05, Delegation of Work to Others, and 9.06, Interpreting Assessment Results).

(b) Psychologists use assessment instruments whose validity and reliability have been established for use with members of the population tested. When such validity or reliability has not been established, psychologists describe the strengths and limitations of test results and interpretation.

The proper use of tests can further principles of fairness and justice by ensuring that all persons benefit from equal quality of assessment measures, procedures, and interpretation (Principle D: Justice and Standard 3.01, Unfair Discrimination). Fair applicability of test results rests on assumptions that the validity and reliability of a test are equivalent for different populations tested. *Validity* refers to the extent to which empirical evidence and psychological theory support the interpretation of test data; that is, whether the test measures the psychological construct it purports to measure. *Reliability* refers to the consistency of test scores when a test is repeated for an individual or for a given population (see AERA, APA, & NCME, 1999).

A test that is a valid and reliable measure of a psychological construct in one population may not adequately measure the same construct in members of a different population, especially if members of the population were represented inadequately in the normative sample or if test validity information has not been established specifically for that group. Standard 9.02b requires psychologists to select assessment instruments whose validity and reliability have been established for use with members of the population tested. This standard applies to psychological assessment of any population, including clients/patients, students, job candidates, legal defendants, and research participants.

To comply with this standard, psychologists, when selecting a test, must be familiar with the specific populations included in the standardization sample and the test's validity and reliability estimates. At minimum, psychologists should determine the applicability of a test to an individual's age group, ethnicity/culture, language, and gender and, where applicable, disability or other population characteristics for which there is scientific or professional evidence to suggest that test scores may not be psychometrically, functionally, or theoretically comparable to the reference groups on which the test was normed.

Psychologists should also be familiar with relevant federal laws on the selection and administration of nondiscriminatory assessment and evaluation procedures (e.g., IDEA, 34 CFR 300.30[c][1][i]).

> ☒ A school psychologist was asked to evaluate a bilingual child whose family recently moved to New York from Puerto Rico. The psychologist used the English version of a well-known intelligence test without considering whether the standardized Spanish version of the test was or was not most appropriate for the child's particular needs.
>
> ☒ A psychologist working in a nursing home always used the Beck Depression Inventory (Beck, Steer, & Brown, 1996) to assess patient depression without considering the appropriateness of other measures specifically standardized on elderly populations or populations with chronic illnesses.

The dynamic and evolving nature of this country's cultural, political, and economic landscape creates situations in which population-valid and reliable tests of a psychological construct may not be available for the individual or group tested. Psychologists asked to evaluate individuals from such groups should select tests validated on other populations with caution because they may produce results that do not adequately assess the qualities or competencies intended to be measured (AERA, APA, & NCME, 1999). Recommendations based on these assessments in turn may lead to unfair denial of educational or employment opportunities, health coverage, legal rights, or necessary services (Principle D: Justice). According to Standard 9.02b, psychologists who use tests without established norms for the individual or population assessed must describe in their reports the strengths of using the specific test results as well as the limitations the use of such tests places on psychologists' interpretations and recommendations.

> ☑ A forensic psychologist was asked to evaluate the competence to stand trial of a prisoner who recently immigrated to the United States from Botswana. The prisoner's English was poor, but there were no tests for competence standardized for individuals from the prisoner's cultural or language group. The psychologist selected the best interview techniques and assessments available and in written conclusions to the court explained the limitations of the tests used.

Selection of "Culture-Free" Tests. School psychologists and neuropsychologists conducting assessments of intellectual, educational, and cognitive abilities may attempt to be culturally sensitive by "stacking" their test batteries with nonverbal visuoperceptual and motor tests when assessing patients who speak languages in which more traditional language-based tests are not available. The use of such tests requires ethical caution since nonverbal tests of cognitive ability can be just as culturally biased as verbal tests (Wong, Strickland, Fletcher-Janzen, Ardila, & Reynolds, 2000).

> ☒   A neuropsychologist was asked to assess a recent Nigerian immigrant who had suf-
> fered brain damage after arriving in America in order to evaluate his ability to carry
> out basic living skills. Because the man had such limited English skills, and no test
> was available in his primary language, the neuropsychologist decided that the most
> culturally sensitive approach would be to assess the man's cognitive capacity with
> an assessment battery composed entirely of visuospatial, perceptual, and motor
> tasks. The psychologist's report did not describe the limitations of test results based
> on the absence of language-based assessments of reasoning and other cognitive
> abilities (adapted from Wong, 2000).

(c) Psychologists use assessment methods that are appropriate to an individual's language preference and competence, unless the use of an alternative language is relevant to the assessment issues.

Language differences are part of the cultural diversity, rich immigration history, and individual differences in hearing and other linguistically relevant disabilities that make up the demographic mosaic of the United States. The validity and applicability of assessment data can be severely compromised when testing is conducted in a language the testee is relatively unfamiliar with or uncomfortable using. Under Standard 9.02c, prior to selecting, administering, or interpreting tests, psychologists must consider both the language preference and language competence of the testee.

Whereas the inappropriateness of English-only-based psychological testing is obvious when testees speak little or no English, the hazards of English-only testing for bilingual persons or oral-language-only assessment of persons with hearing disabilities who can read lips and communicate in sign language are often overlooked. The linguistic competencies of individuals who are bilingual often vary with the mode of communication (e.g., oral vs. written language), language function (e.g., social, educational, or job related), and topical domain (e.g., science, mathematics, interpersonal relationships, self-evaluations). In addition, individuals' language preferences do not always reflect their language competence. Individuals may be embarrassed to reveal that their English, hearing, or oral language is poor; believe non-English or nonhearing testing will negatively affect their evaluations; or misjudge their language proficiency.

The *Standards for Educational and Psychological Testing* (AERA, APA, & NCME, 1999) recommends a number of steps that can help psychologists comply with Standard 9.02c:

- Psychologists can use language tests that assess multiple language domains to determine language dominance and proficiency relevant to different modes of assessment (e.g., written, oral) and topics (e.g., academic, interpersonal).

- Whenever possible, psychologists should use test translations that have been developed according to accepted methods of test construction (see Standard 9.05, Test Construction). For example, the *Standards for Educational and Psychological Testing* recommends the use of an iterative process more akin to test construction and validation rather than sole reliance on back translation (translating the translation of the test back into the original language).

- Additional testing or observation may be necessary to determine whether what appears to be eccentric behavior (e.g., short phrases or reticence in response to test questions) reflects differences in cultural communication styles or an individual characteristic.

- To the extent feasible, psychologists must ensure the language competence of the test administrator (see also Standards 2.05, Delegation of Work to Others, and 9.03c, Informed Consent in Assessments).

- When interpreting assessment results, test norms for native speakers of English should not be used for individuals for whom English is a second language or should be interpreted in part as reflecting a level of English proficiency.

When English or Other Language Proficiency Is Essential. There are instances when proficiency in English or another language is essential to the goal of the assessment. For example, the ability to communicate with English-speaking employees may be a necessary qualification for a successful applicant for a personnel position. Evaluating a student's English proficiency may be necessary to determine appropriate educational placement. The ability to read and speak English may be important to certain service positions responsible for protecting public health, safety, and welfare (AERA, APA, & NCME, 1999). Inclusion of the phrase "unless the use of an alternative language is relevant to the assessment issues" indicates that Standard 9.02c permits psychologists to use tests in a language in which the testee may not be proficient, if effective job performance, school placement, or other goals of assessment require the ability to communicate in that language.

9.03 Informed Consent in Assessments

(a) Psychologists obtain informed consent for assessments, evaluations, or diagnostic services, as described in Standard 3.10, Informed Consent, except when (1) testing is mandated by law or governmental regulations; (2) informed consent is implied because testing is conducted as a routine educational, institutional, or organizational activity (e.g., when participants voluntarily agree to assessment when applying for a job); or (3) one purpose of the testing is to evaluate decisional capacity. Informed consent includes an explanation of the nature and purpose of the assessment, fees, involvement of third parties, and limits of confidentiality and sufficient opportunity for the client/patient to ask questions and receive answers.

To comply with this standard, psychologists must obtain and document, with few exceptions, written or oral consent in the manner set forth in Standard 3.10, Informed Consent. Psychologists must provide individuals who will be assessed and, when appropriate, their legal representative a clear explanation of the nature and purpose of the assessment, fees, involvement of third parties, and the limits of confidentiality.

Core Elements of Informed Consent in Assessments

Nature of the Assessment. The *nature* of an assessment refers to (a) the general category of the assessment (e.g., personality, psychopathology, competency, parenting skills, neuropsychological abilities and deficits, employment skills, developmental disabilities), (b) procedures and testing format (e.g., oral interviews, written self-report checklists, behavioral observation, skills assessment), and (c) duration of the assessment (e.g., hours or multiple assessments).

Purpose of the Assessment. The *purpose* of the assessment refers to its potential use, for example, in employment decisions, school placement, custody decisions, disability benefits, treatment decisions, and plans for or evaluation of rehabilitation of criminal offenders.

Fees. Discussion of *fees* must include the cost of the assessment and payment schedule and should be consistent with requirements of Standard 6.04, Fees and Financial Arrangements. When applicable and to the extent feasible, psychologists must also discuss with relevant parties the extent to which their services will be covered by the individual's health plan, school district, employer, or others (see Standards 6.04a and d, Fees and Financial Arrangements).

Third Parties. Involvement of *third parties* refers to other individuals (e.g., legal guardians), health maintenance organizations (HMOs), employers, organizations, or legal or other governing authorities that have requested the assessment and to whom the results of the assessments will be provided. Psychologists should be familiar with ethical standards, state law, and federal regulations relevant to the appropriate role of third parties and the release and documentation of release of such information to others (see Standard 4.05, Disclosures). Psychologists asked to evaluate a child by one parent should clarify custody issues to determine if another parent must give permission.

Confidentiality. Informed consent to assessments must provide a clear explanation of the extent and limits of *confidentiality,* including (a) when the psychologist must comply with reporting requirements such as mandated child abuse reporting or duty-to-warn laws and (b) in the case of assessments involving minors, guardian access to records (see discussion of parental access involving Health Insurance Portability and Accountability Act, Family Educational Rights and Privacy Act, and other regulations in Standards 3.10, Informed Consent; 4.01, Maintaining Confidentiality; and 4.02, Discussing the Limits of Confidentiality). Psychologists who administer assessments over the Internet must inform clients/patients, research participants, or others about the procedures that will be used to protect confidentiality and the threats to confidentiality unique to this form of electronic transmission of information (see also Standard 4.02c, Discussing the Limits of Confidentiality).

Implications of HIPAA for Confidentiality-Relevant Information

To effectively provide information relevant to confidentiality during informed consent as required in Standard 9.03a, psychologists who will be electronically recording, storing, or disseminating to third parties protected health information (PHI) gathered during an assessment need to be familiar with the Health Insurance Portability and Accountability Act of 1996 (HIPAA; www.hhs.gov/ocr/hipaa/final reg.html). PHI is defined as any information transmitted or maintained in any form or medium relating to the past, present, or future physical or mental health condition, provision of care, or payment for provision of care for an individual that either identifies or can be used to identify the individual (45 CFR 160.102). Not all psychologists who are administering or using assessments are covered entity's under HIPAA. A covered entity is a (a) health plan, (b) health care clearinghouse, or (c) health care provider who transmits any health information in electronic form in connection with a financial or administrative transaction. HIPAA regulations apply to a psychologist's practice and not to individual clients/patients. Therefore, psychologists who are covered entities as that relates to a single client/patient must comply with HIPAA regulations for all their clients/patients.

The HIPAA regulation most relevant to informed consent in assessments is the Notice of Privacy Practices. At the beginning of the professional relationship, covered entities must provide clients/patients a written document detailing routine uses and disclosures of PHI and the individual's rights and the covered entities' legal duties with respect to PHI (45 CFR 164.520). Psychologists conducting assessments should also be familiar with HIPAA-compliant authorization forms for use and release of PHI and HIPAA requirements for Accounting of Disclosures.

These regulations are described in greater detail in the section "A Word About HIPAA" in the Preface of this book and in discussions of Standard 3.10, Informed Consent, in Chapter 6; Standards 4.01, Maintaining Confidentiality, and 4.05, Disclosures, in Chapter 7; Standard 6.01, Documentation of Professional and Scientific Work and Maintenance of Records, in Chapter 9; and Standard 9.04, Release of Test Data, in this chapter. Psychologists conducting assessments may wish to use the HIPAA-compliant model forms developed by the APA Insurance Trust (APAIT) and the APA Practice Directorate (http://www.apapractice.org/apo/hipaa.html#).

Dispensing With Informed Consent

Under Standard 9.03a, informed consent may be waived when consent is implied because testing is conducted as (a) a routine educational activity, such as end-of-term reading or math achievement testing in elementary and high schools; (b) regular institutional activities, such as student and teaching evaluations in academic institutions or consumer satisfaction questionnaires in hospitals or social service agencies; or (c) organizational activity, such as when individuals voluntarily agree to preemployment testing when applying for a job.

Standard 9.03a permits psychologists to dispense with informed consent in assessment when testing is mandated by law or other governing legal authority or when one purpose of testing is to determine the capacity of the individual to give consent. Ethical steps that must be taken in these contexts are discussed next under Standard 9.03b (Moberg & Kniele, 2006).

(b) Psychologists inform persons with questionable capacity to consent or for whom testing is mandated by law or governmental regulations about the nature and purpose of the proposed assessment services, using language that is reasonably understandable to the person being assessed.

Under Standards 3.10b, Informed Consent, and 9.03a, Informed Consent in Assessments, informed consent in assessment is not required when an individual has been determined to be legally incapable of giving informed consent, when testing is mandated by law or other governing legal authority, or when one purpose of testing is to determine consent capacity. These waivers reflect the fact that the term *consent* refers to a person's legal status to make autonomous decisions based on age, mental capacity, or the legal decision under consideration. Consistent with the moral value of respect for the dignity and worth of all persons articulated in Principle E: Respect for People's Rights and Dignity, under Standard 9.03c, psychologists must provide all individuals irrespective of their legal status appropriate explanations of the nature and purpose of the proposed assessment. Readers may also refer to the Hot Topic in Chapter 6, titled "Goodness-of-fit Ethics for Informed Consent Involving Adults With Impaired Decisional Capacity."

Standard 9.03a often applies in situations where assessment is requested by parents of children younger than age 18 years or family members of adults with suspected cognitive impairments. In these situations, the psychologist must provide assent information in a language and at a language level that is reasonably understandable to the child or adult being assessed. When both guardian permission and child or cognitively impaired adult assent are sought, psychologists working with populations for whom English is not a first language should be alert to situations in which prospective clients/patients and their legal guardians may have different language preferences and proficiencies.

Mandated Assessments. Psychologists conducting forensic, military, or other assessments that have been legally mandated should provide *notification of purpose,* which explains to the person being tested the nature and purpose of the testing, who has requested the testing, and who will receive copies of the report. If the examinee is unwilling to proceed following a thorough explanation, according to the Specialty Guidelines for Forensic Psychology, "The forensic practitioner may attempt to conduct the examination, postpone the examination, advise the examinee to contact his or her attorney, or notify the retaining attorney about the examinee's unwillingness to proceed" (Committee on the Revision of the Specialty Guidelines for Forensic Psychology, 2008). The APA Insurance Trust (APAIT) provides a useful sample of a Forensic Informed Consent Contract developed by Jeffrey Younggren, Eric Harris, and Bruce Bennett (http://www.apait.org/apait/).

Defendants who are entering a plea of insanity may not be able to act on their Fifth Amendment right to silence and avoidance of self-incrimination. To avoid compromising the admissibility of a comprehensive forensic evaluation, Bush et al. (2006) suggest that psychologists first assess competency, then sanity, and separate the reports given to the court to provide the court the opportunity to first determine the competence question.

Informed Consent for the Assessment of Malingering

Malingering refers to the intentional production of false symptoms to attain an identifiable external benefit (Iverson, 2006; National Academy of Neuropsychology Policy and Planning Committee, 2000). Some have argued that assessment of malingering is the number one priority of forensic assessment, preceding any professional conclusions in forensic evaluations (Brodsky & Galloway, 2003). Malingering can be manifested through intentional under- or overperformance during psychological assessment. Accurate assessment of malingering is ethically important because errors in diagnosis can assist or impede justice when undetected in forensic procedures or obscure adequate treatment for psychopathology (Principle A: Beneficence and Nonmaleficence).

Some have questioned whether describing the purposes of tests for malingering during informed consent compromises the validity of the assessment or whether failing to include such information during informed consent violates testees' autonomy rights (Principle E: Respect for People's Rights and Dignity and Standard 9.03, Informed Consent in Assessments). Current standards of practice support communicating to testees during informed consent or notification of purpose that measures will be used to assess the examinee's honesty and efforts to do well (Bush et al., 2006).

Research on Coached Malingering. A practical concern in the forensic assessment of defendants or plaintiffs is whether existing tests of malingering can detect over- or underexaggeration of symptoms when the examinee has been coached by individuals familiar with the tests. When researchers attempt to study the extent to which commonly used tests are vulnerable to coached faking, there is a risk that the information provided to research participants or disseminated through publication will be used to improve the success of coached malingers (Berry, Lamb, Wetter, Baier, & Widiger, 1994). Ben-Porath (1994) suggests that to protect against these risks, investigators can (a) coach research participants on items similar but not identical to those on the test under investigation, (b) provide only a brief synopsis of coaching instructions in published articles, and (c) release information on verbatim instructions only to those bound by the APA Ethics Code to protect the integrity of tests (see also Standard 9.11, Maintaining Test Security).

(c) Psychologists using the services of an interpreter obtain informed consent from the client/patient to use that interpreter, ensure that confidentiality of test results and test security are maintained, and include in their recommendations, reports, and diagnostic or evaluative statements, including forensic testimony, discussion of any limitations on the data obtained. (See also Standards 2.05, Delegation of Work to Others; 4.01, Maintaining Confidentiality; 9.01, Bases for Assessments; 9.06, Interpreting Assessment Results; and 9.07, Assessment by Unqualified Persons.)

Compliance with the consent requirements outlined in Standard 3.10 obligates psychologists to provide information in a language and at a language level that is reasonably understandable to the client/patient and, where applicable, his or her legally authorized representative. Psychologists may use the services of an interpreter when they do not possess the skills to obtain consent in the language in which the client/patient is proficient.

When delegating informed consent responsibilities to an interpreter, psychologists must ensure not only that the interpreter is competent in the consent-relevant language (see Standard 2.05, Delegation of Work to Others) but that the interpreter also understands and complies with procedures necessary to protect the confidentiality of test results and test security. An interpreter who revealed the identity of a client/patient or the nature of specific test items used during the assessment would place the psychologist who hired the interpreter in potential violation of this standard. Because test validity and reliability may be vulnerable to errors in interpretation, Standard 9.03c also requires that the involvement of the interpreter and any related limitations on the data obtained be clearly indicated and discussed in any assessment-based report, recommendation, diagnostic or evaluative statement, or forensic testimony.

9.04 Release of Test Data

(a) The term *test data* refers to raw and scaled scores, client/patient responses to test questions or stimuli, and psychologists' notes and recordings concerning client/patient statements and behavior during an examination. Those portions of test materials that include client/patient responses are included in the definition of *test data*. Pursuant to a client/patient release, psychologists provide test data to the client/ patient or other persons identified in the release. Psychologists may refrain from releasing test data to protect a client/patient or others from substantial harm or misuse or misrepresentation of the data or the test, recognizing that in many instances release of confidential information under these circumstances is regulated by law. (See also Standard 9.11, Maintaining Test Security.)

Definition of Test Data

In Standard 9.04a, the term *test data* refers to the client's/patient's actual responses to test items, the raw or scaled scores such responses receive, and a psychologist's written notes or recordings of the client's/patient's specific responses or behaviors during the testing. The term *notes* in this standard is limited to the assessment context and does not include psychotherapy (or process) notes documenting or analyzing the contents of conversation during a private counseling session.

Test Data and Test Materials. Recognizing that availability of test questions and scoring criteria may compromise the validity of a test for future use with a client/patient or other individuals exposed to the information, Standard 9.04a distinguishes *test data,* which under most circumstances must be provided upon a client/patient release, from *test materials,* which under most circumstances should not (see Standard 9.11, Maintaining Test Security). The definition of *test data* does *not* include test manuals, protocols for administering or scoring responses, or test items *unless* these materials include the client's/patient's responses or scores or the psychologist's contemporaneous notes on the client's/patient's testing responses or behaviors. If testing protocols allow, it is good practice for psychologists to record client/patient responses on a form separated from the test items themselves to ensure that upon client/patient request, only the test data and not the test material itself need be released.

The Affirmative Duty to Provide Test Data to Clients/Patients and Others Identified in a Client's/Patient's Release

Release to Clients/Patients. Under Standard 9.04a, psychologists have an affirmative duty to provide test data as defined above to the client/patient or other persons identified in a client/patient release. The obligation set forth by Standard 9.04a to respect clients'/patients' right to their test data is consistent with legal trends toward greater patient autonomy and the self-determination rights of clients/patients as set forth in Principle E: Respect for People's Rights and Dignity. Although not explicitly stated in the standard, it is always good practice for psychologists to have a signed release or authorization from the client/patient even if the data are to be given directly to the client/patient. This standard does not preclude psychologists from discussing with a client/patient the potential for misuse of the information by individuals unqualified to interpret it.

Release to Others. A fundamental tension exists between the desire of psychologists to respect clients'/patients' right to determine who will have access to their assessment results and the desire to ensure that the data are not reviewed by unqualified individuals who might misinterpret or misuse the data or violate contractual agreements designed to protect a test publisher's proprietary interests (Principle A: Beneficence and Nonmaleficence, Principle D: Justice, and Principle E: Respect for People's Rights and Dignity). The language of Standard 9.04 reflects this tension by providing exceptions to the release of test data under conditions in which the release might lead to substantial harm or misuse of the test.

There are several reasons why the standard supports release of test data to clients/patients and those whom they authorize to receive the data. First, whether a person is qualified to use test data is determined by the context of the proposed use. For example, restricting release of test data to individuals with advanced degrees or licensure in professional psychology would preclude other qualified health care professionals from using the information. Broadening but limiting the definition of *qualified* person to health professionals might jeopardize appropriate judicial scrutiny of psychological tests and a client's/patient's right to the discovery process to challenge their use in court. Second, even if a consensus of "qualified" person could be achieved, requiring a psychologist to confirm the education, training, degrees, or certifications of other professionals would pose burdens that might not be possible or feasible to meet. Third, as described below, with few exceptions, HIPAA regulations require that covered entities provide clients/patients and their personal representatives access to PHI.

Withholding Test Data

Standard 9.04a permits psychologists to withhold test data to protect the client/patient or another individual from substantial harm. The standard also permits withholding test data to protect misuse or misrepresentation of the data or the test. Before refusing to release test data under this clause, psychologists should carefully consider the proviso in the standard "that such decisions may be regulated by law." For example, when refusing a client's/patient's request to release test data based on the psychologist's judgment that the data will be misused, psychologists should document in each specific case their rationale for assuming the data will be misused and refrain from behaviors that may be in violation of other standards (e.g., Standard 6.03, Withholding Records for Nonpayment).

Implications of HIPAA. Requiring psychologists to release test data to the client/patient or others pursuant to a client/patient release reflects a sea change in the legal landscape from paternalistic to autonomy-based rules governing access to health records. In particular, HIPAA establishes the right of access of individuals to inspect and receive copies of medical and billing records maintained and used by the provider for decisions about the client/patient (45 CFR 524). This requirement does not include psychotherapy notes or information compiled in reasonable anticipation of or use in civil, criminal, or administrative actions or proceedings. In addition, psychologists who are covered entities under HIPAA must also provide such access to a client's/patient's personal representative (45 CFR 164.502[g][1]).

HIPAA severely limits the ability of covered entities to use professional judgment to determine the appropriateness of releasing test data to clients/patients and their personal representatives. For example, the right of clients/patients to obtain their own test data under HIPAA regulations means in practice that they can pass it on to other individuals of their choice.

Harm. Under HIPAA, psychologists who are covered entities can deny client/patient access to test data only if it is reasonably likely to endanger the life or physical safety of the individual or another person or, in some cases, likely to cause equally substantial harm (Principle A: Beneficence and Nonmaleficence). In addition, psychologists must allow clients/patients the right to have the denial reviewed by a designated licensed health care professional. HIPAA regulations thus severely limit psychologists' ability to exercise their professional judgment as to what constitutes substantial harm to clients/patients.

Misuse or Misrepresentation of the Test. Release of "test data" that include client/patient responses recorded on the test protocol itself can raise issues of copyright protection and fair use by test development companies (Principle B: Fidelity and Responsibility). If testing protocols allow, psychologists may wish to record client/patient responses on a form separated from the test items themselves to comply with contractual agreements with test developers and to maintain test security (Standard 9.11, Maintaining Test Security). When test data cannot be separated from test materials that are protected by copyright law, psychologists' decision to withhold release of test data would be consistent with HIPAA regulations and Standard 9.04a. According to Richard Campanelli, director of the Office for Civil Rights at the U.S. Department of Health and Human Services (DHHS), under Section 1172 (e), withholding protected health information would not be in violation of HIPAA if to do so would violate trade secret laws (http://kspope.com/assess/harcourt-hipaa.php). However, when test data are considered PHI and testees' responses are recorded separately from copyrighted test materials or were not collected using tests protected by trade secret laws, to date HIPAA does not recognize a covered entity's concern about its misuse as a legitimate reason to withhold release.

☒ To protect against the misuse of test data in possible instances when they would be released to clients/patients or another identified person, a psychologist used an idiosyncratic code to record testees' responses. When a client/patient requested the test data be released to another licensed practitioner, it was clear that the test data were undecipherable to others. The psychologist was in violation of Standard 9.04a and HIPAA regulations, because in this particular case there was no reason to assume misuse of test data. The psychologist's failure to appropriately create and store records also violated Standard 6.01, Documentation of Professional and Scientific Work and Maintenance of Records.

Withholding Data in Anticipation of Its Use for Legal Purposes. There are instances, however, when HIPAA constraints are not at issue. For example, HIPAA does not require release of PHI to clients in situations in which information is compiled in reasonable anticipation of, or for use in, civil, criminal, or administrative actions or proceedings. In other instances, such as certain educational evaluations, test data may not come under the PHI classification, and thus the HIPAA Privacy Rule would not apply (see Standard 4.01, Maintaining Confidentiality).

Organizations, Courts, and Government Agencies

The use of the term *client/patient* in this standard refers to the individual testee and not to an organizational client. This standard does not require industrial-organizational or consulting psychologists to release test data to either an organizational client or an employee when testing is conducted to evaluate job candidacy or employee or organization effectiveness and does not assess factors directly related to medical or mental health conditions or services. Psychologists working in these contexts would not be required to provide the test data to the employees themselves under this standard because the organization, not the employee, is the client (see also Standards 3.07, Third-Party Requests for Services; 3.11, Psychological Services Delivered To or Through Organizations; and 9.03, Informed Consent in Assessments). Similarly, forensic psychologists, military psychologists, and others working under governing legal authority are permitted by the Ethics Code to withhold release of test data from a testee when the client is an attorney, the court, or other governing legal authority. Finally, all psychologists are permitted by the Ethics Code to withhold release of test data when required by law (Standard 1.02, Conflicts Between Ethics and Law, Regulations, or Other Governing Legal Authority).

(b) In the absence of a client/patient release, psychologists provide test data only as required by law or court order.

Standard 9.04b recognizes the clients'/patients' right to expect that in the absence of their release or authorization, psychologists will protect the confidentiality of test data. The standard does permit psychologists to disclose test data without the consent of the client/patient in response to a court order (including subpoenas that are court ordered) or in other situations required by law (e.g., an order from an administrative tribunal). In such instances, psychologists are wise to seek legal counsel to determine their legal responsibility to respond to the request (see also Standard 4.05b, Disclosures). Psychologists may also ask the court or other legal authority for a protective order to prevent the inappropriate disclosure of confidential information or suggest that the information be submitted to another psychologist for qualified review.

Implications of HIPAA. Standard 9.04b provides stricter protection of confidential test data than HIPAA. Under the HIPAA Privacy Rule, PHI may be disclosed in response to a subpoena, discovery request, or other lawful process that is not accompanied by an order of a court or administrative tribunal, if the covered entity receives satisfactory assurance from the party seeking the information either that reasonable efforts have been made to ensure that the client/patient has been notified of the request or reasonable efforts have been made to secure a qualified protective order (45 CFR 164.512[e][1]). Psychologists who disclosed information in such an instance would be in violation of 9.04b. The greater protection provided by 9.04b is consistent with most states' more stringent psychotherapist-patient privilege communication statutes.

9.05 Test Construction

Psychologists who develop tests and other assessment techniques use appropriate psychometric procedures and current scientific or professional knowledge for test design, standardization, validation, reduction or elimination of bias, and recommendations for use.

Test development is the foundation of good psychological assessment. Psychologists who construct assessment techniques must be familiar with and apply psychometric methods for establishing the validity and reliability of tests, developing standardized administration instructions, selecting items that reduce or eliminate bias, and drawing on current scientific or professional knowledge for recommendations about the use of test results (see also Standard 2.01, Boundaries of Competence; Turchick, Karpenko, Hammers, & McNamara, 2007).

Standard 9.05 applies to all test development activities, not just those implemented in professional testing services or research settings. Psychologists who develop tests or other assessment techniques to serve private practice clients/patients, organizational clients, or the courts can violate this standard if they fail to use proper psychometric methods for test construction.

Psychometric Procedures

To be in compliance with Standard 9.05, psychologists must be familiar with and competent to implement appropriate psychometric procedures to establish the usefulness of the test (Standard 2.01, Boundaries of Competence). A good resource for complying with this standard in the Ethics Code is the *Standards for Educational and Psychological Testing* (AERA, APA, & NCME, 1999). The following are brief definitions of psychometric procedures presented in greater detail by the AERA, APA, and NCME (1999).

Validity, Reliability, and Standardization. Validity is the degree to which theory and empirical evidence support specific interpretations of test scores. Methods for establishing test validity include content, concurrent, construct, and predictive validity as well as evidence-based response processes, internal structure of a test, and consequences of testing. *Reliability* is the degree to which test scores for a group of test takers are consistent over repeated administrations of a test or for items within a test. Methods for establishing test reliability include internal consistency coefficients, analysis of the standard error of measure, test-retest, split-half, or alternative form comparisons. *Standardization* refers to the establishment of scoring norms based on the test performance of a representative sample of individuals from populations for which the test is intended.

Validity and reliability must be assessed appropriately for each total score, subscore, or combination of scores that will be interpreted. Where relevant, descriptions of the test to users, school personnel, organizational clients, and the courts should include a description of the psychometric procedures used during test development.

> ☒ An industrial-organizational psychologist was hired by a firm to develop a selection system for promotion of line workers to supervisors. The psychologists used appropriate sampling and validation procedures to construct a 20-item measure. When he presented the final measure to the firm's board of trustees, the board president expressed concern that items on attitudes toward the firm were not included. The psychologist agreed to add a few of these to the test without further validation (see Lowman, 2006, Case 3).

> ☒ Over the years, a school psychologist had observed that students who had been removed from their homes because of child abuse or neglect frequently gave a set of common and unique narrative responses to items on the Wechsler Intelligence Scale for Children Comprehension subtest (WISC; Wechsler, 1991). Cognizant of school psychologists' legal duty to report suspected child abuse, she constructed a test composed of 10 narrative statements she believed were typical of abused and neglected children. She developed a scoring system where 0 to 1 indicated that the child was probably not abused or neglected, 2 to 3 suggested that the child should be further observed, and 4 to 10 supported a suspicion of child abuse or neglect that should be reported to child protective services. She began to use the scale to decide whether to make a report of child abuse. When she became district supervisor of psychological and social services, she required all school psychologists and social workers to administer the scale to children with whom they worked despite the lack of evidence of its reliability or validity.

Reduction or Elimination of Test Bias. Test bias may refer to systematic errors in test scoring. The term is associated more frequently with test fairness and refers to assessment norms applied to persons from different populations that fail to establish measurement equivalence: The degree to which reliability and validity coefficients associated with a measure are similar across populations. Depending on the purpose and nature of testing, failure to determine item, functional, scalar, or predictive measurement equivalence when developing a test can lead to over- or underdiagnosis, faulty personnel recommendations, inappropriate educational placements, and misinformation to the courts (AERA, APA, & NCME, 1999; Knight & Hill, 1998).

> ☒ An industrial-organizational psychologist developed a prescreening employment test for a large personnel department. After demonstrating high levels of inter-item and test-retest reliability, the scale was touted as a culture-free measure of employment preparedness. However, the psychologist did not examine whether the factor structure, predictive validity of the test for job performance, or other psychometric factors were equivalent across the members of major ethnic/cultural groups in the city who applied for positions in the company.

Recommendations for Use

In their recommendations for use, test developers must provide adequate guidance to allow users to administer tests in a standardized fashion and score and interpret responses according to established criteria. Psychologists who develop tests or assessment techniques must provide explanations of the meaning and intended interpretation of reported scores by users, school personnel, organizational clients, the courts, and others as appropriate. For example, a test manual might explain how score interpretation can be facilitated through norm-referenced or criterion-referenced scoring, scaling, or cut scores.

☒ A psychologist working for a test company was responsible for developing a test for premorbid speech and language predictors of childhood-onset schizophrenia. Child inpatients who had already been diagnosed with schizophrenia were the only population available for test development. The test yielded good test-retest reliability and was validated on correlations with practitioner diagnoses of childhood schizophrenia. In writing the test manual, the psychologist described the test as useful for identifying children at risk for the disorder. The manual did not indicate that test norms were applicable only to inpatients who had already manifested the disorder.

Psychologists' validity reports should accurately reflect the soundness of the test validation research supporting the use of an assessment procedure. Psychologists should include in their reports limitations of methodological or statistical weaknesses that would limit the usefulness of the test.

☒ A psychologist was hired by a company to develop a work climate questionnaire to help in their restructuring plans. In her validity report to the company, the psychologist buried information indicating problems with sample representativeness and low validity coefficients in a lengthy technical report and failed to include this information in the executive summary (see Lowman, 2006, Case 8; Principle C: Integrity).

Test Revisions

Once tests have been developed, test developers are responsible for monitoring conditions that might warrant test revision, modifications in recommendations for test interpretation, or limitations or withdrawal of test use. According to the *Standards for Educational and Psychological Testing,* tests "should be amended or revised when new research data, significant changes in the domain represented, or newly recommended conditions of test use may lower the validity of test score interpretations" (AERA, APA, & NCME, 1999, Standard 3.25, p. 48).The scope of test revision will depend on the conditions warranting change and may include revisions in test stimuli, administration procedures, scales or units of measure, norms or psychometric features, or applications (Butcher, 2000).

☒ A test company sold a popular test to help determine cognitive decline in newly admitted nursing home patients. The test had been used for more than 15 years. During the past 5 years, the psychologist directing the geropsychological test department of the company had been getting complaints that patients were being underdiagnosed. The psychologist reasoned that the test norms established 15 years ago might not be applicable to a better-educated cohort of elderly persons. However, the company's current 5-year plan focused on the development of new depression inventories and had no budget for revisions of current tests. The psychologists decided not to rock the boat and to wait for the next 5-year plan to recommend a revision of the test (see also Standard 1.03, Conflicts Between Ethics and Organizational Demands).

9.06 Interpreting Assessment Results

When interpreting assessment results, including automated interpretations, psychologists take into account the purpose of the assessment as well as the various test factors, test-taking abilities, and other characteristics of the person being assessed, such as situational, personal, linguistic, and cultural differences, that might affect psychologists' judgments or reduce the accuracy of their interpretations. They indicate any significant limitations of their interpretations. (See also Standards 2.01b and c, Boundaries of Competence, and 3.01, Unfair Discrimination.)

Accurate interpretations of assessment results are critical to ensure that appropriate decisions are made regarding an individual's diagnosis, treatment plan, legal status, educational placement, or employment and promotion opportunities. It is ethically imperative that when providing interpretations, psychologists take into account the purpose of the test and testee characteristics and indicate any significant limitations of their interpretations.

The Purpose of the Test

As required by Standard 9.06, the *purpose* of the assessment must be considered carefully in the interpretation of test scores. At the same time, psychologists must also resist allowing test interpretations to be biased by pressures from school personnel, parents, employers, attorneys, managed care companies, or others with a vested interest in a particular interpretation (AERA, APA, & NCME, 1999).

When offering recommendations, drawing conclusions, or making predictions from test scores, psychologists should refer to test manuals prepared by the test developer as well as relevant research to understand the extent to which tests, in isolation or within the context of other tests, are directly related to the purpose of testing.

> ☒ A neuropsychologist was hired by an insurance claims company to evaluate whether an individual insured by the company had sustained neurological damage following a car accident or whether the individual was feigning symptoms. Following administration of a battery of tests, the psychologist determined that the individual's test scores were at the lower boundaries of normal functioning. Although the psychologist made no effort to obtain information regarding the patient's neurological functioning before the accident, he concluded in his report that there was no evidence to support an injury claim.

Test Factors and Examinee Characteristics. With the exception of perhaps some employment-related screenings, interpretations should never be based solely on test scores. Standard 9.06 requires psychologists to consider factors associated with the testing context, the examinee's test-taking abilities, and other characteristics that may affect or inappropriately bias interpretations. When relevant, psychologists should take into account observations of test-taking styles, fatigue, perceptual and motor impairments, illness, limited fluency in the language of the test, or lack of cultural familiarity with test items that would introduce construct-irrelevant variability into a test score (AERA, APA, & NCME, 1999).

In addition to familiarity with the test itself, psychologists should have the specialized knowledge necessary to formulate professional judgments about the meaning of test scores as they relate to the individual examinee (see Standards 2.01b and c, Boundaries of Competence).

Test takers' scores should not be interpreted in isolation of other information about the characteristics of the person being assessed. Such information may be gained from interviews, additional testing, or collateral information from teachers, employers, supervisors, parents, or school or employment records. Such information may lead to alternative explanations for examinees' test performance.

> ☒ An inpatient at a psychiatric hospital had a Monday appointment with a psychologist to help determine whether he was well enough to go home for the weekend. When he arrived for the appointment, he was obviously distressed and told the psychologist that the patient he shared his room with had threatened to kill him. The psychologist confirmed this story with one of the orderlies. Rather than reschedule the appointment, the psychologist decided to conduct the required standardized assessment and clinical interview. In his report, the psychologist noted that the patient had high scores on the Minnesota Multiphasic Personality Inventory (MMPI; Butcher, Dahlstrom, Graham, Tellegen, & Kaemmer, 2002) indicating paranoid tendencies and high levels of stress that might be interpreted as a lack of readiness to go home. The psychologist's report did not address how the events surrounding the roommate's threats might have influenced MMPI scores and responses to interview questions.
>
> ☑ An industrial-organizational psychologist was responsible for administering and interpreting standardized group tests for employee promotion. During one testing session, two employees got into a shouting match that threatened but did not become a physical fight. In his reporting of the test results to managers, the psychologist mentioned there was a disturbance that could have had a significant detrimental effect on testees' performance and recommended that those who requested should be permitted to retake the tests.

Limitations. Under Standard 9.06, psychologists must indicate any significant limitations of their interpretations. In general, interpretive remarks that are not supported by validity and reliability information should be presented as hypotheses. When test batteries are used, interpretations of patterns of relationships among different test scores should be based on identifiable evidence. If none are available, this must be stated in the report. Interpretations of test results often include recommendations for placement, treatment, employment, or legal status based on validity evidence and professional experience. Psychologists should refrain from implying that empirical relationships exist between test results and recommendations when they do not, as well as distinguish between recommendations based on empirical evidence and those based on professional judgment.

Automated Interpretations. Computer-generated interpretations are based on accumulated empirical data and expert judgment but cannot take into account the special characteristics of the examinee (AERA, APA, & NCME, 1999). Psychologists should use interpretations provided by automated and other types of services with caution and indicate their relevant limitations.

9.07 Assessment by Unqualified Persons

Psychologists do not promote the use of psychological assessment techniques by unqualified persons, except when such use is conducted for training purposes with appropriate supervision. (See also Standard 2.05, Delegation of Work to Others.)

Psychologists' professional and scientific responsibilities to society and those with whom they work (Principle B, Fidelity and Responsibility) include helping to ensure that the administration, scoring, interpretation, and use of psychological tests are conducted only by those who are competent to do so by virtue of their education, training, or experience. Standard 9.07 prohibits psychologists from promoting the use of psychological assessment techniques by unqualified persons. For example, psychologists should not employ persons who have not received formal graduate-level training in psychological assessments to administer, score, or interpret psychological tests that will be used to determine an individual's educational placement, psychological characteristics for employment or promotion, competence to stand trial, parenting skills relevant to child custody, mental health status or diagnosis, or treatment plan.

> ☒ Members of a group practice composed of educational, school, and clinical psychologists specializing in learning disabilities and school-related disorders were finding it difficult to keep up with the hours required to provide individualized treatment, family therapy, and psychological assessment. To meet their needs and keep costs down, they decided to hire and train recent college graduates who had majored in psychology or education to independently administer some of the assessments.

Psychological Assessments Conducted by Trainees

Standard 9.07 does not prohibit psychologists from supervising trainees in the administration, scoring, and interpretation of tests. However, (a) the trainees must be qualified on the basis of their enrollment in a graduate or postdoctoral psychology program or externship or internship, and (b) supervision must be appropriate to their level of training. For example, psychologists teaching a first-year graduate-level personality assessment course that requires students to submit scored protocols of individuals they have independently assessed must ensure that (a) the course adequately prepares students for initial testing situations and (b) students inform persons tested or their legal guardians that the testing is for training purposes only and not for individual assessment.

When students registered in advanced practica, externships, or internships have had a sequence of courses in an assessment program, faculty and site supervisors must nonetheless provide a level of supervision appropriate to the trainees' previous education and experience and see that trainees administer, score, and interpret tests competently (see also Standard 2.05, Delegation of Work to Others).

☑ A psychologist served as an on-site supervisor for externships of third-year psychology graduate students in a large school district. In addition to reviewing their transcripts, during the first weeks of the externship, the psychologist observed each student administer tests and carefully reviewed and provided feedback on their scoring and interpretation of the standard battery of tests they were expected to use. She held weekly supervision meetings with the students and continued to review their reports throughout the year.

9.08 Obsolete Tests and Outdated Test Results

(a) Psychologists do not base their assessment or intervention decisions or recommendations on data or test results that are outdated for the current purpose.

Standard 9.08a prohibits psychologists from making evaluative, intervention, or treatment decisions or recommendations based on outdated data or test results, unless such information is specifically relevant to the diagnostic or placement decision. The standard applies to psychologists who administer, score, and interpret the test as well as to psychologists who use test results for intervention decisions or recommendations. Whether test data or results are outdated for the current purpose may be determined by whether the test from which scores were derived is itself obsolete (see Standard 9.08b, below).

Standard 9.08a is addressed to the use of test scores that may have been derived from currently used tests but are obsolete for the purposes of the evaluation. Previous scores derived from an up-to-date version of a test may be obsolete if individuals might be expected to score differently or require a different test based on (a) the amount of time between the previous administration and the current need for assessment, (b) maturational and other developmental changes, (c) educational advancement, (d) job training or employment experiences, (e) change in health status, (f) new symptomatology, (g) change in work or family status, or (h) an accident or traumatic experience.

☒ A psychologist was asked to provide an assessment of learning disabilities in support of an 18-year-old high school senior's request to be admitted to special learning support programs at the colleges to which he was applying. The psychologist had conducted such an assessment with the student 6 years earlier when he was applying for special educational support in junior high school. The psychologist wrote the report for colleges based on the test data from the earlier test administration.

In some instances, it may be appropriate to use outdated test scores as a basis of comparison with new test results to evaluate the long-term effectiveness of an educational program or intervention or to help identify cognitive decline or a sudden change in mental health or adaptive functioning relevant to treatment, placement in an appropriate educational or health care environment, disability claims, competency hearings, or custody suits. When outdated data or results are used, psychologists' reports and recommendations should include explanations for their use and their limitations (see Standard 9.06, Interpreting Assessment Results).

☑ A neuropsychologist was asked to evaluate cognitive and personality factors that might be responsible for a sudden change in adaptive functioning of an 80-year-old nursing home resident. The resident had been given a battery of intelligence and personality tests 5 years previously upon admission to the nursing home. Advances in geropsychology in the past 5 years had resulted in more developmentally appropriate and sensitive assessment instruments for this age group. The psychologist conducted a new evaluation using the more valid instruments. In her summary, she compared the results of the assessment with the results of the earlier evaluation, accompanied by a discussion of the limitations of comparing current performance with the older test results.

Psychologists should resist pressures to use obsolete test results from schools, health care delivery systems, or other agencies or organizations that seek to cut expenses by using outdated test results for placement or services (see Standard 1.03, Conflicts Between Ethics and Organizational Demands).

(b) Psychologists do not base such decisions or recommendations on tests and measures that are obsolete and not useful for the current purpose.

Test developers often construct new versions of a test to reflect significant (a) advances in the theoretical constructs underlying the psychological characteristic assessed; (b) transformations in cultural, educational, linguistic, or societal influences that challenge the extent to which current test items validly reflect content domains; or (c) changes in the demographic characteristics of the population to be tested, affecting interpretations that can be drawn from standardized scores. Standard 9.08b prohibits psychologists from using outdated versions of tests for assessment or intervention decisions when interpretations drawn from the test are of questionable validity or otherwise not useful for the purpose of testing.

The expense of purchasing the most up-to-date version of a test is not an ethical justification for using obsolete tests when the validity of interpretations drawn from such tests is compromised. Psychologists working with schools, businesses, government agencies, courts, HMOs, and health care delivery systems that resist purchasing updated tests because of costs or ease of record keeping should clarify the nature of the problem, urge organizational reconsideration, and, if such recommendations are not heeded, strive to the extent feasible to limit harms that will arise from misapplication of the test results (see Standards 1.02, Conflicts Between

Ethics and Law, Regulations, or Other Governing Legal Authority, and 1.03, Conflicts Between Ethics and Organizational Demands).

The standard does permit psychologists to use obsolete versions of a test when there is a valid purpose for doing so. In most cases, the purpose will be to compare past and current test performance. When use of an obsolete test is appropriate to the purpose of assessment, psychologists should clarify to schools, courts, or others that will use the test results which version of the test was used, why that version was selected, and the test norms used to interpret the results.

☑ A psychologist asked to evaluate an employee's claim that an industrial accident was responsible for a current disabling psychological disorder learned that the employee had been administered a battery of cognitive and personality tests several years before during preemployment screening. The psychologist decided it would be useful and appropriate to compare the complainant's current performance with his performance on test scores obtained prior to the accident. One of the previous scores was derived from an older version of a test that had been updated and revised recently. The psychologist decided to administer the older version of the test to better determine whether functioning had been affected by the accident. The psychologist's report included a rationale for the use of the older version of the test.

9.09 Test Scoring and Interpretation Services

(a) Psychologists who offer assessment or scoring services to other professionals accurately describe the purpose, norms, validity, reliability, and applications of the procedures and any special qualifications applicable to their use.

Standard 9.09 applies to psychologists who develop or sell computerized, automated, Web-linked, or other test scoring and interpretation services to other professionals. Psychologists offering these services must provide in manuals, instructions, brochures, and advertisements accurate statements about the purpose, basis and method of scoring, validity and reliability of scores derived from the service, the professional contexts in which the scores can be applied, and any special user qualifications necessary to competently use the service.

When test interpretations in addition to scores will be provided to users of the services, psychologists providing the services must document the sources, theoretical rationale, and psychometric evidence for the validity and reliability of the particular interpretation method employed. The *Standards for Educational and Psychological Testing* recommends that scoring services provide a summary of the evidence supporting the interpretations that includes the nature, rationale, and formulas for cutoff scores or configural scoring rules (rules for scoring test items or subtests that depend on a pattern of responses) (AERA, APA, & NCME, 1999). If algorithms or other rules for scoring jeopardize proprietary interests, copyrights, or other intellectual property rights issues, owners of the intellectual property are nevertheless responsible for documenting in some way evidence in support of the validity of score interpretations (AERA, APA, & NCME, 1999; Bersoff & Hofer, 1991).

Descriptions of the application of test scoring and interpretation procedures must include a discussion of their limitations. For example, computer-generated or automated systems may not be able to take into account specific features of the examinee that are relevant to test interpretation such as medical history, gender, age, ethnicity, employment history, education, or competence in the language of the test; motor problems that might interfere with test taking; current life stressors; or special conditions of the testing environment.

(b) Psychologists select scoring and interpretation services (including automated services) on the basis of evidence of the validity of the program and procedures as well as on other appropriate considerations. (See also Standard 2.01b and c, Boundaries of Competence.)

Standard 9.09b applies to psychologists who use computerized, automated, Web-linked, or other test scoring and interpretation services developed by other professionals or test vendors. Psychologists should select only test scoring and interpretation services that provide evidence of the validity of the program and procedures for the types of evaluation or treatment decisions that are to be informed by the assessment and that are appropriate for the individual case under consideration. Psychologists should not use scoring and interpretation services if the psychometric information provided by the test scoring or interpretation services is inadequate or fails to support the applicability of the scoring and interpretation methods to the goals of the particular assessment.

Implications of HIPAA. When the test data to be scored and interpreted by the service come under the HIPAA definition of PHI, psychologists must include this information in the Notice of Privacy Practices or obtain a valid authorization from the client/patient to transmit the information to the service (see more detailed discussion on core requirements for valid HIPAA authorizations under Standard 4.05a, Disclosures). Psychologists must ensure that the service receives, stores, transmits, and discloses client/patient information in a manner that is HIPAA compliant. In most instances, psychologists will enter into a business associate agreement with the testing service (45 CFR 160.103 and 164.504[e]). Under HIPAA, a "business associate" is a person who acts on behalf of a covered entity but not as an employee of the covered entity. As part of the business associate contract, the service must provide assurances to the psychologist that information will be safeguarded appropriately. If a psychologist discovers the service has violated HIPAA regulations in some way, the psychologist must correct the error or terminate the business associate contract.

(c) Psychologists retain responsibility for the appropriate application, interpretation, and use of assessment instruments, whether they score and interpret such tests themselves or use automated or other services.

Irrespective of whether psychologists use a service or score and interpret test data themselves, the psychologist is ultimately responsible for the appropriate selection, administration, scoring, interpretation, and use of the test. Under Standard 9.09c, psychologists must acknowledge this responsibility and take appropriate steps to ensure that tests were properly scored and interpreted.

To be in compliance with Standard 9.09c, psychologists must

• Have sufficient familiarity with scoring and interpretation techniques to adequately perform these tasks themselves, detect errors in test scores provided by a service, and critically evaluate canned interpretations

• Be able to identify the limitations of test service interpretations and know when collateral test scores and other relevant information are necessary to adequately interpret and apply test results. Such information might include an examinee's health status, culture, gender, age, employment history, educational experiences, language competencies, physical disabilities, symptoms of or empirical evidence to assume comorbid disorders, current life stressors, and special conditions of the testing environment.

• Avoid simplified interpretations of test scores that can lead to misdiagnosis, inadequate or iatrogenic treatment plans, or unfair or invalid personnel decisions or that can mislead the trier of fact in judicial and government hearings (AERA, APA, & NCME, 1999)

9.10 Explaining Assessment Results

Regardless of whether the scoring and interpretation are done by psychologists, by employees or assistants, or by automated or other outside services, psychologists take reasonable steps to ensure that explanations of results are given to the individual or designated representative unless the nature of the relationship precludes provision of an explanation of results (such as in some organizational consulting, preemployment or security screenings, and forensic evaluations), and this fact has been clearly explained to the person being assessed in advance.

Psychologists who administer, supervise, or otherwise are responsible for test administration are also responsible for ensuring that the individuals tested, their guardians, or personal representative receive an explanation of the assessment results. The purpose of an explanation is to enable a client/patient to understand the meaning of a test score or test score interpretation as it relates to its purpose, implications, and potential consequences. According to the *Standards for Educational and Psychological Testing,* an appropriate explanation "should describe in simple language what the test covers, what scores mean, the precision of the scores, common misinterpretations of the test scores, and how scores will be used" (AERA, APA, & NCME, 1999, Standard 5.10, p. 65). Whenever possible and clinically appropriate, psychologists assessing children and adolescents should provide feedback to the child as well as his or her guardian; the feedback should be appropriate to the child's developmental level.

Employees and Trainees

According to Standard 9.10, the responsibility for appropriate test explanation lies with the psychologist. It takes into account whether he or she personally scored or interpreted the test, assigned the scoring or interpretation to an employee or assistant, or used an outside service. The standard does not require that psychologists provide the explanation but that they take reasonable steps to ensure that one is given. The term *reasonable steps* is used to acknowledge situations in which the examinee may not wish to or is unable to meet for an explanation of results or an employee has misinformed the psychologist about an explanation taking place. If, however, a psychologist is aware that appropriate staff are unavailable or unable to provide the explanation, the psychologist should do so personally.

> ☒ A psychologist supervised several interns at an outpatient unit of a veterans hospital. The interns were responsible for administering a battery of psychological tests to new patients. Weekly supervision meetings with the interns included discussion of test selection, administration, scoring, and interpretation. The psychologist paid only cursory attention to instructing the supervisees on how to explain test results to patients. The clinic director received several complaints that interns' explanations of test results were confusing and distressing to patients (see also Standard 2.05, Delegation of Work to Others).

Use of Automated Scoring Services

A psychologist who asks a scoring service to send a computerized interpretation to a client/patient should take reasonable steps to ensure that the computerized interpretation provides an explanation adequate for conveying test performance information to examinees. As discussed under Standard 9.09b, psychologists who are covered entities under HIPAA who use scoring services must include this information in the Notice of Privacy Practices or obtain a specific client/patient authorization to use such services and ensure that the service transmits information and protects client/patient privacy in a HIPAA-compliant manner.

> ☑ A psychologist decided to use a popular scoring service for some frequently administered tests after examination of the company's materials indicated that the scoring system was reliable and valid. An added benefit of the service was that it would send test interpretations directly to the client. For the first set of test data the psychologist sent to the service, she asked the service to send her the test interpretation that is usually mailed directly to the client. The psychologist reviewed the interpretive materials and believed the information was too sparse to adequately inform clients and might create confusion. She therefore decided to continue using the service for scoring but did not permit the service to send explanations directly to the client.

Exceptions

Standard 9.10 permits exceptions to this requirement when an explanation of the results is precluded by the psychologist-examinee relationship, such as instances when an organization or legal counsel has retained the psychologist's services or assessment has been ordered by a judicial referral. For example, it is usually inappropriate for psychologists to provide an explanation of test results directly to the examinee when testing is court ordered, when it involves employment testing, or when it involves eligibility for security clearances for government work. Rather, reports are released to the court or retaining party and cannot be released to examinees and their family members, doctors, lawyers, or other representatives without the permission of the retaining party or the court (Bush et al., 2006; National Academy of Neuropsychology Policy and Planning Committee, 2003). In such situations, prior to administering assessments, psychologists are required to inform examinees that the psychologist will not be providing them with an explanation of the test results. If legally permissible, the psychologist should provide the reason why an explanation will not be given (see Standards 3.10c, Informed Consent; 3.11, Psychological Services Delivered To or Through Organizations; and 9.03, Informed Consent in Assessment).

9.11 Maintaining Test Security

The term *test materials* refers to manuals, instruments, protocols, and test questions or stimuli and does not include *test data* as defined in Standard 9.04, Release of Test Data. Psychologists make reasonable efforts to maintain the integrity and security of test materials and other assessment techniques consistent with law and contractual obligations, and in a manner that permits adherence to this Ethics Code.

An assumption of test validity is that individuals take the test under prescribed standardized conditions. For many tests, a critical aspect of standardization is that testees are equally unfamiliar with the test items. When some testees have access to test items prior to the administration of the test, the test norms and thus interpretations based on scaled scores may not be psychometrically defensible. Duplicating test materials or making video or audio recordings of an assessment session that subsequently enters the public domain also threatens the ongoing validity of tests. Individuals who have had uncontrolled access to test content can manipulate or coach others to manipulate test results that harm the public by enabling individuals to malinger or to obtain positions for which they are unqualified. Many tests consist of a static number of items that are costly to develop, take years to construct, and are not easily replaced. Thus, release of test materials can compromise the validity and usefulness of a test and jeopardize the intellectual property rights of test authors and publishers.

Definition of Test Materials and Test Security

Under Standard 9.11, *test materials* are manuals, instruments, protocols, and test questions or stimuli that do not come under the definition of *test data*, as defined in Standard 9.04a, Release of Test Data. Under Standard 9.11, psychologists have a duty to make reasonable efforts to protect the integrity and security of test materials and other assessment techniques. With few exceptions, test materials that do not include client/patient responses should never be released to clients/patients or others unqualified to use the instruments. Unless specifically recommended by the test developer, self-administered tests should not be given to clients/patients to take home. Additional security precautions need to be taken for tests administered through the Internet. Psychologists should consult test developers and, if necessary, seek legal consultation before distributing copyrighted tests over the Internet.

This standard does not prohibit psychologists from discussing individual test items with clients/patients if it assists in explaining test results (Standard 9.10, Explaining Assessment Results). Psychologists may also send test materials to other qualified health professionals bound by their ethical guidelines to protect the security of the instruments, taking appropriate steps not to violate copyright laws.

> ☒   A patient of a psychologist in independent practice was discussing her anxiety about an upcoming psychological evaluation for a job promotion that required security clearance. To reduce the patient's anxiety, the psychologist took out from his files several of the standardized tests that are usually administered for such purposes and went over them with the patient.

Laws Governing Release of Records

Implications of HIPAA. As a matter of practice, psychologists should keep test materials separated from a client's/patient's mental health records so the materials do not come under the HIPAA-defined "designated record set," which may not be withheld pursuant to client/patient release under federal law. Test materials do not have to be included in the patient's record if *test data,* as defined by Standard 9.04, Release of Test Data, are not recorded on the test material itself. *Separated* does not necessarily mean that the test data and test material must be kept in a separate file cabinet, but it does require that they are separated by a folder or binding unit so they are not confused or commingled with the test data records. Psychologists should seek legal advice before making such a determination and be mindful that removing clients'/patients' responses from the test protocol after they have been recorded on the material can constitute unlawful alteration of the patient's record.

Implications of FERPA. School psychologists may also find that laws governing the release of school records supersede the requirements of Standard 9.11. The Family Educational Rights and Privacy Act of 1974 (FERPA) establishes the right of parents to obtain copies of their children's school records where failure to provide the copies would effectively prevent a parent or eligible student from exercising his or her right to inspect and review the education records (20 U.S.C. § 1232G[a][1][A]; 34 CFR § 99.11b; www.ed.gov/offices/OM/fpco/ferpa/index.html). Schools are not required to provide copies of the records unless, because of distance or other considerations, it is impossible for the parent or student to review the records. Psychologists working in schools may also release test materials to attorneys or other nonprofessionals in response to a court order. In these situations, psychologists can request that the court issue a protective order requiring that test items not be duplicated or made available to the public as part of the court record and returned to the psychologist at the end of the proceedings.

Copyright Protection Laws. Release of "test data" that include client/patient responses recorded on the test protocol itself can raise issues of copyright protection and fair use by test development companies. If testing protocols allow, psychologists may wish to record client/patient responses on a form separated from the test items themselves to comply with contractual agreements with test developers and to maintain test security (Standard 9.11, Maintaining Test Security).

When test data consisting of PHI cannot be separated from test materials that are protected by copyright law, psychologists' decision to withhold the release of test data would be consistent with HIPAA regulations and Standard 9.04a. According to Richard Campanelli, director of the Office for Civil Rights at the U.S. DHHS, under Section 1172 (e), withholding protected health information would not be in violation of HIPAA if to do so would violate trade secret laws (http://kspope.com/assess/harcourt-hipaa.php).

In school contexts, reproduction of a test without permission may also be a violation of copyright law, although providing a single copy of a used protocol to parents under FERPA regulations may fall under the "fair use doctrine" provisions of copyright law (Jacob & Hartshorne, 2007; *Newport-Mesa Unified School District v. State of California Department of Education,* 2005).

Psychologists are reminded that Standard 1.02 of the new Ethics Code permits psychologists to adhere to the requirements of the law when such conflicts cannot be resolved and do not justify or defend violating human rights. The release of client/patient and student records is becoming a highly regulated area of health care practice. In this new and evolving legal arena, psychologists are wise to consult with attorneys and to seek guidance from continually updated materials provided by the APA Practice Directorate and APA Insurance Trust.

HOT TOPIC

The Use of Assessments in Expert Testimony: Implications of Case Law and the Federal Rules of Evidence

In 1988, testimony by mental health professionals accepted as experts by the court played a key role in the conviction of Kelly Michaels on 115 counts of sexual offenses involving 20 nursery school children. The "experts" claimed that the responses of children to assessment questions fit the profiles of abuse "documented" by Roland Summit (1983) and Suzanne Sgroi (1982). However, these profiles, drawn from clinical work with sexually abused children, were largely theoretical and had never been subjected to tests of validity or reliability in or out of a forensic context (Fisher, 1995). Five years after Ms. Michael's conviction, the Appellate Division ruled that the data on which the experts' testimonies were based were unreliable, invalid, and not probative of sexual abuse and therefore could not be used as evidence of guilt (*State of New Jersey v. Margaret Kelly Michaels*, 1993).

The Kelly Michaels case served as a wake-up call for psychologists on the ethical and legal consequences of providing expert testimony based on assessment instruments and procedures that have not gained general acceptance within the field and do not have established relevance to the legal question at hand (Klee & Friedman, 2001; Standards 2.04, Bases for Scientific and Professional Judgments, and 9.01, Bases for Assessments). This Hot Topic highlights ethical and legal challenges in selecting forensically valid assessment instruments for expert testimony.

Relevant Case and Federal Law

Mental health professionals are not alone in receiving increased scrutiny of expert opinion in criminal and civil cases. In recent years, there has been an increase in federal and case law requiring judges to determine evidentiary admissibility of expert testimony based on the general acceptance of methods and procedures within the expert's field (Klee & Friedman, 2001; Sales & Shuman, 2007).

The "General Acceptance" Standard. The "general acceptance" standard for admissibility of expert testimony was first established by the Supreme Court in *Frye v. United States* (1923). In *Daubert v. Merrell Dow Pharmaceuticals, Inc.* (1993), the standard was expanded to require specific relevance to the legal question at hand and demonstrated scientific reliability and validity. In *General Electric Co. v. Joiner* (1997), the Court held that judges should exclude from evidence expert testimony when the gap between the data (and the methodology used to substantiate the data) is too great (Grove & Barden, 1999). The "general acceptance" standard was explicitly extended to practitioners in *Kumho Tire Co., Ltd. v. Carmichael* (1999).

As of 2004, the Federal Rules of Evidence (70 FED. R. EVID. 702) require judges to permit expert testimony *only* if it is derived from reliable principles and methods in the expert's field and these principles and methods have been applied reliably to the facts of the case.

In light of case and federal law, appropriate selection of psychological assessment methods for forensic use should be determined by the legal question at hand, the psychometric properties of the instruments and procedures, and admissibility standards established by the court (Bush et al., 2006; Standards 2.01f, Boundaries of Competence; 9.01a, Bases for Assessments; and 9.02, Use of Assessments).

Challenges of the "General Acceptance" Standard to Selection and Use of Assessments in Forensic Contexts

The integration of *Daubert, Kumho,* and *Joiner* into the courts' standard for admissibility of expert testimony has led to ethical and legal debate regarding whether assessments used in clinical settings should be included in forensic opinions if they have not been validated for application to issues before the court. For example, Grove and Barden (1999) argue that diagnostic categories derived from the text revision of the *Diagnostic and Statistical Manual of Mental Disorders* (*DSM-IV-TR;* American Psychiatric Association, 2000), while useful in increasing the reliability of practitioners' agreement on a patient's diagnosis, may not be acceptable under the *Daubert-Kumho-Joiner* evidentiary criteria because they are derived from a process of consensus among a small group of professionals that sometimes draws upon available research but does not require scientific data to validate the existence or etiology of the disorder.

Similar arguments have been made against the use of tests such as the Rorschach Comprehensive System as data for expert testimony regarding psychopathology, based on the fact, among others, that its validity and reliability in and outside of forensic settings continue to be the subject of intense scientific debate (Grove, Barden, Garb, & Lilienfeld, 2002; Ritzler, Erard, & Pettigrew, 2002). Others have challenged whether assessments for neurological injury claims meet the *Daubert-Kumho-Joiner* standard for evidentiary admissibility in the absence of premorbid baselines or empirically established ecological validity of the tests to predict functioning in everyday life (Stern, 2001).

The Limits of Psychological Assessments for Child Custody Disputes. In recent years, courts have begun using the ambiguous standard "best interests of the child" as a means of resolving custody decisions (Elrod & Spector, 2004). Currently, there are no reliable legal criteria or any validated mental health or behavioral criteria on which a psychologist can provide an expert opinion on "best interest" (Krauss & Sales, 2000). Forensic psychologists hired to evaluate the mental health of one or more family members can provide expert opinion on the interpretation of data based on assessment instruments found to be reliable and valid indicators of children's or parents' emotional and cognitive status and their interpersonal interactions with one another. However, there is no established evidence that these instruments can reliably determine whether joint custody or the number of visitations permitted for a noncustodial parent would be in the best interests of the child (Otto & Martindale, 2007). Thus, expert opinion that implies a direct empirical link between the data collected to specific recommendations regarding custody decisions before the court may be inadmissible under the *Daubert-Kumho-Joiner* standard and in violation of Standard 9.01a, Bases for Assessments.

Forensic Assessment Relevant to Violent or Abusive Crimes. In criminal cases, forensic psychologists are often called upon to provide expert testimony based on a defendant's response to assessment instruments designed to measure inclinations toward violence or psychopathologies associated with abusive or other criminal behaviors (Nedopil, 2002; Tolman & Rotzien, 2007). Psychometric techniques for evaluating the validity of such assessment instruments most often depend on probability evidence and comparisons within and between group responses to determine a test's reliability and validity. By contrast, the ultimate decision before the court in such cases is categorical: A defendant is either guilty or innocent. The opinions of psychologists testifying as expert witnesses must therefore reflect the limitations of the methods in which data were obtained. The clinical forensic evaluator can testify as to the degree to which a defendant's test scores reach criteria for psychological characteristics associated with different criminal behaviors but cannot form an opinion as to whether those scores indicate the defendant's guilt or innocence in the legal case at hand (Fisher, 1995; Krauss & Lieberman, 2007).

Ethical and Legal Considerations in the Selection and Use of Assessment Instruments for Expert Testimony

Psychologists providing expert testimony based on psychological assessments with established relevance to the legal question at hand assist the courts in making fair determinations by illuminating data on the legal issue. However, neither justice nor the legal rights of plaintiffs or defendants are well served when psychologists declaring "expert" status present forensic opinions based on assessment instruments and techniques insufficient to substantiate their findings (Principle B: Fidelity and Responsibility; Principle D: Justice; Standards 2.04, Bases for Scientific and Professional Judgments, and 9.01, Bases for Assessments). The following are points psychologists should consider when expert testimony will be based on psychological assessment:

- Select assessment instruments and procedures with established psychometric validity and reliability for the legal question at hand (Standards 9.01a, Bases for Assessments, and 9.02a, Use of Assessments).

- Ensure that established principles of test interpretation have been applied reliably to the facts of the case (Standard 9.06, Interpreting Assessment Results).

- Prepare testimony that reflects awareness of and meets legal criteria for the admissibility of expert testimony based on the reliability of the scientific foundation on which an opinion is based and the established validity and reliability in providing data relevant to the legal question for which their opinion is sought (Bush et al., 2006; *Daubert-Kumho-Joiner;* Standards 2.01f, Boundaries of Competence, and 2.04, Bases for Scientific and Professional Judgments).

- Take full responsibility for ensuring testimony is not flawed by the use of unorthodox assessment procedures and provide the court with reasoning that led from the data to the expert opinion (Grisso, 2003; Heilbrun, 2001).

- Acknowledge limitations in the applicability of the test data to the legal issue (Standard 9.06, Interpreting Assessment Results).

- Avoid omission of relevant data or overemphasis on minor facts to support an opinion (Bush et al., 2006).

- Avoid offering testimony beyond the data collected. Remember, "An expert opinion that answers the ultimate legal question is not an 'expert' opinion, but a personal value judgment" (Grisso, 2003, p. 477).

CHAPTER 13

Standards on Therapy

10. THERAPY

10.01 Informed Consent to Therapy

(a) When obtaining informed consent to therapy as required in Standard 3.10, Informed Consent, psychologists inform clients/patients as early as is feasible in the therapeutic relationship about the nature and anticipated course of therapy, fees, involvement of third parties, and limits of confidentiality and provide sufficient opportunity for the client/patient to ask questions and receive answers. (See also Standards 4.02, Discussing the Limits of Confidentiality, and 6.04, Fees and Financial Arrangements.)

To comply with this standard of the American Psychological Association (APA) Ethics Code (APA, 2002b), psychologists must obtain and document written or oral consent in the manner set forth in Standard 3.10, Informed Consent. Psychologists must also provide prospective therapy clients/patients and, when appropriate, their legal guardians a clear explanation of the nature and anticipated course of therapy, fees, involvement of third parties, and the limits of confidentiality. This information must be presented in a language reasonably understandable to the client/patient, and the consent process must provide sufficient opportunity for questions and answers.

As Early as Feasible. Standard 10.01 explicitly uses the phrase "as early as is feasible" to indicate that in some cases, obtaining informed consent during the first therapy session may not be possible or clinically appropriate. Psychologists may need to wait for feedback from a client's/patient's health maintenance organization (HMO) before consent discussions regarding fees can be completed. Informed consent during the first session may be clinically contraindicated if a new client/patient is suicidal or experiencing some other crisis needing immediate therapeutic attention. In such situations, consent is obtained as soon as all information is available or the crisis has subsided (see also Standard 6.04a, Fees and Financial Arrangements).

> ☑ At the beginning of a first session, it became apparent that a new client was having difficulty communicating in a coherent fashion. With probing, the psychologist learned that the client had a history of schizophrenia and had recently gone off his medications because of the intolerable side effects. The psychologist postponed discussion relevant to informed consent and spent the rest of the session working with the client to determine the best course of action to deal with the immediate situation.

Nature of the Therapy. The *nature* of the therapy refers to information about the therapeutic process that would reasonably be expected to affect clients'/patients' decisions to enter into therapy with the psychologist. Informed consent should include discussion of the duration of each session (e.g., 50 minutes), appointment schedule (e.g., weekly), and the general objectives of treatment (e.g., crisis management, symptom reduction). Depending on the treatment modality, the consent process might inform clients/patients that therapy entails participating in biofeedback sessions, relaxation exercises, behavioral contracts, homework assignments, discussion of dreams and developmental history, collateral treatments, or other aspects of the therapeutic process relevant to an informed consent decision. Psychologists should not assume that all clients/patients are familiar with the nature of psychotherapy.

> ☑ A new patient who had recently immigrated to the United States from West Africa told a psychologist that his general practitioner had recommended that he see the psychologist because of headaches that had not responded to traditional medications. The psychologist explained her cognitive therapy approach to working with such problems, standard confidentiality procedures, and issues relevant to the patient's health plan and then turned to a discussion of issues relevant to the patient's presenting problem. Toward the end of the session, the psychologist asked the patient if he had any additional questions. The patient asked the psychologist if she was ready to give him a prescription for a medication that would cure his headaches. The psychologist then carefully explained in greater detail the nature of cognitive therapy and the difference between such therapy and psychopharmacological approaches.

Anticipated Course of the Therapy. The *anticipated course* of therapy refers to the number of sessions expected given the psychologist's current knowledge of the client's/patient's presenting problem and, when applicable, the company, institutional, or health plan policies that may affect the number of sessions. Depending on the treatment modality, consent discussions would also include expectable modifications such as the evolving nature of systematic desensitization or exposure therapy; the uncovering of as yet unidentified treatment issues, or, if the practitioner is a prescribing psychologist, adjustments in dosage levels of psychopharmacological medications.

In many instances, informed consent to therapy will be an ongoing process determined, for example, by the extent to which the nature of a client's/patient's treatment needs are immediately diagnosed or gradually identified over a series of sessions, cognitive and social maturation in child clients/patients, or functional declines in clients/patients with progressive disorders. Providing clients/patients with an honest evaluation of the anticipated and unanticipated factors that may determine the course of therapy demonstrates respect for their right to self-determination and can promote trust in the therapeutic alliance (Pomerantz, 2005; Principle C: Integrity and Principle E: Respect for People's Rights and Dignity).

☒   A psychologist saw a new client whose presenting problems appeared to be related to a debilitating social phobia. The client was to pay privately for treatment because her health plan did not cover psychotherapy. The client asked the psychologist how long she might have to be in therapy before she saw some relief from her symptoms. The psychologist responded, "We'll just see how it goes."

☑   A psychologist saw a new patient who appeared to be suffering from a mild form of agoraphobia. The psychologist explained his behavioral approach to this type of problem and the average number of sessions after which patients often feel some relief from their symptoms. The psychologist stressed that each individual responds differently and that together they would reassess the patient's progress after a specific number of sessions.

Fees. Discussion of *fees* must include the cost of the therapy, the types of reimbursement accepted (e.g., checks, credit card payments, direct payment from insurance companies), the payment schedule (e.g., weekly, monthly), when fees are reevaluated (e.g., annual raise in rates), and policies regarding late payments and missed appointments.

When appropriate and as soon as such information can be verified, psychologists should also discuss with clients/patients the percentage of therapy costs reimbursed under the client's/patient's health plan and limitations on the number of sessions that can be anticipated because of limitations in insurance or other sources of client/patient financing (see also Standard 6.04, Fees and Financial Arrangements). Psychologists directly contracted with HMOs may have capitated or other types of business agreements that provide financial incentives to limit the number of treatment sessions. When permitted by law and contractual agreement, psychologists should inform clients/patients about such arrangements (Acuff et al., 1999; see also Standard 3.06, Conflict of Interest).

> ☒   On the initial visit, a psychologist told a client her fee for each session and mentioned that she was an approved provider for some managed care organizations. At the end of the first month in treatment when the client asked the psychologist to fill out an insurance form for treatment, he was shocked to learn that the psychologist was not an approved provider for his HMO plan, that she had not called the HMO to inquire about her eligibility, and that she had not informed him of this possibility during the first session.

Involvement of Third Parties. The term *third parties,* as used in this standard, refers to legal guardians, health insurance companies, employers, organizations, or legal or other governing authorities that may be involved in the therapy. Psychologists should inform clients/patients if such parties have requested or ordered mental health treatment, are paying for the therapy, are entitled to receive diagnostic information or details of the therapy based on law or contractual agreement, and to whom information may be provided, contingent on the client's/patient's appropriate written release or authorization (see section below on implications of the Health Insurance Portability and Accountability Act of 1996 [HIPAA]). Psychologists asked to evaluate a child by one parent should clarify, when appropriate, custody issues to determine if the other parent must also give permission.

> ☑   A psychologist was assigned to see a couple for court-ordered therapy following a finding of child abuse and neglect resulting in the removal of the children from their home. The psychologist informed the couple that the treatment was mandatory, that it was paid for by a court-affiliated child protective services agency, and that the psychologist would be providing to the court a summary of the couple's compliance with and progress in therapy.

Confidentiality. Informed consent to therapy must provide a clear explanation of the extent and limits of *confidentiality,* including (a) when the psychologist must comply with reporting requirements such as mandated child abuse reporting or duty-to-warn laws and (b) guardian access to records in the case of therapy involving minors or individuals with impaired consent capacities. Psychologists who provide therapy over the Internet must inform clients/patients about the procedures that will be used to protect confidentiality and the threats to confidentiality unique to this form of electronic transmission of information (see also Standard 4.02c, Discussing the Limits of Confidentiality). Clients/patients enrolled in health plans must be informed about the extent to which treatment plans, diagnosis, or other sensitive information must be disclosed to case managers for precertification or continuing authorization for treatment (Acuff et al., 1999). When appropriate, psychologists providing treatment in forensic settings should inform clients/patients of the possibility that the psychologist may be obligated to disclose statements made in therapy in trial testimony.

☑ A psychologist had an initial appointment with an adolescent and his parents to discuss the 14-year-old's entry into individual psychotherapy for depression. The psychologist discussed with both the prospective patient and his parents what information concerning the adolescent's treatment would and would not be shared with the parents, including her confidentiality and disclosure policies regarding adolescent risk behaviors such as sexual activity and use of illegal drugs. She also informed them about her legal obligations to report suspected child abuse or neglect and her own policy regarding disclosure of information pertaining to patient imminent self-harm or harm to others. In addition, she described the parents' right to access the adolescent's health records under HIPAA (see also the Hot Topic on "Confidentiality and Involvement of Parents in Mental Health Services for Children and Adolescents" in Chapter 7).

☒ A psychologist began therapy with a client over the Internet. The psychologist failed to inform the client of the need to password protect the home computer from which the client would be interacting with the psychologist. The client's spouse opened the files in which therapeutic communications had been saved and printed them out to use against the client in petitioning for divorce.

Informed Consent Involving Children and Adolescent Clients/Patients

Psychologists providing therapy and counseling to children and adolescents face unique informed consent challenges tied to (a) state and federal laws governing the rights of minors to autonomous health care decisions, (b) laws related to the rights and obligations of minors' legal guardians, and (c) developmental changes in children's ability to understand their rights, the nature of their disorder, and the purpose of treatment. When working with children and adolescents, psychologists must constantly balance ethical obligations to protect client/patient welfare and respect client/patient autonomy and privacy (Principle A: Beneficence and Nonmaleficence and Principle E: Respect for People's Rights and Dignity).

When Guardian Consent Is Required by Law. According to Standard 3.10b, Informed Consent, for persons who are legally incapable of providing informed consent, psychologists must obtain guardian consent, provide the client/patient with an appropriate explanation, seek the client's/patient's assent, and consider such person's preferences and best interests. This standard respects the developing autonomy needs and rights of minor children by requiring that they receive developmentally appropriate information regarding the reason for and nature of the treatment and, with some exceptions, are given the right to refuse treatment.

Exceptions to the requirement for child assent arise when children are too young or too impaired at the time treatment is initiated to appreciate their disorder or understand the nature of therapy, especially when treatment is necessary for their well-being. When children's mental health needs indicate that their dissent will not determine whether they will receive treatment, psychologists should provide them with an appropriate explanation but not seek their assent (Fisher & Masty, 2006; Masty & Fisher, 2008).

When Guardian Consent Is Not Permitted or Required by Law. Parents are given significant responsibilities and rights to consent to health care treatments for their children who are under 18 years of age (*Parham v. J.R.,* 1979; Weithorn, 2006; *Wisconsin v. Yoder,* 1972). Psychologists should be familiar with relevant state and federal law before they consider treating a minor client/patient without guardian consent (for a review of state laws, see English & Kenney, 2003). Psychologists providing counseling services in schools should also be aware of district rules and state and federal laws restricting services to children without parental consent (Jacob & Hartshorne, 2007).

Exceptions to state requirements for parental permission to treatment include (a) *emancipated minors* who are legally recognized as adults if they are self-supporting, married, or have children; (b) *mature minors,* who are not granted adult legal status but who may autonomously consent to certain treatments specified in state and federal law (e.g., drug abuse, venereal disease, emotional disorder); and (c) minors for whom there is evidence that their guardians' decisions may not be in their best interests.

According to Standard 3.10b, Informed Consent, when consent by a legally authorized person is not permitted or required by law, psychologists must take reasonable steps to protect the child's rights and welfare. A first step in complying with this standard is to be familiar with research on developmental differences in children's understanding of consent information and clinical methods to evaluate the consent capacity of individual clients/patients. For example, research suggests that by age 14, many children understand consent information as well as adults, although their relative lack of experience with independent health care decision making may place them at a consent disadvantage (Belter & Grisso, 1984; Bluebond-Langner, DiCicco, & Belasco, 2005; Broome, Kodish, Geller, & Siminoff, 2003; Bruzzese & Fisher, 2003; Kaser-Boyd, Adelman, & Taylor, 1985; Masty & Fisher, 2008; Szajnberg & Weiner, 1995; Weithorn & Campbell, 1982).

As a general rule, therefore, psychologists should assume that children younger than age 14 may not be able to provide fully informed consent. In such instances, psychologists should tailor the consent information to the child's level of understanding and may wish to use independent client/patient advocates to help ensure the child's rights are protected.

Informed consent with adolescents must also be fitted to the client's/patient's cognitive and experiential levels of understanding. This may include educating clients/patients about treatment terminology, the nature of treatment, and their right to refuse or withdraw from treatment. Finally, as detailed in the Hot Topic in Chapter 7, even when adolescents have the legal right to consent to their own treatment, parents may have legal access to their child's psychotherapy records. For example, in many instances, if parents are responsible for paying the cost of their child's health care costs directly or through insurers, they will have access to the records irrespective of whether a child has been designated a mature or emancipated minor. Psychologists working with adolescents in the absence of parental consent need to be familiar with state and federal laws governing parental access to records and include this information during informed consent.

Implications of HIPAA

Psychologists who are covered entities under HIPAA (see "A Word About HIPAA" in the Preface of this book) must inform clients/patients about their rights regarding the use and disclosures of their health information. A covered entity is defined as a health care provider who transmits any health information in electronic form in connection with a transaction related to financial or administrative activities related to health care (45 CFR 160.102[a][3] and 160.103). The designation of "covered entity" is not specific to an individual client/patient but to the psychologist's practice. Thus, even if a psychologist is not electronically transmitting health information about a particular client/patient, HIPAA is triggered if the psychologist has conducted any such transactions for other clients/patients.

Notice of Privacy Practices. Clients/patients have certain rights regarding their protected health information (PHI), characterized as individually identifiable health information created or received by a health care provider relating to the past, present, or future health; provision of health care; or payment for health care (45 CFR 160.103 and 160.501). These rights include access to their PHI (excluding psychotherapy notes), the right to amend their PHI, the right to request restriction of uses and disclosures, and the right to an accounting of disclosures made by the provider to others during the past 6 years (45 CFR 164.522, 164.524, 164.526, 164.528; see also discussions under Standard 3.10, Informed Consent, in Chapter 6; Standards 4.01, Maintaining Confidentiality, and 4.05, Disclosures, in Chapter 7; and Standard 6.01, Documentation of Professional and Scientific Work and Maintenance of Records, in Chapter 9). HIPAA requires that if under applicable law a person has authority to act on behalf of a client/patient in decisions related to health care, a covered entity must provide such a person (called a personal representative) with all information that would be given to the client/patient, except if there is reason to believe the client/patient has been abused or is endangered by the personal representative or that treating the individual as a personal representative would not be in the best interests of the client/patient (45 CFR 164.502[g]).

At the beginning of treatment, covered entities are required to provide clients/patients with a Notice of Privacy Practices that explains the uses and disclosures of PHI that may be made by the covered entity, as well as the individual's rights and covered entity's legal duties with respect to PHI (45 CFR 164.520). The notice should be provided to the client/patient in written form and separate from other informed consent procedures or documents.

Authorization. HIPAA requires that covered entities obtain written valid authorization from the individual or his or her personal representative prior to releasing PHI (45 CFR 164.508) to others. The authorization must include the following:

- A specific description of information to be disclosed
- Specific identification of the person or class of persons who can make the authorization
- The specific persons or class of persons to whom information may be disclosed
- A description of each purpose of the use or disclosure
- A statement explaining the client's/patient's rights, including the right to revoke the authorization in writing
- Exceptions to the right to revoke
- An expiration date
- Client/patient signature

The client/patient must also receive a copy of the authorization. In addition, when appropriate release and authorizations are obtained, the HIPAA Privacy Rule requires that psychologists share only the minimum amount of information necessary for billing agencies and non–health provider internal staff to perform their roles (45 CFR 164.502[b]). Psychologists may wish to use the HIPAA-compliant Notice of Privacy Practices and authorization model forms that have been developed by the APA Insurance Trust and the APA Practice Directorate to be compatible with the laws governing practice in each state (see http://apait.org/hipaa and http://apa.org/practice).

Authorization is not required to use or disclose PHI for covered entities to carry out their own treatment, payment, or health care operations as long as appropriate consent has been obtained and a Notice of Privacy Practices provided at the beginning of the professional relationship (164.506[b]).

Psychotherapy Notes. HIPAA is highly protective of psychotherapy notes, defined as notes recorded by a health care provider who is a mental health professional documenting or analyzing the contents of a conversation during a private counseling session or a group, joint, or family counseling session and that are separated from the rest of the individual's medical record. Psychotherapy notes, as defined by HIPAA, do *not* include medication prescription and monitoring, counseling session start and stop times, the modalities and frequencies of treatment furnished, results of clinical tests, and any summary of the following items: diagnosis, functional status, the treatment plan, symptoms, prognosis, and progress to date (45 CFR 164.501).

Patients do *not* have a right of access to psychotherapy notes, and a separate authorization is required for the release of psychotherapy notes when a covered entity agrees to their release. In addition, HMOs are prohibited from requiring patient authorization to disclose psychotherapy notes as a condition for evaluating eligibility. For additional discussion of HIPAA regulations in other chapters, see the standards listed under HIPAA in the topical table of contents.

(b) When obtaining informed consent for treatment for which generally recognized techniques and procedures have not been established, psychologists inform their clients/patients of the developing nature of the treatment, the potential risks involved, alternative treatments that may be available, and the voluntary nature of their participation. (See also Standards 2.01e, Boundaries of Competence, and 3.10, Informed Consent.)

Most techniques that are now accepted practice in the profession of psychology emerged from treatment needs unmet by existing therapies. Standard 10.01b recognizes that innovation in mental health services is critical if a profession is to continue to adequately serve a diverse and dynamic public. The standard also recognizes that during the development and refinement of new therapeutic techniques, the risks and benefits to clients/patients are unknown. Consequently, respect for a client's/patient's right to informed, rational, and voluntary consent requires that when the treatment needs of a client/patient call for innovative techniques, during informed consent, psychologists have the obligation to explain the relatively new and untried nature of the therapy. Furthermore, they must clearly describe alternative established treatments and clarify the client's/patient's right to dissent in favor of more established treatments whether they are offered by the psychologist obtaining the consent or other mental health professionals.

Web-based or e-therapy has been described as a new modality for helping people resolve life and relationship issues using the power and convenience of the Internet to allow synchronous (simultaneous) and asynchronous (time-delayed) communication between client/patient and therapist (Grohol, 2001; Maheu & Gordon, 2000). A primary advantage of e-therapy is that through remote communication, it can provide clients/patients access to qualified mental health professionals regardless of geographical proximity.

To date, e-therapy does not represent a new theoretical approach to psychotherapy in the same vein as cognitive, psychodynamic, behavioral, or other theoretically driven approaches to treatment. Rather, it represents a new modality or process in which these forms of therapy can be provided. While great strides have been made, in many contexts in which Web-based therapies are conducted (i.e., e-mail, chat rooms, videoconferencing), they have yet to emerge as "established treatments (Castelnuovo, Gaggioli, Mantovani, & Riva, 2003). This is due in part to continuously changing technology, use of different Web-based modes of treatment, variability in treatment techniques viewed as compatible with Web-based approaches, the range of disorders treated, and difficulty in obtaining empirical data on the demographics and other characteristics of individuals using Web-based therapies (Heinlen et al., 2003). For these reasons, psychologists providing Web-based services should carefully consider the extent to which their services are considered "established" within the profession and whether their informed consent procedures need to comply with Standard 10.01b.

☑ A psychologist working in a large, underserved rural community found that a number of his clients could not afford to make the 100-mile trip to his office on a weekly basis. After attending an intensive workshop on e-mail therapy and developing a network of colleagues to consult with on behavioral telehealth techniques, the psychologist decided to use this form of therapy. He adopted the procedure of having an initial in-person meeting with each client who might be appropriate for e-mail therapy. During the informed consent provided at this session, he explained the following: (a) e-mail therapy is a new and still-developing form of therapy; (b) although there was reason to believe this form of therapy would serve the client's mental health needs, the extent of such benefits was still largely unknown; (c) current risks associated with e-mail therapy include confidentiality concerns and lack of immediacy; (d) there are traditional treatments available for the client's presenting problem; and (e) if the client preferred to receive a more traditional therapy, the psychologist would try to work out a schedule that could accommodate the client's travel difficulties.

Web-Based Therapy Involving Minors. Since minors constitute a substantial portion of Web users (Kaiser Family Foundation, 2001), psychologists need to have a method for verifying client/patient age and obtaining guardian permission if required by state law. Since state laws vary in these requirements, psychologists also need to verify the state in which the minor resides. When feasible, some practitioners choose to have an initial face-to-face meeting with clients/patients before initiating Web-based treatments. When this is not feasible, an initial videoconference, phone call, or exchange of identifying documents may be useful. Psychologists also need to verify to the best of their ability that the individual they are corresponding with is the same person from whom consent was obtained. Some psychologists have used personalized code names that clients/patients include in their exchanges to address this potential problem.

The Ongoing Nature of Consent

Informed consent should be conceptualized as a continuing process in which the clinically determined need to shift to treatment strategies distinctly different from those that were originally agreed upon during informed consent are discussed with the client/patient at appropriate points during the course of psychotherapy. If, after several sessions, a client's/patient's treatment needs call for a shift to innovative techniques that have not been widely used or accepted by practitioners in the field, psychologists should follow the requirements of Standard 10.01b. The following case illustrates a potential violation of this standard.

☒ A psychologist had just returned from a professional meeting where she heard several other practitioners discuss a new technique for anxiety disorders that involved viewing video clips of people reacting to natural or human-made catastrophes. She decided to try this untested technique with one of her patients who had not been responding to traditional interpersonal approaches to anxiety. At the next session, rather than discussing with the patient the option of trying this new type of approach, she told the patient that as part of his ongoing treatment, they would look at a video together. The patient experienced an anxiety attack following exposure to the video and apologized to the therapist for failing to improve after so many sessions.

(c) When the therapist is a trainee and the legal responsibility for the treatment provided resides with the supervisor, the client/patient, as part of the informed consent procedure, is informed that the therapist is in training and is being supervised and is given the name of the supervisor.

Standard 10.01c applies to therapy conducted and supervised as part of practica, internships, or other training experiences in which the legal responsibility for treatment resides with the supervisor. In these contexts, clients/patients must be informed that the therapist is a trainee and that the therapy is supervised and is given the name and contact information of the supervisor. Both the trainee and the supervisor would be in potential violation of this standard if the supervisee failed to include this information during informed consent. This standard does not apply to therapy conducted by licensed psychologists obtaining postdoctoral training and supervision because in such contexts, the legal responsibility most often resides with the psychologist.

☒   A student interning at a veterans hospital was concerned that her ability to help patients would be compromised if she told them that she was a trainee. When she discussed this with her supervisor, the supervisor told her the decision was up to her.

10.02 Therapy Involving Couples or Families

(a) When psychologists agree to provide services to several persons who have a relationship (such as spouses, significant others, or parents and children), they take reasonable steps to clarify at the outset (1) which of the individuals are clients/patients and (2) the relationship the psychologist will have with each person. This clarification includes the psychologist's role and the probable uses of the services provided or the information obtained. (See also Standard 4.02, Discussing the Limits of Confidentiality.)

Steps required to inform prospective clients/patients in couples or family therapy about the nature of treatment go beyond those described in Standard 10.01, Informed Consent to Therapy. In addition to the features of informed consent described in Standard 10.01, under Standard 10.02, psychologists must identify and explain which members of the couple or family are the primary client/patient. In some treatment modalities, the client/patient is the multiperson unit, and the primary obligation of the psychologist is to the parties as a whole. In other modalities, the primary client/patient is a single individual, with other persons involved only to provide collateral support for the client's/patient's treatment.

☑ A divorced couple with joint custody of their children began family therapy to help their 10-year-old son, who had been having problems in school and in adjusting to living in two different homes. The father indicated that he was just attending sessions to support his son's therapy. The psychologist explained to the father, mother, and child that she offered family therapy in which all members are clients and their feelings and behaviors equally explored during the treatment sessions. She also told them that if there was some indication that the son needed individual therapy, she would recommend an appropriate practitioner specializing in childhood disorders (see also Standard 2.01, Boundaries of Competence).

During informed consent, psychologists also need to ensure that all family members understand the nature of psychotherapy and are voluntarily agreeing to participate.

☑ A 40-year-old woman sought family therapy for herself and her elderly mother. At the initial session, the psychologist learned that the daughter had given up her job to care for her mother and was frustrated by her mother's refusal to do simple chores around the house and their constant arguing. During the informed consent process, the mother appeared anxious. When the psychologist asked her whether she had any questions, she burst into tears and said she found it humiliating to speak to a stranger about family problems. The psychologist explained his role and his obligation to keep whatever he learned in therapy confidential. As the consent discussion continued, the mother became increasingly more agitated about sharing her personal thoughts and feelings. The psychologist concluded that her participation in the therapy would not be voluntary. He discussed his observations with the mother and daughter and recommended they consider seeing a pastoral counselor affiliated with their church as an alternative that might be more acceptable to the mother. He also let them know that he would be available if the mother changed her mind.

Clarifying the Psychologist's Role and Goals of Therapy. In addition to identifying who is the client/patient, discussions at the outset of couple or family therapy must clarify (a) the psychologist's responsibilities in balancing the interests of different individuals, (b) whether the psychologist will conduct individual or conjoint sessions, and (c) how often the psychologist will meet with each party (Principle B: Fidelity and Responsibility). The modifier *reasonable* indicates that a violation of this standard is limited to instances when psychologists do not take steps to clarify information in a manner that would be considered appropriate in the prevailing judgment of other similarly engaged psychologists. Clients'/patients' failure to understand the full implications of this information is not in itself sufficient evidence of violation.

☑   An elderly couple entered therapy to help them address feelings and conflicts arising from the husband's terminal illness. Upon initial assessment of their situation, the psychologist determined that the wife's and husband's emotional reactions to the illness should be explored in individual sessions before it would be helpful for the couple to meet with the therapist together. The therapist outlined a treatment plan that included scheduling of individual and joint sessions.

In many instances, the goals of treatment may be different for the individuals involved. For example, one member of a couple may see therapy as a means of strengthening the relationship, whereas the other sees it as a means of ending the relationship. Psychologists must take reasonable steps to correct such misimpressions.

☑   An interfaith couple began premarital counseling to help resolve conflicts regarding issues such as which clergy should perform their wedding ceremony and the religious upbringing of their children. In the first 10 minutes of the initial session, it became clear that one member of the couple believed the purpose of counseling was to convince his fiancée to agree to conduct the wedding ceremony and to raise the children in his faith. During the process of informed consent and in subsequent sessions, the psychologist continued to clarify that involvement in premarital counseling could not promise the direction the couple's relationship would take.

Confidentiality. Psychologists working with couples and families must take reasonable steps to clarify how confidential information will be handled. Will the psychologist keep information received from one party secret from the other? Or will all information be shared (see Margolin, 1982; Snyder & Doss, 2005)? Psychologists must also clearly articulate their legal obligations and policies regarding confidentiality and disclosure of information about child abuse, domestic abuse, HIV notification, high-risk behaviors of adolescent clients/patients, and other instances of potential harm.

☒   A gay couple had been in couples counseling for several sessions. One member of the couple called the psychologist and revealed that, without the knowledge of his significant other, he had begun seeing his former wife in what was progressing toward a renewal of their sexual relationship. The client asked the psychologist to keep the information secret. Although the psychologist had communicated a general confidentiality policy to the couple at the outset of therapy, she had not specifically discussed with them her policy regarding secrets between her and one member of the couple. She now felt in a terrible bind. If she refused to keep the information secret, she would violate the presumption of confidentiality held by the client who had called. If she respected the request for secrecy, she might be violating the other client's trust and expectation of openness.

(b) If it becomes apparent that psychologists may be called on to perform potentially conflicting roles (such as family therapist and then witness for one party in divorce proceedings), psychologists take reasonable steps to clarify and modify, or withdraw from, roles appropriately. (See also Standard 3.05c, Multiple Relationships.)

It is not unusual for individuals who have sought couples or family therapy to become involved in litigation involving divorce, child custody, child abuse allegations, petitions for child or family services, or mental competency hearings. In such situations, psychologists may be asked by one party to testify on his or her behalf or receive a court order to serve as a fact witness for the legal matter at issue. When such situations arise, under Standard 10.02b, psychologists must first take steps to clarify to clients/patients the nature of the two roles and the potential effect on each party involved in the therapy. To comply with this standard, psychologists will need to be aware of and communicate to their patients/clients the extent to which state law defines as public or private the information revealed in couples or family therapy and whether one or all parties must agree to disclosure of information in court.

As with other forms of multiple relationships, sometimes the request to serve in a dual capacity risks impairing performance of one or both professional roles. In such cases, psychologists are required to take reasonable steps to modify or withdraw from one of the roles to ensure that services continue to be objective and effective and to avoid exploitation or harm to parties involved (Standard 3.05b and c, Multiple Relationships).

☑ A psychologist providing therapy for a family with a terminally ill child received a court order to serve as a fact witness for a case against the couple alleging child neglect. The psychologist informed the parents of the court's request and took steps to clarify the nature of this role to them. The psychologist was concerned that testifying in court would harm the therapeutic relationship achieved with this family and informed the judge in writing of these concerns. The judge refused to comply with the psychologist's request not to testify. The psychologist discussed the situation further with the family, and they mutually agreed to a referral to another therapist.

10.03 Group Therapy

When psychologists provide services to several persons in a group setting, they describe at the outset the roles and responsibilities of all parties and the limits of confidentiality.

In addition to responsibilities described in Standard 10.01, Informed Consent to Therapy, psychologists conducting group therapy must describe at the outset of treatment the unique roles and responsibilities of both therapist and clients/patients in multiperson therapies. Such information may include discussion of (a) differences between the exclusivity of the therapist's attention in individual therapy compared with attention to group dynamics in multiperson treatments; (b) group member responsibilities, including turn taking and prohibitions against group members socializing outside of sessions; and (c) policies regarding such client/patient responsibilities as acceptance of diverse opinions, abusive language, coercive or aggressive behaviors, or member scapegoating.

Confidentiality. A frequently misunderstood aspect of group therapy concerns the limits of confidentiality. Although psychologists are professionally obligated to maintain the confidentiality of most statements made during group therapy sessions, decisions by members of a therapy group to disclose confidential information are neither bound by professional codes nor subject to legal liability. At the outset of group therapy, and each time a new member enters an ongoing group, psychologists must take reasonable steps to clarify that they can request, but not guarantee, that all group members maintain the confidentiality of statements made during sessions. Psychologists should also be familiar with and inform group members about state laws protecting or denying client/patient privilege (the right to limit the psychologist's disclosures to courts) for information shared during group therapy. When group therapy is conducted in response to court-ordered counseling, psychologists must also clarify to group members the parties in the justice system that will receive information learned during group therapy and how such information may be used.

Clients/Patients in Concurrent Single and Group Therapy

Psychologists who see clients/patients concurrently in individual and group therapy must take special precautions to ensure that they do not inadvertently reveal during a group session confidential information gained about a client/patient during an individual session. Psychologists must also clarify in advance to such clients differences between the goals, processes, and therapist-client relationships in single versus group therapy. When recommending that a client/patient seen in individual therapy also participate in group therapy conducted by the psychologist, steps should be taken to ensure that clients/patients understand that such a decision is voluntary and that reluctance to participate in the group will not compromise the current therapeutic relationship. This does not prohibit psychologists from having a policy of only accepting individuals as clients/patients if they participate in group therapy if (a) such multimodal treatment is clinically indicated and (b) clients/patients are informed of this requirement prior to or at the outset of therapy.

10.04 Providing Therapy to Those Served by Others

In deciding whether to offer or provide services to those already receiving mental health services elsewhere, psychologists carefully consider the treatment issues and the potential client's/patient's welfare. Psychologists discuss these issues with the client/patient or another legally authorized person on behalf of the client/patient in order to minimize the risk of confusion and conflict, consult with the other service providers when appropriate, and proceed with caution and sensitivity to the therapeutic issues.

There may be instances when psychologists professionally encounter an individual already receiving mental health services from another professional who might benefit from or is requesting additional therapy with the psychologist. Standard 10.04 recognizes the rights of clients/patients to seek additional services and the potential benefits of collateral therapy, as well as the potential harm that can result from client/patient involvement in concurrent therapies.

Under this standard, careful consideration of the client's/patient's welfare and treatment needs determines the ethical appropriateness of providing therapy to those served by others. In some instances, clients/patients may benefit from consultation with a psychologist when they are uncertain about the effectiveness of their current therapy or uncomfortable with what they perceive as their current provider's boundary violations. In other instances, the expertise of the psychologist may provide needed collateral treatment, for example, when a client/patient who is under the care of a psychiatrist for psychopharmacological treatment of depression would also benefit from psychosocial or behavioral treatment. On the other hand, provision of concurrent services may be harmful if clients/patients consciously or unconsciously seek to use a second therapist as a means of triangulating issues arising in their current therapy, if they begin to receive conflicting therapeutic messages from two different service providers, or if the psychologist's choice to see the patient is governed by the psychologist's own financial interests rather than client/patient welfare (see also Standards 3.06, Conflict of Interest; 3.08, Exploitative Relationships; and 5.06, In-Person Solicitation).

☑   A psychologist had an initial consultation with an individual who was currently in treatment with another provider. During the consultation, the patient frequently asked questions about the appropriateness of certain therapeutic styles. The psychologist asked the patient why he sought the consultation. He stated that he liked his current therapist but thought he would benefit from two different perspectives on his problems. During further discussions, there was no evidence that the patient's current treatment was inadequate or that the psychologist could provide collateral therapy that would be helpful. The psychologist explained this to the patient and told him that under such circumstances, it would not be appropriate for her to see him as a regular patient.

In addition to careful consideration of the treatment issues and client/patient harm, under Standard 10.04, psychologists should take steps to minimize the risk that providing therapy to an individual already receiving mental health services will lead to confusion and conflicts that could jeopardize client/patient welfare. Such steps include discussing with the client/patient or his or her legally authorized representative the potential consequences of entering into a second therapeutic relationship and obtaining authorization from the client/patient to consult with the other service provider about the appropriateness and effectiveness of conjoint services (see discussion of Standard 10.01a for additional information regarding HIPAA).

☑ An individual met with a psychologist to discuss joining one of the psychologist's therapy groups. The client was currently in individual psychotherapy with another practitioner and informed the psychologist that her current therapist suggested that concurrent participation in group therapy might be helpful in addressing some of the social anxiety issues they had been discussing in treatment. The psychologist explained the differences in goals and modalities of group and single therapy and received written authorization from the client to discuss the treatment recommendation with her current therapist. After a conversation with the current therapist, the psychologist agreed that the client could be further helped through participation in group therapy.

Because conflicts and issues associated with providing therapy to those served by others may continue to emerge over the course of treatment, Standard 10.04 also requires that psychologists who decide to offer such services continue to monitor and proceed cautiously and sensitively in response to therapeutic issues that may arise.

10.05 Sexual Intimacies With Current Therapy Clients/Patients

Psychologists do not engage in sexual intimacies with current therapy clients/patients.

Sexual intimacies of any kind with a current therapy client/patient are harmful and prohibited by Standard 10.05. Sexual intimacies are broadly interpreted and include fondling, intercourse, kissing, masturbation in front of a client, telephone sex, touching of genitals, erotic hugging, verbal invitations to engage in sexual relationships, or communications (in person or via electronic transmission) intended to erotically arouse the patient. The ethical obligation to avoid sexual intimacies with clients/patients lies solely with the therapist, not with the client/patient. Any sexual intimacy between psychologists and clients/patients represents a violation of this standard regardless of whether clients/patients initiated sexual contact or voluntarily or involuntarily responded to therapists' overtures.

Sexual intimacies with current clients/patients exploit the explicit power differential and influence that psychologists have over those they treat in therapy and the vulnerabilities that led clients/patients to treatment in the first place. Sexual intimacies further harm clients/patients by impairing the provider's ability to objectively evaluate treatment issues and the client's/patient's ability to trust and respond to the psychologist in his or her professional role. In many cases, therapist-client sex exacerbates the client's/patient's symptoms or leads to more serious mental disorders (Sonne & Pope, 1991).

Nonsexual physical contact with clients/patients such as handshakes or nonerotic hugging is not a violation of Standard 10.05. However, the nonerotic intentions of a therapist are often misperceived as sexualized by clients/patients. In addition, research indicates that for some psychologists, such seemingly minor blurring of boundaries as hugs, self-disclosures, or meetings outside the therapist's office are often precursors of sexual misconduct (Lamb & Catanzaro, 1998; see also section on multiple relationships and nonsexual physical contact in Chapter 6).

10.06 Sexual Intimacies With Relatives or Significant Others of Current Therapy Clients/Patients

Psychologists do not engage in sexual intimacies with individuals they know to be close relatives, guardians, or significant others of current clients/patients. Psychologists do not terminate therapy to circumvent this standard.

Engaging in sexual intimacies with another person who is related to or in a significant relationship with a current client/patient is prohibited. Sexual intimacies with such persons harm the client/patient by impairing the psychologist's treatment objectivity, blurring the therapist-client roles and relationships, and risking exploitation of the client/patient to attain or maintain a sexual relationship with a third party. This standard applies to a client's/patient's parents, siblings, children, legal guardians, and significant others. It may also apply to other relatives if they are emotionally or otherwise close to the client/patient. The phrase "they know to be" applies to the rare instance when psychologists are unaware that someone they are seeing romantically is a close relative, guardian, or significant other of a current client/patient. Standard 10.06 also prohibits psychologists from terminating therapy to circumvent the prohibition.

> ☒   A psychologist began dating the mother of a child who was currently in therapy with the psychologist.
>
> ☒   A psychologist terminated marriage therapy with a couple with the intent to begin a sexual relationship with one of the spouses.

10.07 Therapy With Former Sexual Partners

Psychologists do not accept as therapy clients/patients persons with whom they have engaged in sexual intimacies.

Under 10.07, psychologists are prohibited from providing therapy to former sexual partners. Conducting therapy with individuals with whom psychologists have had a previous sexual relationship risks compromising the effectiveness of professional services. The knowledge gained about the individual from former sexual relationships and romantic and sexualized feelings that may reemerge during therapy can impair the psychologist's ability to objectively evaluate the client's/patient's treatment needs and response to treatment. In addition, intimate and personal knowledge about the psychologist that the client/patient gained during the former relationship can create role confusion and interfere with the client's/patient's ability to benefit from the psychologist's professional communications.

> ☒   A psychologist received a call from a man with whom she had a sexual relationship during college. The man asked if he could see her professionally to discuss some serious problems that had recently arisen in his life. The psychologist told him that she did not think it was a good idea for her to see him professionally because they had been in a previous personal relationship. The man started crying and told the psychologist that he had just moved to the town in which the psychologist practices and she was the only person he could trust with his problems. The psychologist agreed to see him for just one session.

10.08 Sexual Intimacies With Former Therapy Clients/Patients

(a) Psychologists do not engage in sexual intimacies with former clients/patients for at least two years after cessation or termination of therapy.

Standard 10.08a prohibits psychologists from engaging in sexual intimacies for at least 2 years after the therapy has ended. Posttherapy sexual relationships can be

harmful to clients/patients in many ways, including (a) depriving former clients/patients of future services with a practitioner who is familiar with their mental history and with whom they had a good therapeutic rapport, (b) threatening client/patient privilege when the blurring of personal and professional boundaries allows the court to require a psychologist to testify about the former client/patient in his or her personal role, (c) compromising the credibility of previous professional reports written by the psychologist about the client/patient and jeopardizing the credibility of court testimony that may be needed regarding the client's/patient's past mental status, and (d) client/patient exploitation and psychological deterioration.

Two-Year Moratorium. Under Standard 10.08a, any sexual intimacies with a former client/patient within 2 years following the last professional contact are an ethical violation. The standard has a 2-year moratorium period rather than a permanent prohibition against sex with former clients/patients because most complaints involving sexual intimacies with former clients/patients received by the APA Ethics Committee and licensing boards pertain to relationships that began during the first year following the cessation of therapy, and complaints about relationships that began 2 years posttherapy are infrequent. However, as discussed below under Standard 10.08b, such behavior is not unconditionally acceptable after 2 years.

> ☒ A year after therapy ended, a traumatic event in a former patient's life created a need for additional treatment. The patient had begun a sexual relationship with his psychologist a few months following termination of treatment and thus could not reenter therapy with the psychologist. The former patient, fearful that another psychologist would be critical of his relationship with his former therapist, chose not to seek needed treatment.
>
> ☒ A year after therapy terminated, a client entered into a sexual extramarital relationship with her former therapist and continued to discuss her mental health problems in this nonprofessional relationship. During this period, her husband sued her for divorce, naming the therapist as his wife's extramarital partner. The former client wanted to exert her privilege to keep her mental status and thus her involvement in therapy confidential. Due to the blurring of personal and professional boundaries, the judge issued a court order to call the psychologist as a witness.
>
> ☒ A psychologist began a sexual relationship with a former patient soon after therapy was terminated. Several months later, the former patient was injured on the job, and his attorney advised him to pursue a disability insurance claim for mental distress created by the accident. The patient needed the psychologist to testify regarding his mental status prior to the injury. However, the psychologist-client sexual relationship compromised the psychologist's ability to provide or appear to provide objective information to the court.
>
> ☒ A client with a history of child sexual abuse had transferred to the psychologist the feelings of both powerlessness and eroticism that she felt for her childhood abuser.

> The psychologist took advantage of these feelings and told the client that she could overcome the mental health consequences of this early trauma by terminating therapy and becoming his lover. The patient agreed to end therapy. A few weeks into the posttherapy sexual relationship with the psychologist, her depression escalated and she attempted suicide.

(b) Psychologists do not engage in sexual intimacies with former clients/patients even after a two-year interval except in the most unusual circumstances. Psychologists who engage in such activity after the two years following cessation or termination of therapy and of having no sexual contact with the former client/patient bear the burden of demonstrating that there has been no exploitation, in light of all relevant factors, including (1) the amount of time that has passed since therapy terminated; (2) the nature, duration, and intensity of the therapy; (3) the circumstances of termination; (4) the client's/patient's personal history; (5) the client's/patient's current mental status; (6) the likelihood of adverse impact on the client/patient; and (7) any statements or actions made by the therapist during the course of therapy suggesting or inviting the possibility of a posttermination sexual or romantic relationship with the client/patient. (See also Standard 3.05, Multiple Relationships.)

Standard 10.08a prohibits psychologists from engaging in a sexual relationship with a former client/patient for at least 2 years following the termination of therapy. However, sexual intimacies with former clients/patients even 2 years following the cessation of therapy can result in exploitation and harm. If an ethics complaint is made against the psychologist regarding a 2-year posttermination sexual relationship, Standard 10.08b places the ethical burden on the psychologist to demonstrate that the sexual relationship is not exploitative. The standard describes seven relevant factors that could be applied to determine such exploitation. These factors are listed along with examples of how they might be applied to a finding of violation of this standard:

1. *The amount of time that has passed since therapy terminated.* A sexual relationship was initiated immediately following the 24-month period.

2. *The nature, duration, and intensity of the therapy.* The client/patient was seen by the psychologist three times a week for several years in intensive psychodynamic psychotherapy.

3. *The circumstances of termination.* The client/patient abruptly stopped coming to therapy after expressing strong erotic fantasies for the psychologist.

4. *The client's/patient's personal history.* During the therapy, the client/patient had been diagnosed with bipolar disorder marked by periods of mania involving promiscuous and high-risk sexual activity.

5. *The client's/patient's current mental status.* When the posttermination sexual relationship with the psychologist began, the patient was being treated by another psychologist for major depression.

6. *The likelihood of adverse impact on the client/patient.* Based on a sexual abuse history, borderline diagnosis, and current major depression, it was reasonable to assume that a client/patient would be extremely vulnerable to reexperiencing some of the early trauma if engaged in a sexual relationship with his or her former therapist whom he or she perceived as a powerful parent figure.

7. *Any statements or actions made by the therapist during the course of therapy suggesting or inviting the possibility of a posttermination sexual or romantic relationship with the client/patient.* The psychologist had a habit of hugging the client/patient at the end of each therapy session.

10.09 Interruption of Therapy

When entering into employment or contractual relationships, psychologists make reasonable efforts to provide for orderly and appropriate resolution of responsibility for client/patient care in the event that the employment or contractual relationship ends, with paramount consideration given to the welfare of the client/patient. (See also Standard 3.12, Interruption of Psychological Services.)

This standard applies to ethical obligations of psychologists at the time they enter into employment or contractual agreements with other providers, group practices, managed care providers, institutions, or agencies. Employment or contractual agreements can end when psychologists have a time-limited contract or employment period, when they elect to leave for professional or personal reasons, or when the employer or company terminates their position or contract. Under Standard 10.09, psychologists must make reasonable efforts to ensure at the outset that the employment agreement or contract provides for orderly and appropriate resolution of responsibility in the event that the employment or contractual arrangement ends (Principle B: Fidelity and Responsibility).

Psychologists can comply with Standard 10.09 by determining through preemployment discussions whether the organization, group practice, or other entity in which a work arrangement is being considered has policies designed to ensure continuity of care when a practitioner can no longer provide services. If no such policies exist, psychologists can help to develop such policies or include in their employment or contractual agreements permission to resolve treatment responsibility appropriately in the event their employment or contract ends. Steps the psychologist can recommend be taken to protect client/patient welfare when treatment can no longer be provided by the psychologist include providing pretermination counseling and referrals, supervising appropriate transfer and storage of client/patient records, assisting in the transition of the client/patient to a new treatment provider if clinically indicated, or continuing treatment with the client/patient in a different venue. The phrase "make reasonable efforts" recognizes that in some situations, employers, organizations, group practices, or other providers will refuse to promise or follow through on promises to protect client/patient welfare through an orderly and appropriate resolution of care when there is a change in staff.

☑ A school psychologist was hired on a 9-month (October through June) contract to provide counseling services for grade school students who had lost parents in the September 11, 2001, attack on the World Trade Center. It was reasonable to assume that some children might need continued care during the summer. The school psychologist raised this issue when asked to take the position. The school superintendent responded that such services were not available through the schools during the summer. The psychologist worked with the superintendent to develop an agreement with a social services agency to provide treatment for students who needed continued care over the summer. The superintendent also agreed to set up a system that facilitated the appropriate transfer of student records to the social service agency. The psychologist also laid out a plan for identifying children who would need summer services and for informing their guardians about the availability of such services.

Standard 10.09 does not prohibit psychologists from signing a noncompete clause barring the psychologist from continuing to see specific clients/patients after the employment or contractual agreement has ended as long as other provisions for protecting client/patient welfare are in place.

10.10 Terminating Therapy

(a) Psychologists terminate therapy when it becomes reasonably clear that the client/patient no longer needs the service, is not likely to benefit, or is being harmed by continued service.

Psychologists are committed to improving the condition of individuals with whom they work and to do no harm (Preamble; Principle A: Beneficence and Nonmaleficence). In some instances, continued therapy with a client/patient may be nonbeneficial or harmful. Standard 10.10a requires psychologists to terminate therapy under three conditions that either fail to benefit clients/patients or could be harmful if therapy is continued. Although the need to continue or terminate a therapeutic relationship requires professional judgment based on knowledge of the specific treatment context, the phrase "reasonably clear" in this standard indicates that it is ethically inappropriate for a psychologist to continue therapy under conditions in which most psychologists engaged in similar activities in similar circumstances would judge it unnecessary, nonbeneficial, or harmful.

Services Are No Longer Needed. Psychologists who continue to see clients/patients professionally after they no longer need mental health services are in violation of this standard. The need for continued services depends on the nature of the client's/patient's disorder and the goals of treatment as identified during the initial informed consent and throughout the therapeutic process. Psychologists who continue to treat clients/patients when the problems associated with entering treatment have been adequately addressed violate this standard. The standard does not prohibit psychologists and clients/patients from reevaluating treatment needs and continuing in a therapeutic relationship to address additional mental health needs.

However, failure to reevaluate the need for continued therapy after treatment goals are met would violate the standard. Psychologists who continue to see clients/patients solely to fulfill the psychologists' own training requirements or for financial gain violate this standard and also risk violating Standard 3.08, Exploitative Relationships. Psychologists who continue to bill a third-party payor for mental health services when the services are no longer required place themselves at risk for accusations of insurance fraud and are in potential violation of Standards 6.04b, Fees and Financial Arrangements, and 6.06, Accuracy in Reports to Payors and Funding Sources.

☒   A licensed psychologist in independent practice had sought additional training at a prestigious postgraduate psychotherapy institute. The institute required a certain number of hours of supervision with clients with specific disorders to obtain a certificate of completion. The psychologist had 8 more hours of supervision for treatment of anxiety disorders to complete before he could qualify for the certificate. The client who met the diagnostic criteria for supervision had been doing very well in treatment. She had resolved most of the problems at work and at home that had brought her to therapy and viewed terminating treatment with eagerness and a sense of pride. She asked the therapist whether they could have one final session to complete the therapy. The psychologist told her that although she had been doing well, there were a few unresolved issues that would take about eight more sessions to address adequately. The client reluctantly agreed.

The Client/Patient Is Not Likely to Benefit. Psychologists must also terminate therapy when the client/patient is not likely to benefit from the treatment. This criterion applies when, during the course of therapy, it becomes reasonably clear that the client/patient is not responding to treatment, a newly uncovered aspect of the client's/patient's disorder is not amenable to the type of treatment modality in which the psychologist has been trained (see also Standard 2.01a, Boundaries of Competence), or a client/patient is unwilling or unable to comply with treatment (e.g., when a client/patient continuously refuses to follow the terms of a behavioral contract).

☑   A counseling psychologist had been seeing a client for career counseling who was recently fired from a management position that he had held for 10 years. The client was angry and believed that the termination was undeserved. After three sessions, the psychologist determined that there was a clinically paranoid feature to the client's distress and that more intensive psychotherapy was needed before career counseling could be beneficial. The psychologist discussed her concerns with the client and referred him to another practitioner who worked with more seriously disturbed clients. The psychologist also informed the client that her services would be available to him when he was ready to resume career counseling.

The Client/Patient Is Being Harmed by Continued Service. Psychologists are prohibited from continuing therapy if it is reasonably clear that the client/patient is being harmed by the treatment. For example, in some instances, clients/patients may unexpectedly react to a specific treatment modality with major depression, a psychotic episode, or an exacerbation of impulsive or addictive behaviors that do not respond to continued efforts by the psychologist. The phrase "reasonably clear" indicates that the criteria for determining whether a client/patient is being harmed by continued services are determined by what would be the prevailing judgment of psychologists engaged in similar activities in similar circumstances, given the knowledge the psychologist had or should have had at the time. Psychologists who find that a client's/patient's mental health is deteriorating may find it helpful therefore to consult with colleagues regarding whether services should be continued. When it is appropriate to terminate, patients should be referred to alternative treatments that may be more effective.

> ☑ A psychologist was providing psychoanalytic therapy to a patient with narcissistic personality disorder. The treatment appeared to be going well until the patient began to discuss in detail a traumatic rape experience that occurred when she was a young adult. In the weeks that followed, the patient kept putting herself in dangerous situations that appeared to be reenactments of the earlier event. She was engaging in sexual relationships with men she barely knew, having unprotected sex, and frequenting dangerous areas of the city. In therapy during the next 5 weeks, the psychologist continued to explore with the patient her feelings and behaviors associated with the initial trauma. Instead of abating the risky behavior, each session appeared to lead to more extreme behaviors. The psychologist was concerned that the patient might again be raped, assaulted, or contract HIV/AIDS and consulted with several colleagues regarding continuation of services. On the basis of these consultations, he concluded that continuing the therapy would be harmful to this patient and that she might benefit from a different therapeutic approach. He discussed this with the patient over several sessions and referred her to a group practice specializing in treatments for rape trauma.

(b) Psychologists may terminate therapy when threatened or otherwise endangered by the client/patient or another person with whom the client/patient has a relationship.

Standard 10.10b permits psychologists to terminate therapy abruptly if they are threatened or endangered by a client/patient or another person with whom the client/patient has a relationship such as a family member, significant other, friend, employer, or employee. Such situations can include verbal or physical threats or any other evidence that the psychologist is endangered. In such situations, neither advance notification of termination nor pretermination counseling as described in Standard 10.10c is required. Psychologists may also request a protective order against clients/patients or others whom they suspect will threaten or harm them. Prohibitions against revealing confidential information do not apply when psychologists must call on authorities or others to protect them from threats or harm (see Standard 4.05b, Disclosures).

(c) Except where precluded by the actions of clients/patients or third-party payors, prior to termination psychologists provide pretermination counseling and suggest alternative service providers as appropriate.

Termination based on reasonable professional judgment and proper pretermination counseling is ethically appropriate. In addition to the situations described in Standard 10.10a and b above, ethically permissible and professionally appropriate reasons to end a therapeutic relationship include the following: (a) An organized system of health or managed care company rejects a psychologist's recommendations for additional therapy sessions; (b) an unforeseen potentially harmful multiple relationship arises (Standards 3.05b, Multiple Relationships; 10.02b, Therapy Involving Couples or Families); (c) a client/patient repeatedly refuses to pay for services (Standard 6.04e, Fees and Financial Arrangements); (d) a psychologist becomes ill or finds therapy with a particular client/patient stressful in a manner that risks compromising professional services (Standard 2.06b, Personal Problems and Conflicts); (e) during the course of therapy, unexpected treatment needs arise that are outside the psychologist's area of expertise (Standard 2.01, Boundaries of Competence); or (f) the psychologist is relocating or retiring.

Under Standard 10.10c, psychologists must provide pretermination counseling prior to ending a therapeutic relationship. Pretermination counseling includes (a) providing clients/patients sufficient advance notice of termination (when possible), (b) discussing with the client/patient the reasons for the termination, (c) encouraging the client/patient to ask questions regarding termination, and (d) providing referrals to alternate service providers when appropriate. Psychologists need to plan for pretermination counseling for group as well as individual therapies (Mangione, Forti, & Iacuzzi, 2007). Psychologists are not in violation of this standard if pretermination counseling is precluded by client/patient or third-party payor actions. For example, parents may abruptly end their child's therapy, making further contact with the child inappropriate or unfeasible; health plans may prohibit or place restrictions on provider referrals.

> ☑ A psychotherapy patient changed to a health plan that she later realized would not reimburse her current psychologist's services. She told the psychologist that she would not be able to come to any more sessions because she could not afford to pay for therapy out of pocket and thus would be continuing services with a provider covered by her new health plan. The psychologist discussed the patient's concerns about leaving therapy. The patient appeared ready to terminate the relationship. The psychologist told her that he was not familiar with any of her new health plan's approved providers but, with her authorization, would be willing to speak with her new therapist if the need arose.

☑ A psychologist in independent practice accepted a job offer from a treatment center in another state. The psychologist agreed to start the new position in 4 weeks. At their next sessions, the psychologist told each of her clients that she would be relocating at the end of the month and that they would have time to discuss over the next few weeks their feelings about terminating therapy and their plans for the future. At each of the remaining sessions, she encouraged clients to discuss any concerns they might have about the termination. The psychologist provided appropriate referrals to those who wished to continue in therapy with another professional. She told the other clients how to contact her if they wished a referral in the future. One client had serious difficulty adjusting to the termination. The psychologist offered to have phone sessions with this client until a suitable referral could be found.

☑ A patient who recently lost his job had not paid his last two monthly bills for psychotherapy. The psychologist had discussed the issue of nonpayment with the patient several times during the past month. Neither a reduced fee nor payment plan was economically feasible for the patient. The psychologist told the patient that she would not be able to continue to see him pro bono indefinitely and that they would have two more sessions to discuss any questions he might have and his plans for the future. She also provided the patient with a list of several free clinics in the area that offered therapy.

HOT TOPIC

Ethical Issues for the Integration of Religion and Spirituality in Therapy

The past decade has witnessed increased attention to the importance of understanding and respecting client/patient spirituality and religiosity to psychological assessment and treatment, as well as recognition that religious and spiritual factors remain underexamined in research and practice (APA, 2007d). Advances in addressing the clinical relevance of faith in the lives of clients/patients have raised new ethical dilemmas rooted in theoretical models of personality historically isolated from client/patient faith beliefs, the paucity of research on the clinical benefits or harms of injecting faith concepts into treatment practices, group differences in religious practices and values, and individual differences in the salience of religion to mental health (Shafranske & Sperry, 2005; Tan, 2003).

The Secular-Theistic Therapy Continuum

Integration of religion/spirituality in therapy can be characterized on a secular-theistic continuum. Toward the secular end of the continuum are "religiously sensitive therapies" that blend traditional treatment approaches with sensitivity to the relationship of diverse religious/spiritual beliefs and behaviors to mental health. Midway on the continuum are "religiously accommodative therapies" that do not promote faith beliefs but, when clinically relevant, use religious/spiritual language and interventions consistent with clients'/patients' faith values to foster mental health. Toward the other end of the continuum are "theistic therapies" that draw on psychologists' own religious beliefs and use sacred texts and techniques (prayer, forgiveness, and meditation) to promote spiritual health.

The sections that follow highlight ethical challenges that emerge along all points of the secular-theistic therapy continuum.

Competence

All psychologists should have the training and experience necessary to identify when a mental health problem is related to or grounded in religious beliefs (Standards 2.01b, Boundaries of Competence, and 2.03, Maintaining Competence; see also Bartoli, 2007; Johnson, 2004; Plante, 2007; Yarhouse & Tan, 2005). Religious/spiritual therapeutic competencies include

- understanding how religion presents itself in mental health and psychopathology;
- self-awareness of religious bias that may impair therapeutic effectiveness, including awareness that being a member of a faith tradition is not evidence of expertise in the integration of religion/spirituality into mental health treatment;
- techniques to assess and treat clinically relevant religious/spiritual beliefs and emotional reactions; and
- knowledge of data on mental health effectiveness of religious imagery, prayer, or other religious techniques.

Collaboration With Clergy. Collaborations with clergy can help inform psychologists about the origins of the client's beliefs, demonstrate respect for the client's religion, and avoid trespassing into theological domains by increasing the probability that a client's incorrect religious interpretations will be addressed appropriately within his or her faith community (Johnson, Redley, & Nielson, 2000; Standard, 3.09, Cooperation With Other Professionals). When cooperation with clergy will be clinically helpful to a client/patient, psychologists should

- obtain written permission/authorization to speak with a specific identified member of the clergy,
- share only information needed for both to be of optimal assistance to client,
- discuss where roles might overlap (e.g., family counseling, sexual issues), and
- determine ways in which the client can get the best assistance (Richards & Bergin, 2005; Standards 4.01, Maintaining Confidentiality; 4.04, Minimizing Intrusions on Privacy; and 4.05, Disclosures).

Avoiding Secular-Theistic Bias

Psychologists must ensure that their professional and personal biases do not interfere with the provision of appropriate and effective mental health services for persons of diverse religious beliefs (Principle D: Justice and Principle E: Respect for People's Rights and Dignity; Standards 2.06, Personal Problems and Conflicts, and 3.01, Unfair Discrimination).

Disputation or Unquestioned Acceptance of Client/Patient Faith Beliefs

Trivializing or disputing religious values and beliefs can undermine the goals of therapy by threatening those aspects of life that some clients/patients hold sacred, that provide supportive family and community connections, and that form an integral part of their identity (Pargament, Murray-Swank, Magyar, & Ano, 2005; Standard 3.04, Avoiding Harm). Similarly, uncritical acceptance of theistic beliefs, when they indicate misunderstandings or distortions of religious teachings and values, can undercut treatment goals by reinforcing maladaptive ways of thinking or by ignoring signs of psychopathology. To identify if the client harbors distorted religious beliefs, psychologists should explore whether the client's/patient's beliefs (a) create or exacerbate clinical distress, (b) provide a way to avoid reality and responsibility, (c) lead to self-destructive behavior, or (d) create false expectations of God (Johnson et al., 2000).

Imposing Religious Values

Using the therapist's authority to indoctrinate clients/patients to the psychologists' religious beliefs violates their value autonomy and exploits their vulnerability to coercion (Principle E: Respect for People's Rights and Dignity; Standard 3.08, Exploitative Relationships). When clients/patients are grappling with decisions in areas in which religious and secular moral perspectives may conflict (e.g., divorce, sexual orientation, abortion, acceptance of transfusions, end-of-life decisions), therapy needs to distinguish between those moral values that have positive or destructive influences on each individual client's/patient's mental health—not the religious or secular values of the psychologist. Psychologists should guard against discussing religious doctrine when it is irrelevant to the clients'/patients' mental health needs (Richards & Bergin, 2005). Professional license to practice psychology demands that psychologists provide competent professional services and does not give them license to preach (Plante, 2007).

Confusing Religious Values With Psychological Diagnoses. The linking of religious values and psychotherapies involving lesbian, gay, bisexual, and transgendered (LGBT) clients/patients has drawn a considerable amount of public attention. Spiritually sensitive, accommodative, and theistic therapies have a lot to offer LGBT clients/patients (Lease, Horne, & Noffsinger-Frazier, 2005). Ethical problems arise, however, when psychologists confuse religious values with psychological diagnoses. Such ethical challenges have raised considerable professional dialogue as they relate to the application of conversion therapies to alter sexual orientation.

All major professional mental health organizations have affirmed that homosexuality is not a mental disorder (www.apa.org/pi/lgbc/publications/justthefacts.html#2). In addition, to date, empirical data dispute the effectiveness of conversion/reparative therapies aimed at changing sexual orientation (www.Psychology.org.au/ Assets/Files/reparative_therapy.pdf). Psychologists who offer such therapies to LGBT clients/patients risk violating Standard 2.04, Bases for Scientific and Professional Judgments. Moreover, when psychologists offer "cures" for homosexuality, they falsely imply there is established knowledge in the profession that gay/lesbian sexual orientation is a mental disorder. This, in turn, may deprive clients/patients of exploring internalized reactions to a hostile society and risks perpetuating societal prejudices and stereotypes (Haldeman, 1994, 2004; Principle A: Beneficence and Nonmaleficence, Principle B: Fidelity and Responsibility; and Principle D: Justice; Standard 3.04, Avoiding Harm). In addition, when psychologists base their diagnosis on religious doctrines that view homosexual behavior as a "sin," they can be in violation of Standard 9.01, Bases for Assessments, and may be practicing outside the boundaries of their profession.

Multiple Relationships

Multiple relationship challenges arise when clergy who have doctoral degrees in psychology provide mental health services to congregants or nonclergy psychologists who treat members of their faith communities (Standard 3.05, Multiple Relationships).

Clergy-Psychologists

Clergy-psychologists providing therapy for members of their faith over whom they may have ecclesiastical authority should take steps to ensure they and their clients/patients are both aware of and respect the boundaries between their roles as a psychologist and religious leader. Distinguishing role functions becomes particularly important in addressing issues of confidentiality. Psychologists and clergy have different legal and professional obligations when it comes to mandated reporting of abuse and ethically permitted disclosures of information to protect clients/patients and others from harm (Standard 4.05, Disclosures).

Therapists at all points along the secular-theistic continuum who share the faith beliefs of clients/patients or work with fellow congregants must take steps to ensure clients do not misperceive them as having religious or ecclesiastical authority and understand that the psychologists do not act on behalf of the church or its leaders

(Gubi, 2001; Richards & Potts, 1995). Psychologists also need to take steps to ensure that their knowledge of their joint faith community does not interfere with their objectivity and that clients/patients feel safe disclosing and exploring concerns about religion or behaviors that might ostracize them from this community.

Fee-for-Service Quandaries

While psychologists can discuss spiritual issues in therapy, when services are provided as a licensed psychologist eligible for third-party payments, the primary focus must be psychological (Plante, 2007). A focus on religious/spiritual rather than therapeutic goals may risk inappropriately charging third-party payors for nonmental health services not covered by insurance policies (Tan, 2003; see also Principle C: Integrity; Standard 6.04, Fees and Financial Arrangements). Clergy and nonclergy psychologists practicing theistic therapies may find it difficult to clearly differentiate in reports to third-party payors those goals and therapeutic techniques that are accepted mental health practices and those that are spiritually based. Clergy-psychologists should also refrain from encouraging their congregants to see them for fee-for-service therapy (Standard 3.06, Conflict of Interest). When clergy or nonclergy psychologists provide services free of charge in religious settings, they should clarify they are counseling in their ecclesiastical role and that content will be specific to pastoral issues (Richards & Bergin, 2005).

Informed Consent

The role of religion/spirituality in clients'/patients' worldview may determine their willingness to participate in therapies along the secular-theistic continuum. Some may find the interjection of religion into therapy discomforting or coercive, while others may find the absence of religion from therapy alienating.

For psychologists practicing religiously sensitive or accommodative psychotherapies, discussion of the role of spirituality/religion in psychotherapy will often be premature if initiated by the psychologist during informed consent. However, when clients/patients raise the question, psychologists should answer in a clear and clinically appropriate manner and use the discussion as a frame-defining opportunity for both psychologist and client/patient to assess how the psychologist's approach will fit the client's/patient's needs (Tillman, 1998; Principle C: Integrity).

When treatments diverge from established psychological practice, clients/patients have a right to consider this information in their consent decisions. Consequently, informed consent for theistic therapies should explain the religious doctrine and values upon which their treatment is based, the religious methods that will be employed (e.g., prayers, reading of scripture, forgiveness), and the relative emphasis on spiritual versus mental health goals. In addition, since theistic therapies are relatively new and currently lack empirical evidence or disciplinary consensus regarding their use (Plante & Sherman, 2001; Richards & Bergin, 2005), psychologists practicing these therapies should consider whether informed consent requirements for "treatments for which generally recognized techniques and procedures have not been established," described in Standard 10.01b, apply.

Conclusion

There is a welcome increase in research examining the positive and negative influences of religious beliefs and practices on mental health and the clinical outcomes of treatment approaches along the secular-theistic therapy continuum. Ethical commitment to do what is right for each client/patient and well-informed approaches to treatment will reduce but not eliminate ethical challenges that will continue to emerge as scientific and professional knowledge advances. Psychologists conducting psychotherapy with individuals of diverse religious backgrounds and values will need to keep abreast of new knowledge and ethical guidelines that will emerge, continuously monitor the consequences of spirituality and religiously sensitive treatment decisions on client/patient well-being, and have the flexibility and sensitivity to religious contexts, role responsibilities, and client/patient expectations required for effective ethical decision making.

Appendix A

Ethical Principles of Psychologists and Code of Conduct, American Psychological Association (2002, amended June 1, 2010)

Ethical Principles of Psychologists and Code of Conduct
(2002, amended June 1, 2010)

<u>History and Effective Date Footnote</u>

CONTENTS

INTRODUCTION AND APPLICABILITY

The American Psychological Association's (APA's) Ethical Principles of Psychologists and Code of Conduct (herein; referred to as the Ethics Code) consists of an Introduction, a Preamble, five General Principles (A – E), and specific Ethical Standards. The Introduction discusses the intent, organization, procedural considerations, and scope of application of the Ethics Code. The Preamble and General Principles are aspirational goals to guide psychologists t the highest ideals of psychology. Although the Preamble and General Principles are not themselves enforceable rul they should be considered by psychologists in arriving at an ethical course of action. The Ethical Standards set forth enforceable rules for conduct as psychologists. Most of the Ethical Standards are written broadly, in order to apply t psychologists in varied roles, although the application of an Ethical Standard may vary depending on the context. Th Ethical Standards are not exhaustive. The fact that a given conduct is not specifically addressed by an Ethical Stanc does not mean that it is necessarily either ethical or unethical.

This Ethics Code applies only to psychologists' activities that are part of their scientific, educational, or professional as psychologists. Areas covered include but are not limited to the clinical, counseling, and school practice of psychc research; teaching; supervision of trainees; public service; policy development; social intervention; development of assessment instruments; conducting assessments; educational counseling; organizational consulting; forensic activ program design and evaluation; and administration. This Ethics Code applies to these activities across a variety of contexts, such as in person, postal, telephone, Internet, and other electronic transmissions. These activities shall be distinguished from the purely private conduct of psychologists, which is not within the purview of the Ethics Code.

Membership in the APA commits members and student affiliates to comply with the standards of the APA Ethics Co and to the rules and procedures used to enforce them. Lack of awareness or misunderstanding of an Ethical Stand not itself a defense to a charge of unethical conduct.

The procedures for filing, investigating, and resolving complaints of unethical conduct are described in the current R and Procedures of the APA Ethics Committee. APA may impose sanctions on its members for violations of the star of the Ethics Code, including termination of APA membership, and may notify other bodies and individuals of its acti Actions that violate the standards of the Ethics Code may also lead to the imposition of sanctions on psychologists (students whether or not they are APA members by bodies other than APA, including state psychological associatior other professional groups, psychology boards, other state or federal agencies, and payors for health services. In ac APA may take action against a member after his or her conviction of a felony, expulsion or suspension from an affili; state psychological association, or suspension or loss of licensure. When the sanction to be imposed by APA is less expulsion, the 2001 Rules and Procedures do not guarantee an opportunity for an in-person hearing, but generally provide that complaints will be resolved only on the basis of a submitted record.

The Ethics Code is intended to provide guidance for psychologists and standards of professional conduct that can b applied by the APA and by other bodies that choose to adopt them. The Ethics Code is not intended to be a basis c liability. Whether a psychologist has violated the Ethics Code standards does not by itself determine whether the psychologist is legally liable in a court action, whether a contract is enforceable, or whether other legal consequence occur.

The modifiers used in some of the standards of this Ethics Code (e.g., *reasonably, appropriate, potentially*) are inclu the standards when they would (1) allow professional judgment on the part of psychologists, (2) eliminate injustice c inequality that would occur without the modifier, (3) ensure applicability across the broad range of activities conducte psychologists, or (4) guard against a set of rigid rules that might be quickly outdated. As used in this Ethics Code, th *reasonable* means the prevailing professional judgment of psychologists engaged in similar activities in similar circumstances, given the knowledge the psychologist had or should have had at the time.

In the process of making decisions regarding their professional behavior, psychologists must consider this Ethics Cc addition to applicable laws and psychology board regulations. In applying the Ethics Code to their professional worl psychologists may consider other materials and guidelines that have been adopted or endorsed by scientific and professional psychological organizations and the dictates of their own conscience, as well as consult with others wit field. If this Ethics Code establishes a higher standard of conduct than is required by law, psychologists must meet t higher ethical standard. If psychologists' ethical responsibilities conflict with law, regulations, or other governing lega authority, psychologists make known their commitment to this Ethics Code and take steps to resolve the conflict in ¿ responsible manner, in keeping with basic principles of human rights.

PREAMBLE

Psychologists are committed to increasing scientific and professional knowledge of behavior and people's understanding of themselves and others and to the use of such knowledge to improve the condition of individuals, organizations, and society. Psychologists respect and protect civil and human rights and the central importance of freedom of inquiry and expression in research, teaching, and publication. They strive to help the public in developing informed judgments and choices concerning human behavior. In doing so, they perform many roles, such as researcher, educator, diagnostician, therapist, supervisor, consultant, administrator, social interventionist, and expert witness. This Ethics Code provides a common set of principles and standards upon which psychologists build their professional and scientific work.

This Ethics Code is intended to provide specific standards to cover most situations encountered by psychologists. It has as its goals the welfare and protection of the individuals and groups with whom psychologists work and the education of members, students, and the public regarding ethical standards of the discipline.

The development of a dynamic set of ethical standards for psychologists' work-related conduct requires a personal commitment and lifelong effort to act ethically; to encourage ethical behavior by students, supervisees, employees, and colleagues; and to consult with others concerning ethical problems.

GENERAL PRINCIPLES

This section consists of General Principles. General Principles, as opposed to Ethical Standards, are aspirational in nature. Their intent is to guide and inspire psychologists toward the very highest ethical ideals of the profession. General Principles, in contrast to Ethical Standards, do not represent obligations and should not form the basis for imposing sanctions. Relying upon General Principles for either of these reasons distorts both their meaning and purpose.

Principle A: Beneficence and Nonmaleficence

Psychologists strive to benefit those with whom they work and take care to do no harm. In their professional actions, psychologists seek to safeguard the welfare and rights of those with whom they interact professionally and other affected persons, and the welfare of animal subjects of research. When conflicts occur among psychologists' obligations or concerns, they attempt to resolve these conflicts in a responsible fashion that avoids or minimizes harm. Because psychologists' scientific and professional judgments and actions may affect the lives of others, they are alert to and guard against personal, financial, social, organizational, or political factors that might lead to misuse of their influence. Psychologists strive to be aware of the possible effect of their own physical and mental health on their ability to help those with whom they work.

Principle B: Fidelity and Responsibility

Psychologists establish relationships of trust with those with whom they work. They are aware of their professional and scientific responsibilities to society and to the specific communities in which they work. Psychologists uphold professional standards of conduct, clarify their professional roles and obligations, accept appropriate responsibility for their behavior, and seek to manage conflicts of interest that could lead to exploitation or harm. Psychologists consult with, refer to, or cooperate with other professionals and institutions to the extent needed to serve the best interests of those with whom they work. They are concerned about the ethical compliance of their colleagues' scientific and professional conduct. Psychologists strive to contribute a portion of their professional time for little or no compensation or personal advantage.

Principle C: Integrity

Psychologists seek to promote accuracy, honesty, and truthfulness in the science, teaching, and practice of psychology. In these activities psychologists do not steal, cheat, or engage in fraud, subterfuge, or intentional misrepresentation of fact. Psychologists strive to keep their promises and to avoid unwise or unclear commitments. In situations in which deception may be ethically justifiable to maximize benefits and minimize harm, psychologists have a serious obligation to consider the need for, the possible consequences of, and their responsibility to correct any resulting mistrust or other harmful effects that arise from the use of such techniques.

Principle D: Justice

Psychologists recognize that fairness and justice entitle all persons to access to and benefit from the contributions of psychology and to equal quality in the processes, procedures, and services being conducted by psychologists. Psychologists exercise reasonable judgment and take precautions to ensure that their potential biases, the boundaries of their competence, and the limitations of their expertise do not lead to or condone unjust practices.

Principle E: Respect for People's Rights and Dignity

Psychologists respect the dignity and worth of all people, and the rights of individuals to privacy, confidentiality, and self-determination. Psychologists are aware that special safeguards may be necessary to protect the rights and welfare of persons or communities whose vulnerabilities impair autonomous decision making. Psychologists are aware of and respect cultural, individual, and role differences, including those based on age, gender, gender identity, race, ethnicity, culture, national origin, religion, sexual orientation, disability, language, and socioeconomic status and consider these factors when working with members of such groups. Psychologists try to eliminate the effect on their work of biases based on those factors, and they do not knowingly participate in or condone activities of others based upon such prejudices.

ETHICAL STANDARDS

1. Resolving Ethical Issues

1.01 Misuse of Psychologists' Work
If psychologists learn of misuse or misrepresentation of their work, they take reasonable steps to correct or minimize the misuse or misrepresentation.

1.02 Conflicts Between Ethics and Law, Regulations, or Other Governing Legal Authority
If psychologists' ethical responsibilities conflict with law, regulations, or other governing legal authority, psychologists clarify the nature of the conflict, make known their commitment to the Ethics Code and take reasonable steps to resolve the conflict consistent with the General Principles and Ethical Standards of the Ethics Code. Under no circumstances may this standard be used to justify or defend violating human rights.

1.03 Conflicts Between Ethics and Organizational Demands
If the demands of an organization with which psychologists are affiliated or for whom they are in working conflict with this Ethics Code, psychologists clarify the nature of the conflict, make known their commitment to the Ethics Code, and take reasonable steps to resolve the conflict consistent with the General Principles and Ethical Standards of the Ethics Code. Under no circumstances may this standard be used to justify or defend violating human rights.

1.04 Informal Resolution of Ethical Violations
When psychologists believe that there may have been an ethical violation by another psychologist, they attempt to resolve the issue by bringing it to the attention of that individual, if an informal resolution appears appropriate and the intervention does not violate any confidentiality rights that may be involved. (See also Standards 1.02, Conflicts Between Ethics and Law, Regulations, or Other Governing Legal Authority, and 1.03, Conflicts Between Ethics and Organizational Demands.)

1.05 Reporting Ethical Violations
If an apparent ethical violation has substantially harmed or is likely to substantially harm a person or organization and is not appropriate for informal resolution under Standard 1.04, Informal Resolution of Ethical Violations, or is not resolved properly in that fashion, psychologists take further action appropriate to the situation. Such action might include referral to state or national committees on professional ethics, to state licensing boards, or to the appropriate institutional authorities. This standard does not apply when an intervention would violate confidentiality rights or when psychologists have been retained to review the work of another psychologist whose professional conduct is in question. (See also Standard 1.02, Conflicts Between Ethics and Law, Regulations, or Other Governing Legal Authority.)

1.06 Cooperating With Ethics Committees
Psychologists cooperate in ethics investigations, proceedings, and resulting requirements of the APA or any affiliated state psychological association to which they belong. In doing so, they address any confidentiality issues. Failure to cooperate is itself an ethics violation. However, making a request for deferment of adjudication of an ethics complaint pending the outcome of litigation does not alone constitute noncooperation.

1.07 Improper Complaints
Psychologists do not file or encourage the filing of ethics complaints that are made with reckless disregard for or willful ignorance of facts that would disprove the allegation.

1.08 Unfair Discrimination Against Complainants and Respondents
Psychologists do not deny persons employment, advancement, admissions to academic or other programs, tenure, or promotion, based solely upon their having made or their being the subject of an ethics complaint. This does not preclude taking action based upon the outcome of such proceedings or considering other appropriate information.

2. Competence

2.01 Boundaries of Competence
(a) Psychologists provide services, teach, and conduct research with populations and in areas only within the boundaries of their competence, based on their education, training, supervised experience, consultation, study, or professional experience.

(b) Where scientific or professional knowledge in the discipline of psychology establishes that an understanding of factors associated with age, gender, gender identity, race, ethnicity, culture, national origin, religion, sexual orientation, disability, language, or socioeconomic status is essential for effective implementation of their services or research, psychologists have or obtain the training, experience, consultation, or supervision necessary to ensure the competence of their services, or they make appropriate referrals, except as provided in Standard 2.02, Providing Services in Emergencies.

(c) Psychologists planning to provide services, teach, or conduct research involving populations, areas, techniques, or technologies new to them undertake relevant education, training, supervised experience, consultation, or study.

(d) When psychologists are asked to provide services to individuals for whom appropriate mental health services are not available and for which psychologists have not obtained the competence necessary, psychologists with closely related prior training or experience may provide such services in order to ensure that services are not denied if they make a reasonable effort to obtain the competence required by using relevant research, training, consultation, or study.

(e) In those emerging areas in which generally recognized standards for preparatory training do not yet exist, psychologists nevertheless take reasonable steps to ensure the competence of their work and to protect clients/patients, students, supervisees, research participants, organizational clients, and others from harm.

(f) When assuming forensic roles, psychologists are or become reasonably familiar with the judicial or administrative rules governing their roles.

2.02 Providing Services in Emergencies
In emergencies, when psychologists provide services to individuals for whom other mental health services are not available and for which psychologists have not obtained the necessary training, psychologists may provide such services in order to ensure that services are not denied. The services are discontinued as soon as the emergency has ended or appropriate services are available.

2.03 Maintaining Competence
Psychologists undertake ongoing efforts to develop and maintain their competence.

2.04 Bases for Scientific and Professional Judgments
Psychologists' work is based upon established scientific and professional knowledge of the discipline. (See also Standards 2.01e, Boundaries of Competence, and 10.01b, Informed Consent to Therapy.)

2.05 Delegation of Work to Others
Psychologists who delegate work to employees, supervisees, or research or teaching assistants or who use the services of others, such as interpreters, take reasonable steps to (1) avoid delegating such work to persons who have a multiple relationship with those being served that would likely lead to exploitation or loss of objectivity; (2) authorize only those responsibilities that such persons can be expected to perform competently on the basis of their education, training, or experience, either independently or with the level of supervision being provided; and (3) see that such persons perform these services competently. (See also Standards 2.02, Providing Services in Emergencies; 3.05, Multiple Relationships; 4.01, Maintaining Confidentiality; 9.01, Bases for Assessments; 9.02, Use of Assessments; 9.03, Informed Consent in Assessments; and 9.07, Assessment by Unqualified Persons.)

2.06 Personal Problems and Conflicts
(a) Psychologists refrain from initiating an activity when they know or should know that there is a substantial likelihood that their personal problems will prevent them from performing their work-related activities in a competent manner.

(b) When psychologists become aware of personal problems that may interfere with their performing work-related duties adequately, they take appropriate measures, such as obtaining professional consultation or assistance, and determine whether they should limit, suspend, or terminate their work-related duties. (See also Standard 10.10, Terminating Therapy.)

3. Human Relations

3.01 Unfair Discrimination
In their work-related activities, psychologists do not engage in unfair discrimination based on age, gender, gender identity, race, ethnicity, culture, national origin, religion, sexual orientation, disability, socioeconomic status, or any basis proscribed by law.

3.02 Sexual Harassment
Psychologists do not engage in sexual harassment. Sexual harassment is sexual solicitation, physical advances, or verbal or nonverbal conduct that is sexual in nature, that occurs in connection with the psychologist's activities or roles as a psychologist, and that either (1) is unwelcome, is offensive, or creates a hostile workplace or educational environment, and the psychologist knows or is told this or (2) is sufficiently severe or intense to be abusive to a reasonable person in

the context. Sexual harassment can consist of a single intense or severe act or of multiple persistent or pervasive acts. (See also Standard 1.08, Unfair Discrimination Against Complainants and Respondents.)

3.03 Other Harassment
Psychologists do not knowingly engage in behavior that is harassing or demeaning to persons with whom they interact in their work based on factors such as those persons' age, gender, gender identity, race, ethnicity, culture, national origin, religion, sexual orientation, disability, language, or socioeconomic status.

3.04 Avoiding Harm
Psychologists take reasonable steps to avoid harming their clients/patients, students, supervisees, research participants, organizational clients, and others with whom they work, and to minimize harm where it is foreseeable and unavoidable.

3.05 Multiple Relationships
(a) A multiple relationship occurs when a psychologist is in a professional role with a person and (1) at the same time is in another role with the same person, (2) at the same time is in a relationship with a person closely associated with or related to the person with whom the psychologist has the professional relationship, or (3) promises to enter into another relationship in the future with the person or a person closely associated with or related to the person.

A psychologist refrains from entering into a multiple relationship if the multiple relationship could reasonably be expected to impair the psychologist's objectivity, competence, or effectiveness in performing his or her functions as a psychologist, or otherwise risks exploitation or harm to the person with whom the professional relationship exists.

Multiple relationships that would not reasonably be expected to cause impairment or risk exploitation or harm are not unethical.

(b) If a psychologist finds that, due to unforeseen factors, a potentially harmful multiple relationship has arisen, the psychologist takes reasonable steps to resolve it with due regard for the best interests of the affected person and maximal compliance with the Ethics Code.

(c) When psychologists are required by law, institutional policy, or extraordinary circumstances to serve in more than one role in judicial or administrative proceedings, at the outset they clarify role expectations and the extent of confidentiality and thereafter as changes occur. (See also Standards 3.04, Avoiding Harm, and 3.07, Third-Party Requests for Services.)

3.06 Conflict of Interest
Psychologists refrain from taking on a professional role when personal, scientific, professional, legal, financial, or other interests or relationships could reasonably be expected to (1) impair their objectivity, competence, or effectiveness in performing their functions as psychologists or (2) expose the person or organization with whom the professional relationship exists to harm or exploitation.

3.07 Third-Party Requests for Services
When psychologists agree to provide services to a person or entity at the request of a third party, psychologists attempt to clarify at the outset of the service the nature of the relationship with all individuals or organizations involved. This clarification includes the role of the psychologist (e.g., therapist, consultant, diagnostician, or expert witness), an identification of who is the client, the probable uses of the services provided or the information obtained, and the fact that there may be limits to confidentiality. (See also Standards 3.05, Multiple Relationships, and 4.02, Discussing the Limits of Confidentiality.)

3.08 Exploitative Relationships
Psychologists do not exploit persons over whom they have supervisory, evaluative, or other authority such as clients/patients, students, supervisees, research participants, and employees. (See also Standards 3.05, Multiple Relationships; 6.04, Fees and Financial Arrangements; 6.05, Barter With Clients/Patients; 7.07, Sexual Relationships With Students and Supervisees; 10.05, Sexual Intimacies With Current Therapy Clients/Patients; 10.06, Sexual Intimacies With Relatives or Significant Others of Current Therapy Clients/Patients; 10.07, Therapy With Former Sexual Partners; and 10.08, Sexual Intimacies With Former Therapy Clients/Patients.)

3.09 Cooperation With Other Professionals
When indicated and professionally appropriate, psychologists cooperate with other professionals in order to serve their clients/patients effectively and appropriately. (See also Standard 4.05, Disclosures.)

3.10 Informed Consent
(a) When psychologists conduct research or provide assessment, therapy, counseling, or consulting services in person or via electronic transmission or other forms of communication, they obtain the informed consent of the individual or individuals using language that is reasonably understandable to that person or persons except when conducting such activities without consent is mandated by law or governmental regulation or as otherwise provided in this Ethics Code.

(See also Standards 8.02, Informed Consent to Research; 9.03, Informed Consent in Assessments; and 10.01, Informed Consent to Therapy.)

(b) For persons who are legally incapable of giving informed consent, psychologists nevertheless (1) provide an appropriate explanation, (2) seek the individual's assent, (3) consider such persons' preferences and best interests, and (4) obtain appropriate permission from a legally authorized person, if such substitute consent is permitted or required by law. When consent by a legally authorized person is not permitted or required by law, psychologists take reasonable steps to protect the individual's rights and welfare.

(c) When psychological services are court ordered or otherwise mandated, psychologists inform the individual of the nature of the anticipated services, including whether the services are court ordered or mandated and any limits of confidentiality, before proceeding.

(d) Psychologists appropriately document written or oral consent, permission, and assent. (See also Standards 8.02, Informed Consent to Research; 9.03, Informed Consent in Assessments; and 10.01, Informed Consent to Therapy.)

3.11 Psychological Services Delivered To or Through Organizations

(a) Psychologists delivering services to or through organizations provide information beforehand to clients and when appropriate those directly affected by the services about (1) the nature and objectives of the services, (2) the intended recipients, (3) which of the individuals are clients, (4) the relationship the psychologist will have with each person and the organization, (5) the probable uses of services provided and information obtained, (6) who will have access to the information, and (7) limits of confidentiality. As soon as feasible, they provide information about the results and conclusions of such services to appropriate persons.

(b) If psychologists will be precluded by law or by organizational roles from providing such information to particular individuals or groups, they so inform those individuals or groups at the outset of the service.

3.12 Interruption of Psychological Services

Unless otherwise covered by contract, psychologists make reasonable efforts to plan for facilitating services in the event that psychological services are interrupted by factors such as the psychologist's illness, death, unavailability, relocation, or retirement or by the client's/patient's relocation or financial limitations. (See also Standard 6.02c, Maintenance, Dissemination, and Disposal of Confidential Records of Professional and Scientific Work.)

4. Privacy and Confidentiality

4.01 Maintaining Confidentiality

Psychologists have a primary obligation and take reasonable precautions to protect confidential information obtained through or stored in any medium, recognizing that the extent and limits of confidentiality may be regulated by law or established by institutional rules or professional or scientific relationship. (See also Standard 2.05, Delegation of Work to Others.)

4.02 Discussing the Limits of Confidentiality

(a) Psychologists discuss with persons (including, to the extent feasible, persons who are legally incapable of giving informed consent and their legal representatives) and organizations with whom they establish a scientific or professional relationship (1) the relevant limits of confidentiality and (2) the foreseeable uses of the information generated through their psychological activities. (See also Standard 3.10, Informed Consent.)

(b) Unless it is not feasible or is contraindicated, the discussion of confidentiality occurs at the outset of the relationship and thereafter as new circumstances may warrant.

(c) Psychologists who offer services, products, or information via electronic transmission inform clients/patients of the risks to privacy and limits of confidentiality.

4.03 Recording

Before recording the voices or images of individuals to whom they provide services, psychologists obtain permission from all such persons or their legal representatives. (See also Standards 8.03, Informed Consent for Recording Voices and Images in Research; 8.05, Dispensing With Informed Consent for Research; and 8.07, Deception in Research.)

4.04 Minimizing Intrusions on Privacy

(a) Psychologists include in written and oral reports and consultations, only information germane to the purpose for which the communication is made.

(b) Psychologists discuss confidential information obtained in their work only for appropriate scientific or professional purposes and only with persons clearly concerned with such matters.

4.05 Disclosures
(a) Psychologists may disclose confidential information with the appropriate consent of the organizational client, the individual client/patient, or another legally authorized person on behalf of the client/patient unless prohibited by law.

(b) Psychologists disclose confidential information without the consent of the individual only as mandated by law, or where permitted by law for a valid purpose such as to (1) provide needed professional services; (2) obtain appropriate professional consultations; (3) protect the client/patient, psychologist, or others from harm; or (4) obtain payment for services from a client/patient, in which instance disclosure is limited to the minimum that is necessary to achieve the purpose. (See also Standard 6.04e, Fees and Financial Arrangements.)

4.06 Consultations
When consulting with colleagues, (1) psychologists do not disclose confidential information that reasonably could lead to the identification of a client/patient, research participant, or other person or organization with whom they have a confidential relationship unless they have obtained the prior consent of the person or organization or the disclosure cannot be avoided, and (2) they disclose information only to the extent necessary to achieve the purposes of the consultation. (See also Standard 4.01, Maintaining Confidentiality.)

4.07 Use of Confidential Information for Didactic or Other Purposes
Psychologists do not disclose in their writings, lectures, or other public media, confidential, personally identifiable information concerning their clients/patients, students, research participants, organizational clients, or other recipients of their services that they obtained during the course of their work, unless (1) they take reasonable steps to disguise the person or organization, (2) the person or organization has consented in writing, or (3) there is legal authorization for doing so.

5. Advertising and Other Public Statements

5.01 Avoidance of False or Deceptive Statements
(a) Public statements include but are not limited to paid or unpaid advertising, product endorsements, grant applications, licensing applications, other credentialing applications, brochures, printed matter, directory listings, personal resumes or curricula vitae, or comments for use in media such as print or electronic transmission, statements in legal proceedings, lectures and public oral presentations, and published materials. Psychologists do not knowingly make public statements that are false, deceptive, or fraudulent concerning their research, practice, or other work activities or those of persons or organizations with which they are affiliated.

(b) Psychologists do not make false, deceptive, or fraudulent statements concerning (1) their training, experience, or competence; (2) their academic degrees; (3) their credentials; (4) their institutional or association affiliations; (5) their services; (6) the scientific or clinical basis for, or results or degree of success of, their services; (7) their fees; or (8) their publications or research findings.

(c) Psychologists claim degrees as credentials for their health services only if those degrees (1) were earned from a regionally accredited educational institution or (2) were the basis for psychology licensure by the state in which they practice.

5.02 Statements by Others
(a) Psychologists who engage others to create or place public statements that promote their professional practice, products, or activities retain professional responsibility for such statements.

(b) Psychologists do not compensate employees of press, radio, television, or other communication media in return for publicity in a news item. (See also Standard 1.01, Misuse of Psychologists' Work.)

(c) A paid advertisement relating to psychologists' activities must be identified or clearly recognizable as such.

5.03 Descriptions of Workshops and Non-Degree-Granting Educational Programs
To the degree to which they exercise control, psychologists responsible for announcements, catalogs, brochures, or advertisements describing workshops, seminars, or other non-degree-granting educational programs ensure that they accurately describe the audience for which the program is intended, the educational objectives, the presenters, and the fees involved.

5.04 Media Presentations
When psychologists provide public advice or comment via print, internet, or other electronic transmission, they take precautions to ensure that statements (1) are based on their professional knowledge, training, or experience in accord with appropriate psychological literature and practice; (2) are otherwise consistent with this Ethics Code; and (3) do not indicate that a professional relationship has been established with the recipient. (See also Standard 2.04, Bases for Scientific and Professional Judgments.)

5.05 Testimonials
Psychologists do not solicit testimonials from current therapy clients/patients or other persons who because of their particular circumstances are vulnerable to undue influence.

5.06 In-Person Solicitation
Psychologists do not engage, directly or through agents, in uninvited in-person solicitation of business from actual or potential therapy clients/patients or other persons who because of their particular circumstances are vulnerable to undue influence. However, this prohibition does not preclude (1) attempting to implement appropriate collateral contacts for the purpose of benefiting an already engaged therapy client/patient or (2) providing disaster or community outreach services.

6. Record Keeping and Fees

6.01 Documentation of Professional and Scientific Work and Maintenance of Records
Psychologists create, and to the extent the records are under their control, maintain, disseminate, store, retain, and dispose of records and data relating to their professional and scientific work in order to (1) facilitate provision of services later by them or by other professionals, (2) allow for replication of research design and analyses, (3) meet institutional requirements, (4) ensure accuracy of billing and payments, and (5) ensure compliance with law. (See also Standard 4.01, Maintaining Confidentiality.)

6.02 Maintenance, Dissemination, and Disposal of Confidential Records of Professional and Scientific Work
(a) Psychologists maintain confidentiality in creating, storing, accessing, transferring, and disposing of records under their control, whether these are written, automated, or in any other medium. (See also Standards 4.01, Maintaining Confidentiality, and 6.01, Documentation of Professional and Scientific Work and Maintenance of Records.)

(b) If confidential information concerning recipients of psychological services is entered into databases or systems of records available to persons whose access has not been consented to by the recipient, psychologists use coding or other techniques to avoid the inclusion of personal identifiers.

(c) Psychologists make plans in advance to facilitate the appropriate transfer and to protect the confidentiality of records and data in the event of psychologists' withdrawal from positions or practice. (See also Standards 3.12, Interruption of Psychological Services, and 10.09, Interruption of Therapy.)

6.03 Withholding Records for Nonpayment
Psychologists may not withhold records under their control that are requested and needed for a client's/patient's emergency treatment solely because payment has not been received.

6.04 Fees and Financial Arrangements
(a) As early as is feasible in a professional or scientific relationship, psychologists and recipients of psychological services reach an agreement specifying compensation and billing arrangements.

(b) Psychologists' fee practices are consistent with law.

(c) Psychologists do not misrepresent their fees.

(d) If limitations to services can be anticipated because of limitations in financing, this is discussed with the recipient of services as early as is feasible. (See also Standards 10.09, Interruption of Therapy, and 10.10, Terminating Therapy.)

(e) If the recipient of services does not pay for services as agreed, and if psychologists intend to use collection agencies or legal measures to collect the fees, psychologists first inform the person that such measures will be taken and provide that person an opportunity to make prompt payment. (See also Standards 4.05, Disclosures; 6.03, Withholding Records for Nonpayment; and 10.01, Informed Consent to Therapy.)

6.05 Barter With Clients/Patients
Barter is the acceptance of goods, services, or other nonmonetary remuneration from clients/patients in return for psychological services. Psychologists may barter only if (1) it is not clinically contraindicated, and (2) the resulting arrangement is not exploitative. (See also Standards 3.05, Multiple Relationships, and 6.04, Fees and Financial Arrangements.)

6.06 Accuracy in Reports to Payors and Funding Sources
In their reports to payors for services or sources of research funding, psychologists take reasonable steps to ensure the accurate reporting of the nature of the service provided or research conducted, the fees, charges, or payments, and where applicable, the identity of the provider, the findings, and the diagnosis. (See also Standards 4.01, Maintaining Confidentiality; 4.04, Minimizing Intrusions on Privacy; and 4.05, Disclosures.)

6.07 Referrals and Fees
When psychologists pay, receive payment from, or divide fees with another professional, other than in an employer-employee relationship, the payment to each is based on the services provided (clinical, consultative, administrative, or other) and is not based on the referral itself. (See also Standard 3.09, Cooperation With Other Professionals.)

7. Education and Training

7.01 Design of Education and Training Programs
Psychologists responsible for education and training programs take reasonable steps to ensure that the programs are designed to provide the appropriate knowledge and proper experiences, and to meet the requirements for licensure, certification, or other goals for which claims are made by the program. (See also Standard 5.03, Descriptions of Workshops and Non-Degree-Granting Educational Programs.)

7.02 Descriptions of Education and Training Programs
Psychologists responsible for education and training programs take reasonable steps to ensure that there is a current and accurate description of the program content (including participation in required course- or program-related counseling, psychotherapy, experiential groups, consulting projects, or community service), training goals and objectives, stipends and benefits, and requirements that must be met for satisfactory completion of the program. This information must be made readily available to all interested parties.

7.03 Accuracy in Teaching
(a) Psychologists take reasonable steps to ensure that course syllabi are accurate regarding the subject matter to be covered, bases for evaluating progress, and the nature of course experiences. This standard does not preclude an instructor from modifying course content or requirements when the instructor considers it pedagogically necessary or desirable, so long as students are made aware of these modifications in a manner that enables them to fulfill course requirements. (See also Standard 5.01, Avoidance of False or Deceptive Statements.)

(b) When engaged in teaching or training, psychologists present psychological information accurately. (See also Standard 2.03, Maintaining Competence.)

7.04 Student Disclosure of Personal Information
Psychologists do not require students or supervisees to disclose personal information in course- or program-related activities, either orally or in writing, regarding sexual history, history of abuse and neglect, psychological treatment, and relationships with parents, peers, and spouses or significant others except if (1) the program or training facility has clearly identified this requirement in its admissions and program materials or (2) the information is necessary to evaluate or obtain assistance for students whose personal problems could reasonably be judged to be preventing them from performing their training- or professionally related activities in a competent manner or posing a threat to the students or others.

7.05 Mandatory Individual or Group Therapy
(a) When individual or group therapy is a program or course requirement, psychologists responsible for that program allow students in undergraduate and graduate programs the option of selecting such therapy from practitioners unaffiliated with the program. (See also Standard 7.02, Descriptions of Education and Training Programs.)

(b) Faculty who are or are likely to be responsible for evaluating students' academic performance do not themselves provide that therapy. (See also Standard 3.05, Multiple Relationships.)

7.06 Assessing Student and Supervisee Performance
(a) In academic and supervisory relationships, psychologists establish a timely and specific process for providing feedback to students and supervisees. Information regarding the process is provided to the student at the beginning of supervision.

(b) Psychologists evaluate students and supervisees on the basis of their actual performance on relevant and established program requirements.

7.07 Sexual Relationships With Students and Supervisees
Psychologists do not engage in sexual relationships with students or supervisees who are in their department, agency, or training center or over whom psychologists have or are likely to have evaluative authority. (See also Standard 3.05, Multiple Relationships.)

8.   Research and Publication

8.01 Institutional Approval

When institutional approval is required, psychologists provide accurate information about their research proposals and obtain approval prior to conducting the research. They conduct the research in accordance with the approved research protocol.

8.02 Informed Consent to Research

(a) When obtaining informed consent as required in Standard 3.10, Informed Consent, psychologists inform participants about (1) the purpose of the research, expected duration, and procedures; (2) their right to decline to participate and to withdraw from the research once participation has begun; (3) the foreseeable consequences of declining or withdrawing; (4) reasonably foreseeable factors that may be expected to influence their willingness to participate such as potential risks, discomfort, or adverse effects; (5) any prospective research benefits; (6) limits of confidentiality; (7) incentives for participation; and (8) whom to contact for questions about the research and research participants' rights. They provide opportunity for the prospective participants to ask questions and receive answers. (See also Standards 8.03, Informed Consent for Recording Voices and Images in Research; 8.05, Dispensing With Informed Consent for Research; and 8.07, Deception in Research.)

(b) Psychologists conducting intervention research involving the use of experimental treatments clarify to participants at the outset of the research (1) the experimental nature of the treatment; (2) the services that will or will not be available to the control group(s) if appropriate; (3) the means by which assignment to treatment and control groups will be made; (4) available treatment alternatives if an individual does not wish to participate in the research or wishes to withdraw once a study has begun; and (5) compensation for or monetary costs of participating including, if appropriate, whether reimbursement from the participant or a third-party payor will be sought. (See also Standard 8.02a, Informed Consent to Research.)

8.03 Informed Consent for Recording Voices and Images in Research

Psychologists obtain informed consent from research participants prior to recording their voices or images for data collection unless (1) the research consists solely of naturalistic observations in public places, and it is not anticipated that the recording will be used in a manner that could cause personal identification or harm, or (2) the research design includes deception, and consent for the use of the recording is obtained during debriefing. (See also Standard 8.07, Deception in Research.)

8.04 Client/Patient, Student, and Subordinate Research Participants

(a) When psychologists conduct research with clients/patients, students, or subordinates as participants, psychologists take steps to protect the prospective participants from adverse consequences of declining or withdrawing from participation.

(b) When research participation is a course requirement or an opportunity for extra credit, the prospective participant is given the choice of equitable alternative activities.

8.05 Dispensing With Informed Consent for Research

Psychologists may dispense with informed consent only (1) where research would not reasonably be assumed to create distress or harm and involves (a) the study of normal educational practices, curricula, or classroom management methods conducted in educational settings; (b) only anonymous questionnaires, naturalistic observations, or archival research for which disclosure of responses would not place participants at risk of criminal or civil liability or damage their financial standing, employability, or reputation, and confidentiality is protected; or (c) the study of factors related to job or organization effectiveness conducted in organizational settings for which there is no risk to participants' employability, and confidentiality is protected or (2) where otherwise permitted by law or federal or institutional regulations.

8.06 Offering Inducements for Research Participation

(a) Psychologists make reasonable efforts to avoid offering excessive or inappropriate financial or other inducements for research participation when such inducements are likely to coerce participation.

(b) When offering professional services as an inducement for research participation, psychologists clarify the nature of the services, as well as the risks, obligations, and limitations. (See also Standard 6.05, Barter With Clients/Patients.)

8.07 Deception in Research

(a) Psychologists do not conduct a study involving deception unless they have determined that the use of deceptive techniques is justified by the study's significant prospective scientific, educational, or applied value and that effective nondeceptive alternative procedures are not feasible.

(b) Psychologists do not deceive prospective participants about research that is reasonably expected to cause physical pain or severe emotional distress.

(c) Psychologists explain any deception that is an integral feature of the design and conduct of an experiment to participants as early as is feasible, preferably at the conclusion of their participation, but no later than at the conclusion of the data collection, and permit participants to withdraw their data. (See also Standard 8.08, Debriefing.)

8.08 Debriefing
(a) Psychologists provide a prompt opportunity for participants to obtain appropriate information about the nature, results, and conclusions of the research, and they take reasonable steps to correct any misconceptions that participants may have of which the psychologists are aware.

(b) If scientific or humane values justify delaying or withholding this information, psychologists take reasonable measures to reduce the risk of harm.

(c) When psychologists become aware that research procedures have harmed a participant, they take reasonable steps to minimize the harm.

8.09 Humane Care and Use of Animals in Research
(a) Psychologists acquire, care for, use, and dispose of animals in compliance with current federal, state, and local laws and regulations, and with professional standards.

(b) Psychologists trained in research methods and experienced in the care of laboratory animals supervise all procedures involving animals and are responsible for ensuring appropriate consideration of their comfort, health, and humane treatment.

(c) Psychologists ensure that all individuals under their supervision who are using animals have received instruction in research methods and in the care, maintenance, and handling of the species being used, to the extent appropriate to their role. (See also Standard 2.05, Delegation of Work to Others.)

(d) Psychologists make reasonable efforts to minimize the discomfort, infection, illness, and pain of animal subjects.

(e) Psychologists use a procedure subjecting animals to pain, stress, or privation only when an alternative procedure is unavailable and the goal is justified by its prospective scientific, educational, or applied value.

(f) Psychologists perform surgical procedures under appropriate anesthesia and follow techniques to avoid infection and minimize pain during and after surgery.

(g) When it is appropriate that an animal's life be terminated, psychologists proceed rapidly, with an effort to minimize pain and in accordance with accepted procedures.

8.10 Reporting Research Results
(a) Psychologists do not fabricate data. (See also Standard 5.01a, Avoidance of False or Deceptive Statements.)

(b) If psychologists discover significant errors in their published data, they take reasonable steps to correct such errors in a correction, retraction, erratum, or other appropriate publication means.

8.11 Plagiarism
Psychologists do not present portions of another's work or data as their own, even if the other work or data source is cited occasionally.

8.12 Publication Credit
(a) Psychologists take responsibility and credit, including authorship credit, only for work they have actually performed or to which they have substantially contributed. (See also Standard 8.12b, Publication Credit.)

(b) Principal authorship and other publication credits accurately reflect the relative scientific or professional contributions of the individuals involved, regardless of their relative status. Mere possession of an institutional position, such as department chair, does not justify authorship credit. Minor contributions to the research or to the writing for publications are acknowledged appropriately, such as in footnotes or in an introductory statement.

(c) Except under exceptional circumstances, a student is listed as principal author on any multiple-authored article that is substantially based on the student's doctoral dissertation. Faculty advisors discuss publication credit with students as early as feasible and throughout the research and publication process as appropriate. (See also Standard 8.12b, Publication Credit.)

8.13 Duplicate Publication of Data
Psychologists do not publish, as original data, data that have been previously published. This does not preclude republishing data when they are accompanied by proper acknowledgment.

8.14 Sharing Research Data for Verification
(a) After research results are published, psychologists do not withhold the data on which their conclusions are based from other competent professionals who seek to verify the substantive claims through reanalysis and who intend to use such data only for that purpose, provided that the confidentiality of the participants can be protected and unless legal rights concerning proprietary data preclude their release. This does not preclude psychologists from requiring that such individuals or groups be responsible for costs associated with the provision of such information.

(b) Psychologists who request data from other psychologists to verify the substantive claims through reanalysis may use shared data only for the declared purpose. Requesting psychologists obtain prior written agreement for all other uses of the data.

8.15 Reviewers
Psychologists who review material submitted for presentation, publication, grant, or research proposal review respect the confidentiality of and the proprietary rights in such information of those who submitted it.

9.   Assessment

9.01 Bases for Assessments
(a) Psychologists base the opinions contained in their recommendations, reports, and diagnostic or evaluative statements, including forensic testimony, on information and techniques sufficient to substantiate their findings. (See also Standard 2.04, Bases for Scientific and Professional Judgments.)

(b) Except as noted in 9.01c, psychologists provide opinions of the psychological characteristics of individuals only after they have conducted an examination of the individuals adequate to support their statements or conclusions. When, despite reasonable efforts, such an examination is not practical, psychologists document the efforts they made and the result of those efforts, clarify the probable impact of their limited information on the reliability and validity of their opinions, and appropriately limit the nature and extent of their conclusions or recommendations. (See also Standards 2.01, Boundaries of Competence, and 9.06, Interpreting Assessment Results.)

(c) When psychologists conduct a record review or provide consultation or supervision and an individual examination is not warranted or necessary for the opinion, psychologists explain this and the sources of information on which they based their conclusions and recommendations.

9.02 Use of Assessments
(a) Psychologists administer, adapt, score, interpret, or use assessment techniques, interviews, tests, or instruments in a manner and for purposes that are appropriate in light of the research on or evidence of the usefulness and proper application of the techniques.

(b) Psychologists use assessment instruments whose validity and reliability have been established for use with members of the population tested. When such validity or reliability has not been established, psychologists describe the strengths and limitations of test results and interpretation.

(c) Psychologists use assessment methods that are appropriate to an individual's language preference and competence, unless the use of an alternative language is relevant to the assessment issues.

9.03 Informed Consent in Assessments
(a) Psychologists obtain informed consent for assessments, evaluations, or diagnostic services, as described in Standard 3.10, Informed Consent, except when (1) testing is mandated by law or governmental regulations; (2) informed consent is implied because testing is conducted as a routine educational, institutional, or organizational activity (e.g., when participants voluntarily agree to assessment when applying for a job); or (3) one purpose of the testing is to evaluate decisional capacity. Informed consent includes an explanation of the nature and purpose of the assessment, fees, involvement of third parties, and limits of confidentiality and sufficient opportunity for the client/patient to ask questions and receive answers.

(b) Psychologists inform persons with questionable capacity to consent or for whom testing is mandated by law or governmental regulations about the nature and purpose of the proposed assessment services, using language that is reasonably understandable to the person being assessed.

(c) Psychologists using the services of an interpreter obtain informed consent from the client/patient to use that interpreter, ensure that confidentiality of test results and test security are maintained, and include in their recommendations, reports, and diagnostic or evaluative statements, including forensic testimony, discussion of any limitations on the data obtained. (See also Standards 2.05, Delegation of Work to Others; 4.01, Maintaining Confidentiality; 9.01, Bases for Assessments; 9.06, Interpreting Assessment Results; and 9.07, Assessment by Unqualified Persons.)

9.04 Release of Test Data
(a) The term *test data* refers to raw and scaled scores, client/patient responses to test questions or stimuli, and psychologists' notes and recordings concerning client/patient statements and behavior during an examination. Those portions of test materials that include client/patient responses are included in the definition of *test data*. Pursuant to a client/patient release, psychologists provide test data to the client/patient or other persons identified in the release. Psychologists may refrain from releasing test data to protect a client/patient or others from substantial harm or misuse or misrepresentation of the data or the test, recognizing that in many instances release of confidential information under these circumstances is regulated by law. (See also Standard 9.11, Maintaining Test Security.)

(b) In the absence of a client/patient release, psychologists provide test data only as required by law or court order.

9.05 Test Construction
Psychologists who develop tests and other assessment techniques use appropriate psychometric procedures and current scientific or professional knowledge for test design, standardization, validation, reduction or elimination of bias, and recommendations for use.

9.06 Interpreting Assessment Results
When interpreting assessment results, including automated interpretations, psychologists take into account the purpose of the assessment as well as the various test factors, test-taking abilities, and other characteristics of the person being assessed, such as situational, personal, linguistic, and cultural differences, that might affect psychologists' judgments or reduce the accuracy of their interpretations. They indicate any significant limitations of their interpretations. (See also Standards 2.01b and c, Boundaries of Competence, and 3.01, Unfair Discrimination.)

9.07 Assessment by Unqualified Persons
Psychologists do not promote the use of psychological assessment techniques by unqualified persons, except when such use is conducted for training purposes with appropriate supervision. (See also Standard 2.05, Delegation of Work to Others.)

9.08 Obsolete Tests and Outdated Test Results
(a) Psychologists do not base their assessment or intervention decisions or recommendations on data or test results that are outdated for the current purpose.

(b) Psychologists do not base such decisions or recommendations on tests and measures that are obsolete and not useful for the current purpose.

9.09 Test Scoring and Interpretation Services
(a) Psychologists who offer assessment or scoring services to other professionals accurately describe the purpose, norms, validity, reliability, and applications of the procedures and any special qualifications applicable to their use.

(b) Psychologists select scoring and interpretation services (including automated services) on the basis of evidence of the validity of the program and procedures as well as on other appropriate considerations. (See also Standard 2.01b and c, Boundaries of Competence.)

(c) Psychologists retain responsibility for the appropriate application, interpretation, and use of assessment instruments, whether they score and interpret such tests themselves or use automated or other services.

9.10 Explaining Assessment Results
Regardless of whether the scoring and interpretation are done by psychologists, by employees or assistants, or by automated or other outside services, psychologists take reasonable steps to ensure that explanations of results are given to the individual or designated representative unless the nature of the relationship precludes provision of an explanation of results (such as in some organizational consulting, preemployment or security screenings, and forensic evaluations), and this fact has been clearly explained to the person being assessed in advance.

9.11. Maintaining Test Security
The term *test materials* refers to manuals, instruments, protocols, and test questions or stimuli and does not include *test data* as defined in Standard 9.04, Release of Test Data. Psychologists make reasonable efforts to maintain the integrity and security of test materials and other assessment techniques consistent with law and contractual obligations, and in a manner that permits adherence to this Ethics Code.

10.   Therapy

10.01 Informed Consent to Therapy
(a) When obtaining informed consent to therapy as required in Standard 3.10, Informed Consent, psychologists inform clients/patients as early as is feasible in the therapeutic relationship about the nature and anticipated course of therapy, fees, involvement of third parties, and limits of confidentiality and provide sufficient opportunity for the client/patient to ask

questions and receive answers. (See also Standards 4.02, Discussing the Limits of Confidentiality, and 6.04, Fees and Financial Arrangements.)

(b) When obtaining informed consent for treatment for which generally recognized techniques and procedures have not been established, psychologists inform their clients/patients of the developing nature of the treatment, the potential risks involved, alternative treatments that may be available, and the voluntary nature of their participation. (See also Standards 2.01e, Boundaries of Competence, and 3.10, Informed Consent.)

(c) When the therapist is a trainee and the legal responsibility for the treatment provided resides with the supervisor, the client/patient, as part of the informed consent procedure, is informed that the therapist is in training and is being supervised and is given the name of the supervisor.

10.02 Therapy Involving Couples or Families
(a) When psychologists agree to provide services to several persons who have a relationship (such as spouses, significant others, or parents and children), they take reasonable steps to clarify at the outset (1) which of the individuals are clients/patients and (2) the relationship the psychologist will have with each person. This clarification includes the psychologist's role and the probable uses of the services provided or the information obtained. (See also Standard 4.02, Discussing the Limits of Confidentiality.)

(b) If it becomes apparent that psychologists may be called on to perform potentially conflicting roles (such as family therapist and then witness for one party in divorce proceedings), psychologists take reasonable steps to clarify and modify, or withdraw from, roles appropriately. (See also Standard 3.05c, Multiple Relationships.)

10.03 Group Therapy
When psychologists provide services to several persons in a group setting, they describe at the outset the roles and responsibilities of all parties and the limits of confidentiality.

10.04 Providing Therapy to Those Served by Others
In deciding whether to offer or provide services to those already receiving mental health services elsewhere, psychologists carefully consider the treatment issues and the potential client's/patient's welfare. Psychologists discuss these issues with the client/patient or another legally authorized person on behalf of the client/patient in order to minimize the risk of confusion and conflict, consult with the other service providers when appropriate, and proceed with caution and sensitivity to the therapeutic issues.

10.05 Sexual Intimacies With Current Therapy Clients/Patients
Psychologists do not engage in sexual intimacies with current therapy clients/patients.

10.06 Sexual Intimacies With Relatives or Significant Others of Current Therapy Clients/Patients
Psychologists do not engage in sexual intimacies with individuals they know to be close relatives, guardians, or significant others of current clients/patients. Psychologists do not terminate therapy to circumvent this standard.

10.07 Therapy With Former Sexual Partners
Psychologists do not accept as therapy clients/patients persons with whom they have engaged in sexual intimacies.

10.08 Sexual Intimacies With Former Therapy Clients/Patients
(a) Psychologists do not engage in sexual intimacies with former clients/patients for at least two years after cessation or termination of therapy.

(b) Psychologists do not engage in sexual intimacies with former clients/patients even after a two-year interval except in the most unusual circumstances. Psychologists who engage in such activity after the two years following cessation or termination of therapy and of having no sexual contact with the former client/patient bear the burden of demonstrating that there has been no exploitation, in light of all relevant factors, including (1) the amount of time that has passed since therapy terminated; (2) the nature, duration, and intensity of the therapy; (3) the circumstances of termination; (4) the client's/patient's personal history; (5) the client's/patient's current mental status; (6) the likelihood of adverse impact on the client/patient; and (7) any statements or actions made by the therapist during the course of therapy suggesting or inviting the possibility of a posttermination sexual or romantic relationship with the client/patient. (See also Standard 3.05, Multiple Relationships.)

10.09 Interruption of Therapy
When entering into employment or contractual relationships, psychologists make reasonable efforts to provide for orderly and appropriate resolution of responsibility for client/patient care in the event that the employment or contractual relationship ends, with paramount consideration given to the welfare of the client/patient. (See also Standard 3.12, Interruption of Psychological Services.)

10.10 Terminating Therapy

(a) Psychologists terminate therapy when it becomes reasonably clear that the client/patient no longer needs the service, is not likely to benefit, or is being harmed by continued service.

(b) Psychologists may terminate therapy when threatened or otherwise endangered by the client/patient or another person with whom the client/patient has a relationship.

(c) Except where precluded by the actions of clients/patients or third-party payors, prior to termination psychologists provide pretermination counseling and suggest alternative service providers as appropriate.

History and Effective Date Footnote

This version of the APA Ethics Code was adopted by the American Psychological Association's Council of Representatives during its meeting, August 21, 2002, and is effective beginning June 1, 2003. Inquiries concerning the substance or interpretation of the APA Ethics Code should be addressed to the Director, Office of Ethics, American Psychological Association, 750 First Street, NE, Washington, DC 20002-4242. The Ethics Code and information regarding the Code can be found on the APA web site, http://www.apa.org/ethics. The standards in this Ethics Code will be used to adjudicate complaints brought concerning alleged conduct occurring on or after the effective date. Complaints regarding conduct occurring prior to the effective date will be adjudicated on the basis of the version of the Ethics Code that was in effect at the time the conduct occurred.

The APA has previously published its Ethics Code as follows:

American Psychological Association. (1953). Ethical standards of psychologists. Washington, DC: Author.

American Psychological Association. (1959). Ethical standards of psychologists. *American Psychologist, 14,* 279–282.

American Psychological Association. (1963). Ethical standards of psychologists. *American Psychologyist, 18,* 56–60.

American Psychological Association. (1968). Ethical standards of psychologists. *American Psychologyist, 23,* 357–361.

American Psychological Association. (1977, March). Ethical standards of psychologists. *APA Monitor ,* 22–23.

American Psychological Association. (1979). *Ethical standards of psychologists.* Washington, DC: Author.

American Psychological Association. (1981). Ethical principles of psychologists. *American Psychologist, 36,* 633–638.

American Psychological Association. (1990). Ethical principles of psychologists (Amended June 2, 1989). *American Psychologist, 45,* 390–395.

American Psychological Association. (1992). Ethical principles of psychologists and code of conduct. *American Psychologist, 47,* 1597–1611.

SOURCE: American Psychological Association. (2010a). Ethical principles of psychologists and code of conduct (2002, amended June 1, 2010). Retrieved from http://www.apa.org/ethics/code/index.aspx. Reprinted with permission.

Request copies of the APA's Ethical Principles of Psychologists and Code of Conduct from the APA Order Department, 750 First Street, NE, Washington, DC 20002-4242, or phone (202) 336-5510.

Appendix B

*Relevant Readings Regarding
Ethics and Human Rights*

READING 1

**U.N. Human Rights Council: Resolution on Torture and other
Cruel, Inhuman, or Degrading Treatment or Punishment**

READING 2

Careful Training Creates Soldiers Who Torture

READING 3

5 International Treaties Ban Torture

READING 4

Is Torture Ever Justified: 2 Views

READING 1

U.N. Human Rights Council: Resolution on Torture and other Cruel, Inhuman, or Degrading Treatment or Punishment. March 2009.

UNITED NATIONS

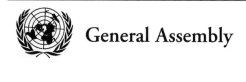 **General Assembly**

Distr.
LIMITED

A/HRC/10/L.32
20 March 2009

Original: ENGLISH

HUMAN RIGHTS COUNCIL
Tenth session
Agenda item 3

PROMOTION AND PROTECTION OF ALL HUMAN RIGHTS, CIVIL, POLITICAL, ECONOMIC, SOCIAL AND CULTURAL RIGHTS, INCLUDING THE RIGHT TO DEVELOPMENT

Argentina, Australia*, Austria*, Belgium*, Bosnia and Herzegovina, Bulgaria*, Cameroon, Canada, Chile, Costa Rica*, Croatia*, Cyprus*, Czech Republic*, Denmark*, Estonia*, Finland*, France, Germany, Greece*, Guatemala*, Hungary*, Iceland*, Ireland*, Italy, Latvia*, Liechtenstein*, Lithuania*, Luxembourg*, Malta*, Mexico, Monaco*, Netherlands, New Zealand*, Norway*, Panama*, Peru*, Poland*, Portugal*, Republic of Moldova*, Romania*, Slovakia, Slovenia, Spain*, Sweden*, Switzerland, the former Yugoslav Republic of Macedonia*, Turkey*, Ukraine, United Kingdom of Great Britain and Northern Ireland, Uruguay: draft resolution

10/...   Torture and other cruel, inhuman or degrading treatment or punishment: the role and responsibility of medical and other health personnel

The Human Rights Council,

Recalling all resolutions on torture and other cruel, inhuman or degrading treatment or punishment and on forensic science adopted by the General Assembly, the Commission on Human Rights and the Human Rights Council,

   Recalling also the Principles of Medical Ethics relevant to the Role of Health Personnel, particularly Physicians, in the Protection of Prisoners and Detainees against Torture and other Cruel, Inhuman or Degrading Treatment or Punishment,

   Reaffirming that no one shall be subjected to torture or to other cruel, inhuman or degrading treatment or punishment,

---

* Non-member State of the Human Rights Council.

Recalling that freedom from torture and other cruel, inhuman or degrading treatment or punishment is a non-derogable right that must be protected under all circumstances, including in times of international or internal armed conflict or disturbance and state of emergency, and that the absolute prohibition of torture and other cruel, inhuman or degrading treatment or punishment is affirmed in relevant international instruments,

Noting the duty of medical and other health personnel to practice for the good of the patients and never do harm or injustice pursuant to the Hippocratic Oath and their respective professional codes of ethics,

Recalling that it is a gross contravention of medical ethics, for medical and other health personnel to engage, actively or passively, in acts which constitute participation in, complicity in, incitement to or attempts to commit torture or other cruel, inhuman or degrading treatment or punishment pursuant to the Principles of Medical Ethics,

Stressing that medical and other health personnel have a duty to provide competent medical service in full professional and moral independence, with compassion and respect for human dignity, and to always bear in mind human life and to act in the patient's best interest under their respective professional codes of ethics,

Noting the duty of all medical and other health personnel to report or denounce acts of torture or cruel, inhuman or degrading treatment of which they are aware to relevant medical, judicial, national or international authorities as appropriate under and consistent with their respective professional codes of ethics,

Noting also that, under the Geneva Conventions of 1949, torture and inhuman treatment are a grave breach and that under the statute of the International Tribunal for the Prosecution of Persons Responsible for Serious Violations of International Humanitarian Law Committed in the Territory of the Former Yugoslavia since 1991, the statute of the International Criminal Tribunal for the Prosecution of Persons Responsible for Genocide and Other Serious Violations of International Humanitarian Law Committed in the Territory of Rwanda and Rwandan Citizens Responsible for Genocide and Other Such Violations Committed in the Territory of Neighbouring States between 1 January and 31 December 1994 and the Rome Statute of the International Criminal Court, acts of torture can constitute crimes against humanity and, when committed in a situation of armed conflict, constitute war crimes,

1. *Condemns* all forms of torture and other cruel, inhuman or degrading treatment or punishment, including through intimidation, which are and shall remain prohibited at any time and in any place whatsoever and can thus never be justified, and calls upon all States to implement fully the absolute prohibition of torture and other cruel, inhuman or degrading treatment or punishment;

2. *Emphasizes* that States must take persistent, determined and effective measures to prevent and combat torture and other cruel, inhuman or degrading treatment or punishment, and stresses that all acts of torture must be made offences under domestic criminal law;

3. *Stresses* that an order or instruction from a superior officer or a public authority should not be invoked as a justification of torture or other cruel, inhuman or degrading treatment or punishment and that States must never request or require anyone, including any medical or other health personnel, to commit any act of torture or other cruel, inhuman or degrading treatment or punishment;

4. *Urges* States to respect the professional and moral independence, duties and responsibilities of medical and other health personnel;

5. *Also urges* States to ensure that all medical and other health personnel may fulfil their duty to report or denounce acts of torture or cruel, inhuman or degrading treatment of which they are aware to

relevant medical, judicial, national or international authorities as appropriate under and consistent with their respective codes of ethics without fear of retribution or harassment;

6. *Stresses* that all allegations of torture and other cruel, inhuman or degrading treatment or punishment must be examined promptly and impartially by the competent domestic authority, including where relevant through examination by forensic experts and other relevant medical personnel, in order for those who encourage, order, tolerate or perpetrate such acts to be held responsible, brought to justice and punished commensurate with the severity of the offence;

7. *Urges* States to establish effective investigation and documentation procedures, and takes note of the Principles on the Effective Investigation and Documentation of Torture and other Cruel, Inhuman or Degrading Treatment or Punishment as a useful tool in this respect;

8. *Stresses* that States must not punish or otherwise intimidate medical and other health personnel for not obeying orders or instructions to commit, facilitate or conceal acts amounting to torture or other cruel, inhuman or degrading treatment or punishment or for speaking out against it;

9. *Urges* all States to provide all persons deprived of their liberty, in prisons or any other detention facility, with a professional medical examination at their admission to and transfer between such facilities and thereafter on a regular basis as a means to help prevent torture or other cruel, inhuman or degrading treatment or punishment;

10. *Also urges* all States to provide all persons deprived of their liberty with protection of their physical and mental health, treatment of any disease or care specifically needed by persons with disabilities of the same quality and standard as is afforded to persons not deprived of their liberty as a means to help prevent torture or other cruel, inhuman or degrading treatment or punishment;

11. *Recognizes* that forensic investigation can play an important role in combating impunity by providing the evidentiary basis on which prosecutions can successfully be brought against persons responsible for violations of human rights and, in times of armed conflict, international humanitarian law and encourages further coordination concerning, inter alia, the planning and realization of such investigations, as well as the protection of forensic and related experts, between Governments, intergovernmental organizations and non-governmental organizations;

12. *Calls upon* all States to ensure that education and information regarding the absolute prohibition of torture and cruel, inhuman or degrading treatment or punishment are fully included in the training of medical and other health personnel who may be involved in the custody, interrogation and treatment of any individual subjected to any form of arrest, detention or imprisonment;

13. *Urges* all States that have not yet done so to become parties to the Convention against Torture and other Cruel, Inhuman or Degrading Treatment or Punishment as a matter of priority and calls upon States parties to give early consideration to signing and ratifying the Optional Protocol to the Convention;

14. *Welcomes* the designation or establishment of independent national preventive mechanisms to prevent torture, with the participation of relevant medical and other health personnel, encourages all States that have not yet done so to establish such mechanisms and calls upon States parties to the Optional Protocol to the Convention against Torture and other Cruel, Inhuman or Degrading Treatment or Punishment to fulfil their obligation to designate or establish truly independent and effective national preventive mechanisms;

15. *Requests* the Special Rapporteur on torture and other relevant special procedures and invites relevant treaty bodies, within their respective mandates:

(*a*) To remain vigilant with regard to medical and other health personnel's active or passive participation in torture and other cruel, inhuman or degrading treatment or punishment and to their functional independence of the institution in which they serve;

(*b*) To discuss possible areas of cooperation with the relevant United Nations bodies, specialized agencies and programmes, in particular the World Health Organization, to address the role and responsibility of medical and other health personnel in the documentation and prevention of torture and other cruel, inhuman or degrading treatment or punishment;

(*c*) To respond effectively to credible and reliable information submitted to their attention regarding alleged cases of the active or passive participation of medical and other health personnel in torture and other cruel, inhuman or degrading treatment or punishment;

(*d*) To consider including in their reports submitted to the Council information on the problem of medical and other health personnel's participation in torture and other cruel, inhuman or degrading treatment or punishment;

16. *Also requests* States to cooperate fully and in good faith with the relevant special procedures;

17. *Calls upon* the Office of the United Nations High Commissioner for Human Rights to continue to provide advisory services to States for the prevention of torture and cruel, inhuman or degrading treatment or punishment, including concerning tools such as the Principles on the Effective Investigation and Documentations of Torture and other Cruel, Inhuman or Degrading Treatment or Punishment for the investigation of alleged cases of torture;

18. *Takes note* of the report of the Special Rapporteur (A/HRC/10/44).

SOURCE: U.N. Human Rights Council: Resolution on Torture and other Cruel, Inhuman, or Degrading Treatment or Punishment. March 2009. http://blog.unwatch.org/wp-content/uploads/2009/03/march-hrc-torture.pdf

READING 2

Careful Training Creates Soldiers Who Torture

Most defy sadistic stereotype.

Torturers are made, not born. That was the finding of a Greek psychology professor who studied the military regime that came to power in Greece after a 1967 coup.

Until it fell in 1974, the dictatorship carefully trained soldiers to gather information and squelch dissent through torture. That's when Professor Mika Haritos-Fatouros tried to understand how the soldiers had been turned into torturers. In one of the most in-depth studies of torturers ever conducted, she interviewed 16 former soldiers and reviewed the testimony of 21 others and their victims.[1]

Many of her interviewees defy the stereotype of sadistic men who take pleasure in abuse. Haritos-Fatouros found that the torturers were simply plucked from the ranks of ordinary soldiers and trained. One, from a farm family, was a 33-year-old high school teacher married with two children by the time Haritos-Fatouros interviewed him. But for 18 months he had tortured prisoners and ordered others to do so.

The army sought young recruits from rural, conservative families who were physically healthy, of normal intelligence, conformist in nature and compliant. They underwent three months of intensive "training," during which they were broken down physically and mentally — a process that began almost before they arrived at the training facility. The abuse of the torturers-in-training intensified during the subsequent weeks as they were allowed little sleep and ordered to run or hop everywhere they went.

The aim "was to minimize all resistance by instilling in the cadets the habit of obeying without question an order without logic," Haritos-Fatouros wrote.[2] In short, they were programmed to blindly obey authority and dehumanize their victims.

Gradually, they were desensitized to torture. First, they participated in group beatings. One of the torturers said the first time he participated in a group beating he went to his cousin's house and cried. But it got easier each time, he said. Later, they ratcheted up to inflicting electric shocks and other serious abuse.

The underlying goal, Haritos-Fatouros concluded, was making the torturers believe they were "not, in fact, inflicting a savage and horrifying violation upon another human being."

"They brainwashed us," one torturer said. "It was only later we realized that what we did was inhuman. It was only after I finished my military service that it occurred to me that most of us beat up prisoners because we'd been beaten up ourselves."[3]

Another torturer told her, "When I tortured, basically, I felt it was my duty. A lot of the time I found myself repeating the phrases I'd heard in the lessons, like 'bloody communists' and so on. I think I became worse as time went on. I became more a part of the system. I believed in the whole system."[4]

Haritos-Fatouros' chilling conclusion: "We are all, under the right conditions, capable of becoming torturers."[5]

---

[1] Mika Haritos-Fatouros, The Psychological Origins of Institutionalized Torture (2003).

[2] Ibid., p. 46.

[3] Ibid., p. 95.

[4] Ibid., p. 82.

[5] Ibid., p. 229.

SOURCE: Stern, S. (2007, September 1). Torture debate. *CQ Global Researcher, 1,* 211–236.

READING 3

5 International Treaties Ban Torture

Five International Treaties Ban Torture

Torture has been banned by international treaties since 1948. Key provisions include:

Universal Declaration of Human Rights (1948)

"No one shall be subjected to torture or to cruel, inhuman or degrading treatment or punishment."

*Adopted by the U.N. General Assembly on Dec. 10, 1948, **www.un.org/Overview/rights.html**.*

Third Geneva Convention, Common Article 3 (1949)

Regarding the treatment of civilians and prisoners of war, "the following acts are and shall remain prohibited at any time:

  (a) violence to life and person, in particular murder of all kinds, mutilation, cruel treatment and torture;
  (b) taking of hostages;
  (c) outrages upon personal dignity, in particular humiliating and degrading treatment . . ."

Adopted on Aug. 12, 1949, by the Diplomatic Conference for the Establishment of International Conventions for the Protection of Victims of War, held in Geneva, Switzerland; effective Oct. 21, 1950,
***www.icrc.org/ihl.nsf/0/e160550475c4b133c12563cd0051aa66?OpenDocument**.*

International Covenant on Civil and Political Rights (1966)

Article 7
No one shall be subjected to torture or to cruel, inhuman or degrading treatment or punishment. In particular, no one shall be subjected without his free consent to medical or scientific experimentation.

Article 10
All persons deprived of their liberty shall be treated with humanity and with respect for the inherent dignity of the human person.

*Adopted by the U.N. General Assembly on Dec. 16, 1966, and opened for signature and ratification; became effective on March 23, 1976, **www.unhchr.ch/html/menu3/b/a_ccpr.htm**.*

Protocol Additional to the Geneva Conventions of Aug. 12, 1949, relating to the Protection of Victims of International Armed Conflicts (1977)

Article 75: Fundamental guarantees

1. ". . . persons who are in the power of a Party to the conflict . . . shall be treated humanely in all circumstances and shall enjoy, as a minimum, the protection provided by this Article without any adverse distinction based upon race, colour, sex, language, religion or belief, political or other opinion, national or social origin, wealth, birth or other status, or on any other similar criteria. Each Party shall respect the person, honour, convictions and religious practices of all such persons.

2. The following acts are and shall remain prohibited at any time and in any place whatsoever, whether committed by civilian or by military agents:

  (a) Violence to the life, health, or physical or mental well-being of persons, in particular:
    (i) Murder;
    (ii) Torture of all kinds, whether physical or mental;
    (iii) Corporal punishment; and
    (iv) Mutilation;
  (b) Outrages upon personal dignity, in particular humiliating and degrading treatment, enforced prostitution and any form of indecent assault;
  (c) The taking of hostages;
  (d) Collective punishments; and
  (e) Threats to commit any of the foregoing acts."

*Adopted by the Diplomatic Conference on the Reaffirmation and Development of International Humanitarian Law applicable in Armed Conflicts on June 8, 1977; became effective on Dec. 7, 1979, **www.unhchr.ch/html/menu3/b/93.htm**.*

Convention Against Torture and other Cruel, Inhuman or Degrading Treatment or Punishment (1984)

Article 1

". . . the term 'torture' means any act by which severe pain or suffering, whether physical or mental, is intentionally inflicted on a person for such purposes as obtaining from him or a third person information or a confession, punishing him for an act he or a third person has committed or is suspected of having committed, or intimidating or coercing him or a third person, or for any reason based on discrimination of any kind, . . .

Article 2

1. Each State Party shall take effective legislative, administrative, judicial or other measures to prevent acts of torture in any territory under its jurisdiction.
2. No exceptional circumstances whatsoever, whether a state of war or a threat of war, internal political instability or any other public emergency, may be invoked as a justification of torture.
3. An order from a superior officer or a public authority may not be invoked as a justification of torture.

Article 3

1. No State Party shall expel, return ("refouler") or extradite a person to another State where there are substantial grounds for believing that he would be in danger of being subjected to torture.
2. For the purpose of determining whether there are such grounds, the competent authorities shall take into account all relevant considerations including, where applicable, the existence in the State concerned of a consistent pattern of gross, flagrant or mass violations of human rights."

*Adopted by the U.N. General Assembly on Dec. 10, 1984, and opened for signature and ratification; became effective on June 26, 1987, **www.unhchr.ch/html/menu3/b/h_cat39.htm**.*

SOURCE: Stern, S. (2007, September 1). Torture debate. *CQ Global Researcher, 1,* 211–236.

READING 4

Is Torture Ever Justified: 2 Views

Mirko Bagaric

Professor of Law, Deakin University Melbourne, Australia

Written for *CQ Global Researcher*, August 2007

Despite its pejorative overtone, we should never say never to torture. Torture is bad. Killing innocent people is worse. Some people are so depraved they combine these evils and torture innocent people to death. Khalid Shaikh Mohammed, who is still gloating about personally beheading American journalist Daniel Pearl with his "blessed right hand," is but just one exhibit.

Torture opponents must take responsibility for the murder of innocent people if they reject torture if it is the only way to save innocent lives. We are responsible not only for what we do but also for the things we can, but fail, to prevent.

Life-saving torture is not cruel. It is morally justifiable because the right to life of innocent people trumps the physical integrity of wrongdoers. Thus, torture has the same moral justification as other practices in which we sacrifice the interests of one person for the greater good. A close analogy is life-saving organ and tissue transplants. Kidney and bone marrow transplants inflict high levels of pain and discomfort on donors, but their pain is normally outweighed by the benefit to the recipient.

Such is the case with life-saving compassionate torture. The pain inflicted on the wrongdoer is manifestly outweighed by the benefit from the lives saved. The fact that wrongdoers don't consent to their mistreatment is irrelevant. Prisoners and enemy soldiers don't consent to being incarcerated or shot at, yet we're not about to empty our prisons or stop trying to kill enemy soldiers.

Most proponents of banning torture say it does not produce reliable information. Yet there are countless counter-examples. Israeli authorities claim to have foiled 90 terrorist attacks by using coercive interrogation. In more mundane situations, courts across the world routinely throw out confessions that are corroborated by objective evidence because they were only made because the criminals were beaten up.

It is also contended that life-saving torture will lead down the slippery slope of other cruel practices. This is an intellectually defeatist argument. It tries to move the debate from what is on the table (life-saving torture) to situations where torture is used for reasons of domination and punishment — which is never justifiable.

Fanatics who oppose torture in all cases are adopting their own form of extremism. It is well-intentioned, but extremism in all its manifestations can lead to catastrophic consequences. Cruelty that is motivated by misguided kindness hurts no less.

Sune Segal

Head of Communications Unit, International Rehabilitation Council for Torture Victims, Copenhagen, Denmark

Written for *CQ Global Researcher*, August 2007

Taking a utilitarian "greater good" approach in the wake of 9/11/2001, some scholars argue that torture is justified if used to prevent large-scale terror attacks. That argument rests on several flawed assumptions.

The claim that torture — or what is now euphemistically referred to as "enhanced interrogation techniques" — extracts reliable information is unfounded. The 2006 U.S. Army Field Manual states that "the use of force . . . yields unreliable results [and] may damage subsequent collection efforts." As laid out in a recent Vanity Fair article, it was humane treatment — not torture — of a detainee that led to the arrest of alleged 9/11 mastermind Khalid Shaikh Mohammed. In the same article, a U.S. Air Force Reserve colonel and expert in human-intelligence operations, drives home the point: "When [CIA psychologists argue that coercive interrogation] can make people talk, I have one question: 'About what?' "

But even if torture did "work," is it justified when a suspect is in custody and presumed to possess information about an imminent attack likely to kill thousands of people?

No, for several reasons. First, the above scenario assumes the person in custody has the pertinent information — a presumption that is never foolproof. Thus, by allowing torture there would be cases in which innocent detainees would be at risk of prolonged torture because they would not possess the desired information.

Second, it might be argued that mere circumstantial evidence suggesting the detainee is the right suspect is enough to justify torture or that torturing a relative into revealing the suspect's whereabouts is acceptable.

Third, if one form of torture — such as "waterboarding" — is allowed to preserve the "greater good," where do we go if it doesn't work? To breaking bones? Ripping out nails? Torturing the suspect's 5-year-old daughter?

Fourth, torture is not a momentary infliction of pain. In most cases the victim — innocent or guilty — is marked for life, as is the torturer. As a former CIA officer and friend of one of Mohammed's interrogators told The New Yorker in an Aug. 13, 2007, article: "[My friend] has horrible nightmares. . . . When you cross over that line, it's hard to come back. You lose your soul."

That's why we refrain from torture: to keep our souls intact. Torture is the hallmark of history's most abhorrent regimes and a violation of civilized values. Taking the "greater good" approach to torture is intellectually and morally bankrupt.

SOURCE: Stern, S. (2007, September 1). Torture debate. *CQ Global Researcher, 1,* 211–236.

References

Acuff, C., Bennett, B. E., Bricklin, P. M., Canter, M. B., Knapp, S. J., & Moldawsky, S. (1999). Considerations for ethical practice in managed care. *Professional Psychology: Research and Practice, 30,* 563–565.

Adkins, D. C. (1952). Proceedings of the sixteenth annual business meeting of the American Psychological Association, Inc., Washington, DC. *American Psychologist, 7,* 645–670.

Age Discrimination in Employment Amendments of 1996, Pub. L. No. 104–208, div. A, title I, §101(a) [title I, §119], 110 Stat. 3009 (1996).

Alleman, J. R. (2002). Online counseling: The Internet and mental health treatment. *Psychotherapy: Theory, Research & Practice, 39,* 199–209.

Althouse, R. (2000). Standards for psychological services in jails, prisons, correctional facilities, and agencies. *Criminal Justice & Behavior, 27,* 433–494.

American Academy of Clinical Neuropsychology. (2001). Policy statement on the presence of third party observers in neuropsychological assessments. *The Clinical Neuropsychologists, 15,* 433–439.

American Academy of Clinical Neuropsychology. (2003). Official position of the American Academy of Clinical Neuropsychology on ethical complaints made against clinical neuropsychologists during adversarial proceedings. *The Clinical Neuropsychologist, 17,* 443–445.

American Association of Correctional Psychology (AACP). (2000). U.S. standards for psychology services in jails, prisons, correctional facilities, and agencies. *Criminal Justice & Behavior, 27,* 433–494.

American Educational Research Association (AERA), American Psychological Association, & National Council on Measurement in Education. (1999). *Standards for educational and psychological testing.* Washington, DC: American Educational Research Association.

American Psychiatric Association. (2000). *Diagnostic and statistical manual of mental disorders* (4th ed., text rev.). Washington, DC: Author.

American Psychiatric Association. (2003). *Practice guidelines for the assessment and treatment of patients with suicidal behavior.* Washington, DC: Author.

American Psychiatric Association & American Psychological Association. (1985). *Against torture: Joint resolution of the American Psychiatric Association and the American Psychological Association.* Retrieved August 26, 2008, from http://www.psych.org/Departments/EDU/Library/APAOfficialDocumentsandRelated/PositionStatements/198506.aspx

American Psychological Association. (1981). Ethical principles of psychologists. *American Psychologist, 36,* 633–638.

American Psychological Association. (1992). Ethical principles of psychologists and code of conduct. *American Psychologist, 47,* 1597–1611.

American Psychological Association. (1993). Guidelines for providers of psychological services to ethnic, linguistic, and culturally diverse populations. *American Psychologist, 48,* 45–48.

American Psychological Association. (1994). Guidelines for child custody evaluations in divorce proceedings. *American Psychologist, 49,* 677–680.

American Psychological Association. (1995). Report of the Ethics Committee, 1994. *American Psychologist, 50,* 706–713.

American Psychological Association. (1996). Report of the Ethics Committee, 1995. *American Psychologist, 51,* 1279–1286.

American Psychological Association. (2000). Guidelines for psychotherapy with lesbian, gay, & bisexual clients. *American Psychologist, 55,* 1440–1451.

American Psychological Association. (2001). *Publication manual of the American Psychological Association* (5th ed.).Washington, DC: Author.

American Psychological Association. (2002a). Criteria for evaluating treatment guidelines. *American Psychologist, 57,* 1052–1059.

American Psychological Association. (2002b). Ethical principles of psychologists and code of conduct. *American Psychologist, 57,* 1060–1073.

American Psychological Association. (2003). Guidelines on multicultural education, training, research, practice, and organizational change for psychologists. *American Psychologist, 58,* 377–402.

American Psychological Association. (2006). *Editor's handbook: Operating procedures and policies for APA publications.* Retrieved March 13, 2008, from http://www.apa.org/journals/authors/pubmed-deposit .html (Handbook available by request from http://www.apa.org/about/division/chapter8.html)

American Psychological Association. (2007a). Guidelines for education and training at the doctoral and postdoctoral levels in consulting psychology/organizational consulting psychology. *American Psychologist, 62,* 980–992.

American Psychological Association. (2007b). Guidelines for psychological practice with girls and women. *American Psychologist, 62,* 949–979.

American Psychological Association. (2007c). Record keeping guidelines. *American Psychologist, 62,* 992–1004.

American Psychological Association. (2007d, August 16). *Resolution on religious, religion-based, and/or religion-derived prejudice.* Retrieved April 15, 2008, from http://www.apa.org/pi/religious_discrimi nation_resolution.pdf

American Psychological Association. (2010a). *Ethical Principles of Psychologists and Code of Conduct with the 2010 amendments.* Retrieved June 3, 2010, from http://www.apa.org/ethics/code/index.aspx

American Psychological Association. (2010b). *American Psychological Association amends Ethics Code to address potential conflicts among professional ethics, legal authority and organizational demands.* Retrieved June 3, 2010, from http://www.apa.org/news/press/releases/2010/02/ethics-code.aspx

American Psychological Association Committee on Animal Research and Ethics. (1996). *Guidelines for ethical conduct in the care and use of animals* [Brochure]. Retrieved October 2, 2002, from http://www.apa.org/science/anguide.html

American Psychological Association Committee on Legal Issues. (2006). Strategies for private practitioners coping with subpoenas or compelled testimony for client records or test data. *Professional Psychology: Research and Practice, 37,* 215–222.

American Psychological Association Council of Representatives. (1986). *American Psychological Association resolution against torture.* Retrieved February 21, 2008, from http://www.apa.org/ about/division/cpminternatl.html#3

American Psychological Association Council of Representatives. (2006). *The resolution against torture and other cruel, inhuman, and degrading treatment or punishment.* Retrieved February 21, 2008, from http://www.apa.org/governance/resolutions/notortureres.html

American Psychological Association Practice Directorate and the American Psychological Association Insurance Trust. (2002). *Getting ready for HIPAA: What you need to know now.* Washington, DC: American Psychological Association.

American Psychological Association Presidential Task Force. (2005, February). *The report of the Presidential Task Force on Psychological Ethics and National Security (PENS).* Washington, DC: American Psychological Association. Retrieved February 21, 2008, from http://www.apa.org/ releases/PENSTaskForceReportFinal.pdf

Americans with Disabilities Act of 1990 (ADA), Pub. L. No. 101–336, 104 Stat. 327, codified at 42 U.S.C. §12101 *et seq.* (1990).

Andberg, M. M. (2004, August). *Caught in the middle: Ethical/legal mandates and test security.* Paper presented at the annual meeting of the American Psychological Association, Honolulu, HI. Retrieved June 18, 2008, from www.caveon.com/ethical.pdf

Anderson, S. K., & Kitchener, K. S. (1996). Nonromantic, nonsexual posttherapy relationships between psychologists and former clients: An exploratory study of critical incidents. *Professional Psychology: Research and Practice, 27,* 59–66.

Anno, B. J. (2001). National correctional health standards. In J. B. Ashford, B. D. Sales, & W. H. Reid (Eds.), *Treating adult and juvenile offender with special needs* (pp. 31–49). Thousand Oaks, CA: Sage.

Appelbaum, P. S., & Grisso, T. (2001). *MacArthur Competence Assessment Tool for Clinical Research (MacCAT-CR).* Sarasota, FL: Professional Resource Press.

Appelbaum, P. S., Grisso, T., Frank, E., O'Donnell, S., & Kupfer, D. J. (1999). Competence of depressed patients for consent to research. *American Journal of Psychiatry, 156,* 1380–1384.

Appelbaum, P. S., Lidz, W. L., & Grisso, T. (2004). Therapeutic misconception in clinical research: Frequency and risk factors. *IRB: Ethics & Human Research, 26*, 1–8.

Appelbaum, P. S., & Rosenbaum, A. (1989). *Tarasoff* and the researcher: Does the duty to protect apply in the research setting? *American Psychologist, 44*, 885–894.

Appelbaum, P. S., Roth, L. H., & Lidz, C. (1982). The therapeutic misconception: Informed consent in psychiatric research. *International Journal of Law and Psychiatry, 5*, 319–329.

Arredondo, P. (1999). Multicultural competencies as tools to address oppression and racism. *Journal of Counseling and Development, 77*, 102–108.

Baier, A. (1985). What do women want in a moral theory? *Nous, 19*, 53–63.

Barak, A., & English, N. (2002). Prospects and limitations of psychological testing on the Internet. *Journal of Technology in Human Services, 19*, 65–89.

Barnett, J. E., Cornish, J. A. E., Goodyear, R. K., & Lichtenberg, J. W. (2007). Commentaries on the ethical and effective practice of clinical supervision. *Professional Psychology: Research & Practice, 38*, 268–275.

Barnett, J. E., & Hillard, D. (2001). Psychologist distress and impairment: The availability, nature, and use of colleague assistance programs for psychologists. *Professional Psychology: Research and Practice, 32*, 205–210.

Bartoli, E. (2007). Religious and spiritual issues in psychotherapy practice: Training the trainer. *Psychotherapy: Theory, Research, Practice, Training, 44*, 54–65.

Baumrind, D. (1985). Research using intentional deception: Ethical issues revisited. *American Psychologist, 40*, 165–174.

Beauchamp, T. L., & Childress, J. F. (2001). *Principles of biomedical ethics* (5th ed.). New York: Oxford University Press.

Beck, A. T., Steer, R. A., & Brown, G. K. (1996). *The Beck Depression Inventory—second edition (BDI-II).* San Antonio, TX: Psychological Corporation.

Begley, A. M. (2006). Facilitating the development of moral insight in practice: Teaching ethics and teaching virtue. *Nursing Philosophy, 7*, 257–265.

Belter, R. W., & Grisso, T. (1984). Children's recognition of rights violations in counseling. *Professional Psychology: Research & Practice, 15*, 899–910.

Bennett, B. E., Bricklin, P. M., Harrism, E., Knapp, S., VandeCreek, L., & Younggren, J. N. (2006). *Assessing and managing risk in psychological practice: An individualized approach.* Rockville, MD: The Trust.

Ben-Porath, Y. S. (1994). The ethical dilemma of coached malingering research. *Psychological Assessment, 6*, 14–15.

Bernard, J. M., & Goodyear, R. K. (2004). *Fundamentals of clinical supervision* (3rd ed.). New York: Allyn & Bacon.

Berry, D. T. R., Lamb, G. L., Wetter, M. W., Baier, R. A., & Widiger, T. A. (1994). Ethical considerations in research on coached malingering. *Psychological Assessment, 6*, 16–17.

Bersoff, D. N. (1976). Therapists as protectors and policemen: New roles as a result of *Tarasoff? Professional Psychology: Research and Practice, 7*, 267–273.

Bersoff, D. N. (1994). Explicit ambiguity: The 1992 ethics code as an oxymoron. *Professional Psychology: Research and Practice, 25*, 382–387.

Bersoff, D. N., & Hofer, P. J. (1991). *Legal issues in computerized psychological testing: The computer and the decision-making process.* Mahwah, NJ: Lawrence Erlbaum.

Bixler, R., & Seeman, J. (1946). Suggestions for a code of ethics for consulting psychologists. *Journal of Abnormal Psychology, 41*, 486–490.

Blau, T. J. (1984). Psychological tests in the courtroom. *Professional Psychology: Research & Practice, 47*, 176–186.

Bluebond-Langner, M., DiCicco, A., & Belasco, J. (2005). Involving children with life-shortening illnesses in decisions about participation in clinical research: A proposal for shuttle diplomacy and negotiation. In E. Kodish (Ed.), *Ethics and research with children: A case-based approach* (pp. 323–343). New York: Oxford University Press.

Bongar, B., Beutler, L., Zimbardo, P., Breckenridge, J., Brown, L., Sullivan, G., et al. (2002). *Behavioral emergencies update: Psychology & terrorism.* Retrieved August 26, 2008, from http://topmdi.com/cerita/war/Psychology.of.Terrorism.pdf

Bordnick, P. S., Elkins, R. L., Orr, T. Edward, Walters, P., & Thyer, B. A. (2004). Evaluating the relative effectiveness of three aversion therapies designed to reduce craving among cocaine abusers. *Behavioral Interventions, 19*, 1–24.

Brabeck, M. (Ed.). (2000). *Practicing feminist ethics in psychology.* Washington, DC: American Psychological Association.

Braun, S. A., & Cox, J. A. (2005). Managed mental health care: Intentional misdiagnosis of mental disorders. *Journal of Counseling and Development, 83,* 425–433.

Brodsky, S. L., & Galloway, V. A. (2003). Ethical and professional demands for forensic mental health professionals in the post-Atkins era. *Ethics & Behavior, 13,* 3–9.

Broome, M. E., Kodish, E., Geller, G., & Siminoff, L. A. (2003). Children in research: New perspectives and practices for informed consent. *IRB: Ethics & Human Research, 25*(Suppl. 5), S20–S25.

Brotman, L. E., Liberi, W. P., & Wasylyshyn, K. M. (1998). Executive coaching: The need for standards of competence. *Consulting Psychology Journal: Practice and Research, 50,* 40–46.

Brown v. Board of Education of Topeka, 347 U.S. 483 (1954) (USSC+).

Brownlee, K. (1996). Ethics in community mental health care: The ethics of non-sexual dual relationships: A dilemma for the rural mental health profession. *Community Mental Health Journal, 32,* 497–503.

Bruzzese, J. M., & Fisher, C. B. (2003). Assessing and enhancing the research consent capacity of children and youth. *Applied Developmental Science, 7,* 13–26.

Buchanan, T. (2002). Online assessment: Desirable or dangerous? *Professional Psychology: Research and Practice, 33,* 138–154.

Buelow, G. D., & Chafetz, M. D. (1996). Proposed ethical practice guidelines for clinical pharmacopsychology: Sharpening a new focus in psychology. *Professional Psychology: Research and Practice, 27,* 53–58.

Burian, B. K., & Slimp, A. O. (2000). Social dual-role relationships during internship: A decision-making model. *Professional Psychology: Research & Practice, 31,* 332–338.

Bush, S. S. (2006). Neurocognitive enhancement: Ethical considerations for an emerging subspeciality. *Applied Neuropsychology, 13,* 125–136.

Bush, S. S., Connell, M. A., & Denney, R. L. (2006). *Ethical practice in forensic psychology: A systematic model for decision-making.* Washington, DC: American Psychological Association.

Butcher, J. N. (2000). Revising psychological tests: Lessons learned from revisions of the MMPI. *Psychological Assessment, 12,* 263–271.

Butcher, J. N., Dahlstrom, W. G., Graham, J. R., Tellegen, A., & Kaemmer, B. (2002). *Minnesota Multiphasic Personality Inventory (MMPI-2): Manual for administration, scoring, and interpretation* (Rev. ed.). Minneapolis: University of Minnesota Press.

Callahan, D. (1982). Should there be an academic code of ethics? *Journal of Higher Education, 53,* 335–344.

Canter, M. B., Bennett, B. E., Jones, S. E., & Nagy, T. F. (1994). *Ethics for psychologists: A commentary on the APA ethics code.* Washington, DC: American Psychological Association.

Carpenter, W. T., Gold, J. M., Lahti, A. C., Queem, C. A., Conley, R. R., Bartko, J. J., et al. (2000). Decisional capacity for informed consent in schizophrenia research. *Archives of General Psychiatry, 57,* 533–538.

Castelnuovo, G., Gaggioli, A., Mantovani, F., & Riva, G. (2003). New and old tools in psychotherapy: The use of technology for the integration of traditional clinical treatments. *Psychotherapy: Theory, Research, Practice, Training, 40,* 33–44.

Cea, C., & Fisher, C. B. (2003). Health care decision-making by adults with mental retardation. *Mental Retardation, 41,* 78–87.

Chafetz, M. D., & Buelow, G. D. (1994). A training model for psychologists with prescription privileges: Clinical pharmacopsychologists. *Professional Psychology: Research and Practice, 25,* 149–153.

Chenneville, T. (2000). HIV, confidentiality, and duty to protect: A decision-making model. *Professional Psychology: Research and Practice, 31,* 661–670.

Child Abuse Prevention and Treatment Act of 1976, P.L. 93–247.

Childs, R. A., & Eyde, L. D. (2002). Assessment training in clinical psychology doctoral programs: What should we teach? *Journal of Personality Assessment, 78,* 130–144.

The Civil Rights Act of 1964, Pub. L. No. 88–352, 42 U.S.C. § 2000d (1964).

Cohen, C. (1986). The case for the use of animals in biomedical research. *New England Journal of Medicine, 315,* 865–870.

Cohen, D. J., & Cicchetti, D. (2006). *Developmental psychopathology.* New York: John Wiley.

Combs, D. R., Penn, D. L., & Fenigstein, A. (2002). Ethnic differences in subclinical paranoia: An expansion of norms of the Paranoia Scale. *Cultural Diversity & Ethnic Minority Psychology, 8,* 248–256.

Committee on Ethical Guidelines for Forensic Psychologists. (1991). Specialty guidelines for forensic psychologists. *Law and Human Behavior, 15,* 655–665.

Committee on Legal Issues. (1996). Strategies for private practitioners coping with subpoenas or compelled testimony for client records or test data. *Professional Psychology: Research and Practice, 27,* 245–251.

Committee on the Revision of the Specialty Guidelines for Forensic Psychology. (2008). *Specialty guidelines for forensic psychology, revised.* Retrieved February 28, 2008, from http://www.ap-ls.org/links/professionalsgfp.html

Cornell University Law School, Legal Information Institute. (2007). *Employment discrimination.* Retrieved March 13, 2008, from http://www.law.cornell.edu/wex/index.php/Employment_discrimination

Council of National Psychological Associations for the Advancement of Ethnic Minority Interests. (2000). *Guidelines for research in ethnic minority communities.* Washington, DC: American Psychological Association.

Daniels, J. A., & Larson, L. M. (2001). The impact of performance feedback on counseling self-efficacy and counselor anxiety. *Counselor Education & Supervision, 41,* 120–130.

Daubert v. Merrell Dow Pharmaceuticals, Inc. 509 U.S. 579 (1993).

De Vries, R., DeBruin, D. A., & Goodgame, A. (2004). Ethics review of social, behavioral and economic research: Where should we go from here? *Ethics & Behavior, 14,* 351–368.

Deidan, C., & Bush, S. S. (2002). Addressing perceived ethical violations by colleagues. In S. S. Bush & M. L. Drexler (Eds.), *Ethical issues in clinical neuropsychology* (pp. 81–305). Lisse, The Netherlands: Swes & Zeitlinger.

DeLeon, P. H., Bennett, B. E., & Bricklin, P. M. (1997). Ethics and public policy formulation: A case example related to prescription privileges. *Professional Psychology: Research and Practice, 28,* 518–525.

Democracy Now. (2007, August). *American Psychological Association rejects blanket ban on participation in interrogation of U.S. detainees.* Retrieved June 28, 2008, from www.democracynow.org/2007/8/20/american_psychological_association_rejects_blanket_ban

Denney, R. L., & Wynkoop, T. F. (2000). Clinical neuropsychology in the criminal forensic setting. *Journal of Head Trauma Rehabilitation, 15,* 804–828.

Department of Health and Human Services. (2003, February 20). Health insurance reform: Security standards; final rule [Rules and Regulations]. *Federal Register, 68,* 8333–8381.

Department of Health and Human Services. (2005, June). *Title 45 Public Welfare, Part 46, Code of Federal Regulations, Protection of Human Subjects.* Washington, DC: Government Printing Office. Retrieved March 11, 2008, from http://www.nihtraining.com/ohsrsite/guidelines/45cfr46.html

Dickens v. Johnson County Board of Education, 661 F.Supp. 155 (E.D. Tenn. 1987).

Dickert, N., & Grady, C. (1999). What's the price of a research subject? Approaches to payment for research participation. *New England Journal of Medicine, 341,* 198–203.

Diedrich, R. C. (2008). Still more about coaching. *Consulting Psychology Journal: Practice and Research, 60,* 4–6.

Dillon, R. (1992). Care and respect. In E. B. Cole & S. Coultrap-McQuin (Eds.), *Explorations in feminist ethics* (pp. 69–81). Bloomington: Indiana University Press.

Donner, M. B.; VandeCreek, L., Gonsiorek, J. C., & Fisher, C. B. (2008). Balancing confidentiality: Protecting privacy and protecting the public. *Professional Psychology: Research and Practice, 39,* 369–376.

DuBois, J. (2006). Is compliance a professional virtue of researchers? Reflections on promoting the responsible conduct of research. *Ethics & Behavior, 14,* 383–395.

Dunn, L. B., Nowrangi, M. A., Palmer, B. A., Jeste, D. V., & Saks, E. R. (2006). Assessing decisional capacity for clinical research or treatment: A review of instruments. *American Journal of Psychiatry, 163,* 1323–1334.

Education for All Handicapped Children Act of 1975, Pub. L. No. 94–142 (1975).

Eissenberg, T., Paniker, S., Berenbaum, S., Epley, N., Fendrich, M., Kelso, R., et al. (2004). *IRBs and psychological science: Ensuring a collaborative relationship.* Retrieved February 21, 2008, from http://www.apa.org/science/rcr/irbs_psychsci.html

Elementary and Secondary Education Act of 1965, Pub. L. 89–10, 79 Stat. 77 (1965).

Elrod, L. D., & Spector, R. G. (2004). A review of the year in family law: Children's issues remain the focus. *Family Law Quarterly, 37,* 527–578.

English, A., & Kenney, K. E. (2003). *State minor consent laws: A summary* (2nd ed.). Chapel Hill, NC: Center for Adolescent Health and the Law.

Equal Employment Opportunity Act of 1972, Pub. L. No. 92–261 (1972).

Everly, G. S., Flannery, R. B., & Mitchell, J. T. (2000). Critical incident stress management (CISM): A review of the literature. *Aggressive Violent Behavior, 5,* 23–40.

Executive Order No. 11246, 3 C.F.R 339 (1964–1965 Compilation).

Falender, C. A., Cornish, J. A., Goodyear, R., Hatcher, R., Kaslow, N. J., Leventhal, G., et al. (2004). Defining competencies in psychology supervision: A consensus statement. *Journal of Clinical Psychology, 60,* 771–787.

Falender, C. A., & Shafranske, E. P. (2007). Competence in competency-based supervision practice: Construct and application. *Professional Psychology: Research & Practice, 38,* 232–240.

False Claims Amendments Act of 1986, 31 U.S.C. § 3701 (1986).

Family and Medical Leave Act of 1993, Pub. L. No. 103–3 (1993).

Family Educational Rights and Privacy Act of 1974 (FERPA), 20 U.S.C. § 1232g; 34 CFR Part 99 (1974).

Ferreri, S. J., Tamm, L., & Wier, K. G. (2006). Using food aversion to decrease severe pica by a child with autism. *Behavior Modification, 30,* 456–471.

Field, M. J., & Behrman, R. E. (Eds.). (2004). *Ethical conduct of clinical research involving children.* Washington, DC: National Academies Press.

Fine, M. A., & Kurdek, L. A. (1993). Reflections on determining authorship credit and authorship order on faculty-student collaborations. *American Psychologist, 48,* 1141–1147.

Fisher, C. B. (1995). American Psychological Association's (1992) ethics code and the validation of child abuse in day-care settings. *Psychology, Public Policy, & Law, 1,* 461–478.

Fisher, C. B. (1999). Relational ethics and research with vulnerable populations. In National Bioethics Advisory Commission (Ed.), *Reports on research involving persons with mental disorders that may affect decision-making capacity* (Vol. 2, pp. 29–49). Rockville, MD: National Bioethics Advisory Commission.

Fisher, C. B. (2000). Relational ethics in psychological research: One feminist's journey. In M. Brabeck (Ed.), *Practicing feminist ethics in psychology* (pp. 125–142). Washington, DC: American Psychological Association.

Fisher, C. B. (2002a). A goodness-of-fit ethic of informed consent. *Urban Law Journal, 30,* 159–171.

Fisher, C. B. (2002b). Respecting and protecting mentally impaired persons in medical research. *Ethics & Behavior, 12,* 279–284.

Fisher, C. B. (2003a). Adolescent and parent perspectives on ethical issues in youth drug use and suicide survey research. *Ethics & Behavior, 13,* 302–331.

Fisher, C. B. (2003b). A goodness-of-fit ethic for informed consent to research involving persons with mental retardation and developmental disabilities. *Mental Retardation and Developmental Disabilities Research Reviews, 9,* 27–31.

Fisher, C. B. (2004). Ethics in drug abuse and related HIV risk research. *Applied Developmental Science, 8,* 90–102.

Fisher, C. B. (2005). Deception research involving children: Ethical practice and paradox. *Ethics & Behavior, 15,* 271–287.

Fisher, C. B., Cea, C. D., Davidson, P. W., & Fried, A. L. (2006). Capacity of persons with mental retardation to consent to participation in randomized clinical trials. *American Journal of Psychiatry, 163,* 1813–1821.

Fisher, C. B., & Fyrberg, D. (1994). Participant partners: College students weigh the costs and benefits of deceptive research. *American Psychologist, 49,* 417–427.

Fisher, C. B., & Goodman, S. J. (in press). Goodness-of-fit ethics for non-intervention research involving dangerous and illegal behaviors. In D. Buchanan, C. B. Fisher, & L. Gable (Eds.), *Ethical and legal issues in research with high risk populations.* Washington, DC: American Psychological Association Press.

Fisher, C. B., Hatashita-Wong, M., & Isman, L. (1999). Ethical and legal issues. In W. K. Silverman & T. H. Ollendick (Eds.), *Developmental issues in the clinical treatment of children and adolescents* (pp. 470–486). Needham Heights, MA: Allyn & Bacon.

Fisher, C. B., Higgins-D'Alessandro, A., Rau, J. M. B., Kuther, T., & Belanger, S. (1996). Reporting and referring research participants: The view from urban adolescents. *Child Development, 67,* 2086–2099.

Fisher, C. B., Hoagwood, K., Duster, T., Frank, D. A., Grisso, T., Macklin, R., et al. (2002). Research ethics for mental health science involving ethnic minority children and youth. *American Psychologist, 57,* 1024–1040.

Fisher, C. B., Hoagwood, K., & Jensen, P. S. (1996). Casebook on ethical issues in research with children and adolescents with mental disorders. In K. Hoagwood, P. S. Jensen, & C. B. Fisher (Eds.), *Ethical issues in mental health research with children and adolescents* (pp. 135–238). Mahwah, NJ: Lawrence Erlbaum.

Fisher, C. B., Kornetsky, S. Z., & Prentice, E. D. (2007). Determining risk in pediatric research with no prospect of direct benefit: Time for a national consensus on the interpretation of federal regulations. *American Journal of Bioethics, 7,* 5–10.

Fisher, C. B., & Masty, J. K. (2006). A goodness-of-fit ethic for informed consent to pediatric cancer research. In R. T. Brown (Ed.), *Comprehensive handbook of childhood cancer and sickle cell disease: A biopsychosocial approach* (pp. 205–217). New York: Oxford University Press.

Fisher, C. B., Oransky, M., Mahadevan, M., Singer, M., Mirhej, G., & Hodge, G. D. (2008). Experimental realism, experimental mistrust and therapeutic misconception in marginalized populations' understanding of drug addiction research. *IRB: Ethics & Human Research, 28,* 1–9.

Fisher, C. B., Oransky, M., Mahadevan, M., Singer, M., Mirhej, G., & Hodge, G. D. (in press). Do drug abuse researchers have a "Duty to Protect" third parties from HIV transmission? Moral perspectives of street drug users. In D. Buchanan, C. B. Fisher, & L. Gable (Eds.), *Ethical and legal responsibilities in research with high-risk populations: Addressing threats of suicide, child abuse, and violence.* Washington, DC: American Psychological Association Press.

Fisher, C. B., & Ragsdale, K. (2006). A goodness-of-fit ethics for multicultural research. In J. Trimble & C. B. Fisher (Eds.), *The handbook of ethical research with ethnocultural populations and communities* (pp. 3–26). Thousand Oaks, CA: Sage.

Fisher, C. B., & Whiting, K. A. (1998). How valid are child sexual abuse validations? In S. J. Ceci & H. Hembrooke (Eds.), *Expert witnesses in child abuse cases: What can and should be said in court* (pp. 159–184). Washington, DC: American Psychological Association.

Fisher, C. B., & Younggren, J. (1997). The value and utility of the APA ethics code. *Professional Psychology: Research and Practice, 28,* 582–592.

Flanagan, J. C. (1954). The critical incident technique. *Psychological Bulletin, 54,* 327–358.

Flowers, B. J., & Davidov, B. J. (2006). The virtue of multiculturalism: Personal transformation, character, and openness to the other. *American Psychologist, 61,* 581–594.

Fox, R. E., Schwelitz, F. D., & Barclay, A. G. (1992). A proposed curriculum for psychopharmacology for professional psychologists. *Professional Psychology: Research and Practice, 23,* 216–219.

Frankel, M. S. (1996). Developing ethical standards for responsible research: Why? Form? Functions? Process? Outcomes? *Journal of Dental Research, 75,* 832–835.

Friedrich, J., & Douglass, D. (1998). Ethics and persuasive enterprise of teaching psychology. *American Psychologist, 53,* 549–562.

Frye v. United States, 293 F. 1013 (54 App. D.C. 1923).

General Electric Co. v. Joiner, 522 U.S. 136 (1997).

Gilligan, C. (1982). *In a different voice.* Cambridge, MA: Harvard University Press.

Ginsberg, K. R., Winn, R. J., Rudy, B. J., Crawford, J., Zhao, H., & Schwarz, D. (2002). How to reach sexual minority youth in the health care setting: The teens offer guidance. *Journal of Adolescent Health, 31,* 407–416.

Gizara, S. S., & Forest, L. (2004). Supervisors' experiences of trainee impairment and incompetence in APA-accredited internship sites. *Professional Psychology: Research and Practice, 3,* 131–140.

Glass, T. A. (1998). Ethical issues in group therapy. In R. M. Anderson, T. L. Needels, & H. V. Hall (Eds.), *Avoiding ethical misconduct in psychology specialty areas* (pp. 95–126). Springfield, IL: Charles C Thomas.

Glosoff, H. L., Herlihy, S. B., Herlihy, B., & Spence, E. B. (1997). Privileged communication in the psychologist-client relationship. *Professional Psychology: Research and Practice, 28,* 573–581.

Gluck, J. P., Bell, J. B., & Pearson-Bish, M. (2003). Confronting ethical issues in the use of animals in biomedical and behavioral research. In W. O'Donohue & K. Ferguson (Eds.), *Handbook of professional ethics for psychologists* (pp. 257–274). Thousand Oaks, CA: Sage.

Goldman, J., & Choy, A. (2001). *Privacy and confidentiality in health research.* Paper commissioned by the National Bioethics Advisory Commission. Retrieved August 26, 2008 from http://govinfo.library.unt.edu/nbac/human/overvol2.html

Goss v. Lopez, 419 U.S. 565 (1975).

Gostin, L. O. (2007). Biomedical research involving prisoners: Ethical values and legal regulation. *Journal of the American Medical Association, 297,* 737–740.

Gottlieb, M. C. (1993). Multiple-role dilemmas for military mental health care providers: Avoiding exploitative dual relationships: A decision-making model. *Psychotherapy, 30,* 41–48.

Gottlieb, M. C., Robinson, K., & Younggren, J. N. (2007). Multiple relations in supervision: Guidance for administrators, supervisors, and students. *Professional Psychology: Research & Practice, 38,* 241–247.

Graham, T. A. (2001). Teaching child development via the Internet: Opportunities and pitfalls. *Teaching Psychology, 28,* 67–71.

Green, R. J., & Mitchell, V. (2002). Gay and lesbian couples in therapy: Homophobia, relational ambiguity, and social support. In A. S. Gurman & N. S. Jacobson (Eds.), *Clinical handbook of couple therapy* (pp. 536–568). New York: Guilford.

Greenberg, S. A., & Shuman, D. W. (1997). Irreconcilable conflict between therapeutic and forensic roles. *Professional Psychology: Research & Practice, 28,* 50–57.

Griggs v. Duke Power, 401 U.S. 424 (1971).

Grisso, T. (2003). *Evaluating competencies* (2nd ed.). New York: Plenum.

Grisso, T., & Appelbaum, P. S. (1998). *Assessing competence to consent to treatment: A guide for physicians and other health professionals.* New York: Oxford University Press.

Grohol, J. H. (2001). *Best practices in e-therapy: Clarifying the definition.* Retrieved March 11, 2008, from http://www.psychcentral.com/best/best3.htm

Grove, W. M., & Barden, R. C. (1999). Protecting the integrity of the legal system: The admissibility of testimony from mental health experts under *Daubert/Kumho* analyses. *Psychology, Public Policy, and Law, 5,* 224–242.

Grove, W. M., Barden, R. C., Garb, H. N., & Lilienfeld, S. O. (2002). Failure of Rorschach-Comprehensive-System-Based Testimony to be admissible under the *Daubert-Joiner-Kumho* Standard. *Psychology, Public Policy, and Law, 8,* 216–234.

Gubi, P. M. (2001). An exploration of the use of Christian prayer in mainstream counseling. *British Journal of Guidance and Counseling, 29,* 425–434.

Gutheil, T. G., & Gabbard, G. O. (1993). The concept of boundaries in clinical practice: Theoretical and risk-management dimensions. *American Journal of Psychiatry, 150,* 188–196.

Gutheil, T. G., & Simon, R. L. (2004). Avoiding bias in expert testimony. *Contemporary Psychiatry, 34,* 260–270.

Haas, L. J., & Cummings, N. A. (1991). Managed outpatient mental health plans: Clinical, ethical, and practical guidelines for participation. *Professional Psychology: Research and Practice, 22,* 45–51.

Hadjistavropoulos, T., & Bieling, P. (2001). File review consultation in the adjudication of mental health and chronic pain disability claims. *Consulting Psychology Journal: Practice and Research, 53,* 52–63.

Haldeman, D. C. (1994). The practice and ethics of sexual orientation conversion therapy. *Journal of Consulting and Clinical Psychology, 62,* 221–227.

Haldeman, D. C. (2004). When sexual and religious orientation collide. *Counseling Psychologist, 32,* 691–715.

Hall, R. C. W., & Hall, R. C. W. (2007). A profile of pedophilia: Definition, characteristics of offenders, recidivism, treatment outcomes, and forensic issues. *Mayo Clinic Proceedings, 82,* 457–471.

Hauerwas, S. (1981). *A community of character.* Notre Dame, IN: University of Notre Dame Press.

Hayes v. Unified School District No. 377, 877 F. 2d 809, 811 (10th Cir. 1989).

Health Insurance Portability and Accountability Act of 1996 (HIPAA), Pub. L. No. 104–191, 110 Stat. 1936 (1996).

Health Research Extension Act of 1985, Pub. L. No. 99–158 (1985).

Heilbrun, K. (2001). *Principles of forensic mental health assessment.* New York: Kluwer Academic/Plenum.

Heinlen, K., Welfel, E. R., Richmond, E. N., & O'Donell, M. D. (2003). The nature, scope, and ethics of psychologists' e-therapy Web sites: What consumers find when surfing the Web. *Psychotherapy, Theory, Research Practice, Training, 40,* 112–124.

Hellkamp, D., & Lewis, J. (1995). The consulting psychologist as an expert witness in sexual harassment and retaliation cases. *Consulting Psychology Journal: Practice and Research, 47,* 150–159.

Helms, J. E. (1993). I also said White racial identity influences White researchers. *The Counseling Psychologist, 21,* 240–243.

Hennan, M. R., Dornbusch, S. M., Herron, M. C., & Herting, J. R. (1997). The influence of family regulation, connection, and psychological autonomy on six measures of adolescent functioning. *Journal of Adolescent Research, 12,* 34–67.

Hess, A. K. (1998). Accepting forensic case referrals: Ethical and professional considerations. *Professional Psychology: Research and Practice, 29,* 109–114.

Hobbs, N. (1948). The development of a code of ethical standards for psychology. *American Psychologist, 3,* 80–84.

Individuals with Disabilities Education Improvement Act of 2004, Pub. L. No. 108–446, 118 Stat. 2647 (2004).

Iverson, G. L. (2006). Ethical issues associated with the assessment of exaggeration, poor effort and malingering. *Applied Neuropsychology, 13,* 77–90.

Jacob, S., & Hartshorne, T. S. (2007). *Ethics and law for school psychologists* (5th ed.). New York: John Wiley.

Jeffrey, T. B., Rankin, R. J., & Jeffrey, L. K. (1992). In service of two masters: The ethical-legal dilemma faced by military psychologists. *Professional Psychology: Research and Practice, 23,* 91–95.

Jerome, L. W. (1998). *Seclusion and restraint: Avoiding ethical misconduct in psychology specialty areas.* Springfield, IL: Charles C Thomas.

Jeste, D. V., & Saks, E. (2006). Decisional capacity in mental illness and substance use disorders: Empirical database and policy implications. *Behavioral Sciences and the Law, 24,* 607–628.

Johnson, W. B. (1995). Perennial ethical quandaries in military psychology: Toward American Psychological Association–Department of Defense collaboration. *Professional Psychology: Research and Practice, 26,* 281–287.

Johnson, W. B. (2004). Rational emotive behavior therapy for disturbance about sexual orientation. In P. S. Richards & A. E. Bergin (Eds.), *Casebook for a spiritual strategy in counseling and psychotherapy* (pp. 247–265). Washington, DC: American Psychological Association.

Johnson, W. B., Bacho, R., Heim, M., & Ralph, J. (2006). Multiple-role dilemmas for military mental health care providers. *Military Medicine, 171,* 311–315.

Johnson, W. B., Redley, C. R., & Nielson, S. L. (2000). Religiously sensitive rational emotive behavior therapy: Elegant solutions and ethical risks. *Professional Psychology: Research & Practice, 31,* 14–20.

Jones, J. H. (1993). *Bad blood: The Tuskegee syphilis experiment* (Rev. ed.). New York: Free Press.

Jordan, A. E., & Meara, N. M. (1990). Ethics and the professional practice of psychologists: The role of virtues and principles. *Professional Psychology: Research and Practice, 21,* 107–114.

Josephson Institute of Ethics. (1999). *Making ethical decisions.* Marina del Rey, CA: Author.

Kaiser Family Foundation. (2001). *Generation Rx.com: How young people use the Internet for health information.* Retrieved March 11, 2008, from http://www.kaisernetwork.org/health_cast/hcast_index.cfm?display=detail&hc=405

Kampa-Kokesch, S., & Anderson, M. Z. (2001). Executive coaching: A comprehensive review of the literature. *Consulting Psychology Journal: Practice and Research, 53,* 205–228.

Kant, I. (1959). *Foundations of the metaphysics of morals.* Indianapolis, IN: Bobbs-Merrill. (Original work published 1785)

Karraker v. Rent-a-Center, 411 F. 3d 831 (7th Cir. 2005).

Kaser-Boyd, N., Adelman, H. S., & Taylor, L. (1985). Minors' ability to identify risks and benefits of therapy. *Professional Psychology: Research and Practice, 16,* 411–417.

Keenan, J. (1995). Proposing cardinal virtues. *Theological Studies, 56,* 709–729.

Kilburg, R .R. (1996). Toward a conceptual understanding and definition of executive coaching. *Consulting Psychology Journal: Practice and Research, 48,* 134–144.

Kitchener, K. S. (1984). Intuition, critical evaluation and ethical principles: The foundation for ethical decisions in counseling psychology. *The Counseling Psychologist, 12,* 43–55.

Klee, C. H., & Friedman, H. J. (2001). Neurolitigation: A perspective on the elements of expert testimony for extending the *Daubert* challenge. *NeuroRehabilitation, 16,* 79–85.

Knapp, S., Gottlieb, M., Berman, J., & Handelsman, M. M. (2007). When laws and ethics collide: What should psychologists do? *Professional Psychology, Research and Practice, 38,* 54–59.

Knapp, S., & VandeCreek, L. (1997). *Jaffee v. Redmond:* The Supreme Court recognizes a psychotherapist-patient privilege in federal courts. *Professional Psychology: Research and Practice, 28,* 567–572.

Knapp, S., & VandeCreek, L. (2003). Legal and ethical issues in billing patients and collecting fees. *Psychotherapy: Theory Research, Practice, Training, 30,* 25–31.

Knight, G. P., & Hill, N. E. (1998). Measurement equivalence in research involving minority adolescents. In V. C. McLoyd & L. Steinberg (Eds.), *Studying minority adolescents: Conceptual, methodological, and theoretical issues* (pp. 183–211). Mahwah, NJ: Lawrence Erlbaum.

Koocher, G. P. (2006, February 2). Speaking against torture: President's column. *Monitor on Psychology, 37,* 5. Retrieved February 28, 2008, from http://www.apa.org/monitor/feb06/pc.html

Koocher, G. P., & Keith-Spiegel, P. (1998). *Ethics in psychology: Professional standards and cases* (2nd ed.). New York: Oxford University Press.

Krauss, D., & Lieberman, H. (2007). Expert testimony on risk and future dangerousness. In M. Costano, D. Krauss, & K. Pezdek (Eds.), *Expert psychological testimony for the courts* (pp. 227–250). Mahwah, NJ: Lawrence Erlbaum.

Krauss, D. A., & Sales, D. B. (2000). Legal standards, expertise and experts in the resolution of contested child custody cases. *Psychology, Public Policy, and Law, 6,* 843–879.

Krivacska, J. J., & Margolis, H. (1995, Summer). The special education consultant in due process hearings: Ethics and expertise. *Consulting Psychologist Journal: Practice and Research,* pp. 173–183.

Kuehnle, K., & Sparta, S. N. (2006). Assessing child sexual abuse allegations. In S. N. Sparta & G. P. Koocher (Eds.), *Forensic mental health assessment of children and adolescents* (pp. 129–148). New York: Oxford University Press.

Kumho Tire Co., Ltd. v. Carmichael, 119 S. Ct. 1167 (March 23, 1999). 119 S. Ct. 1167; 143 L. Ed. 2d 238 (1999).

Lakin, M. (1994). Morality in group and family therapies: Multiperson therapies and the 1992 ethics code. *Professional Psychology: Research and Practice, 25,* 344–348.

Lamb, D. H., & Catanzaro, S. J. (1998). Sexual and nonsexual boundary violations involving psychologists, clients, supervisees, and students: Implications for professional practice. *Professional Psychology: Research and Practice, 29,* 498–503.

Lang, S. (1993). Questions of scientific responsibility: The Baltimore case. *Ethics & Behavior, 3,* 3–72.

Larrabee, G. J. (2007). *Assessment of malingered neuropsychological deficits.* New York: Oxford University Press.

Latane, B., & Darley, J. M. (1970). *The unresponsive bystander: Why doesn't he help?* New York: Appleton-Century-Crofts.

Lease, S. H., Horne, S. G., & Noffsinger-Frazier, N. (2005). Affirming faith experiences and psychological health for Caucasian lesbian, gay and bisexual individuals. *Journal of Counseling Psychology, 52,* 378–388.

Leigh, I. W., Corbett, C. A., Gutman, V., & Morere, D. A. (1996). Providing psychological services to deaf individuals: A response to new perceptions of diversity. *Professional Psychology: Research and Practice, 27,* 364–371.

Lemoire, S. J., & Chen, C. P. (2005). Applying person-centered counseling to sexual minority adolescents. *Journal of Counseling & Development, 83,* 146–154.

Levant, R. (2005). *Report of the 2005 Presidential Task Force on Evidence-Based Practice.* Washington, DC: American Psychological Association.

Liss, M. (1994). State and federal laws governing reporting for researchers. *Ethics & Behavior, 4,* 133–146.

Lowman, R. L. (Ed.). (2006). *The ethical practice of psychology in organizations* (2nd ed.). Washington, DC: American Psychological Association and the Society for Industrial and Organizational Psychology, Inc.

Lyon, A. R., & Cotler, S. (2007). Toward reduced bias and increased utility in the assessment of school refusal behavior: The case for diverse samples and evaluations of context. *Psychology in the Schools, 44,* 551–565.

MacIntyre, A. (1984). *After virtue* (2nd ed.). Notre Dame, IN: University of Notre Dame Press.

MacIntyre, A. (1989). *Whose justice? Which rationality?* Notre Dame, IN: University of Notre Dame Press.

Macklin, R. (1981). 'Due' and 'undue' inducements: On paying money to research subjects. *Ethics and Human Research, 3,* 1–6.

Macklin, R. (1999). *Against relativism: Cultural diversity and the search for ethical universals in medicine.* New York: Oxford University Press.

Maheu, M. M. (2001). *Exposing the risk, yet moving forward: A behavioral e-health model.* Retrieved August 26, 2008 from http://www3.interscience.wiley.com/cgi-bin/fulltext/120837826/HTMLSTART

Maheu, M. M., & Gordon, B. L. (2000). Counseling and therapy on the Internet. *Professional Psychology: Research and Practice, 31,* 484–489.

Mangione, L., Forti, R., & Iacuzzi, C. M. (2007). Ethics and endings in group psychotherapy: Saying good-bye and saying it well. *International Journal of Group Psychotherapy, 57,* 25–40.

Margolin, G. (1982). Ethical and legal considerations in marital and family therapy. *American Psychologist, 37,* 788–801.

Martelli, M. F., Bush, S. S., & Sasler, N. D. (2003). Identifying, avoiding, and addressing ethical misconduct in neuropsychological medicolegal practice. *International Journal of Forensic Psychology, 1,* 26–44.

Masty, J., & Fisher, C. B. (2008). A goodness of fit approach to parent permission and child assent pediatric intervention research. *Ethics & Behavior, 18,* 139–160.

May, W. F. (1984). The virtues in a professional setting. *Soundings, 67,* 245–266.

McAllister, P. H. (1991). Overview of state legislation to regulate standardized testing. *Educational Measurement: Issues and Practice, 10,* 19–22.

Melton, G. (1990). Ethical dilemmas in playing by the rules: Applied developmental research and the law. In C. B. Fisher & W. W. Tryon (Eds.), *Ethics in applied developmental psychology: Emerging issues in an emerging field* (pp. 145–161). Norwood, NJ: Ablex.

Mental Health and Developmental Disabilities Confidentiality Act of 1979, 740 Ill. Comp. Stat. 110/1 *et seq.* (1979).

Mill, J. S. (1957). *Utilitarianism.* New York: Bobbs-Merrill. (Original work published 1861)

Miller, F. G., & Emanuel, E. J. (2008). Quality-improvement research and informed consent. *New England Journal of Medicine, 358,* 765-767.

Mitchell, C. W., Disque, J. G., & Robertson, P. (2002). When parents want to know: Responding to parental demands for confidential information. *Professional School Counseling, 6,* 156–161.

Mittal, D., Palmer, B. W., Dunn, L. B., Landes, R., Ghormley, C., Beck, C., et al. (2007). Comparison of two enhanced consent procedures for patients with mild Alzheimer disease or mild cognitive impairment. *American Journal of Geriatric Psychiatry, 15,* 163–168.

Moberg, P. J., & Kniele, K. (2006). Evaluation of competency: Ethical considerations for neuropsychologists. *Applied Neuropsychology, 13,* 101–114.

Mohatt, G. V., & Thomas, L.R. (2006). "I wonder, why would you do it that way?" Ethical dilemmas in doing participatory research with Alaska Native communities. In J. E. Trimble & C. B. Fisher (Eds.), *The handbook of ethical research with ethnocultural populations and communities* (pp. 93–116). Thousand Oaks, CA: Sage.

Monshi, B., & Zieglmayer, V. (2004). The problem of privacy in transcultural research: Reflections on an ethnographic study in Sri Lanka. *Ethics & Behavior, 14,* 305–312.

Morris, R. J., & Mather, N. (Eds.). (2007). *Evidence-based interventions for students with learning and behavioral challenges.* Oxford, UK: Taylor & Francis.

Munsey, C. (2007). *Stay involved or get out? Monitor on psychology, 38.* Retrieved June 27, 2008, from www.apa.org/monitor/oct07/stayinvolved.html

National Academy of Neuropsychology Policy and Planning Committee. (2000). Presence of third party observers during neuropsychological testing: Official statement of the National Academy of Neuropsychology. *Archives of Clinical Neuropsychology, 15,* 379–380.

National Academy of Neuropsychology Policy and Planning Committee. (2003). *Test security: An update. Official statement of the National Academy of Neuropsychology.* Retrieved August 26, 2008 http://www.nanonline.org/NAN/Files/PAIC/PDFs/NANTestSecurityUpdate.pdf

National Academy of Sciences. (1995). *On being a scientist: Responsible conduct in research.* Washington, DC: National Academy Press.

National Association of School Psychologists. (2000). Principles for professional ethics: Guidelines for the provision of school psychological services. In *Professional conduct manual for school psychology* (pp. 13–62). Bethesda, MD: Author. Retrieved November 30, 2007, http://www.nasponline.org/standards/ProfessionalCond.pdf

National Bioethics Advisory Committee (NBAC). (2001). *Ethical and policy issues in international research: Clinical trials in developing countries* (Vol. 1). Retrieved March 11, 2008, from http://www.bioethics.gov/reports/past_commissions/nbac_international.pdf

National Research Council (NRC). (2003). *Protecting participants and facilitating social and behavioral sciences research.* Washington, DC: National Academies Press.

Nedopil, N. (2002). The boundaries of courtroom experience. *Journal of Forensic Psychiatry & Psychology, 13,* 494–498.

Needleman, H. M. (1993). Reply to Ernhart, Scarr, and Geneson. *Ethics & Behavior, 3,* 95–101.

Newman, J. L., Gray, E. A., & Fuqua, D. R. (1996). Beyond ethical decision making. *Consulting Psychology Journal: Practice and Research, 48,* 230–236.

Newport-Mesa Unified School District v. State of California Department of Education, 371 F. Supp. 2d 1170 (C.D. Cal. 2005).

Nickelson, D.W. (1998). Telehealth and the evolving health care system: Strategic opportunities for professional psychology. *Professional Psychology: Research and Practice, 29,* 527–535.

No Child Left Behind Act of 2001, Pub. L. No. 107–110, 115 Stat. 1425 (2001).

Noe, T. D., Manson, S. M., Croy, C. D., McGough, H., Henderson, J. A., & Buchwald, D. S. (2006). In their own voices: American Indian decisions to participate in health research. In J. E. Trimble & C. B. Fisher (Eds.), *Handbook of ethical research with ethnocultural populations and communities* (pp. 93–116). Thousand Oaks, CA: Sage.

Norris, D. M., Gutheil, T. G., & Strasburger, L. H. (2003). This couldn't happen to me: Boundary problems and sexual misconduct in the psychotherapy relationship. *Psychiatric Services, 54,* 517–522.

The Nuremberg Code. (1949). In A. Mitscherlich & F. Mielke (Eds.), *Doctors of infamy: The story of the Nazi medical crimes* (pp. xxiii–xxv). New York: Schuman.

Oberlander, S. E., & Barnett, J. E. (2005). Multiple relationships between graduate assistants and students: Ethical and practical considerations. *Ethics & Behavior, 15,* 49–63.

O'Connor, M. F. (2001). On the etiology and effective management of professional distress and impairment among psychologists. *Professional Psychology: Research and Practice, 32,* 345–350.

Oetzel, K. B., & Scherer, D. G. (2003). Therapeutic engagement with adolescents in psychotherapy. *Psychotherapy: Theory, Research, Practice, Training, 40,* 215–225.

Office for Protection From Research Risks, Department of Health and Human Services, National Institutes of Health. (1993). *Protecting human research subjects: Institutional review board guidebook.* Washington, DC: Government Printing Office.

Okorodudu, C., Strickland, W. J., Van Hoorn, J. L., & Wiggins, E. C. (2007). A call to action: APA's 2007 Resolution Against Torture. *Monitor on Psychology, 38,* 2.

Olivieri, N. (2003). Patients' health or company profits? The commercialization of academic research. *Science & Engineering Ethics, 9,* 29–41.

Olson, B., & Soldz, S. (2007). Positive illusions and the necessity of a bright line forbidding psychologist involvement in detainee interrogations. *Analyses of Social Issues and Public Policy, 7,* 1–10.

Olson, B., Soldz, S., & Davis, M. (2008). The ethics of interrogation and the American Psychological Association: A critique of policy and process. *Philosophy, Ethics, and Humanities in Medicine, 3,* 3. Retrieved June 28, 2008, from http://www.peh-med.com/content/3/1/3

Oransky, M., Fisher, C. B, Mahadevan, M., & Singer, M. (in press). Barriers and opportunities for recruitment for non-intervention studies on HIV risk: Perspectives of street drug users. *Substance Use & Misuse.*

Orendi, J. M., Boer, K., van Loon, A. M., Borleffs, J. C., van Oppen, A. C., & Boucher, C. A. (1999). Vertical HIV-1-transmission.1.Risk and prevention in pregnancy. *Ned Tidjschr Geneeskd, 8,* 434–436. English translation retrieved August 21, 2008, from http://www.ncbi.nlm.nih.gov/pubmed/1006 5235?ordinalpos=6&itool=EntrezSystem2.PEntrez.Pubmed.Pubmed_ResultsPanel.Pubmed_RVDocSum.

Orme, D. R., & Doerman, A. L. (2001). Ethical dilemmas in the U.S. Air Force clinical psychologists: A survey. *Professional Psychology: Research and Practice, 32,* 305–311.

O'Sullivan, C., & Fisher, C. B. (1997). The effect of confidentiality and reporting procedures on parent-child agreement to participate in adolescent risk research. *Applied Developmental Science, 1,* 185–197.

Otto, R. K., & Martindale, D. A. (2007). The law, process, and science of child custody evaluation. In M. Costanzo, D. Krauss, & K. Pezdek (Eds.), *Expert psychological testimony for the courts* (pp. 251–275). Englewood Cliffs, NJ: Lawrence Erlbaum.

Pachter, W. S., Fox, R. E., Zimbardo, P., & Antonuccio, D. O. (2007). Corporate funding and conflicts of interest: A primer for psychologists. *American Psychologist, 62,* 1005–1015.

Palma, T. V., & Iannelli, R. J. (2002). Therapeutic reactivity to confidentiality with HIV positive clients: Bias or epidemiology? *Ethics & Behavior, 12,* 353–370.

Pargament, K. I., Murray-Swank, N. A., Magyar, G. M., & Ano, C. G. (2005). Spiritual struggle: A phenomenon of interest to psychology and religion. In W. R. Miller & H. D. Delaney (Eds.), *Judeo-Christian perspectives on psychology: Human nature, motivation, and change* (pp. 245–268). Washington, DC: American Psychological Association.

Parham v. J.R., 442 U.S. 584 (1979).

Patterson, D. R., & Hanson, S. L. (1995). Joint Division 22 and ACRM guidelines for postdoctoral training in rehabilitation psychology. *Rehabilitation Psychology, 40,* 299–310.

Pearlman, L. A., & Saakvitne, K. W. (1995). Treating therapists with vicarious traumatization and secondary traumatic stress disorders. In C. R. Figley (Ed.), *Compassion fatigue: Coping with secondary traumatic stress disorder in those who treat the traumatized* (pp. 150–177). Philadelphia: Brunner/Mazel.

Pellegrino, E. D. (1989). Can ethics be taught? An essay. *Mount Sinai Journal of Medicine, 56,* 490–494.

Pellegrino, E. D. (1995). Toward a virtue-based normative ethics for the health professions. *Kennedy Institute Journal of Ethics, 5,* 253–278.

Perrin, G. I., & Sales, B. D. (1994). Forensic standards in the American Psychological Association's new ethics code. *Professional Psychology: Research and Practice, 25,* 376–381.

Peterson, D. B. (2007). Executive coaching in cross-cultural context. *Consulting Psychology Journal: Practice and Research, 59,* 261–271.

Pipes, R. B., Holstein, J. E., & Aguirre, M. G. (2005). Examining the personal-professional distinction: Ethics codes and the difficulty of drawing a boundary. *American Psychologist, 60,* 325–334.

Plante, T. G. (2007). Integrating spirituality and psychotherapy: Ethical issues and principles to consider. *Journal of Clinical Psychology, 63,* 891–902.

Plante, T. G., & Sherman, A. C. (Eds.). (2001). *Faith and health: Psychological perspectives.* New York: Guilford.

Pomerantz, A. M. (2005). Increasingly informed consent: Discussing distinct aspects of psychotherapy at different points in time. *Ethics & Behavior, 15,* 351–360.

Ponterotto, J. G., Casas, J. M., Suzuki, L. A., & Alexander, C. M. (Eds.). (2001). *Handbook of multicultural counseling* (2nd ed.). Thousand Oaks, CA: Sage.

Pope, K. S., & Brown, L. (1996). *Recovered memories of abuse: Assessment, therapy, forensics.* Washington, DC: American Psychological Association.

Pope, K. S., & Vasquez, M. J. T. (2007). *Ethics in psychotherapy and counseling: A practical guide* (3rd ed.). New York: John Wiley.

Powers, K. A., Poole, C., Pettifor, A. E., & Cohen, M. S. (2008). Rethinking the heterosexual infectivity of HIV-1: A systematic review and meta-analysis. August 4, Retrieved August 21, 2008, from http://www.ncbi.nlm.nih.gov/pubmed/18684670?ordinalpos=4&itool=EntrezSystem2 .PEntrez.Pubmed.Pubmed_ResultsPanel.Pubmed_RVDocSum.

Pregnancy Discrimination Act, Pub. L. No. 95–555, 92 Stat. 2076 (42 U.S.C. 2000e(k)) (1978).

Prilleltensky, I. (1997). Values, assumptions, and practices: Assessing the moral implications of psychological discourse and action. *American Psychologist, 52,* 517–535.

Protection of Pupil Rights Amendment (PPRA) of 2004 (20 U.S.C. § 1232–34 CFR Part 98).

Public Health Service Act 3.01(d), 42 U.S.C. § 241(d) (1946).

Quattrocchi, M. R., & Schopp, R. F. (2005). Tarasaurus Rex: A standard of care that could not adapt. *Psychology, Public Policy & Law, 11,* 109–137.

Rada, R. (2003). *HIPAA in 24 hours: Small healthcare entity HIPAA manual.* Liverpool, England: Hypermedia Solutions Limited.

Ramsey, P. (2002). *The patient as person: Explorations in medical ethics* (2nd ed.). New Haven, CT: Yale University Press.

Randsdell, S. (2002). Teaching psychology as a laboratory science in the age of the Internet. *Behavior Research Methods, Instruments & Computers, 34,* 145–150.

Rappo, P. D. (2002). Coding for mental health and behavioral problems: The arcane elevated to the ranks of the scientific. *Pediatrics, 110,* 167–169.

Reddy, M., Borum, R., Berglund, J., Vossekuil, B., Fein, R., & Modzeleski, W. (2001). Evaluating risk for targeted violence in schools: Comparing risk assessment, threat assessment and other approaches. *Psychology in the Schools, 38,* 157–172.

Regan, T. (1983). *The case for animal rights.* Berkeley: University of California Press.

Rest, J. (1983). Morality. In P. H. Mussen (Series Ed.) & J. Flavell & E. Markham (Vol. Eds.), *Handbook of child psychology: Vol. 4. Cognitive development* (pp. 520–629). New York: John Wiley.

Reutter, E. E. (1994). *The law of public education.* Westbury, NY: Foundation Press.

Richards, P. S., & Bergin, A. E. (2005). *A spiritual strategy for counseling and psychotherapy* (2nd ed.). Washington, DC: American Psychological Association.

Richards, P. S., & Potts, R. W. (1995). Using spiritual interventions in psychotherapy: Practices, successes, failures, and ethical concerns of Mormon psychotherapists. *Professional Psychology: Research and Practice, 26,* 163–170.

Ridley, C. R., Liddle, M. C., Hill, C. K. L., & Li, L. C. (2001). Ethical decision making in multicultural counseling. In J. G. Ponterotto, J. M. Casas, L. A. Suzuki, & C. M. Alexander (Eds.), *Handbook of multicultural counseling* (2nd ed., pp. 165–188). Thousand Oaks, CA: Sage.

Ritzler, B., Erard, R., & Pettigrew, G. (2002). Protecting the integrity of Rorschach expert witnesses: A reply to Grove and Barden (1999) Re: The admissibility of testimony under *Daubert/Kumho* analyses. *Psychology, Public Policy, and Law, 8,* 201–215.

Roeher Institute. (1996). *Building bridges: Inclusive postsecondary education for people with intellectual disabilities.* North York, Ontario, Canada: Author.

Romans, J. S. C., Boswell, D. L., Carlozzi, A. F., & Ferguson, D. B. (1995). Training and supervision practices in clinical, counseling, and school psychology programs. *Professional Psychology: Research and Practice, 26,* 407–412.

Russell, C. S., & Peterson, C. M. (1998, December). The management of personal and professional boundaries in marriage and family therapy training programs. *Contemporary Family Therapy, 20,* 457–470.

Saks, M. J., & Lanyon, R. I. (2007). Pitfalls and ethics of expert testimony. In M. Costanzo, D. Krauss, & K. Pezdek (Eds.), *Expert psychological testimony for the courts* (pp. 277–296). Mahwah, NJ: Lawrence Erlbaum.

Sales, B. D., & Shuman, D. W. (2007). Science, experts and law: Reflections on the past and the future. In M. Costano, D. Krauss, & K. Pezdek (Eds.), *Expert psychological testimony for the courts* (pp. 9–30). Mahwah, NJ: Lawrence Erlbaum.

Sarason, S. B. (1984). If it can be studied or developed, should it? *American Psychologist, 39,* 477–485.

Savin-Williams, R. C., & Diamond, L. M. (1999). Sexual orientation. In W. K. Silverman & T. H. Ollendick (Eds.), *Developmental issues in the clinical treatment of children and adolescents* (pp. 241–258). Boston: Allyn & Bacon.

Scarr, S. (1988). Race and gender as psychological variables: Social and ethical issues. *American Psychologist, 43,* 56–59.

Schur, G. M. (1982). Toward a code of ethics for academics. *Journal of Higher Education, 53,* 319–334.

Scott, P. A. (2003). Virtue, nursing, and the moral domain of practice. In V. Tschudin (Ed.), *Approaches to ethics* (pp. 25–32). London: Butterworth Heinemann.

Scott, K. J., Ingram, K. M., Vitanza, S. A., & Smith, N. G. (2000). Training in supervision: A survey of current practices. *The Counseling Psychologist, 28,* 403–422.

Sechrest, L., & Coan, J. A. (2002). Preparing psychologists to prescribe. *Journal of Clinical Psychology, 58,* 649–658.

Section 504 of the Rehabilitation Act of 1973, as amended 29 U.S.C. § 794 (1993).

Seitz, J., & O'Neill, P. (1996). Ethical decision-making and the code of ethics of the Canadian Psychological Association. *Canadian Psychology, 37,* 23–30.

Seligman, L. (1999). Twenty years of diagnosis and the *DSM* [Electronic version]. *Journal of Mental Health Counseling, 21,* 229–240.

Sgroi, S. M. (Ed.). (1982). *Handbook of clinical intervention in child sexual abuse.* Lexington, MA: Lexington Books.

Shafranske, E. P., & Sperry, L. (2005). Addressing the spiritual dimension in psychotherapy: Introduction and overview. In L. Sperry & E. P. Shafranske (Eds.), *Spiritually oriented psychotherapy* (pp. 11–29). Washington, DC: American Psychological Association.

Shapiro, E., & Ginzberg, R. (2003). To accept or not to accept: Referrals and the maintenance of boundaries. *Professional Psychology: Research & Practice, 34,* 258–263.

Shapiro, D. E., & Schulman, C. E. (1996). Ethical and legal issues in e-mail therapy. *Ethics & Behavior, 6,* 107–124.

Shead, N. W., & Dobson, K. S. (2004). Psychology for sale: The ethics of advertising professional services. *Canadian Psychology, 45,* 125–136.

Sherman, M. D., & Thelen, M. H. (1998). Distress and professional impairment among psychologists in clinical practice. *Professional Psychology: Research and Practice, 29,* 79–85.

Shuman, D. W., & Greenberg, S. A. (2003). The expert witness, the adversarial system, and the voice of reason: Reconciling impartiality and advocacy. *Professional Psychology: Research and Practice, 34,* 219–224.

Sieber, J. E. (1982). Kinds of deception and the wrongs they may involve. *IRB: A Review of Human Subjects Research, 4,* 1–5.

Sinclair, C., Poizner, S., Gilmour-Barrett, K., & Randall, D. (1987). The development of a code of ethics for Canadian psychologists. *Canadian Psychology, 28,* 1–8.

Singer, M., Marshall, P., Trotter, R., Schensul, J., Weeks, M., Simmons, J. E., et al. (1999). Ethics, ethnography, drug use and AIDS: Dilemmas and standards in federally funded research. In P. Marshall, M. Singer, & M. Clatts (Eds.), *Cultural, observational, and epidemiological approaches in the prevention of drug abuse and HIV/AIDS* (pp. 198–222). Bethesda, MD: National Institute on Drug Abuse.

Singer, M., Stopka, T., Siano, C., Springer, K., Barton, G., Khoshnood, D., et al. (2000). The social geography of AIDS and hepatitis risk: Qualitative approaches for assessing local differences in sterile-syringe access among injection users. *American Journal of Public Health, 90,* 1049–1056.

Sireci, S. G., & Parker, P. (2006). Validity on trial: Psychometric and legal conceptualizations of validity. *Educational Measurement: Issues and Practice, 25,* 27–34.

Skorupa, J., & Agresti, A. A. (1993). Ethical beliefs about burnout and continued professional practice. *Professional Psychology: Research and Practice, 24,* 281–285.

Snyder, K. D., & Doss, B. D. (2005). Treating infidelity: Clinical and ethical directions. *Journal of Clinical Psychology: In Session, 61,* 1383–1391.

Soisson, E. L., VandeCreek, L., & Knapp, S. (1987). Thorough record keeping: A good defense in a litigious era. *Professional Psychology: Research and Practice, 18,* 498–502.

Sonne, J. L., & Pope, K. S. (1991). Treating victims of therapist-patient sexual involvement. *Psychotherapy, 28,* 174–187.

Sprague, R. L. (1993). Whistleblowing: A very unpleasant avocation. *Ethics & Behavior, 3,* 103–134.

Staal, M. A., & King, R. E. (2000). Managing a multiple relationship environment: The ethics of military psychology. *Professional Psychology: Research and Practice, 31,* 698–705.

State of New Jersey v. Margaret Kelly Michaels, 625 A.2d 489 (N.J. Superior A.D. 1993).

Steele, K. D., & Morlin, B. (2007). *Spokane psychologists linked to CIA: Congress probes role in controversial interrogations.* Retrieved August 26, 2008, from http://www.spokesmanreview.com/news/archives.asp

Steinbock, B., Arras, J. D., & London, A. J. (Eds.). (2003). *Ethical issues in modern medicine.* New York: McGraw-Hill.

Stern, B. H. (2001). Admissibility of neuropsychological testimony after *Daubert* and *Kumho. NeuroRehabilitation, 16,* 93–101.

Stratton, J. S., & Smith, R. D. (2006). Supervision of couples cases. *Psychotherapy: Theory, Research, Practice, Training, 43,* 337–348.

Striefel, S. S. (2007). Ethical practice issues in treating pain. *Biofeedback, 35,* 44–47.

Sue, D. W., & Sue, D. (2003). *Counseling the culturally diverse.* New York: John Wiley.

Summit, R. C. (1983). The child sexual abuse accommodation syndrome. *Child Abuse & Neglect, 7,* 177–193.

Szajnberg, N. M., & Weiner, A. (1995). The child's conception of psychiatric cure. *Child Psychiatry and Human Development, 26,* 247–255.

Tan, S. (2003). Integrating spiritual direction into psychotherapy: Ethical issues and guidelines. *Journal of Psychology & Theology, 31,* 14–23.

Tarasoff v. Regents of the University of California (Tarasoff II), 17 Cal. 3d 425, 551 P.2d 334 (Cal. 1976).

Taylor, L., & Adelman, H. S. (1989). Reframing the confidentiality dilemma to work in children's best interests. *Professional Psychology: Research and Practice, 20,* 79–83.

Taylor, R. E., & Gazda, G. M. (1991). Concurrent individual and group therapy: The ethical issues. *Journal of Group Psychotherapy, Psychodrama, & Sociometry, 44,* 51–59.

Thompson, J., Baird, P., & Downie, J. (2001). *The Olivieri Report: The complete text of the report of the independent inquiry commissioned by the CAUT.* Toronto: James Lorimer & Company.

Thurber, S. (1985). Effect size estimates in chemical aversion treatments of alcoholism. *Journal of Clinical Psychology, 41,* 285–287.

Tillman, J. G. (1998). Psychodynamic psychotherapy, religious beliefs, and self-disclosure. *American Journal of Psychotherapy, 52,* 273–286.

Tolman, A. O., & Rotzien, A. L. (2007). Conducting risk evaluations for future violence: Ethical practice is possible. *Professional Psychology: Research & Practice, 38,* 71–79.

Trimble, J. E., & Fisher, C. B. (Eds.). (2006). *The handbook of ethical research with ethnocultural populations & communities.* Thousand Oaks, CA: Sage.

Turchik, J. A., Karpenko, V., Hammers, D., & McNamara, J. R. (2007). Practical and ethical assessment issues in rural, impoverished, and managed care settings. *Professional Psychology: Research and Practice, 38,* 158–168.

Uniformed Services Employment and Reemployment Rights Act of 1994 (USERRA), 38 U.S.C. §§ 4301–4333 (1994).

U.S. Department of Defense (DoD). (1997a). *Mental health evaluations of members of the armed forces* (DoD Directive 6490.1).Washington, DC: Government Printing Office.

U.S. Department of Defense (DoD). (1997b). *Requirements for mental health evaluations of members of the armed forces* (DoD Instruction 6490.4).Washington, DC: Government Printing Office.

VandeCreek, L., & Knapp, S. (1993). Tarasoff *and beyond: Legal and clinical considerations in the treatment of life-endangering patients* (Rev. ed.). Sarasota, FL: Professional Resource Press.

VandenBos, G. R. (2001). *Disguising case material for publication.* (Unpublished manuscript, available from American Psychological Association, 750 First Street, NE, Washington, DC 20002–4242).

van Emmerick, A. A. P., Kamphuis, J. H., Hulsbosch, A. M., & Emmelkamp, P. M. G. (2002). Single session debriefing after psychological trauma: A meta-analysis. *The Lancet, 360,* 766–771.

Walker, M. W. (1992). Moral understandings: Alternative "epistemology" for a feminist ethic. In E. B. Cole & S. Coultrap-McQuin (Eds.), *Explorations in feminist ethics* (pp. 165–175). Bloomington: Indiana University Press.

Walzer, M. (1983). *Spheres of justice: A defense of pluralism and equality.* New York: Basic Books.

Wards Cove Packing Company v. Antonio, 490 U.S. 642, Certiorari to the United States Court of Appeals for the Ninth Circuit, No. 87-1387 (1989).

Webber, D. W. (1999). *AIDS and the law: 1999 cumulative supplement* (3rd ed.). New York: Panel.

Wechsler, D. (1991). *Wechsler Intelligence Scale for Children, third edition (WISC-III).* San Antonio, TX: Psychological Corporation.

Weinberger, L. E., & Sreenivasan, S. (2003). Ethical principles of correctional psychology. In W. O'Donohue & K. Ferguson (Eds.), *Handbook of professional ethics for psychologists* (pp. 359–375). Thousand Oaks, CA: Sage.

Weisz, J. R., & Hawley, K. M. (2002). Developmental factors in the treatment of adolescents. *Journal of Consulting and Clinical Psychology, 70,* 21–43.

Weithorn, L. (2006). The legal contexts of forensic assessment of children and families. In S. N. Sparta & G. P. Koocher (Eds.), *Forensic mental health assessment of children and adolescents* (pp. 11–19). New York: Oxford University Press.

Weithorn, L. A., & Campbell, S. B. (1982). The competency of children and adolescents to make informed treatment decisions. *Child Development, 53,* 1589–1598.

Wisconsin v. Yoder, 406 U.S. 205 (1972).

Wong, T. M. (2000). Neuropsychological assessment and intervention with Asian Americans. In E. Fletcher-Janzen, T. L. Strickland, & C. R. Reynolds (Eds.), *Handbook of cross-cultural neuropsychology* (pp. 43–53). New York: Kluwer Academic/Plenum.

Wong, T. M., Strickland, T. L., Fletcher-Janzen, E., Ardila, A., & Reynolds, C. R. (2000). Theoretical and practical issues in the neuropsychological assessment and treatment of culturally dissimilar patients. In E. Fletcher-Janzen, T. L. Strickland, & C. R. Reynolds (Eds.), *Handbook of cross-cultural neuropsychology* (pp. 3–18). New York: Kluwer Academic/Plenum.

Workforce Investment Act of 1988, 29 U.S.C. 2938 (1988).

Wylie, M. S. (1995, May–June). The power of *DSM-IV:* Diagnosing for dollars. *Family Therapy Networker,* pp. 23–33, 65–69.

Yarhouse, M. A., & Tan, E. S. N. (2005). Addressing religious conflicts in adolescents who experience sexual identity confusion. *Professional Psychology: Research and Practice, 36,* 530–536.

Yell, M. L. (1994). Timeout and students with behavior disorders: A legal analysis. *Education and Treatment of Children, 17,* 293–301.

Younggren, J. N., & Gottlieb, D. (2004). Managing risk when contemplating multiple relationships. *Professional Psychology: Research and Practice, 35,* 255–260.

Zuckerman, E. L. (2005). *Clinician's thesaurus: The guide to conducting interviews and writing psychological reports* (6th ed.). New York: Guilford.

Index

About the Author

Celia B. Fisher, PhD, Director of the Fordham University Center for Ethics Education and the Marie Ward Doty University Chair and Professor of Psychology, served as Chair of the American Psychological Association's (APA's) Ethics Code Task Force responsible for the 2002 revision of the APA Ethical Principles of Psychologists and Code of Conduct. She has served as Chair of the Environmental Protection Agency's Human Subjects Research Board, the New York State Board for Licensure in Psychology, the National Task Force on Applied Developmental Science, and the Society for Research in Child Development Committee for Ethical Conduct in Child Development Research. Dr. Fisher was also a member of the APA Ethics Committee, the National Institute of Mental Health (NIMH) Data Safety and Monitoring Board, the Institute of Medicine Committee on Clinical Research Involving Children, numerous federal grant review committees, and the Department of Health and Human Services Secretary's Advisory Committee on Human Research Protections (SACHRP), for which she co-chaired the SACHRP Subcommittee on Research Involving Children. She also served as the founding director of the Fordham University Doctoral Program in Applied Developmental Psychology and is a co-founding editor of the journal *Applied Developmental Science.*

Dr. Fisher has written commissioned papers on research ethics with mentally impaired and vulnerable populations for President Clinton's National Bioethics Advisory Commission, for NIMH on points for consideration in the ethical conduct of suicide research and research involving children and adolescents, and for the National Institute on Drug Abuse (NIDA) on HIV education, treatment, and referrals for research participants. She co-chaired the APA, NIMH, Fordham University co-sponsored national conference on Research Ethics for Mental Health Science Involving Ethnic Minority Children and Youth (*American Psychologist,* December 2002) and the first National Conference on Graduate Education in Applied Developmental Science (*Journal of Applied Developmental Psychology,* 1993).

Dr. Fisher has co-edited eight books and authored more than 150 scholarly chapters and empirical articles on cognitive and social development across the life span and on research and professional ethics with special emphasis on the rights of racial/ethnic minorities, children and adults with impaired decision making, and socially marginalized populations. With support from the National Institute for

Child Health and Human Development (NICHD), she has studied how to assess and enhance the abilities of adults with developmental disabilities to consent to research. With funding from the National Science Foundation (NSF) and the National Institutes of Health (NIH), she has developed research ethics instructional materials for undergraduates, graduate students, senior scientists, and institutional review boards. She has developed assessment instruments to evaluate how teenagers and parents from different racial/ethnic backgrounds prepare for and react to racial discrimination, examined the validity of child abuse assessment techniques in institutional and forensic settings, and, with support from the NSF, NIDA, and the National Center for Research Resources (NCRR), has partnered with culturally diverse community members to understand their perspectives on the ethics of adolescent risk research and research involving adults on street drug use and related HIV risk. With support from NIAID and the Office of Research Integrity she has developed and validated measures assessing mentoring behaviors and departmental climates nurturing the responsible conduct of research in psychology graduate programs. Her research on intervention programs to reduce college students' drinking behaviors has been supported by the Department of Education and the National Institute on Alcohol Abuse and Alcoholism (NIAAA).